CIVIL LIBERTIES IN AMERICA

Civil Liberties
in
America

★ ★ ★ ★ ★

A CASEBOOK

★ ★ ★ ★ ★

by

ESTHER C. SWEET

Tufts University

D. VAN NOSTRAND COMPANY, INC.

PRINCETON, NEW JERSEY

TORONTO   LONDON   MELBOURNE

VAN NOSTRAND REGIONAL OFFICES: *New York, Chicago, San Francisco*

D. VAN NOSTRAND COMPANY, LTD., *London*

D. VAN NOSTRAND COMPANY (Canada), LTD., *Toronto*

D. VAN NOSTRAND AUSTRALIA PTY. LTD., *Melbourne*

First Published October 1966
Reprinted August 1967

PRINTED IN THE UNITED STATES OF AMERICA

To my husband

PREFACE

★ ★ ★

THIS BOOK HAS grown out of the author's experience in teaching civil liberties to college students over the past decade. Recent Supreme Court decisions in the field have been numerous, lengthy, and very important. Simultaneously, civil liberties issues have become among the most pressing and difficult of American political problems. In spite of this, no inexpensive, specialized collection of civil liberties case materials has been published. This book has been designed to help fill that gap.

Although the principal emphasis of the book rests on contemporary cases and problems, a certain amount of background material has been included. In this way, I hope, the book fulfills two purposes. First, it will help students with little or no background in law to understand the complexity and variety of problems which reach the United States Supreme Court in the civil liberties field. Second, it will help the student explore the thought processes of the Justices against a background of some 175 years of decisions. This approach should assist the student to a better understanding of the restrictions upon both courts and government.

Several variants from the usual casebook approach have been used. First, in most cases I have included the Court's own statement of the facts it considered relevant to the decision rather than my own summary. I felt that an editor's summary of facts which have already been summarized by the Court might be too restrictive for the decision. The complex facts might be simplified so much that the decision would seem both obvious and inevitable to the student.

Second, dissenting opinions are presented, not only because they may one day become majority opinions, but also, and more particularly because they reveal the other side of the coin: the problems and conflicts in the law and in the viewpoints of the Justices in their own words. Third, procedural restrictions and limitations upon the power of the Court have been described and explained where relevant because they are ever-present and important factors underlying, influencing, and often circumscribing Supreme Court decisions.

Finally, in order to help the student see the latest decisions in the perspective of history, I have included some of the older cases which either initiated a trend or to which the Court has returned.

I am happy to acknowledge the assistance of the following people: Miss June Bezjian; Miss Ann Van Ummersen; Miss Carolyn Clinton; Mrs. Gertrude Andelman; Mrs. Katharine Dempster; Mrs. Stella Briere;

and Mrs. Edna Nelson, all of whom contributed materially in relieving me of the burdens of the tedious parts of preparing a text. I am particularly grateful to my colleague, Dr. William A. Andrews, whose extremely valuable advice and criticism have been given with kindness. Finally, I am especially thankful for the help and forbearance of my husband for these past several months.

ESTHER C. SWEET

* * *

Contents

* * *

CHAPTER ONE

*   *   *

Background

CIVIL LIBERTIES CASES do not exist in isolation. They are part of the broad spectrum of constitutional law, and enmeshed in the complexities and limitations of our federal political and legal system. One of the complexities arises from the existence of 51 governmental systems, and also 51 judicial systems, in the United States. In some respects federal and state governments differ in their powers, in some they are parallel, and in others they overlap. Violations of federal laws are within the jurisdiction of the federal courts, and ultimately may be reviewed by the United States Supreme Court. Certain state actions which violate rights protected by the federal Constitution may also be reviewed by the United States Supreme Court.

Uncertainties and disputes about particular powers give rise to questions which are often highly technical. The very existence of a claimed power may be disputed. There are also constant conflicts between the rights of the individual and the power of the state or federal government, and between the conflicting rights of individuals.

There seems to be a growing tendency on the part of the United States Supreme Court to interpret the "due process" clause of the Fourteenth Amendment so that substantially similar duties and obligations are imposed upon state and federal governments, thus reducing the diversity of standards by which individuals in different states may be judged.

Since the adoption of the Constitution, the Supreme Court has been engaged in both definition and clarification of the rights, powers, and duties of the federal government, the states, and the individual. Although the standard for such determinations is the federal Constitution and the amendments thereto, interpretations of that document have developed and changed over the years. Additions to the Constitution itself (particularly the Thirteenth, Fourteenth, and Fifteenth Amendments) have required interpretation. Different interpretations of history, or new light upon it, sometimes subtle differences in the meaning of words, vast changes in the economic, social, and political structure of the nation have also changed the interpretation of the Constitution. In addition, the points of view of the Justices, as well as Justice Holmes' "felt necessities of the times" have contributed their share to the development of constitutional interpretation. In studying a decision of the Court, therefore, it is most helpful to have some idea of the climate of the times in which the decision was made. The Dred Scott decision was as much a product of its time as were the School Desegregation cases of 1954.

We may need to remind ourselves that we live in a world vastly different from that of the Founding Fathers. We have almost two hundred years of history behind us, the area of our country and our population have expanded enormously, and we are no longer isolated from other nations or from one another. We have a greater need than even fifty years ago to be one nation. As individuals, we depend infinitely more upon federal and state governments for our economic welfare, and accept infinitely more of their control, subtle or obvious. We cannot have the freedom of action, as individuals, that we enjoyed in a rural economy, for each person's action impinges too quickly upon the rights of others. The sphere of freedom for all, including the dissident, the solitary, and the individualist, has become enormously restricted. Government, in some form, has become ever-present and frequently limits the lives of each individual, from the necessity of recording a birth through compulsory school attendance to the official certification of death. And government, of course, exists and acts through the individuals who combine in groups to make and enforce laws.

Certainly, the more laws and people there are, the more violations of the law there will be, from sheer ignorance of the law if for no other reason. No one can hope to keep up with the yearly changes in statutes, state and national, to say nothing of the court cases which interpret both statutes and constitutions. Although the general meaning and import of many changes are widely publicized, details are not, nor are applications to the particular situation of a particular individual. We are informed, in general terms, of the necessity to insure automobiles, register for the draft and for social security, obtain a permit to add a room to a home or to carry certain weapons, and hordes of other statutory limitations upon our freedom. But as laws proliferate so do their interstices, for what is not covered, or is only partially covered by statute, is often as important as what is detailed. Laws also have conflicts: conflicts between laws, and often conflicting requirements in a particular law. State and federal laws may cover essentially the same subject matter, but from differing points of view. Myriads of laws on the statute books have never been interpreted and are, because of their phraseology, subject to a number of interpretations. In addition, literally thousands of administrative rulings may have the force and effect of law. This vast jungle of law is the despair of both layman and lawyer.

Finally, there are court opinions, particularly those of state and federal courts of last resort. But again, the meaning and import of the decisions are not always clear. The ambiguity is not necessarily the fault of the Court. The difficulty may lie with the statute or the section of the statute interpreted, or with the relation of the court's opinion to other cases. Even the naiveté or attitude toward law of a person who is unaware of the technicalities in a particular opinion may cause him seriously to misinterpret a decision. In other instances, a person's emotional attitude may make it impossible for him to accept the clear meaning of the Court's opinion. The meaning of a particular case interpreting a section of a statute or of the Constitution may therefore depend, at least in part, upon the approach and sophistication of the reader.

A number of problems in connection with the interpretation of the federal Constitution appear from time to time, and need to be kept in mind. First, there is a question of the meanings of words. Perhaps certain words or phrases had fixed meanings when the Constitution was written, but they have changed. Or possibly their meanings were not fixed; the words were vague enough to allow more than one interpretation. In either case, the words may now be invested with new meanings, thereby allowing a new interpretation of an old problem.

Second, there has been a long-continued discussion of whether the Constitution was a compact of the states, or of individuals without respect to their domicile. If it was the latter, states may be considered administrative conveniences which express the will of the people of the nation. This point of view weakens the "states' rights" argument, and strengthens the nation.

Third, a study of the older cases may disclose prejudices of the times unknowingly written into certain decisions of the Court. If so, the old decisions may be more easily overturned in favor of statements more consonant with our present ideas. These ideas may be as prejudiced as those expressed in the older case, but of course we do not see them in this light.

Fourth, it is sometimes argued that the vast changes in our life require that the Constitution be interpreted in the light of present needs.

Buttressing this argument is the idea that court decisions are based upon the facts of each case, so that a change in interpretation of the Constitution is justified, and indeed may be required, because the facts of no two cases are identical.

Finally, the Court itself gives constant thought to the place of the Court in the federal system and the limitations upon it. The viewpoints of individual justices influence this thought: their philosophies of law and government, their ideas of the purposes and limitations of the Supreme Court, their definitions of such abstract concepts as law and justice.

The limitations upon the Court are more restrictive than the layman knows, in many instances accounting for particular decisions, as well as for numerous dissents. Some limitations are imposed by the Constitution itself or by the Court's interpretation of the Constitution; some are products of congressional action; and some have been evolved by the Justices over the years. An understanding of these restrictions is basic to a comprehension of the Court's decisions.

According to Article III, Section 2, 1,

> The judicial Power shall extend to all Cases, in Law and Equity, arising under this Constitution, the Laws of the United States, and Treaties made, or which shall be made, under their Authority . . . to Controversies. . . .

What is a "case" or "controversy"? It is simple to say what it is not: it is not an advisory opinion. Chief Justice Marshall in *Marbury* v. *Madison* (1 Cranch 137, 1803) pointed out that the Constitution did not give the Court power to render an advisory opinion. And the "case" or "controversy" must be a genuinely adversary proceeding: those who want a decision cannot bring a "friendly" suit. The limitations upon the cases accepted by the Supreme Court are summarized by Mr. Justice Brandeis in his concurring opinion in *Ashwander* v. *Tennessee Valley Authority*, 297 U.S. 288, 345 *et seq.*; 56 S. Ct. 466, 482 *et seq.* He said:

Ashwander v. *Tennessee Valley Authority*

> The Court developed, for its own governance in the cases confessedly within its jurisdiction, a series of rules under which it has avoided passing upon a large part of all the constitutional questions pressed upon it for decision. They are:
> 1. The Court will not pass upon the constitutionality of legislation in a friendly, non-adversary, proceeding, declining because to decide such questions "is legitimate only in the last resort, and as a necessity in the determination of real, earnest and vital controversy between individuals. It never was the thought that, by means of a

friendly suit, a party beaten in the legislature could transfer to the courts an inquiry as to the constitutionality of the legislative act." *Chicago & Grand Trunk Ry.* v. *Wellman*, 143 U.S. 339, 345. . . .

2. The Court will not "anticipate a question of constitutional law in advance of the necessity of deciding it." *Liverpool, N.Y. & P.S.S. Co.* v. *Emigration Commissioners*, 113 U.S. 33, 39. . . .

3. The Court will not "formulate a rule of constitutional law broader than is required by the precise facts to which it is to be applied." *Liverpool, N.Y. & P.S.S. Co.* v. *Emigration Commissioners, supra.* . . .

4. The Court will not pass upon a constitutional question although properly presented by the record, if there is also present some other ground upon which the case may be disposed of. This rule has found most varied application. Thus, if a case can be decided on either of two grounds, one involving a constitutional question, the other a question of statutory construction or general law, the Court will decide only the latter. *Siler* v. *Louisville & Nashville R. Co.*, 213 U.S. 175, 191. . . .

5. The Court will not pass upon the validity of a statute upon complaint of one who fails to show that he is injured by its operation. *Tyler* v. *The Judges*, 179 U.S. 405. . . . Among the many applications of this rule, none is more striking than the denial of the right of challenge to one who lacks a personal or property right. Thus, the challenge by a public official interested only in the performance of his official duty will not be entertained. *Columbus & Greenville Ry.* v. *Miller*, 283 U.S. 96, 99–100. . . .

. . . In *Massachusetts* v. *Mellon*, 262 U.S. 447, the challenge of the federal Maternity Act was not entertained although made by the Commonwealth on behalf of all its citizens.

6. The Court will not pass upon the constitutionality of a statute at the instance of one who has availed himself of its benefits. *Great Falls Mfg. Co.* v. *Attorney General*, 124 U.S. 581. . . .

7. "When the validity of an act of the Congress is drawn in question, and even if a serious doubt of constitutionality is raised, it is a cardinal principle that this Court will first ascertain whether a construction of the statute is fairly possible by which the question may be avoided." *Crowell* v. *Benson*, 285 U.S. 22, 62. . . .

The Supreme Court adheres to other limitations upon its great power. One fundamental rule is that a case or controversy must be "justiciable"; that is, there must be injury to a legally protected right. The controversy must also be determinable by a decree that is conclusive in character, and the decision will be no broader than necessary for the facts before the Court. This last requirement is also a source of disagreement among the members of the Court, for they do not always agree about what facts are properly before the Court or even what facts are essential to the decision. Lest it seem that the Justices are in constant and unnecessary conflict, it is well to remember that the record before the Court may be as long as 16,000 pages as in *Dennis* v. *United States* (341 U.S. 494, 71 S. Ct. 857; 1951). With this quantity of material, there will inevitably be certain disagreements concerning the essentiality of specific facts. Since the decision is based upon facts before the Court, disagreement concerning their relevance can lead to differences of opinion in the Court's decision.

If the constitutionality of a statute is called into question, the statute is presumed valid, and the burden of proof is on the party that claims it is invalid. In addition, if the case comes from a state, the U.S. Supreme Court will respect the state court's interpretation of the statute, or, if no interpretation has been made, and one is necessary, the Court will return the case to the state court for interpretation of the state law. The federal court may, however, find that the state statute, as interpreted, conflicts with the federal Constitution. If a state court has interpreted a federal statute, the U.S. Supreme Court is not, of course, bound by the state's viewpoint.

The Court does not pass upon the expediency or wisdom of statutes, at least in theory, but it does pass upon the power of the legislative branch to enact particular statutes. But "expediency" or "wisdom" to some may be "power" to others, and hence another source of dissenting opinions.

Finally, the Court does not pass upon "political" questions. But when is a problem a "political" question, and when is it a denial of equal protection or due process of law under the Fourteenth Amendment? The distinction has been a particularly fertile source of dissent since *Colegrove* v. *Green* (328 U.S. 549, 66 S. Ct. 1198; 1946), in which the majority held, over Mr. Justice Black's dissent, that the reapportionment of congressional districts was "political," and not appropriate for decision.

An elementary knowledge of certain procedures is also required to understand Supreme Court decisions, for the procedures may limit the decisions' scope. Cases now reach the U.S. Supreme Court by one of two methods: writ of certiorari or appeal. Although cases which may be appealed are limited, when appeal is appropriate the Court may not refuse to take the case. The more common method is by writ of certiorari, a procedure which allows the Court to accept or refuse a case, and to limit the issues it will hear. In *Dennis* v. *United States*, for example, a writ of certiorari was issued, but the Court considered only two of the many questions raised.

Before the Supreme Court is reached, the litigants may have a hearing or trial "on the merits." The average person is familiar with this procedure: witnesses are examined and cross-examined, the attorneys object to the admission of evidence, a decision is made. However, this trial stage may not be reached. One party may file a technical pleading, usually either a motion to dismiss, or a demurrer, which may be granted after a limited hearing at which the attorneys and the judge are present and the argument is highly technical. The losing party may appeal a decision. When the case reaches a court of last resort, the record is much shorter, for there has been no parade of witnesses, no voluminous objections in the trial court. There has been no introduction of evidence, and there is a different set of technicalities for the appellate court to consider. If the basic problems revealed by the motion to dismiss or the demurrer are settled, a trial may not be needed or may at least be restricted in scope. On the other hand, these pleadings are frequently dangerous for the parties.

In addition to the rules and technicalities discussed briefly in the preceding paragraphs, the differing personalities, backgrounds, experiences, and points of view of the Justices produce varying perceptions and evaluations of problems. There are, therefore, numerous opinions in which the Justices concur in the decision, but disagree on the reasons for the decision. Even this simple explanation of the problems and technicalities shows that there are many reasons for dissenting opinions. Given nine men of the independence of mind possessed by Supreme Court Justices, perhaps we should be surprised that there are not more dissents. The almost infinite possibilities for disagreement make it certain that a unanimous opinion expresses a truly common ground.

Probably one of the deepest divisions in viewpoint on the present Court is between those who give primacy to the rights of the individual under the Bill of Rights and the Fourteenth Amendment, and those who, although they believe strongly that the rights of the individual are usually of primary importance, believe also that at times the power of government must be dominant in order to preserve the form of government which makes the rights of the individual possible. In other words, the rights of the individual should be balanced against those of society. The right and duty of the government to maintain itself against violent change is fundamental. Equally fundamental is the right of the individual to the protections of the Bill of Rights, including the First Amendment rights of freedom of speech, assembly, and religion. A constantly recurring problem is the question of the point at which the government may abrogate or punish certain forms of speech in order to diminish the possibility of violent change in our form of government.

A great many conflicts which give rise to civil rights cases begin as the exercise of what is known as the "police power." The term may conjure up a vision of uniformed men directing traffic, but it includes the right of the government to regulate or even forbid a great many activities of the individual in order to protect the health, safety, morals, and general welfare of the community. The regulation of traffic, requirements for safety in public and rented buildings, limitations on construction, sanitation control, food inspection, reporting of contagious diseases, the regulation or even elimination of businesses which may be dangerous to the health or safety of the public, and requirements for the licensing of the practitioners of certain skills and professions are only a few examples. Although no such express power is given to the national government in the Constitution, it is in fact exercised under a variety of granted powers.

Admitting this power to regulate, the question in most instances is whether in its efforts to protect the community the government has exceeded its powers, and has interfered with the constitutional rights of particular members of society. A decision will, of course, depend upon the facts of each case. During a crisis such as war, for example, the Court may not object to restrictions that would not be acceptable in peacetime.

As a practical matter, community disapproval of an idea or of the person holding an idea may prevent its expression. Conversely, statutes or ordinances may compel an expression or action which reflects the viewpoint of the majority of the community. Since these laws are presumed to be valid, they may be enforced until they are repealed, or until a court of last resort finds them unconstitutional.

CHAPTER TWO

Due Process and Fair Procedure

Due Process

THE FIFTH AMENDMENT of the Bill of Rights, adopted in 1791, provides in part, "No person shall . . . be deprived of life, liberty or property, without due process of law; nor shall private property be taken for public use, without just compensation." This Amendment does not specifically limit its reach to the national government, as does the First, which begins, "Congress shall make no law. . . ." Even though the Bill of Rights was adopted as a limitation on the federal government, it might also include, because of its vagueness, state governments as well. That, at least, was the contention of the plaintiff in *Barron* v. *The Mayor and City Council of Baltimore,* 7 Peters 243 (1833). When the city improved its streets, certain streams were diverted from their natural courses, causing earth and sand to be deposited beside the plaintiff's wharf. These deposits made the water so shallow that large vessels could not use the wharf, thereby reducing the plaintiff's business. This he considered to be a taking of his private property for public use, without the just compensation required by the Fifth Amendment. But Chief Justice Marshall did not agree with him.

Barron v. *Baltimore*

The question thus presented is, we think, of great importance, but not of much difficulty. . . .

The constitution was ordained and established by the people of the United States for themselves, for their own government and not for the government of the individual States. Each State established a constitution for itself, and, in that constitution, provided such limitations and restrictions on the powers of its particular government as its judgment dictated. The people of the United States framed such a government for the United States as they supposed best adapted to their situation, and best calculated to promote their interests. The powers they conferred on this government were to be exercised by itself; and the limitations on power, if expressed in general terms, are naturally, and, we think, necessarily applicable to the government created by the instrument. They are limitations of power granted in the instrument itself; not of distinct governments, framed by different persons and for different purposes.

If these propositions be correct, the 5th amendment must be understood as restraining the power of the general government, not as applicable to the States. In their several constitutions they have imposed such restrictions on their respective governments as their own wisdom suggested; such as they deemed most proper for themselves. It is a subject on which they judge exclusively, and with which others interfere no further than they are supposed to have a common interest. * * *

If the original constitution, in the 9th and 10th sections of the 1st article, draws this plain and marked line of discrimination between the limitations it imposes on the powers of the general government, and on those of the States; if in every inhibition intended to act on state power, words are employed which directly express that intent; some strong reason must be assigned for departing from this safe and judicious course in framing the amendments, before that departure can be assumed.

We search in vain for that reason.

Had the people of the several States . . . required additional safeguards to liberty from the apprehended encroachments of their particular governments; the remedy was in their own hands, and would have been applied by themselves. . . .

. . . In almost every convention by which the constitution was adopted, amendments to guard against the abuse of power were recommended. These amendments demanded security against the apprehended encroachments of the general government, not against those of the local governments. . . .

. . . These amendments contain no expression indicating an intention to apply them to the state governments. This court cannot so apply them. . . .

We are of opinion that the provision in the 5th amendment to the constitution, declaring that private property shall not be taken for public use without just compensation, is intended solely as a limitation on the exercise of power by the government of the United States, and is not applicable to the legislation of the States. . . . This court, therefore, has no jurisdiction of the cause; and it is dismissed.

In 1857 the Court found other restrictions upon the power of the federal government. The case was *Dred Scott* v. *Sandford,* 19 Howard 393, a decision which required 234 pages to set forth the strong views of the Court. As is not uncommon, the basic arguments were on technicalities: whether Dred Scott had a right to bring action at all and what questions were open to the Court for decision. But those are not the points for which the decision is remembered today. It is remembered because of

Mr. Justice Taney's opinion which held not only that a slave could not become a citizen of the United States (even though in fact freed slaves had been considered citizens of particular states) but also that the Congress was without power to pass the law commonly known as the Missouri Compromise.

> . . . An Act of Congress, which deprives a citizen of the United States of his liberty or property, merely because he came himself or brought his property into a particular Territory of the United States, and who had committed no offense against the laws, could hardly be dignified with the name of due process of law.[1]

In the phraseology of Justice Taney, "a negro, whose ancestors were imported into this country, and sold as slaves" could not "become a member of the political community formed and brought into existence by the Constitution of the United States. . . ."[2]

"Dred Scott was not a citizen of Missouri within the meaning of the Constitution of the United States, and was not entitled as such to sue in its courts. . . ."[3] He was property, and the attempt to deprive his owner of this property was without "due process of law."

What is "due process of law"? The phrase appears in the Fifth Amendment, applicable to the national government, and in the Fourteenth, applicable to the states. It is difficult to define, in part because definitions are spelled out by the Court on a case-by-case basis, and in part because the Court has held that the Fourteenth Amendment limitation upon the states is not necessarily identical with the standard of the national government. Beyond these difficulties are others: the effort to differentiate between "substantive" and "procedural" due process, which seem to be distinguishable, at best, only toward the extremes; the unstated, unresolved, but ever-present and ever-changing conflict between the rights of the individual and the rights of government; and the impossibilities of reducing the complexities of human nature and human relations to a formula more meaningful than the "due process of law" phrase itself. Neither negative definitions (definitions by exclusions) nor positive ones are adequate. Derived from, or a descendant of, Magna Charta's "law of the land," the due process concept has been defined in such words as the following:

> . . . those settled usages and modes of proceeding existing in the common and statute law of England before the emigration of our ancestors, and which are shown not to have been unsuited to their

[1]*Dred Scott v. Sandford,* 19 Howard 393, p. 450.
[2]*Ibid.,* p. 403.
[3]*Ibid.,* p. 429.

civil and political condition by having been acted on by them after the settlement of this country.[4]

. . . any legal proceeding enforced by public authority, whether sanctioned by age and custom, or newly devised in the discretion of the legislative power, in furtherance of the general public good, which regards and preserves these principles of liberty and justice, must be held to be due process of law.[5]

. . . those canons of decency and fairness which express the notions of justice of English-speaking peoples even toward those charged with the most heinous offenses.[6]

The requirement of "due process" is not a fair-weather or timid assurance. It must be respected in periods of calm and in times of trouble; it protects aliens as well as citizens. But "due process," unlike some legal rules, is not a technical conception with a fixed content unrelated to time, place and circumstances. Expressing as it does in its ultimate analysis respect enforced by law for that feeling of just treatment which has been evolved through centuries of Anglo-American constitutional history and civilization, "due process" cannot be imprisoned within the treacherous limits of any formula. Representing a profound attitude of fairness between man and man, and more particularly between the individual and government, "due process" is compounded of history, reason, the past course of decisions, and stout confidence in the strength of the democratic faith which we profess. Due process is not a mechanical instrument. It is not a yardstick. It is a process. It is a delicate process of adjustment inescapably involving the exercise of judgment by those whom the Constitution entrusted with the unfolding of the process.[7]

Within these broad and uncertain boundaries the details are pricked out, case by case.

With the adoption of the Thirteenth, Fourteenth, and Fifteenth Amendments many questions concerning the meaning and application of these amendments, and particularly the Fourteenth, reached the Supreme Court. Not all the problems arose in connection with the status of former slaves. In *The Slaughterhouse Cases,* 16 Wall. 36 (1873), for instance, the Court distinguished between the two kinds of citizenship, state and national, mentioned in Section One of the Fourteenth Amendment. The Court's interpretation left the definition and enforcement of civil liberties largely to the discretion of the states.

Ten years later, in *The Civil Rights Cases,* 109 U.S. 3, 3 S. Ct. 18 (1883), the Fourteenth Amendment was limited to the literal meaning

[4]*Murray's Lessees* v. *Hoboken, etc.,* 18 How. 272, 276–77.
[5]*Hurtado* v. *California,* 110 U.S. 516, 537, 4 S. Ct. 111 (1883).
[6]*Adamson* v. *California,* 332 U.S. 46, 67–8; 67 S. Ct. 1672, 1683 (1947).
[7]Mr. Justice Frankfurter, *Joint Anti-Fascist Refugee Committee* v. *McGrath,* 341 U.S. 123, 162; 71 S. Ct. 624, 643 (1951).

of its words: "no state." The Civil Rights Act passed by the Congress in 1875 was intended to continue national power to prevent discrimination based upon race. Under its terms, it was a crime as well as a civil wrong for any person to deny anyone

> . . . the full and equal enjoyment of any accommodations, advantages, facilities and privileges of inns, public conveyances on land or water, theaters and other places of public amusement; subject only to the conditions and limitations established by law, and applicable alike to citizens of every race and color. . . .

Individuals who were denied "full and equal enjoyment of certain accommodations" brought suit.

The Civil Rights Cases, 109 U.S. 3, 3 S.Ct. 18 (1883)

The first section of the Fourteenth Amendment (which is the one relied on) . . . is prohibitory in its character, and is prohibitory upon the States. . . .

It is State action of a particular character that is prohibited. Individual invasion of individual rights is not the subject-matter of the amendment. It has a deeper and broader scope. It nullifies and makes void all State legislation, and State action of every kind, which impairs the privileges and immunities of citizens of the United States, or which injures them in life, liberty or property without due process of law, or which denies to any of them the equal protection of the laws. . . .

Positive rights and privileges are undoubtedly secured by the Fourteenth Amendment; but they are secured by way of prohibition against State laws and State proceedings affecting those rights and privileges, and by power given to Congress to legislate for the purpose of carrying such prohibition into effect: and such legislation must necessarily be predicated upon such supposed State laws or State proceedings, and be directed to the correction of their operation and effect. * * *

And so in the present case, until some State law has been passed, or some State action through its officers or agents has been taken, adverse to the rights of citizens sought to be protected by the Fourteenth Amendment, no legislation of the United States under said amendment, nor any proceeding under such legislation, can be called into activity: for the prohibitions of the amendment are against State laws and acts done under State authority. . . .

An inspection of the law shows that it makes no reference whatever to any supposed or apprehended violation of the Fourteenth Amendment on the part of the States. It is not predicated on any such view. It proceeds *ex directo* to declare that certain acts committed by individuals shall be deemed offences, and shall be prosecuted and punished by proceedings in the courts of the United States. It does not profess to be corrective of any constitutional wrong committed by the States; it does not make its operation to depend upon any such wrong committed. * * *

In this connection it is proper to state that civil rights, such as are guaranteed by the Constitution against State aggression, cannot be impaired by the wrongful acts of individuals, unsupported by State authority in the shape of laws, customs, or judicial or executive proceedings. The wrongful act of an individual, unsupported by any such authority, is simply a private wrong, or a crime of that individual . . . but if not sanctioned in some way by the State, or not done under State authority, his rights remain in full force, and may presumably be vindicated by resort to the laws of the State for redress. * * *

. . . [I]t is assumed, that the power vested in Congress to enforce the article by appropriate legislation, clothes Congress with power to pass all laws necessary and proper for abolishing all badges and incidents of slavery in the United States: and upon this assumption it is claimed, that this is sufficient authority for declaring by law that all persons shall have equal accommodations and privileges in all inns, public conveyances, and places of amusement; the argument being, that the denial of such equal accommodations and privileges is, in itself, a subjection to a species of servitude within the meaning of the amendment. * * *

After giving to these questions all the consideration which their importance demands, we are forced to the conclusion that such an act of refusal has nothing to do with slavery or involuntary servitude, and that if it is violative of any right of the party, his redress is to be sought under the laws of the State; or if those laws are adverse to his rights and do not protect him, his remedy will be found in the corrective legislation which Congress has adopted, or may adopt, for counteracting the effect of State laws, or State action, prohibited by the Fourteenth Amendment. * * *

MR. JUSTICE HARLAN, dissenting.

. . . I cannot resist the conclusion that the substance and spirit of the recent amendments of the Constitution have been sacrificed by a subtle and ingenious verbal criticism. * * * I mean only . . . to express an earnest conviction that the court has departed from the familiar rule requiring, in the interpretation of constitutional provisions, that full effect be given to the intent with which they were adopted.

The purpose of the first section of the act of Congress of March 1, 1875, was to prevent *race* discrimination in respect of the accommodations and facilities of inns, public conveyance, and places of public amusement. . . . The second section provides a penalty against any one denying, or aiding or inciting the denial, to any citizen, of that equality of right given by the first section, except for reasons by law applicable to citizens of every race or color regardless of any previous condition of servitude. . . .

The court adjudges, I think erroneously, that Congress is without power, under either the Thirteenth or Fourteenth Amendment, to establish such regulations. * * *

Congress has not . . . entered the domain of State control and supervision. . . . It simply declares, in effect, that since the nation has established universal freedom in this country, for all time, there shall be no discrimination, based merely upon race or color, in respect of the accommodations and advantages of public conveyances, inns, and places of public amusement.

I am of the opinion that such discrimination practised by corporations and individuals in the exercise of their public or quasi-public functions is a badge of servitude the imposition of which Congress may prevent under its power . . . to enforce the Thirteenth Amendment; and, consequently, without reference to its enlarged power under the Fourteenth Amendment, the act of March 1, 1875, is not, in my judgment, repugnant to the Constitution. * * *

. . . I agree that government has nothing to do with social, as distinguished from technically legal, rights of individuals. . . . What I affirm is that no State, nor the officers of any State, nor any corporation or individual wielding power under State authority for the public benefit or the public convenience, can, consistently either with the freedom established by the fundamental law, or with that equality of civil rights which now belongs to every citizen, discriminate against freemen or citizens, in those rights, because of their race, or because they once labored under the disabilities of slavery imposed upon them as a race. The rights which Congress, by the act of 1875, endeavored to secure and protect are legal, not social rights. The right, for instance, of a colored citizen to use the accommodations of a public highway, upon the same terms as are permitted to white citizens, is no more a social right than his right, under the law, to use the public streets of a city or a town, or a turnpike road, or a public market. . . .

The court, in its opinion, reserves the question whether Congress, in the exercise of its power to regulate commerce amongst the several States, might or might not pass a law regulating rights in public conveyances passing from one State to another. . . . I beg to suggest that that precise question was substantially presented here in the only one of these cases relating to railroads — *Robinson and Wife* v. *Memphis & Charleston Railroad Company.* * * *

Fair Procedure

Often "procedure" is disparaged by preceding the word with "only." But some procedural rights are so fundamental that they must be followed; attention to these rights helps to implement the broad statements of the Bill of Rights. A number of due process and equal protection decisions have been made on the basis of a denial of "fair procedure." It is a difficult concept to define, and is, of course, developed on a case-by-case basis. A brief statement of the legal framework within which fair procedure is worked out may be helpful.

Fundamental to any trial is a right of action in a civil case, or the commission of a crime in a criminal case. Although the definitions of what constitutes a right of action or a crime have been spelled out over the years by courts and legislatures, the definition of a crime is not always clear. Serious crimes require "intent"; if the definition of the crime is unclear, the required intent to commit the criminal act may be lacking. Also, more than one interpretation for a definition may be possible, or the phraseology may be so unclear that the accused could not know that his actions were forbidden. Every person is presumed to know the law, but that maxim applies only to law clearly defined. Lack of such clarity was one reason for the decision in the Watkins case (*Watkins* v. *U.S.*, 354 U.S. 178, 77 S. Ct. 1173; 1957).

Crimes are commonly classified as "misdemeanors" or "felonies." The exact difference between the two classes is determined by each state and by the federal government, but the penalty imposed provides a practical common boundary line. A death sentence or imprisonment in a state or federal penitentiary commonly distinguishes a felony from a misdemeanor.

In a serious criminal case the accusatory process usually begins formally with the arraignment of the accused before a magistrate after a grand jury has found probable cause or a police investigation has shown it to be probable that the accused committed the crime in question. Although arraignment may be the technical beginning of the case in court, the accused already may have been in the custody of the police for a matter of hours or days before arraignment, as Culombe was (*Culombe* v. *Connecticut*). The procedure followed in his case is not uncommon. In addition to such detention to obtain information which may help solve a particular crime, other information may be obtained which will enable the prosecution to prepare a more convincing case, or which may solve other crimes or implicate other people.

Once arraigned, the accused may be released on bail, or if he cannot post bail, he may be remanded to jail to await trial. One handicap of the bail system is that the well-to-do person can afford to post bail, but the poor, however innocent, rarely can. Weeks or months spent in jail awaiting trial can mean financial disaster for the defendant and his family, even though he is ultimately found innocent.

In at least one jurisdiction, research showed that those who were not out on bail were more often found guilty than those who were. The Vera Foundation, working with the New York University School of

Law, investigated persons accused of crime and has recommended the release of many on their own recognizance (that is, without the posting of bail money or bond as an assurance that the accused will return for the trial). The course of action pursued after arraignment varies somewhat, depending upon the jurisdiction, the gravity of the crime, and the character and financial ability of the accused.

In certain instances the accused may avoid a trial completely by pleading guilty, or he may waive a jury trial. A waiver of a jury trial is supposed to be "intelligent," but it may be difficult to determine, as a matter of fact, whether a particular waiver was intelligent, or the result of coercion, stupidity, ignorance, or of reliance upon a prosecutor's advice. If the accused is uneducated, emotionally upset, or without counsel, he may not understand the legal consequences of such a waiver, or of a plea of guilty, even though the judge explains them to him. If the accused has been in custody, has been persuaded that he is isolated from his friends and family, or has been put in fear, he may hear the words the judge uses, but he may not be able to evaluate them, even though he would ordinarily have the intelligence for a proper understanding.

If the accused does have a jury trial, a number of problems center around the choice of the jurors. Although some standards for qualification can be established, they cannot include a systematic exclusion of person, otherwise qualified, on grounds of race (*Norris* v. *Alabama*, 294 U.S. 587, 55 S. Ct. 579; 1935), or national origin (*Hernandez* v. *Texas*, 347 U.S. 475, 74 S. Ct. 667; 1954). Other exclusions are not a denial of fair trial or equal protection: those made on the basis of age; non-citizens; non-residents of the county in which the juror is to serve; those convicted of a felony; those not able to read and write the English language understandingly; those not of sound mind and good character; those not in possession of their natural faculties. Although these exclusions change the character of the jury (and one or two might be used for purposes of discrimination), they are needed in order to have a jury capable of functioning with reasonable effectiveness. Certain other groups are exempt: for example, physicians, dentists, clergymen, attorneys, members of the armed services, firemen and policemen.

Beyond these restrictions, the "blue ribbon" jury of New York has been upheld. The special limitations on that type of jury were found to be "reasonably and closely related to the juror's suitability for the kind of service the special panel requires or to his fitness to judge the kind of case for which it is most frequently utilized," and in addition many of "the standards of elimination . . . are those the court would have to apply to excuse a juror on challenge for cause."[8] There was no denial of due process of law, or of equal protection in the use of such a jury.

Fair procedure requires a public trial (*In re Oliver*, 333 U.S. 257, 68 S. Ct. 499; 1948), before an impartial judge (*Tumey* v. *Ohio*, 273 U.S. 510, 47 S. Ct. 437; 1927) and an impartial jury (*Irvin* v. *Dowd*, 359 U.S. 394, 79 S. Ct. 825; 1959), as well as one from which members of the accused's race have not been systematically excluded (*Norris* v. *Alabama*, 294 U.S. 587, 55 S. Ct. 579; 1935). He is entitled to a prosecutor who is neither suppressing evidence favorable to him nor knowingly allowing false testimony (*Alcorta* v. *Texas*, 355 U.S. 28, 78 S. Ct. 103; 1957); *Napue* v. *Illinois*, 360 U.S. 264, 79 S. Ct. 1173; 1959). He is entitled to have an effective means of appeal to the highest court, even though he cannot afford the court costs, attorney's fees, or even the filing fee. On such appeal, he is entitled to have an adequate record on which to base his case. Refusal of a request for a change of venue may prevent a fair trial, and may amount to a denial of due process (*Rideau* v. *Louisiana*, 373 U.S. 373, 83 S. Ct. 1417; 1963). Various technical matters of proof may violate fair procedure and amount to a lack of due process, as, for example, when the burden of proving non-advocacy of violent overthrow of the government in a criminal case is put upon the taxpayer, contrary to the presumption of innocence until proof of guilt (*Speiser* v. *Randall*, 357 U.S. 513, 78 S. Ct. 1332; 1958).

With modern means of communication, a fair trial may be difficult or even impossible to obtain, because state-wide (or even nation-wide) publicity may so prejudice prospective jurors that it is impossible to obtain an impartial jury. Although the judge in any case may bar cameras and typewriters from the courtroom, a court has relatively little control over what is published in a newspaper or broadcast over the radio or television. But allowing radio or television broadcasts to originate in the courtroom presents a different problem. In fact, such broadcasts have been forbidden in most states. Texas is an exception: the judge may, in his sound discretion, allow direct broadcasting from the courtroom. The *Estes* case, which follows, is the first to reach the Supreme Court on the issue of whether such coverage, over the defendant's objections, denies him a fair trial or due process of law. The case was a notorious one. Well known in Texas before the difficulties which occasioned the case occurred, the defendant was charged with making certain false and fraudulent representations which led several farmers to buy non-existent equipment, and to sign and deliver to the accused

---

[8]*Fay* v. *People of State of New York,* 332 U.S. 261, pp. 270, 271, 67 S. Ct. 1613; 1947.

chattel mortgages on the non-existent property. When the scheme was discovered, there was extensive nation-wide publicity.

Estes v. *State of Texas*, 381 U.S. 532, 85 S. Ct. 1628 (1965)

MR. JUSTICE CLARK delivered the opinion of the Court.

The question presented here is whether the petitioner, who stands convicted in the District Court for the Seventh Judicial District of Texas at Tyler for swindling, was deprived of his right under the Fourteenth Amendment to due process by the televising and broadcasting of his trial. Both the trial court and the Texas Court of Criminal Appeals found against the petitioner. . . . We hold to the contrary and reverse his conviction.

. . . [P]etitioner . . . contend[s]   that . . . the   time-honored principles of a fair trial were not followed in his case and that he was convicted without due process of law. . . . [T]he question here is . . . whether petitioner was tried in a manner which comports with the due process requirement of the Fourteenth Amendment.

Petitioner's case was originally called for trial on September 24, 1962, in Smith County after a change of venue from Reeves County, some 500 miles west. Massive pretrial publicity totaling 11 volumes of press clippings, which are on file with the Clerk, had given it national notoriety. All available seats in the courtroom were taken and some 30 persons stood in the aiseles. However, at that time a defense motion to prevent telecasting, broadcasting by radio and news photography and a defense motion for continuance were presented, and after a two-day hearing the former was denied and the latter granted.

These initial hearings were carried live by both radio and television, and news photography was permitted throughout. The videotapes of these hearings clearly illustrate that the picture presented was not one of that judicial serenity and calm to which the petitioner was entitled. . . . Indeed, at least 12 cameramen were engaged in the courtroom throughout the hearing taking motion and still pictures and televising the proceedings. Cables and wires were snaked across the courtroom floor, three microphones were on the judge's bench and others were beamed at the jury box and the counsel table. It is conceded that the activities of the television crews and news photographers led to considerable disruption of the hearings. Moreover, a venire of jurymen had been summoned and was present in the courtroom during the entire hearing but was later released after petitioner's motion for continuance had been granted. The court also had the names of the witnesses called, and some answered but the absence of others led to a continuance of the case until October 22, 1962. It is contended that this two-day pretrial hearing cannot be considered in determining the question before us. We cannot agree. Pretrial can create a major problem for the defendant in a criminal case. Indeed, it may be more harmful than publicity during the trial for it may well set the community opinion as to guilt or innocence.

Though the September hearings dealt with motions to prohibit television coverage and to postpone the trial, they are unquestionably relevant to the issue before us. All of this two-day affair was highly publicized and could only have impressed those present, and also the community at large, with the notorious character of the petitioner as well as the proceeding. The trial witnesses present at the hearing, as well as the original jury panel, were undoubtedly made aware of the peculiar public importance of the case by the press and television coverage being provided, and by the fact that they themselves were televised live and their pictures rebroadcast on the evening show.

When the case was called for trial on October 22 the scene had been altered. A booth had been constructed at the back of the courtroom which was painted to blend with the permanent structure of the room. It had an aperture to allow the lens of the cameras an unrestricted view of the courtroom. All television cameras and newsreel photographers were restricted to the area of the booth when shooting film or telecasting.

Because of continual objection, the rules governing live telecasting, as well as radio and still photos, were changed as the exigencies of the situation seemed to require. As a result, live telecasting was prohibited during a great portion of the actual trial. Only the opening and closing arguments of the State, the return of the jury's verdict and its receipt by the trial judge were carried live with sound. Although the order allowed videotapes of the entire proceeding without sound, the cameras operated only intermittently, recording various portions of the trial for broadcast on regularly scheduled newscasts later in the day and evening. At the request of the petitioner, the trial judge prohibited coverage of any kind, still or television, of the defense counsel during their summations to the jury.

Because of the varying restrictions placed on sound and live telecasting the telecasts of the trial were confined largely to film clips shown on the stations' regularly scheduled news programs. The news commentators would use the film of a particular part of the day's trial activities as a backdrop for their reports. Their commentary included excerpts from testimony and the usual reportorial remarks. On one occasion the videotapes of the September hearings were rebroadcast in place of the "late movie."

In *Rideau* v. *State of Louisiana*, 373 U.S. 723, this Court constructed a rule that the televising of a defendant in the act of confessing to a crime was inherently invalid under the Due Process Clause of the Fourteenth Amendment even without a showing of prejudice or a demonstration of the nexus between the televised confession and the trial. . . . Here, although there was nothing so dramatic as a home-viewed confession, there had been a bombardment of the community with the sights and sounds of a two-day hearing during which the original jury panel, the petitioner, the lawyers and the judge were highly publicized. The petitioner was subjected to characterization and minute electronic scrutiny to such an extent that at one point the photographers were found attempting to picture the page of the paper from which he was reading while sitting at the counsel table. The two-day hearing and the order permitting television at the actual trial were widely known throughout the community. This emphasized the notorious character that the trial would take and, therefore, set it apart in the public mind as an extraordinary case or, as Shaw would say, something "not conventionally unconventional." When the new jury was empaneled at the trial four of the jurors selected had seen and heard all or part of the broadcasts of the earlier proceedings. . . .

We start with the proposition that it is a "public trial" that the Sixth Amendment guarantees to the "accused." The purpose of the requirement of a public trial was to guarantee that the accused would be fairly dealt with and not unjustly condemned. History had proven that secret tribunals were effective instruments of oppression. . . .

The free press has been a mighty catalyst in awakening public interest in governmental affairs. . . . While maximum freedom must be allowed the press in carrying on this important function in a democratic society its exercise must necessarily be subject to the maintenance of absolute fairness in the judicial process. . . .

Nor can the courts be said to discriminate where they permit the newspaper reporter access to the courtroom. The television and radio reporter has the same privilege. All are entitled to the same rights as the general public. . . .

Court proceedings are held for the solemn purpose of endeavoring to ascertain the truth which is the *sine qua non* of a fair trial. Over the centuries Anglo-American courts have devised careful safeguards by rule and otherwise to protect and facilitate the performance of this high function. As a result, at this time those safeguards do not permit the televising and photographing of a criminal trial, save in two States and there only under restriction. The federal courts prohibit it by specific rule. . . . We have always held that the atmosphere essential to the preservation of a fair trial—the most fundamental of all freedoms—must be maintained at all costs. . . . Here the remedy is clear and certain of application and it is our duty to continue to enforce the principles that from time immemorial have proven efficacious and necessary to a fair trial. . . .

The State contends that the televising of portions of a criminal trial does not constitute a denial of due process. Its position is that because no prejudice has been shown by the petitioner as resulting from the televising, it is permissible; . . . that psychological considerations are for psychologists, not courts, because they are purely hypothetical. . . .

At the outset the notion should be dispelled that telecasting is dangerous because it is new. . . . However, the nub of the question is not its newness but, as Mr. Justice Douglas says, "the insidious influences which it puts to work in the administration of justice."

Douglas, *The Public Trial and the Free Press,* 33 *Rocky Mt. L. Rev.* 1 (1960). . . .

It is true that the public has the right to be informed as to what occurs in its courts, but reporters of all media, including television, are always present if they wish to be and are plainly free to report whatever occurs in open court through their respective media. . . .

The State, however, says that the use of television in the instant case was "without injustice to the person immediately concerned," basing its position on the fact that the petitioner has established no isolatable prejudice and that this must be shown in order to invalidate a conviction in these circumstances. The State paints too broadly in this contention, for this Court itself has found instances in which a showing of actual prejudice is not a prerequisite to reversal. This is such a case. . . .[A]t times a procedure employed by the State involves such a probability that prejudice will result that it is deemed inherently lacking in due process. . . .

This rule was followed in *Rideau, supra,* and in *Turner* v. *State of Louisiana,* 379 U.S. 466. . . . In *Rideau* and *Turner* the Court did not stop to consider the actual effect of the practice but struck down the conviction on the ground that prejudice was inherent in it. . . .

In this case it is even clearer that such a rule must be applied. . . . In *Turner* . . . [n]o prejudice was shown but the circumstances were held to be inherently suspect, and therefore, such a showing was not held to be a requisite to reversal. Likewise in this case the application of this principle is especially appropriate. Television in its present state and by its very nature, reaches into a variety of areas in which it may cause prejudice to an accused. Still one cannot put his finger on its specific mischief and prove with particularity wherein he was prejudiced. . . . Forty-eight of our States and the Federal Rules have deemed the use of television improper in the courtroom. This fact is most telling in buttressing our conclusion that any change in procedure which would permit its use would be inconsistent with our concepts of due process in this field. . . .

As has been said, the chief function of our judicial machinery is to ascertain the truth. The use of television, however, cannot be said to contribute materially to this objective. Rather its use amounts to the injection of an irrelevant factor into court proceedings. In addition experience teaches that there are numerous situations in which it might cause actual unfairness — some so subtle as to defy detection by the accused or control by the judge. We enumerate some in summary:

1. The potential impact of television on the jurors is perhaps of the greatest significance. They are the nerve center of the fact-finding process. . . . From the moment the trial judge announces that a case will be televised it becomes a *cause célèbre.* . . . The approaching trial immediately assumes an important status in the public press and the accused is highly publicized along with the offense with which he is charged. Every juror carries with him into

the jury box these solemn facts and thus increases the chance of prejudice that is present in every criminal case. And we must remember that realistically it is only the notorious trial which will be broadcast, because of the necessity for paid sponsorship. The conscious or unconscious effect that this may have on the juror's judgment cannot be evaluated, but experience indicates that it is not only possible but highly probable that it will have a direct bearing on his vote as to guilt or innocence. Where pretrial publicity of all kinds has created intense public feeling which is aggravated by the telecasting or picturing of the trial the televised jurors cannot help but feel the pressures of knowing that friends and neighbors have their eyes upon them. If the community be hostile to an accused a televised juror, realizing that he must return to neighbors who saw the trial themselves, may well be led "not to hold the balance nice, clear and true between the State and the accused. * * *"

Moreover, while it is practically impossible to assess the effect of television on jury attentiveness, those of us who know juries realize the problem of jury "distraction.". . . . It is the awareness of the fact of telecasting that is felt by the juror throughout the trial. . . . Not only will a juror's eyes be fixed on the camera, but also his mind will be preoccupied with the telecasting rather than the testimony.

Furthermore, in many States the jurors serving in the trial may see the broadcasts of the trial proceedings. . . . They would also be subjected to reenactment and emphasis of the selected parts of the proceedings which the requirements of the broadcasters determined would be telecast and would be subconsciously influenced the more by that testimony. Moreover, they would be subjected to the broadest commentary and criticism and perhaps the well-meant advice of friends, relatives and inquiring strangers who recognized them on the streets.

Finally, new trials plainly would be jeopardized in that potential jurors will often have seen and heard the original trial when it was telecast. . . .

2. The quality of the testimony in criminal trials will often be impaired. The impact upon a witness of the knowledge that he is being viewed by a vast audience is simply incalculable. . . . There is little wonder that the defedant cannot "prove" the existence of such factors. Yet we all know from experience that they exist. . . .

Indeed, the mere fact that the trial is to be televised might render witnesses reluctant to appear and thereby impede the trial as well as the discovery of the truth. . . .

3. A major aspect of the problem is the additional responsibilities the presence of television places on the trial judge. His job is to make certain that the accused receives a fair trial. This most difficult task requires his undivided attention. Still when television comes into the courtroom he must also supervise it. In this trial, for example, the judge on several different occasions—aside from the two days of pretrial—was obliged to have a hearing or enter an order made

necessary solely because of the presence of television. Thus . . . his task is made much more difficult and exacting. And, as happened here, such rulings may unfortunately militate against the fairness of the trial. In addition, laying physical interruptions aside, there is the ever-present distraction that the mere awareness of television's presence prompts. Judges are human beings also and are subject to the same psychological reactions as laymen. Telecasting is particularly bad where the judge is elected, as is the case in all save a half dozen of our States. The telecasting of a trial becomes a political weapon, which along with other distractions inherent in broadcasting, diverts his attention from the task at hand—the fair trial of the accused.

But this is not all. There is the initial decision that must be made as to whether the use of television will be permitted. This is perhaps an even more crucial consideration. Our judges are highminded men and women. But it is difficult to remain oblivious to the pressures that the news media can bring to bear on them both directly and through the shaping of public opinion. Moreover, where one judge in a district or even in a State permits telecasting, the requirement that the others do the same is almost mandatory. Especially is this true where the judge is selected at the ballot box.

4. Finally, we cannot ignore the impact of courtroom television on the defendant. Its presence is a form of mental—if not physical—harassment, resembling a police line-up or the third degree. . . . The heightened public clamor resulting from radio and television coverage will inevitably result in prejudice. Trial by television is, therefore, foreign to our system. Furthermore, telecasting may also deprive an accused of effective counsel. The distractions, intrusions into confidential attorney-client relationships and the temptation offered by television to play to the public audience might often have a direct effect not only upon the lawyers, but the judge, the jury and the witnesses. . . .

The television camera is a powerful weapon. Intentionally or inadvertently it can destroy an accused and his case in the eyes of the public. While our telecasters are honorable men, they too are human. The necessity for sponsorship weighs heavily in favor of the televising of only notorious cases, such as this one, and invariably focuses the beam of the lens upon the unpopular or infamous accused. Such a selection is necessary in order to obtain a sponsor willing to pay a sufficient fee to cover the costs and return a profit. . . .

The State would dispose of all these observations with the simple statement that they are for psychologists because they are purely hypothetical. . . . But we cannot afford the luxury of saying that, because these factors are difficult of ascertainment in particular cases, they must be ignored. . . . They are real enough to have convinced the Judicial Conference of the United States, this Court and the Congress that television should be barred in federal trials by the Federal Rules of Criminal Procedure; in addition they have persuaded all but two of our States to prohibit television in the courtroom. . . .

The facts in this case demonstrate clearly the necessity for the application of the rule announced in *Rideau*. The sole issue before the court for two days of pretrial hearing was the question now before us. The hearing was televised live and repeated on tape in the same evening, reaching approximately 100,000 viewers. . . . The selection of the jury took an entire week. As might be expected, a substantial amount of that time was devoted to ascertaining the impact of the pretrial televising on the prospective jurors. As we have noted, four of the jurors selected had seen all or part of those broadcasts. The trial, on the other hand, lasted only three days. . . .

Moreover, the trial judge was himself harassed. After the initial decision to permit telecasting he apparently decided that a booth should be built at the broadcasters' expense to confine its operations; he then decided to limit the parts of the trial that might be televised live; then he decided to film the testimony of the witnesses without sound in an attempt to protect those under the rule; and finally he ordered that defense counsel and their argument not be televised, in the light of their objection. Plagued by his original error—recurring each day of the trial—his day-to-day orders made the trial more confusing to the jury, the participants and to the viewers. Indeed, it resulted in a public presentation of only the State's side of the case. . . .

It is said that the ever-advancing techniques of public communication and the adjustment of the public to its presence may bring about a change in the effect of telecasting upon the fairness of criminal trials. But we are not dealing here with future developments in the field of electronics. Our judgment cannot be rested on the hypothesis of tomorrow but must take the facts as they are presented today.

The judgment is therefore reversed. *Reversed*

MR. CHIEF JUSTICE WARREN, whom MR. JUSTICE DOUGLAS and MR. JUSTICE GOLDBERG join, concurring.

While I join the Court's opinion and agree that the televising of criminal trials is inherently a denial of due process, I desire to express additional views on why this is so. In doing this, I wish to emphasize that our condemnation of televised criminal trials is not based on generalities or abstract fears. The record in this case presents a vivid illustration of the inherent prejudice of televised criminal trials and supports our conclusion that this is the appropriate time to make a definitive appraisal of television in the courtroom.

Petitioner, a much publicized financier, was indicted by a Reeves County, Texas, grand jury for obtaining property through false pretenses. * * *

With photographers roaming at will through the courtroom, petitioner's counsel made his motion that all cameras be excluded. As he spóke a cameraman wandered behind the judge's bench and snapped his picture. * * *

On October 1, 1963, the trial judge issued an order explaining what coverage he would permit during the trial. The judge delivered the order in his chambers for the benefit of television cameramen so that they could film him. . . . The judge did not explain how he decided which television cameramen and which still photographers were to be permitted in the courtroom and which were to be excluded. * * *

The trial judge reaffirmed his prior ruling to permit cameramen in the courtroom. In response to petitioner's argument that his rights under the Constitution of the United States were being violated, the judge remarked that the "case [was] not being tried under the Federal Constitution." * * *

Significantly, in the Sixth Amendment the words "speedy and public" qualify the term *trial* and the rest of the Amendment defines specific protections the accused is to have at his *trial* . . . a word with a meaning of its own, see *Bridges* v. *State of California*, 314 U.S. 252, 271. . . .

[I]t also has been agreed that neither the Sixth nor the Fourteenth Amendment is to be read formalistically, for the clear intent of the amendments is that these specific rights be enjoyed at a constitutional trial. In the words of Justice Holmes, even though "every form [be] preserved," the forms may amount to no "more than an empty shell" when considered in the context or setting in which they were actually applied. * * *

For the Constitution to have vitality, this Court must be able to apply its principles to situations that may not have been foreseen at the time those principles were adopted. . . .

I believe that it violates the Sixth Amendment for federal courts and the Fourteenth Amendment for state courts to allow criminal trials to be televised to the public at large. I base this conclusion on three grounds: (1) that the televising of trials diverts the trial from its proper purpose in that it has an inevitable impact on all the trial participants; (2) that it gives the public the wrong impression about the purpose of trials, thereby detracting from the dignity of court proceedings and lessening the reliability of trials; and (3) that it singles out certain defendants and subjects them to trials under prejudicial conditions not experienced by others. * * *

The very presence of the cameras at the September hearing tended to impress upon the trial judge the power of the communications media and the criticism to which he would have been subjected if he had ruled that the presence of the cameras was inconsistent with petitioner's right to a fair trial. The prejudice to petitioner did not end here. . . . No one could forget that he was constantly in the focus of the "all-seeing eye." . . .

It is common knowledge that "television * * * can * * * work * * * profound changes in the behavior of the people it focuses on. . . . And, even if all participants make a conscientious and studied effort to be unaffected by the presence of television, this effort in itself prevents them from giving their full attention to their proper functions at trial. Thus, the evil of televised trials, as demonstrated by this case, lies not in the noise and appearance of the cameras, but in the trial participants' awareness that they are being televised. To the extent that television has such an inevitable impact it undercuts the reliability of the trial process. . . .

The television industry might also decide that the bareboned trial itself does not contain sufficient drama to sustain an audience. It might provide expert commentary on the proceedings and hire persons with legal backgrounds to anticipate possible trial strategy, as the football expert anticipates plays for his audience. . . .

There would be a real threat to the integrity of the trial process if the television industry and trial judges were allowed to become partners in the staging of criminal proceedings. . . .

Broadcasting in the courtroom would give the television industry an awesome power to condition the public mind either for or against an accused. . . . Moreover, if the case should end in a mistrial, the showing of selected portions of the trial, or even of the whole trial, would make it almost impossible to select an impartial jury for a second trial. . . . To permit this powerful medium to use the trial process itself to influence the opinions of vast numbers of people, before a verdict of guilt or innocence has been rendered, would be entirely foreign to our system of justice.

The sense of fairness, dignity and integrity that all associate with the courtroom would become lost with its commercialization. Thus, the televising of trials would not only have an effect on those participating in the trial that is being televised, but also on those who observe the trials and later become trial participants.

It is argued that television not only entertains but also educates the public. But the function of trial is not to provide an educational experience. . . .

Finally, if the televising of criminal proceedings were approved, trials would be selected for television coverage for reasons having nothing to do with the purpose of trial. A trial might be televised because a particular judge has gained the fancy of the public by his unorthodox approach; or because the district attorney has decided to run for another office . . . [T]he most important factor that would draw television to the courtroom would be the nature of the case. The alleged perpetrator of the sensational murder, the fallen idol . . . are the very persons who encounter the greatest difficulty in securing an impartial trial, even without the presence of television. ° ° °

I believe petitioner in this case has shown that he was actually prejudiced by the conduct of these proceedings, but I cannot agree with those who say that a televised trial deprives a defendant of a fair trial only if "actual prejudice" can be shown. The prejudice of television may be so subtle that it escapes the ordinary methods of proof, but it would gradually erode our fundamental conception of trial. . . . More importantly, the tapes or films, even if unedited, could give a wrong impression of the proceedings. . . . The most the camera can show is that a formally correct trial took place, but our Constitution requires more than form.

I recognize that the television industry has shown in the past that it can be an enlightening and informing institution, but like other institutions it must respect the rights of others and cannot demand that we alter fundamental constitutional conceptions for its benefit. We must take notice of the inherent unfairness of television in the courtroom and rule that its presence is inconsistent with the "fundamental conception" of what a trial should be. . . .

Nothing in this opinion is inconsistent with the constitutional guarantees of a public trial and the freedoms of speech and the press. . . .

In summary, television is one of the great inventions of all time and can perform a large and useful role in society. But the television camera, like other technological innovations, is not entitled to pervade the lives of everyone in disregard of constitutionally protected rights. . . . On entering that hallowed sanctuary, where the lives, liberty and property of people are in jeopardy, television representatives have only the rights of the general public, namely, to be present, to observe the proceedings, and thereafter, if they choose, to report them.

MR. JUSTICE HARLAN, concurring.

I concur in the opinion of the Court, subject, however, to the reservations and only to the extent indicated in this opinion. . . .

The question is fraught with unusual difficulties. . . . My conclusion is that there is no constitutional requirement that television be allowed in the courtroom, and at least as to a notorious criminal trial such as this one, the considerations against allowing television in the courtroom so far outweigh the countervailing factors advanced in its support as to require a holding that what was done in this case infringed the fundamental right to a fair trial assured by the Due Process Clause of the Fourteenth Amendment. * * *

The Estes trial was a heavily publicized and highly sensational affair. I therefore put aside all other types of cases; in so doing, however, I wish to make it perfectly clear that I am by no means prepared to say that the constitutional issue should ultimately turn upon the nature of the particular case involved. . . . The resolution of those further questions should await an appropriate case; the Court should proceed only step by step in this unplowed field. The opinion of the Court necessarily goes no farther, for only the four members of the majority who unreservedly join the Court's opinion would resolve those questions now. * * *

. . . At the present juncture I can only conclude that televised trials, at least in cases like this one, possess such capabilities for interfering with the even course of the judicial process that they are constitutionally banned. On these premises I concur in the opinion of the Court. . . .

MR. JUSTICE STEWART, whom MR. JUSTICE BLACK, MR. JUSTICE BRENNAN, and MR. JUSTICE WHITE join, dissenting.

I cannot agree with the Court's decision that the circumstances of this trial led to a denial of the petitioner's Fourteenth Amendment rights. I think that the introducton of television into a courtroom is, at least in the present state of the art, an extremely unwise policy. It invites many constitutional risks, and it detracts from the inherent dignity of a courtroom. But I am unable to escalate this personal view into a *per se* constitutional rule. And I am unable to find, on the specific record of this case, that the circumstances attending the limited televising of the petitioner's trial resulted in the denial of any right guaranteed to him by the United States Constitution. . . .

[A]s the Court rightly says, the problem before us is . . . rooted in the Due Process Clause of the Fourteenth Amendment. We deal here with matters subject to continuous and unforeseeable change—the techniques of public communication. In an area where all the variables may be modified tomorrow, I cannot at this time rest my determination on hypothetical possibilities not present in the record of this case. There is no claim here based upon any right guaranteed by the First Amendment. But it is important to remember that we move in an area touching the realm of free communication, and for that reason, if for no other, I would be wary of imposing any *per se* rule which, in the light of future technology, might serve to stifle or abridge true First Amendment rights. * * *

It is important to bear in mind the precise limits of the question before us in this case. The petition for a writ of certiorari asked us to review four separate constitutional claims. We declined to review three of them. . . . We thus left undisturbed the determination of the Texas Court of Criminal Appeals that the members of the jury were *not* prejudiced by the widespread publicity which preceded the petitioner's trial. One ingredient of this pretrial publicity was the telecast of the September hearings. Despite the confusion in the courtroom during those hearings, all that a potential juror could have possibly learned from watching them on television was that the petitioner's case had been called for trial, and that motions had been made and acted upon for a continuance, and to exclude cameras and television. . . .

Under the limited grant of certiorari in this case, the sole question before us is . . . only the regulated presence of television and still photography at the trial itself, which began on October 22, 1962. Any discussion of pretrial events can do no more than obscure the important question which is actually before us. * * *

It is obvious that the introduction of television and news cameras into criminal trial invites many serious constitutional hazards. . . .

Some of those risks are catalogued in the *amicus curiae* brief filed in this case by the American Bar Association. . . .

The plain fact of the matter, however, is that none of these things happened or could have happened in this case. . . .

What ultimately emerges from this record, therefore, is one bald question—whether the Fourteenth Amendment of the United States Constitution prohibits all television cameras from a state courtroom whenever a criminal trial is in progress. In the light of this record and what we now know about the impact of television on a criminal trial, I can find no such prohibition in the Fourteenth Amendment or in any other provision of the Constitution. If what occurred did not deprive the petitioner of his constitutional right to a fair trial, then the fact that the public could view the proceeding on television has no constitutional significance. The Constitution does not make us arbiters of the image that a televised state criminal trial projects to the public.

. . . The idea of imposing upon any medium of communications the burden of justifying its presence is contrary to where I had always thought the presumption must lie in the area of First Amendment freedoms. . . . And the proposition that nonparticipants in a trial might get the "wrong impression" from unfettered reporting and commentary contains an invitation to censorship which I cannot accept. Where there is no disruption of the "essential requirement of the fair and orderly administration of justice," "[f]reedom of discussion should be given the widest range." *Pennekamp* v. *State of Florida*, 328 U.S. 331, 347.

. . . I cannot now hold that the Constitution absolutely bars television cameras from every criminal courtroom, even if they have no impact upon the jury, no effect upon any witness, and no influence upon the conduct of the judge.

For these reasons I would affirm the judgment.

MR. JUSTICE WHITE, with whom MR. JUSTICE BRENNAN joins, dissenting.

I agree with MR. JUSTICE STEWART that a finding of constitutional prejudice on this record entails erecting a flat ban on the use of cameras in the courtroom and believe that it is premature to promulgate such a broad constitutional principal at the present time. . . . In my view, the currently available materials assessing the effect of cameras in the courtroom are too sparse and fragmentary to constitute the basis for a constitutional judgment permanently barring any and all forms of television coverage. . . .

The opinion of the Court in effect precludes further opportunity for intelligent assessment of the probable hazards imposed by the use of cameras at criminal trials. . . . Here, although our experience is inadequate and our judgment correspondingly infirm, the Court discourages further meaningful study of the use of television at criminal trials. Accordingly, I dissent.

Mr. Justice Brennan.

I write merely to emphasize that only four of the five Justices voting to reverse rest on the proposition that televised criminal trials are constitutionally infirm, whatever the circumstances. Although the opinion announced by my Brother CLARK purports to be an "opinion of the Court," my Brother HARLAN subscribes to a significantly less sweeping proposition. . . .

Thus today's decision is *not* a blanket constitutional prohibition against the televising of state criminal trials.

While I join the dissents of my Brothers STEWART and WHITE, I do so on the understanding that their use of the expressions "the Court's opinion" or "the opinion of the Court" refers only to those views of our four Brethren which my Brother HARLAN explicitly states he shares. . . .

CHAPTER THREE

★　　★　　★

Religion

THE FIRST AMENDMENT to the Constitution provides that "Congress shall make no law respecting an establishment of religion, or prohibiting the free exercise thereof . . . ", a deceptively simple statement. On the face of it, "no law . . . prohibiting the free exercise thereof" would seem to allow the individual to act in accordance with the dictates of his religious beliefs. But the word "religion" is not defined in the Constitution, nor is "prohibiting the free exercise thereof," nor is the right to act on one's beliefs spelled out.

Without defining "religion," the *Reynolds* case (*Reynolds* v. *U.S.*, 98 U.S. 145; 1878) distinguished between freedom to believe and freedom to act on one's belief. Mr. Reynolds was convicted under a federal statute which made it a crime for a person having a spouse to marry another in a Territory under the exclusive jurisdiction of the United States. A resident of the Territory of Utah, Mr. Reynolds was a member of the Mormon Church, and accepted its doctrines, including that of plural marriage. With church permission he took a second wife, although he knew it was illegal, asserting that he was acting on his religious beliefs and was therefore immune from prosecution. The Court did not agree, saying that although Mr. Reynolds had a right to his religious beliefs, he had no right to act in violation of the law. His conviction was therefore affirmed.

Freedom to believe the tenets of a particular faith would seem to include the right to teach them to the believer's own children. A natural extension of this right is to employ others to teach, and to establish a school where both religious and secular subjects are taught.

But the state has an obvious interest in having a healthy and informed body of citizens, and may therefore impose certain restrictions upon those who would organize and operate a school. In the exercise of its police power, certain standards of health and safety may be required. Since an informed body of citizens is necessary to maintain

32

government, instruction in a specified minimum of subjects may also be required. But in a private school, what limitations may be placed upon learning?

Our religious and other private schools have been built upon the legal foundation of the *Meyer* and *Pierce* cases, both of which show the indirect influence Supreme Court decisions can have. In the *Meyer* case, what was in issue was the right of a teacher to pursue his calling and in the *Pierce* case the right of a corporation not to be deprived of its property without due process of law. The decisions gave both religious and other private schools legal justification for their special programs.

In *Meyer* v. *Nebraska* (262 U.S. 390; 43 S. Ct. 625; 1923) the Court struck down a statute which restricted the teaching of the German language to children who had successfully passed the eighth grade. Mr. Meyer had taught the language to a religious school child of ten. The Court said,

> The problem for our determination is whether the statute as construed and applied unreasonably infringes the liberty guaranteed to the plaintiff in error by the Fourteenth Amendment. * * *
> . . . Mere knowledge of the German language cannot reasonably be regarded as harmful. . . . Plaintiff in error taught this language in school as part of his occupation. His right thus to teach and the right of parents to engage him so to instruct their children, we think, are within the liberty of the Amendment. * * *
> . . . The Supreme Court of the State has held that "the so-called ancient or dead languages" are not "within the spirit or the purpose of the act." . . . Evidently the legislature has attempted materially to interfere with the calling of modern language teachers, with the opportunities of pupils to acquire knowledge, and with the power of parents to control the education of their own. . . .
> That the State may do much, go very far, indeed, in order to improve the quality of its citizens, physically, mentally and morally, is clear; but the individual has certain fundamental rights which must be respected. . . .
> The power of the State to compel attendance at some school and to make reasonable regulations for all schools, including a requirement that they shall give instructions in English, is not questioned. . . . No emergency has arisen which renders knowledge by a child of some language other than English so clearly harmful as to justify its inhibition with the consequent infringement of rights long freely enjoyed. We are constrained to conclude that the statute as applied is arbitrary and without reasonable relation to any end within the competency of the State. * * *   *Reversed.*

Mr. Justice Holmes, dissenting in a companion case (*Bartels* v. *Iowa,* 262 U.S. 404, 412), disagreed with his brethren.

* * * The only question is whether the means adopted deprive teachers of the liberty secured to them by the Fourteenth Amendment. . . . I cannot bring my mind to believe that in some circumstances . . . the statute might not be regarded as a reasonable or even necessary method of reaching the desired result. . . . But if it is reasonable it is not an undue restriction of the liberty either of teacher or scholar. . . . [T]he only criterion of [a teacher's] liberty under the Constitution that I can think of is "whether, considering the end in view, the statute passes the bounds of reason and assumes the character of a merely arbitrary fiat." *Purity Extract & Tonic Co.* v. *Lynch*, 226 U.S. 192, 204. . . . I think I appreciate the objection to the law but it appears to me to present a question upon which men reasonably differ and therefore I am unable to say that the Constitution of the United States prevents the experiment being tried.

Two years later, in *Pierce* v. *Society of the Sisters of the Holy Name* (268 U.S. 510; 45S. Ct. 571; 1925) an attempt on the part of Oregon to prohibit both private and parochial schools failed, not on religious or educational grounds, but on the grounds that the owners of such schools were deprived of their property without due process of law. The Court reasoned that the schools owned physical facilities which were of no use without pupils; they had, in fact, already suffered a loss of enrollment. If the statute were enforced, the schools would perish. The Court then went on to say:

. . . The fundamental theory of liberty upon which all governments in this Union repose excludes any general power of the state to standardize its children by forcing them to accept instruction from public teachers only. The child is not the mere creature of the state; those who nurture him and direct his destiny have the right, coupled with the high duty, to recognize and prepare him for additional obligations.
Appellees are corporations, and therefore, it is said, they cannot claim for themselves the liberty which the Fourteenth Amendment guarantees. Accepted in the proper sense, this is true. . . . But they have business and property for which they claim protection. These are threatened with destruction through the unwarranted compulsion which appellants are exercising over present and prospective patrons of their schools. And this court has gone very far to protect against loss threatened by such action. . . .[1]

On the basis of these cases it would seem that parents who want the special training for their children offered by private and religious schools may have it not because of an unrestricted power to direct the education of their offspring, but because these schools, and the teach-

---

[1]*Pierce* v. *Society of the Sisters of the Holy Name,* 268 U.S. 510, pp. 535, 536.

ing profession, have property rights which cannot be destroyed by the exercise of the state's police power.

Ever since the great depression of 1929 an increasing variety of services has been made available to public school children. One area of disagreement has been the extent to which these services, which are paid for by the state or federal government, should be available to private school children. Although both religious and secular schools, charitable and non-charitable, are included in the term "private school," the conflict actually is largely focussed on services to children who attend religious schools. It is relatively simple to state: In providing free books, lunches, and medical services to such children, the state is aiding a particular religion. These services involve some expense to the government; if they are given to religious schools on the same basis as to public schools, the state is spending money to help support the educational policies and beliefs of a particular religion, in violation of the First Amendment as that is a part of the Fourteenth Amendment. The counter-argument is that the services are not given to the schools but to children who happen to go to school. Must a child be denied benefits because his parents have chosen not to send him to public school—in fact, believe they have chosen a superior education? A child is no less a child because he attends a private school.

Each community in fact resolves the problem in its own fashion, often taking into account the strongly expressed viewpoints of its citizens. But attempts to resolve the conflict have also been a motivating force in legislation, and in certain cases which have reached the United States Supreme Court.

According to the First Amendment, made applicable to the states through the Fourteenth, "Congress shall make no law respecting an establishment of religion, or prohibiting the free exercise thereof. . . ." Violation of the "establishment clause" and the "free exercise clause" have been claimed in numerous cases. The next cases were related to school problems.

Although the pattern of *Zorach* v. *Clauson* has been widely used, one of the basic questions raised by Justice Black still remains unanswered: Who has the right to define what a "duly constituted religious body" is?

The last two—*Schempp* and *Murray*—were companion cases. In the *Schempp* case there had been a trial on the merits; in the *Murray* case there had not, for the respondents demurred, thus admitting all facts well pleaded by the petitioners. In this case the petition of the Murrays for a writ of mandamus and the demurrer were before the Court, but there was no evidence of experts and no confirmation, denial, or elaboration of the facts set forth in the petition and answer. A writ of mandamus is a technical proceeding in which the petitioner asks that the respondent perform a purely ministerial act: an act which requires the exercise of no judgment or discretion. In effect, the Murrays were saying that the city was obligated to rescind the rule providing for opening exercises which included reading the Bible or a recitation of the Lord's Prayer. The questions open to the Court in the *Murray* case were, therefore, much more restricted in the law and in the facts before the Court than in the *Schempp* case.

These cases illustrate constantly recurring problems in the techniques of decision making. The first is, of course, whether the United States Constitution has been violated: a mere allegation that it has been is not sufficient. A second problem is whether the issues raised in two (or more) cases are similar enough to be part of one decision. A third problem is that of putting the case in historical and constitutional perspective, as well as explaining not only the logic which compels the decision and the reasons why such a decision was required by the facts, but also what was not decided. A Supreme Court decision in an area of particular concern to the public now seems to be directed almost as much to that public as it is to the experts whose life is in the law.

In the *Engel* case, in spite of the care of the Court and the clarity of the opinion, there was an immediate outcry — so immediate, in fact, that those objecting to the decision obviously had not read it before castigating the Court. Second thoughts, undoubtedly accompanied in many instances by a reading of the case, have made approval of the opinion prominent. Many have come to recognize that not only is any kind of "establishment" of religion forbidden, but that such establishment would proscribe the "free exercise" of religion.

Everson v. *Board of Education of the Township of Ewing et al.* 330 U.S. 1, 67 S. Ct. 504 (1947)

MR. JUSTICE BLACK delivered the opinion of the Court.

A New Jersey statute authorizes its local school districts to make rules and contracts for the transportation of children to and from schools. The appellee, a township board of education, acting pursuant to this statute, authorized reimbursement to parents of money expended by them for the bus transportation of their children on regular busses operated by the public transportation system. Part of this money was for the payment of transportation of some children in the community to Catholic parochial schools. These church schools give their students, in addition to secular education, regular religious instruction conforming to the religious tenets and modes of worship of the Catholic Faith. The superintendent of these schools is a Catholic priest.

The appellant, in his capacity as a district taxpayer, filed suit in a state court challenging the right of the Board to reimburse parents of parochial school students. He contended that the statute and the resolution passed pursuant to it violated both the State and the Federal Constitutions. That court held that the legislature was without power to authorize such payment under the state constitution. 132 N. J. L. 98. The New Jersey Court of Errors and Appeals reversed, holding that neither the statute nor the resolution passed pursuant to it was in conflict with the State constitution or the provisions of the Federal Constitution in issue. 133 N. J. L. 350. The case is here on appeal under 28 U.S. C. § 344 (a).

Since there has been no attack on the statute on the ground that a part of its language excludes children attending private schools operated for profit from enjoying State payment for their transportation, we need not consider this exclusionary language; it has no relevancy to any constitutional question here presented. . . .

The only contention here is that the state statute and the resolution, insofar as they authorized reimbursement to parents of children attending parochial schools, violate the Federal Constitution in these two respects, which to some extent overlap. *First.* They authorize the State to take by taxation the private property of some and bestow it upon others, to be used for their own private purposes.This, it is alleged, violates the due process clause of the Fourteenth Amendment. *Second.* The statute and the resolution forced inhabitants to pay taxes to help support and maintain schools which are dedicated to, and which regularly teach, the Catholic Faith. This is alleged to be a use of state power to support church schools contrary to the prohibition of the First Amendment which the Fourteenth Amendment made applicable to the states.

First. The due process argument that the state law taxes some people to help others carry out their private purposes is framed in two phases. The first phase is that a state cannot tax A to reimburse B for the cost of transporting his children to church schools. This is said to violate the due process clause because the children are sent to these church schools to satisfy the personal desires of their parents, rather than the public's interest in the general education of all children. This argument, if valid, would apply equally to prohibit state payment for the transportation of children to any non-public school, whether operated by a church or any other non-government individual or group. But, the New Jersey legislature has decided that a public purpose will be served by using tax-raised funds to pay the bus fares of all school children, including those who attend parochial schools. The New Jersey Court of Errors and Appeals has reached the same conclusion. The fact that a state law, passed to satisfy a public need, coincides with the personal desires of the individuals most directly affected is certainly an inadequate reason for us to say that a legislature has erroneously appraised the public need.

It is true that this Court has, in rare instances, struck down state statutes on the ground that the purpose for which tax-raised funds were to be expended was not a public one. *Loan Association* v. *Topeka,* 20 Wall. 655. . . . But the Court has also pointed out that this far-reaching authority must be exercised with the most extreme caution. *Green* v. *Frazier,* 253 U.S. 233, 240. Otherwise, a state's power to legislate for the public welfare might be seriously curtailed, a power which is a primary reason for the existence of states. . . .

It is much too late to argue that legislation intended to facilitate the opportunity of children to get a secular education serves no public purpose. *Cochran* v. *Louisiana State Board of Education,* 281 U. S. 370. . . . The same thing is no less true of legislation to reimburse needy parents, or all parents, for payment of the fares of their children so that they can ride in public busses to and from schools rather than run the risk of traffic and other hazards incident to walking or "hitchhiking." . . . Nor does it follow that a law has a private rather than a public purpose because it provides that tax-raised funds will be paid to reimburse individuals on account of money spent by them in a way which furthers a public program. . . .

Insofar as the second phase of the due process argument may differ from the first, it is by suggesting that taxation for transportation of children to church schools constitutes support of a religion by the State. But if the law is invalid for this reason, it is because it violates the First Amendment's prohibition against the establishment of religion by law. This is the exact question raised by appellant's second contention, to consideration of which we now turn.

Second. The New Jersey statute is challenged as a "law respecting an establishment of religion." The First Amendment, as made applicable to the states by the Fourteenth, *Murdock* v. *Pennsylvania,* 319 U. S. 105, commands that a state "shall make no law respecting an establishment of religion, or prohibiting the free exercise thereof. . . ." These words of the First Amendment reflected in the minds of early Americans a vivid mental picture of conditions and practices which they fervently wished to stamp out in order to preserve liberty for themselves and for their posterity. . . . Whether this New Jersey law is one respecting an "establishment of religion" requires an understanding of the meaning of that language, particularly with respect to the imposition of taxes. Once again, therefore, it is not inappropriate briefly to review the background and environment of the period in which that constitutional language was fashioned and adopted.

. . . No one locality and no one group throughout the Colonies can rightly be given entire credit for having aroused the sentiment that culminated in adoption of the Bill of Rights' provisions embracing religious liberty. But Virginia, where the established church had achieved a dominant influence in political affairs and where many excesses attracted wide public attention, provided a great stimulus and able leadership for the movement. . . .

This Court has previously recognized that the provisions of the First Amendment, in the drafting and adoption of which Madison and Jefferson played such leading roles, had the same objective and were intended to provide the same protection against governmental intrusion on religious liberty as the Virginia statute. *Reynolds* v. *United States*. . . . Prior to the adoption of the Fourteenth Amendment, the First Amendment did not apply as a restraint against the states. Most of them did soon provide similar constitutional protections for religious liberty. But some states persisted for about half a century in imposing restraints upon the free exercise of religion and in discriminating against particular religious groups. In recent years, so far as the provision against the establishment of a religion is concerned, the question has most frequently arisen in connection with proposed state aid to church schools and efforts to carry on religious teachings in the public schools in accordance with the tenets of a particular sect. Some churches have either sought or accepted state financial support for their schools. Here again the efforts to obtain state aid or acceptance of it have not been limited to any one particular faith. . . . The broad meaning given the Amendment by these earlier cases has been accepted by this Court in its decisions concerning an individual's religious freedom rendered since the Fourteenth Amendment was interpreted to make the prohibitions of the First applicable to state action abridging religious freedom. There is every reason to give the same application and broad interpretation to the "establishment of religion" clause. . . .

The "establishment of religion" clause of the First Amendment means at least this: Neither a state nor the Federal Government can set up a church. Neither can pass laws which aid one religion, aid all religions, or prefer one religion over another. Neither can force nor influence a person to go to or to remain away from church against his will or force him to profess a belief or disbelief in any religion. No person can be punished for entertaining or professing religious beliefs or disbeliefs, for church attendance or non-attendance. No tax in any amount, large or small, can be levied to support any religious activities or institutions, whatever they may be called, or whatever form they may adopt to teach or practice religion. Neither a state nor the Federal Government can, openly or secretly, participate in the affairs of any religious organizations or groups and *vice versa*. In the words of Jefferson, the clause against establishment of religion by law was intended to erect "a wall of separation between church and State." *Reynolds* v. *United States, supra* at 164.

We must consider the New Jersey statute in accordance with the foregoing limitations imposed by the First Amendment. But we must not strike that state statute down if it is within the State's constitutional power even though it approaches the verge of that power. . . .

While we do not mean to intimate that a state could not provide transportation only to children attending public schools, we must be careful, in protecting the citizens of New Jersey against state-established churches, to be sure that we do not inadvertently prohibit New Jersey from extending its general state law benefits to all its citizens without regard to their religious belief.

Measured by these standards, we cannot say that the First Amendment prohibits New Jersey from spending tax-raised funds to pay the bus fares of parochial school pupils as a part of a general program under which it pays the fares of pupils attending public and other schools. . . .

Of course, cutting off church schools from these services, so separate and so indisputably marked off from the religious function, would make it far more difficult for the schools to operate. But such is obviously not the purpose of the First Amendment. That Amendment requires the state to be a neutral in its relations with groups of religious believers and non-believers; it does not require the state to be their adversary. State power is no more to be used so as to handicap religions than it is to favor them. . . .

This Court has said that parents may, in the discharge of their duty under state compulsory education laws, send their children to a religious rather than a public school if the school meets the secular educational requirements which the state has power to impose. See *Pierce* v. *Society of Sisters*, 268 U.S. 510. It appears that these parochial schools meet New Jersey's requirements. The State contributes no money to the schools. It does not support them. Its legislation, as applied, does no more than provide a general program to help parents get their children, regardless of their religion, safely and expeditiously to and from accredited schools.

The First Amendment has erected a wall between church and state. That wall must be kept high and impregnable. We could not approve the slightest breach. New Jersey has not breached it here.

Affirmed.

MR. JUSTICE JACKSON, dissenting.

I find myself, contrary to first impressions, unable to join in this decision. I have a sympathy, though it is not ideological, with Catholic citizens who are compelled by law to pay taxes for public schools, and also feel constrained by conscience and discipline to support other schools for their own children. Such relief to them as this case involves is not in itself a serious burden to taxpayers and I had assumed it to be as little serious in principle. Study of this case convinces me otherwise. . . .

In fact, the undertones of the opinion, advocating complete and uncompromising separation of Church from State, seem utterly discordant with its conclusion yielding support to their commingling in educational matters. The case which irresistibly comes to mind as the most fitting precedent is that of Julia who, according to Byron's reports, "whispering 'I will ne'er consent,'—consented." . . . .

The Court sustains this legislation by assuming two deviations from the facts of this particular case; first, it assumes a state of facts the record does not support, and secondly, it refuses to consider facts which are inescapable on the record.

The Court concludes that this "legislation, as applied, does no more than provide a general program to help parents get their children, regardless of their religion, safely and expeditiously to and from accredited schools," and it draws a comparison between "state provisions intended to guarantee free transportation" for school children with services such as police and fire protection, and implies that we are here dealing with "laws authorizing new types of public services . . . ." This hypothesis permeates the opinion. The facts will not bear that construction.

The Township of Ewing is not furnishing transportation to the children in any form; it is not operating school buses itself or contracting for their operation; and it is not performing any public service of any kind with this taxpayer's money. All school children are left to ride as ordinary paying passengers on the regular busses operated by the public transportation system. What the Township does, and what the taxpayer complains of, is at stated intervals to reimburse parents for the fares paid, provided the children attend either public schools or Catholic Church schools. This expenditure of tax funds has no possible effect on the child's safety or expedition in transit. As passengers on the public busses they travel as fast and no faster, and are as safe and no safer, since their parents are reimbursed as before.

In addition to thus assuming a type of service that does not exist, the Court also insists that we must close our eyes to a discrimination which does exist. The resolution which authorizes disbursement of this taxpayer's money limits reimbursement to those who attend public schools and Catholic schools. That is the way the Act is applied to this taxpayer.

The New Jersey Act in question makes the character of the school, not the needs of the children, determine the eligibility of parents to reimbursement. The Act permits payment for transportation to parochial schools or public schools but prohibits it to private schools operated in whole or in part for profit. . . . If all children of the state were objects of impartial solicitude, no reason is obvious for denying transportation reimbursement to students of this class, for these often are as needy and as worthy as those who go to public or parochial schools. . . . Thus, under the Act and resolution brought to us by this case, children are classified according to the schools they attend and are to be aided if they attend the public schools or private Catholic schools, and they are not allowed to be aided if they attend private secular schools or private religious schools of other faiths.

. . . [T]his case. . . is one of a taxpayer urging that he is being taxed for an unconstitutional purpose. I think he is entitled to have us consider the Act just as it is written. . . .

If we are to decide this case on the facts before us, our question is simply this: Is it constitutional to tax this complainant to pay the cost of carrying pupils to Church schools of one specified denomination? . . .

Whether the taxpayer constitutionally can be made to contribute aid to parents of students because of their attendance at parochial schools depends upon the nature of those schools and their relation to the Church. The Constitution says nothing of education. It lays no obligation on the states to provide schools and does not undertake to regulate state systems of education if they see fit to maintain them. But they cannot, through school policy any more than through other means, invade rights secured to citizens by the Constitution of the United States. *West Virginia State Board of Education* v. *Barnette*, 319 U.S. 624. One of our basic rights is to be free of taxation to support a transgression of the constitutional command that the authorities "shall make no law respecting an establishment of religion, or prohibiting the free exercise thereof . . . ." U. S. Const., Amend. I; *Cantwell* v. *Connecticut*, 310 U.S. 296.

The function of the Church school is a subject on which this record is meager. . . . But we know that such schools are parochial only in name — they, in fact, represent a world-wide and age-old policy of the Roman Catholic Church. . . .

It is no exaggeration to say that the whole historic conflict in temporal policy between the Catholic Church and non-Catholics comes to a focus in their respective school policies. The Roman Catholic Church, counseled by experience in many ages and many lands and with all sorts and conditions of men, takes what, from the viewpoint of its own progress and the success of its mission, is a wise estimate of the importance of education to religion. It does not leave the individual to pick up religion by chance. It relies on early and indelible indoctrination in the faith and order of the Church by the word and example of persons consecrated to the task. . . .

I should be surprised if any Catholic would deny that the parochial school is a vital, if not the most vital, part of the Roman Catholic Church. . . . Catholic education is the rock on which the whole structure rests, and to render tax aid to its Church school is indistinguishable to me from rendering the same aid to the Church itself. . . .

It is of no importance in this situation whether the beneficiary of this expenditure of tax-raised funds is primarily the parochial school and incidentally the pupil, or whether the aid is directly bestowed on the pupil with indirect benefits to the school. The state cannot maintain a Church and it can no more tax its citizens to furnish free carriage to those who attend a Church. The prohibition against establishment of religion cannot be circumvented by a subsidy, bonus or reimbursement of expense to individuals for receiving religious instruction and indoctrination. . . .

It seems to me that the basic fallacy in the Court's reasoning, which accounts for its failure to apply the principles it avows, is in ignoring the essentially religious test by which beneficiaries of this expenditure are selected. * * *

There is no answer to the proposition, more fully expounded by MR. JUSTICE RUTLEDGE, that the effect of the religious freedom Amendment to our Constitution was to take every form of propagation of religion out of the realm of things which could directly or indirectly be made public business and thereby be supported in whole or in part at taxpayers' expense. That is a difference which the Constitution sets up between religion and almost every other subject matter of legislation, a difference which goes to the very root of religious freedom and which the Court is overlooking today. This freedom was first in the Bill of Rights because it was first in the forefathers' minds; it was set forth in absolute terms, and its strength is its rigidity. It was intended not only to keep the states' hands out of religion, but to keep religion's hands off the state, and, above all, to keep bitter religious controversy out of public life by denying to every denomination any advantage from getting control of public policy or the public purse. Those great ends I cannot but think are immeasurably compromised by today's decision. ° ° ° °

. . . I cannot read the history of the struggle to separate political from ecclesiastical affairs, well summarized in the opinion of MR. JUSTICE RUTLEDGE in which I generally concur, without a conviction that the Court today is unconsciously giving the clock's hands a backward turn.

MR. JUSTICE FRANKFURTER joins in this opinion.

MR. JUSTICE RUTLEDGE, with whom MR. JUSTICE FRANKFURTER, MR. JUSTICE JACKSON and MR. JUSTICE BURTON agree, dissenting.

. . . Neither so high nor so impregnable today as yesterday is the wall raised between church and state by Virginia's great statute of religious freedom and the First Amendment, now made applicable to all the states by the Fourteenth. New Jersey's statute sustained is the first, if indeed it is not the second breach to be made by this Court's action. That a third, and a fourth, and still others will be attempted, we may be sure. . . .

This case forces us to determine squarely for the first time what was "an establishment of religion" in the First Amendment's conception; and by that measure to decide whether New Jersey's action violates its command. . . .

Named parents have paid the cost of public conveyance of their children from their homes in Ewing to three public high schools and four parochial schools outside the district. Semiannually the Board has reimbursed the parents from public school funds raised by general taxation. Religion is taught as part of the curriculum in each of the four private schools, as appears affirmatively by the testimony of the superintendent of parochial schools in the Diocese of Trenton. . . .

Not simply an established church, but any law respecting an establishment of religion is forbidden. The Amendment was broadly but not loosely phrased. . . .

The Amendment's purpose . . . was to create a complete and permanent separation of the spheres of religious activity and civil authority by comprehensively forbidding every form of public aid or support for religion. In proof the Amendment's wording and history unite with this Court's consistent utterances whenever attention has been fixed directly upon the question. ° ° °

New Jersey's action . . . exactly fits the type of exaction and the kind of evil at which Madison and Jefferson struck. Under the test they framed it cannot be said that the cost of transportation is no part of the cost of education or of the religious instruction given. * * *

For me, therefore, the feat is impossible to select so indispensable an item from the composite of total costs, and characterize it as not aiding, contributing to, promoting or sustaining the propagation of beliefs which it is the very end of all to bring about. Unless this can be maintained, and the Court does not maintain it, the aid thus given is outlawed. * * *

This is not therefore just a little case over bus fares. In paraphrase of Madison, distant as it may be in its present form from a complete establishment of religion, it differs from it only in degree; and is the first step in that direction. * * *

I have chosen to place my dissent upon the broad ground I think decisive, though strictly speaking the case might be decided on narrower issues. The New Jersey statute might be held invalid on its face for the exclusion of children who attend private, profit-making schools. . . .

Two great drives are constantly in motion to abridge, in the name of education, the complete division of religion and civil authority which our forefathers made. One is to introduce religious education and observances into the public schools. The other, to obtain public funds for the aid and support of various private religious schools. . . . In my opinion both avenues were closed by the Constitution. Neither should be opened by this Court. . . . We should not be less strict to keep strong and untarnished the one side of the shield of religious freedom than we have been of the other.

The judgment should be reversed.

Illinois ex rel. McCollum v. *Board of Education of School District No. 71, Champaign County, Illinois, et al.,* 333 U.S. 203, 68 S. Ct. 461 (1948)

MR. JUSTICE BLACK delivered the opinion of the Court.

This case relates to the power of a state to utilize its tax-supported public school system in aid of religious instruction insofar as that power may be restricted by the First and Fourteenth Amendments to the Federal Constitution.

The appellant, Vashti McCollum, began this action for mandamus against the Champaign Board of Education in the Circuit Court of Champaign County, Illinois. Her asserted interest was that of a resident and taxpayer of Champaign and of a parent whose child was then enrolled in the Champaign public schools. Illinois has a compulsory education law which, with exceptions, requires parents to send their children, aged seven to sixteen, to its tax-supported public schools where the children are to remain in attendance during the hours when the schools are regularly in session. Parents who violate this law commit a misdemeanor punishable by fine unless the children attend private or parochial schools which meet educational standards fixed by the State. District boards of education are given general supervisory powers over the use of the public school buildings within the school districts. . . .

Appellant's petition for mandamus alleged that religious teachers, employed by private religious groups, were permitted to come weekly into the school buildings during the regular hours set apart for secular teaching, and then and there for a period of thirty minutes substitute religious teaching for the secular education provided under the compulsory education law. The petitioner charged that this joint public-school religious-group program violated the First and Fourteenth Amendments to the United States Constitution. The prayer of her petition was that the Board of Education be ordered to "adopt and enforce rules and regulations prohibiting all instruction in and teaching of religious education in all public schools in Champaign School District Number 71, . . . and in all public school houses and buildings in said district when occupied by public schools."

. . . An answer . . . admitted that regular weekly religious instruction was given during school hours to those pupils whose parents consented and that those pupils were released temporarily from their regular secular classes for the limited purpose of attending the religious classes. The answer denied that this coordinated program of religious instruction violated the State or Federal Constitution. . . . [T]he petition for mandamus was denied on the ground that the school's religious instruction program violated neither the federal nor state constitutional provisions invoked by the appellant. . . . Appellant appealed to this Court. . . .

Although there are disputes between the parties as to various inferences that may or may not properly be drawn from the evidence concerning the religious program, the following facts are shown by the record without dispute. In 1940 interested members of the Jewish, Roman Catholic, and a few of the Protestant faiths formed a voluntary association called the Champaign Council on Religious Education. They obtained permission from the Board of Education to offer classes in religious instruction to public school pupils in grades four to nine inclusive. Classes were made up of pupils whose parents signed printed cards requesting that their children be permitted to attend; they were held weekly, thirty minutes for the lower grades, forty-five minutes for the higher. The council employed the religious teachers at no expense to the school authorities, but the instructors were subject to the approval and supervision of the superintendent of schools. The classes were taught in three separate religious groups by Protestant teachers, Catholic priests, and a Jewish rabbi, although for the past several years there have apparently been no classes instructed in the Jewish religion. Classes were conducted in the regular classrooms of the school building. Students who did not choose to take the religious instruction were not released from public school duties; they were required to leave their classrooms and go to some other place in the school building for pursuit of their secular studies. On the other hand, students who were released from secular study for the religious instructions were required to be present at the religious classes. Reports of their presence or absence were to be made to their secular teachers.

The foregoing facts, without reference to others that appear in the record, show the use of tax-supported property for religious instruction and the close cooperation between the school authorities and the religious council in promoting religious education. The operation of the State's compulsory education system thus assists and is integrated with the program of religious instruction carried on by separate religious sects. Pupils compelled by law to go to school for secular education are released in part from their legal duty upon the condition that they attend the religious classes. This is beyond all question a utilization of the tax-established and tax-supported public school system to aid religious groups to spread their faith. And it falls squarely under the ban of the First Amendment (made applicable to the States by the Fourteenth) as we interpreted it in *Everson* v. *Board of Education,* 330 U. S. 1. . . . The majority in the *Everson* case, and the minority . . . agreed that the First Amendment's language, properly interpreted, had erected a wall of separation between Church and State. They disagreed as to the facts shown by the record and as to the proper application of the First Amendment's language to those facts.

. . . [C]ounsel for the respondents . . . argue that historically the First Amendment was intended to forbid only government preference of one religion over another, not an impartial governmental assistance of all religions. In addition they ask that we distinguish or overrule our holding in the *Everson* case that the Fourteenth Amendment made the "establishment of religion" clause of the First Amendment applicable as a prohibition against the States. After giving full consideration to the arguments presented we are unable to accept either of these contentions.

To hold that a state cannot consistently with the First and Fourteenth Amendments utilize its public school system to aid any or all religious faiths or sects in the dissemination of their doctrines and ideals does not, as counsel urge, manifest a governmental hostility to religion or religious teachings. . . . For the First Amendment rests upon the promise that both religion and government can best work to achieve their lofty aims if each is left free from the other within its respective sphere. Or, as we said in the *Everson* case, the First Amendment has erected a wall between Church and State which must be kept high and impregnable.

Here not only are the State's tax-supported public school buildings used for the dissemination of religious doctrines. The State also affords sectarian groups an invaluable aid in that it helps to provide pupils for their religious classes through use of the State's compulsory public school machinery. This is not separation of Church and State.

The cause is reversed and remanded to the State Supreme Court for proceedings not inconsistent with this opinion.

Reversed and remanded.

MR. JUSTICE FRANKFURTER delivered the following opinion, in which MR. JUSTICE JACKSON, MR. JUSTICE RUTLEDGE and MR. JUSTICE BURTON join.

We dissented in *Everson* v. *Board of Education,* 330 U.S. 1, because in our view the Constitutional principle requiring separation of Church and State compelled invalidation of the ordinance sustained by the majority. Illinois has here authorized the commingling of sectarian with secular instruction in the public schools. The Constitution of the United States forbids this.

This case, in the light of the *Everson* decision, demonstrates anew that the mere formulation of a relevant Constitutional principle is the beginning of the solution of a problem, not its answer. This is so because the meaning of a spacious conception like that of the separation of Church from State is unfolded as appeal is made to the principle from case to case. We are all agreed that the First and the Fourteenth Amendments have a secular reach far more penetrating in the conduct of Government than merely to forbid an "established church." But agreement, in the abstract, . . . does not preclude a clash of views as to what the wall separates. Involved is not only the Constitutional principle but the implications of judicial review in its enforcement. Accommodation of legislative freedom and Constitutional limitations upon that freedom cannot be achieved by a mere phrase. . . . Traditionally, organized education in the Western world was Church education. It could hardly be otherwise when the education of children was primarily study of the Word and the ways of God. . . .

The emigrants who came to these shores brought this view of education with them. . . . The upshot of these controversies, often long and fierce, is fairly summarized by saying that long before the Fourteenth Amendment subjected the States to new limitations, the prohibition of furtherance by the State of religious instruction became the guiding principle, in law and feeling, of the American people. . . .

Separation in the field of education, then, was not imposed upon unwilling States by force of superior law. In this respect the Fourteenth Amendment merely reflected a principle then dominant in our national life. To the extent that the Constitution thus made it binding upon the States, the basis of the restriction is the whole experience of our people. Zealous watchfulness against fusion of secular and religious activities by Government itself, through any of its instruments but especially through its educational agencies, was the democratic response of the American community to the particular needs of a young and growing nation, unique in the composition of its people. . . .

It is pertinent to remind that the establishment of this principle of Separation in the field of education was not due to any decline in the religious beliefs of the people. . . .

This development of the public school as a symbol of our secular unity was not a sudden achievement nor attained without violent conflict. . . .

Enough has been said to indicate that we are dealing not with a full-blown principle, nor one having the definiteness of a surveyor's metes and bounds. But by 1875 the separation of public education from Church entanglements, of the State from the teaching of religion, was firmly established in the consciousness of the nation.

. . . "[R]eleased time" has attained substantial proportions. . . . According to responsible figures almost 2,000,000 in some 2,200 communities participated in "released time" programs during 1947. . . . But to the extent that aspects of these programs are open to Constitutional objection, the more extensively the movement operates, the more ominous the breaches in the wall of separation. . . . If no provision is made for religious instruction in the particular faith of a child, or if for other reasons the child is not enrolled in any of the offered classes, he is required to attend a regular school class, or a study period during which he is often left to his own devices. . . .

Religious education so conducted on school time and property is patently woven into the working scheme of the school. The Champaign arrangement thus presents powerful elements of inherent pressure by the school system in the interest of religious sects. The fact that this power has not been used to discriminate is beside the point. Separation is a requirement to abstain from fusing functions of Government and of religious sects, not merely to treat them all equally. That a child is offered an alternative may reduce the constraint; it does not eliminate the operation of influence by the school in matters sacred to conscience and outside the school's domain. The law of imitation operates, and non-conformity is not an outstanding characteristic of children. The result is an obvious pressure upon children to attend. Again, . . . not even all the practicing sects in Champaign are willing or able to provide religious instruction. . . . As a result, the public school system of Champaign actively furthers inculcation in the religious tenets of some faiths, and in the process sharpens the consciousness of religious differences at least among some of the children committed to its care. These are consequences not amenable to statistics. But they are precisely the consequences against which the Constitution was directed when it prohibited the Government common to all from becoming embroiled, however innocently, in the destructive religious conflicts of which the history of even this country records some dark pages. . . .

The momentum of the whole school atmosphere and school planning is presumably put behind religious instruction, as given in Champaign, precisely in order to secure for the religious instruction such momentum and planning. To speak of "released time" as being only half or three quarters of an hour is to draw a thread from a fabric. . . .

Separation means separation, not something less. Jefferson's metaphor in describing the relation between Church and State speaks of a "wall of separation," not of a fine line easily overstepped. The public school is at once the symbol of our democracy and the most pervasive means for promoting our common destiny. In no activity of the State is it more vital to keep out divisive forces than in its schools, to avoid confusing, not to say fusing, what the Constitution sought to keep strictly apart. . . .

We renew our conviction that "we have staked the very existence of our country on the faith that complete separation between the state and religion is best for the state and best for religion." *Everson* v. *Board of Education,* 330 U.S. at 59. If nowhere else, in the relation between Church and State, "good fences make good neighbors."

MR. JUSTICE JACKSON, concurring.

I join the opinion of MR. JUSTICE FRANKFURTER, and concur in the result reached by the Court, but with these reservations: I think it is doubtful whether the facts of this case establish jurisdiction in this Court, but in any event that we should place some bounds on the demands for interference with local schools that we are empowered or willing to entertain. . . .

A Federal Court may interfere with local school authorities only when they invade either a personal liberty or a property right protected by the Federal Constitution. Ordinarily this will come about in either of two ways:

First. When a person is required to submit to some religious rite or instruction or is deprived or threatened with deprivation of his freedom for resisting such unconstitutional requirement. We may then set him free or enjoin his prosecution. Typical of such cases was *West Virginia State Board of Education* v. *Barnette,* 319 U.S. 624. . . .

Second. Where a complainant is deprived of property by being taxed for unconstitutional purposes, such as directly or indirectly to support a religious establishment. We can protect a taxpayer against such a levy. This was the *Everson Case,* 330 U.S. 1, as I saw it then and see it now. . . .

In this case, however, any cost of this plan to the taxpayers is incalculable and negligible. . . . I think it is doubtful whether the taxpayer in this case has shown any substantial property injury.

If, however, jurisdiction is found to exist, it is important that we circumscribe our decision with some care. . . . The relief demanded in this case is the extraordinary writ of mandamus to tell the local Board of Education what it must do. . . .

This Court is directing the Illinois courts generally to sustain plaintiff's complaint without exception of any of these grounds of complaint, without discriminating between them and without laying down any standards to define the limits of the effect of our decision. . . .

While we may and should end such formal and explicit instruction as the Champaign plan and can at all times prohibit teaching of creed and catechism and ceremonial and can forbid forthright proselyting in the schools, I think it remains to be demonstrated whether it is possible, even if desirable, to comply with such demands as plaintiff's completely to isolate and cast out of secular education all that some people may reasonably regard as religious instruction. . . .

The fact is that, for good or for ill, nearly everything in our culture worth transmitting, everything which gives meaning to life, is saturated with religious influences, derived from paganism, Judaism, Christianity — both Catholic and Protestant — and other faiths accepted by a large part of the world's peoples. One can hardly respect a system of education that would leave the student wholly ignorant of the currents of religious thought that move the world society for a part in which he is being prepared.

. . . While I agree that the religious classes involved here go beyond permissible limits, I also think the complaint demands more than plaintiff is entitled to have granted. So far as I can see this Court does not tell the State court where it may stop, nor does it set up any standards by which the State court may determine that question for itself.

The task of separating the secular from the religious in education is one of magnitude, intricacy and delicacy.

. . . If with no surer legal guidance we are to take up and decide every variation of this controversy, . . . we are likely to have much business of the sort. And, more importantly, we are likely to make the legal "wall of separation between church and state" as winding as the famous serpentine wall designed by Mr. Jefferson for the University he founded.

MR. JUSTICE REED, dissenting.

. . . As I am convinced that this interpretation of the First Amendment is erroneous, I feel impelled to express the reasons for my disagreement. By directing attention to the many instances of close association of church and state in American society and by recalling that many of these relations are so much a part of our tradition and culture that they are accepted without more, this dissent may help in an appraisal of the meaning of the clause of the First Amendment concerning the establishment of religion and of the reasons which lead to the approval or disapproval of the judgment below. . . .

. . . I find it difficult to extract from the opinions any conclusion as to what it is in the Champaign plan that is unconstitutional. . . .

. . . From the holding and the language of the opinions, I can only deduce that religious instruction of public school children during school hours is prohibited. The history of American education is against such an interpretation of the First Amendment.

The opinions do not say in words that the condemned practice of religious education is a law respecting an establishment of religion contrary to the First Amendment. . . . That was the basis of *Everson* v. *Board of Education*, 330 U.S. 1. It seems obvious that the action of the School Board in permitting religious education in certain grades of the schools by all faiths did not prohibit the free exercise of religion. . . . As no issue of prohibition upon the free exercise of religion is before us, we need only examine the School Board's action to see if it constitutes an establishment of religion. . . .

It seems clear to me that the "aid" referred to by the Court in the *Everson* case could not have been those incidental advantages that religious bodies, with other groups similarly situated, obtain as a by-product of organized society. This explains the well-known fact that all churches receive "aid" from government in the form of freedom from taxation. . . .

With the general statements in the opinions concerning the constitutional requirement that the nation and the states, by virtue of the First and Fourteenth Amendments, may "make no law respecting an establishment of religion," I am in agreement. But, in the light of the meaning given to those words by the precedents, customs, and practices which I have detailed above, I cannot agree with the Court's conclusion that when pupils compelled by law to go to school for secular education are released from school so as to attend the religious classes, churches are unconstitutionally aided. . . . The prohibition of enactments respecting the establishment of religion do not bar every friendly gesture between church and state. It is not an absolute prohibition against every conceivable situation where the two may work together, any more than the other provisions of the First Amendment—free speech, free press—are absolutes. . . . Devotion to the great principle of religious liberty should not lead us into a rigid interpretation of the constitutional guarantee that conflicts with accepted habits of our people. This is an instance where, for me, the history of past practices is determinative of the meaning of a constitutional clause, not a decorous introduction to the study of its text. The judgment should be affirmed.

Zorach v. *Clauson*, 343 U.S. 306, 72 S. Ct. 679 (1952)

MR. JUSTICE DOUGLAS delivered the opinion of the Court.

New York City has a program which permits public schools to release students during the school day so that they may leave the school buildings and school grounds and go to religious centers for religious instruction or devotional exercises. A student is released on written request of his parents. Those not released stay in the classrooms. The churches make weekly reports to the schools, sending a list of children who have been released from public school but who have not reported for religious instruction.

This "released time" program involves neither religious instruction in public school classrooms nor the expenditure of public funds. All costs, including the application blanks, are paid by the religious organizations. The case is therefore unlike *McCollum* v. *Board of Education,* 333 U.S. 203, which involved a "released time" program from Illinois. . . .

Appellants, who are taxpayers and residents of New York City and whose children attend its public schools, challenge the present law, contending it is in essence not different from the one involved in the McCollum case. Their argument, stated elaborately in various ways, reduces itself to this: the weight and influence of the school is put behind a program for religious instruction; public school teachers police it, keeping tab on students who are released; the classroom activities come to a halt while the students who are released for religious instruction are on leave; the school is a crutch on which the churches are leaning for support in their religious training; without the cooperation of the schools this "released time" program, like the one in the *McCollum* case, would be futile and ineffective. The New York Court of Appeals sustained the law against this claim of unconstitutionality, 303 N.Y. 161. The case is here on appeal. . . . [O]ur problem reduces itself to whether New York by this system has either prohibited the "free exercise" of religion or has made a law "respecting an establishment of religion" within the meaning of the First Amendment.

It takes obtuse reasoning to inject any issue of the "free exercise" of religion into the present case. No one is forced to go to the religious classroom and no religious exercise or instruction is brought to the classrooms of the public schools. A student need not take religious instruction. He is left to his own desires as to the manner or time of his religious devotions, if any.

There is a suggestion that the system involves the use of coercion to get public school students into religious classrooms. There is no evidence in the record before us that supports that conclusion. The present record indeed tells us that the school authorities are neutral in this regard and do no more than release students whose parents so request. If in fact coercion were used, if it were established that any one or more teachers were using their office to persuade or force students to take the religious instruction, a wholly different case would be presented. Hence we put aside that claim of coercion both as respects the "free exercise" of religion and "an establishment of religion" within the meaning of the First Amendment.

Moreover, apart from that claim of coercion, we do not see how New York by this type of "released time" program has made a law respecting an establishment of religion within the meaning of the First Amendment. . . . There cannot be the slightest doubt that the First Amendment reflects the philosophy that Church and State should be separated. And so far as interference with the "free exercise" of religion and an "establishment" of religion are concerned, the separation must be complete and unequivocal. The First Amendment within the scope of its coverage permits no exception; the prohibition is absolute. The First Amendment, however, does not say that in every and all respects there shall be a separation of Church and State. Rather, it studiously defines the manner, the specific ways, in which there shall be no concert or union or dependency one on the other. That is the common sense of the matter. . . .

We would have to press the concept of separation of Church and State to these extremes to condemn the present law on constitutional grounds. * * *

We are a religious people whose institutions presuppose a Supreme Being. We guarantee the freedom to worship as one chooses. We make room for as wide a variety of beliefs and creeds as the spiritual needs of man deem necessary. We sponsor an attitude on the part of government that shows no partiality to any one group and that lets each flourish according to the zeal of its adherents and the appeal of its dogma. When the state encourages religious instruction or cooperates with religious authorities by adjusting the schedule of public events to sectarian needs, it follows the best of our traditions. For it then respects the religious nature of our people and accommodates the public service to their spiritual needs. To hold that it may not would be to find in the Constitution a requirement that the government show a callous indifference to religious groups. That would be preferring those who believe in no religion over those who do believe.

The government must be neutral when it comes to competition between sects. . . . But it can close its doors or suspend its operations as to those who want to repair to their religious sanctuary for worship or instruction. No more than that is undertaken here.

This program may be unwise and improvident from an educational or a community viewpoint. . . . The constitutional standard is the separation of Church and State. The problem, like many problems in constitutional law, is one of degree. See *McCollum* v. *Board of Education, supra*, p. 231. . . . We follow the *McCollum* case. But we cannot expand it to cover the present released time program unless separation of Church and State means that public institutions can make no adjustments of their schedules to accommodate the religious needs of the people. We cannot read into the Bill of Rights such a philosophy of hostility to religion.

Affirmed.

Mr. Justice Black, dissenting.

Illinois ex rel. McCollum v. *Board of Education,* 333 U.S. 203, held invalid as an "establishment of religion" an Illinois system under which school children, compelled by law to go to public schools, were freed from some hours of required school work on condition that they attend special religious classes held in the school buildings. . . .

I see no significant difference between the invalid Illinois system and that of New York here sustained. Except for the use of the school buildings in Illinois, there is no difference between the systems which I consider even worthy of mention. . . . *McCollum* . . . held that Illinois could not constitutionally manipulate the compelled classroom hours of its compulsory school machinery so as to channel children into sectarian classes. Yet that is exactly what the Court holds New York can do.

. . . In dissenting today, I mean to do more than give routine approval to our *McCollum* decision. I mean also to reaffirm my faith in the fundamental philosophy expressed in *McCollum* and *Everson v. Board of Education*, 330 U.S. 1. That reaffirmance can be brief because of the exhaustive opinions in those recent cases. . . . Here the sole question is whether New York can use its compulsory education laws to help religious sects get attendants presumably too unenthusiastic to go unless moved to do so by the pressure of this state machinery. That this is the plan, purpose, design and consequence of the New York program cannot be denied. The state thus makes religious sects beneficiaries of its power to compel children to attend secular schools. Any use of such coercive power by the state to help or hinder some religious sects or to prefer all religious sects over nonbelievers or vice versa is just what I think the First Amendment forbids. In considering whether a state has entered this forbidden field the question is not whether it has entered too far but whether it has entered at all. New York is manipulating its compulsory education laws to help religious sects get pupils. This is not separation but combination of Church and State. * * *

. . . The First Amendment was . . . to insure that no one powerful sect or combination of sects could use political or governmental power to punish dissenters whom they could not convert to their faith. Now as then, it is only by wholly isolating the state from the religious sphere and compelling it to be completely neutral, that the freedom of each and every denomination and of all nonbelievers can be maintained. It is this neutrality the Court abandons today when it treats New York's coercive system as a program which *merely* "encourages religious instruction or cooperates with religious authorities." The abandonment is all the more dangerous to liberty because of the Court's legal exaltation of the orthodox and its derogation of unbelievers. . . .

. . . Before today, our judicial opinions have refrained from drawing invidious distinctions between those who believe in no religion and those who do believe. The First Amendment has lost much if the religious follower and the atheist are no longer to be judicially regarded as entitled to equal justice under law.

State help to religion injects political and party prejudices into a holy field. It too often substitutes force for prayer, hate for love, and persecution for persuasion. Government should not be allowed, under cover of the soft euphemism of "co-operation," to steal into the sacred area of religious choice.

MR. JUSTICE FRANKFURTER, dissenting.

By way of emphasizing my agreement with MR. JUSTICE JACKSON'S dissent, I add a few words.

The Court tells us that in the maintenance of its public schools, "[The State government] can close its doors or suspend its operations" so that its citizens may be free for religious devotions or instruction. If that were the issue, it would not rise to the dignity of a constitutional controversy. Of course, a State may provide that the classes in its schools shall be dismissed, for any reason, or no reason, on fixed days, or for special occasions. The essence of this case is that the school system did not "close its doors" and did not "suspend its operations." There is all the difference in the world between letting the children out of school and letting some of them out of school into religious classes. . . .

The pith of the case is that formalized religious instruction is substituted for other school activity which those who do not participate in the released-time program are compelled to attend. The school system is very much in operation during this kind of released time. If its doors are closed, they are closed upon those students who do not attend the religious instruction, in order to keep them within the school. That is the very thing which raises the constitutional issue. It is not met by disregarding it. Failure to discuss this issue does not take it out of the case.

Again, the Court relies upon the absence from the record of evidence of coercion in the operation of the system. "If in fact coercion were used," according to the Court, "if it were established that any one or more teachers were using their office to persuade or force students to take the religious instruction, a wholly different case would be presented." Thus, "coercion" in the abstract is acknowledged to be fatal. But the Court disregards the fact that as the case comes to us, there could be no proof of coercion, for the appellants were not allowed to make proof of it. Appellants alleged that "The operation of the released time program has resulted and inevitably results in the exercise of pressure and coercion upon parents and children to secure attendance by the children for religious instruction." This allegation—that coercion was in fact present and is inherent in the system, no matter what disavowals might be made in the operating regulations—was denied by appellees. Thus were drawn issues of fact which cannot be determined, on any conceivable view of judicial notice, by judges out of their own knowledge or experience. Appellants sought an opportunity to adduce evidence in support of these allegations at an appropriate trial. And though the courts below cited the concurring opinion in *McCollum* v. *Board of Education,* 333 U.S. 203, 226, to "emphasize the importance of detailed analysis of the facts to which the Constitutional test of Separation is to be applied," they denied that opportunity on the ground that such proof was irrelevant to the issue of constitutionality. . . .

When constitutional issues turn on facts, it is a strange procedure indeed not to permit the facts to be established. When such is the case, there are weighty considerations for us to require the State court to make its determination only after a thorough canvass of all the circumstances and not to bar them from consideration. * * *

MR. JUSTICE JACKSON, dissenting.

This released time program is founded upon a use of the State's power of coercion, which, for me, determines its unconstitutionality. Stripped to its essentials, the plan has two stages: first, that the State compel each student to yield a large part of his time for public secular education; and, second, that some of it be "released" to him on condition that he devote it to sectarian religious purposes.

No one suggests that the Constitution would permit the State directly to require this "released" time to be spent "under the control of a duly constituted religious body." This program accomplishes that forbidden result by indirection. . . .

The greater effectiveness of this system over voluntary attendance after school hours is due to the truant officer who, if the youngster fails to go to the Church school, dogs him back to the public schoolroom. Here schooling is more or less suspended during the "released time" so the nonreligious attendants will not forge ahead of the churchgoing absentees. But it serves as a temporary jail for a pupil who will not go to Church. It takes more subtlety of mind than I possess to deny that this is governmental constraint in support of religion. It is as unconstitutional, in my view, when exerted by indirection as when exercised forthrightly.

As one whose children, as a matter of free choice, have been sent to privately supported Church schools, I may challenge the Court's suggestion that opposition to this plan can only be antireligious, atheistic, or agnostic. My evangelistic brethren confuse an objection to compulsion with an objection to religion. It is possible to hold a faith with enough confidence to believe that what should be rendered to God does not need to be decided and collected by Caesar.

The day that this country ceases to be free for irreligion it will cease to be free for religion — except for the sect that can win political power. . . . And, after all, if we concede to the State power and wisdom to single out "duly constituted religious" bodies as exclusive alternatives for compulsory secular instruction, it would be logical to also uphold the power and wisdom to choose the true faith among those "duly constituted." We start down a rough road when we begin to mix compulsory public education with compulsory godliness. . . . The wall which the Court was professing to erect between Church and State has become even more warped and twisted than I expected. Today's judgment will be more interesting to students of psychology and of the judicial processes than to students of constitutional law.

Engel v. *Vitale*, 370 U.S. 431, 82 S. Ct. 1261 (1962)

MR. JUSTICE BLACK delivered the opinion of the Court.

The respondent Board of Education of Union Free School District No. 9, New Hyde Park, New York, acting in its official capacity under state law, directed the School District's principal to cause the following prayer to be said aloud by each class in the presence of a teacher at the beginning of each school day:

"Almighty God, we acknowledge our dependence upon Thee, and we beg Thy blessings upon us, our parents, our teachers and our country."

This daily procedure was adopted on the recommendation of the State Board of Regents, a governmental agency created by the State Constitution to which the New York Legislature has granted broad supervisory, executive, and legislative powers over the State's public school system. These state officials composed the prayer which they recommended and published as a part of their "Statement on Moral and Spiritual Training in the Schools," saying: "We believe that this Statement will be subscribed to by all men and women of good will, and we call upon them to aid in giving life to our program."

Shortly after the practice of reciting the Regents' prayer was adopted by the School District, the parents of ten pupils brought this action in a New York State Court insisting that use of this official prayer in the public schools was contrary to the beliefs, religions, or religious practices of both themselves and their children. Among other things, these parents challenged the constitutionality of both the state law authorizing the School District to direct the use of prayer in public schools and the School District's regulation ordering the recitation of this particular prayer on the ground that these actions of official governmental agencies violate that part of the First Amendment of the Federal Constitution which commands that "Congress shall make no law respecting an establishment of religion" — a command which was "made applicable to the State of New York Court of Appeals . . . sustained an order of the lower state courts which had upheld the power of New York to use the Regents' prayer as a part of the daily procedures of its public schools so long as the schools did not compel any pupil to join in the prayer over his or his parents' objection. We granted certiorari to review this important decision involving rights protected by the First and Fourteenth Amendments.

We think that by using its public school system to encourage recitation of the Regents' prayer, the State of New York has adopted a practice wholly inconsistent with the Establishment Clause. There can, of course, be no doubt that New York's program of daily classroom invocation of God's blessings as prescribed in the Regents' prayer is a religious activity. . . . The nature of such a prayer has always been religious, none of the respondents has denied this and the trial court expressly so found. . . .

The petitioners contend among other things that the state laws requiring or permitting use of the Regents' prayer must be struck down as a violation of the Establishment Clause because that prayer was composed by governmental officials as a part of a governmental program to further religious beliefs. For this reason, petitioners argue, the State's use of the Regents' prayer in its public school system breaches the constitutional wall of separation between Church and State. We agree with that contention since we think that the constitutional prohibition against laws respecting an establishment of religion must at least mean that in this country it is no part of the business of government to compose official prayers for any group of the American people to recite as a part of a religious program carried on by government.

It is a matter of history that this very practice of establishing governmentally composed prayers for religious services was one of the reasons which caused many of our early colonists to leave England and seek religious freedom in America. . . .

There can be no doubt that New York's state prayer program officially establishes the religious beliefs embodied in the Regents' prayer. . . . Neither the fact that the prayer may be denominationally neutral, nor the fact that its observance on the part of the students is voluntary can serve to free it from the limitations of the Establishment Clause, as it might from the Free Exercise Clause, of the First Amendment, both of which are operative against the States by virtue of the Fourteenth Amendment. . . . The Establishment Clause, unlike the Free Exercise Clause, does not depend upon any showing of direct governmental compulsion and is violated by the enactment of laws which establish an official religion whether those laws operate directly to coerce nonobserving individuals or not. . . . But the purposes underlying the Establishment Clause go much further than that. Its first and most immediate purpose rested on the belief that a union of government and religion tends to destroy government and to degrade religion. . . . The Establishment Clause thus stands as an expression of principle on the part of the Founders of our Constitution that religion is too personal, too sacred, too holy, to permit its "unhallowed perversion" by a civil magistrate. Another purpose of the Establishment Clause rested upon an awareness of the historical fact that governmentally established religions and religious persecutions go hand in hand. . . . The New York laws officially prescribing the Regents' prayer are inconsistent both with the purposes of the Establishment Clause and with the Establishment Clause itself. . . .

It is true that New York's establishment of its Regents' prayer as an officially approved religious doctrine of that State does not amount to a total establishment of one particular religious sect to the exclusion of all others. . . . To those who may subscribe to the view that because the Regents' official prayer is so brief and general there can be no danger to religious freedom in its governmental establishment, however, it may be appropriate to say in the words of James Madison, the author of the First Amendment:

"It is proper to take alarm at the first experiment on our liberties. * * * Who does not see that the same authority which can establish Christianity, in exclusion of all other Religions, may establish with the same ease any particular sect of Christians, in exclusion of all other Sects?". . . .   *Reversed and remanded.* . . .

MR. JUSTICE DOUGLAS, concurring.

. . . The point for decision is whether the Government can constitutionally finance a religious exercise. Our system at the federal and state levels is presently honeycombed with such financing. Nevertheless, I think it is an unconstitutional undertaking whatever form it takes. . . .

The question presented by this case is . . . an extremely narrow one. It is whether New York oversteps the bounds when it finances a religious exercise. . . .

. . . I cannot say that to authorize this prayer is to establish a religion in the strictly historic meaning of those words. Yet once government finances a religious exercise it inserts a divisive influence into our communities. . . .

The First Amendment leaves the Government in a position not of hostility to religion but of neutrality. . . . The First Amendment teaches that a government neutral in the field of religion better serves all religious interests.

My problem today would be uncomplicated but for *Everson* v. *Board of Education*, 330 U.S. 1, 17. . . . The *Everson* case seems in retrospect to be out of line with the First Amendment. . . . Mr. Justice Rutledge stated in dissent what I think is durable First Amendment philosophy:

". . . The great condition of religious liberty is that it be maintained free from sustenance, as also from other interferences, by the state. For when it comes to rest upon that secular foundation it vanishes with the resting. . . ."

MR. JUSTICE STEWART, dissenting. . . .

With all respect, I think the Court has misapplied a great constitutional principle. I cannot see how an "official religion" is established by letting those who want to say a prayer say it. On the contrary, I think that to deny the wish of these school children to join in reciting this prayer is to deny them the opportunity of sharing in the spiritual heritage of our Nation. . . .

The Court today says that the state and federal governments are without constitutional power to prescribe any particular form of words to be recited by any group of the American people on any subject touching religion. . . . In 1954 Congress added a phrase to the Pledge of Allegiance to the Flag so that it now contains the words "one Nation *under God*, indivisible, with liberty and justice for all". . . .

Countless similar examples could be listed. . . .

I do not believe that this Court, or the Congress, or the President has by the actions and practices I have mentioned established an "official religion" in violation of the Constitution. And I do not believe the State of New York has done so in this case. What each has done has been to recognize and to follow the deeply entrenched and highly cherished spiritual traditions of our Nation—traditions which come down to us from those who almost two hundred years ago avowed their "firm reliance on the Protection of Divine Providence" when they proclaimed the freedom and independence of this brave new world. . . . I dissent.

School District of Abington Township, Pennsylvania, et al. v. Edward Lewis Schempp et al.;
William J. Murray III, etc., et al., v. John N. Curlett, President, et al., Individually and Constituting the Board of School Commissioners of Baltimore City, Nos. 142 and 119.
374 U.S. 203, 83 S. Ct. 1560 (1963).

MR. JUSTICE CLARK delivered the opinion of the Court.

Once again we are called upon to consider the scope of the provision of the First Amendment to the United States Constitution which declares that "Congress shall make no law respecting an establishment of religion, or prohibiting the free exercise thereof. . ." . . . *No. 142.* The Commonwealth of Pennsylvania by law, 24 Pa. Stat. § 15-1516, as amended, Pub. Law 1928 (Supp. 1960) Dec. 17, 1959, requires that "At least ten verses from the Holy Bible shall be read, without comment, at the opening of each public school on each school day. Any child shall be excused from such Bible reading or attending such Bible reading, upon the written request of his parent or guardian." The Schempp family . . . brought suit to enjoin enforcement of the statute, contending that their rights under the Fourteenth Amendment to the Constitution of the United State are, have been, and will continue to be violated unless this statute be declared unconstitutional as violative of these provisions of the First Amendment. They sought to enjoin the appellant school district. . . . A three-judge statutory District Court for the Eastern District of Pennsylvania held that the statute is violative of the Establishment Clause of the First Amendment as applied to the States by the Due Process Clause of the Fourteenth Amendment and directed that appropriate injunctive relief issue. . . . •

The appellees . . . are of the Unitarian faith and are members of the Unitarian Church in Germantown, Philadelphia, Pennsylvania, where they, as well as another son, Ellory, regularly attend religious services. . . .

On each school day at the Abington Senior High School between 8:15 and 8:30 A.M., while the pupils are attending their home rooms or advisory sections, opening exercises are conducted pursuant to the statute. The exercises are broadcast into each room in the school building through an intercommunications system. . . . Selected students . . . gather each morning in the school's workshop studio for the exercises, which include readings by one of the students of 10 verses of the Holy Bible, broadcast to each room in the building. This is followed by the recitation of the Lord's Prayer, likewise over the intercommunications system, but also by the students in the various classrooms, who are asked to stand and join in repeating the prayer in unison. The exercises are closed with the flag salute and such pertinent announcements as are of interest to the students. . . . The student reading the verses from the Bible may select the passages and read from any version he chooses, although the only copies furnished by the school are the King James version, copies of which were circulated to each teacher by the school district. . . . There are . . . no comments or explanations made. . . . The students and parents are advised that the student may absent himself from the classroom or, should he elect to remain, not participate in the exercises. . . .

At the first trial Edward Schempp and the children testified as to specific religious doctrines purveyed by a literal reading of the Bible "which were contrary to the religious beliefs which they hold and to their familial teaching." . . .

The trial court, in striking down the practices and the statute requiring them, made specific findings of fact that the children's attendance at Abington Senior High School is compulsory and that the practice of reading 10 verses from the Bible is also compelled by law. It also found that:

"The reading of the verses, even without comment, possesses a devotional and religious character and constitutes in effect a religious observance. . . . Since the statute requires the reading of the 'Holy Bible', a Christian document, the practice . . . prefers the Christian religion. . . ."

No. 119. In 1905 the Board of School Commissioners of Baltimore City adopted a rule pursuant to Art. 77, § 202 of the Annotated Code of Maryland. . . . The petitioners, Mrs. Madalyn Murray and her son, William J. Murray, III, are both professed atheists. Following unsuccessful attempts to have the respondent school board rescind the rule this suit was filed for mandamus to compel its rescission and cancellation. It was alleged that William was a student in a public school of the city and Mrs. Murray, his mother, was a taxpayer therein; that it was the practice under the rule to have a reading on each school morning from the King James version of the Bible; that at petitioners' insistence the rule was amended to permit children to be excused from the exercise on request of the parent and that William had been excused pursuant thereto; that nevertheless the rule as amended was in violation of the petitioners' rights "to freedom of religion under the First and Fourteenth Amendments" and in violation of "the principle of separation between church and state, contained therein.* * * "

The petition particularized the petitioners' atheistic beliefs and stated that the rule, as practiced, violated their rights "in that it threatens their religious liberty by placing a premium on belief as against non-belief and subjects their freedom of conscience to the rule of the majority. . . ."

The respondents demurred and the trial court, recognizing that the demurrer admitted all facts well pleaded, sustained it without leave to amend. The Maryland Court of Appeals affirmed. * * *

Before examining this "neutral" position in which the Establishment and Free Exercise Clauses of the First Amendment place our government it is well that we discuss the reach of the Amendment under the cases of this Court.

First, this Court has decisively settled that the First Amendment's mandate that "Congress shall make no law respecting an establishment of religion, or prohibiting the free exercise thereof" has been made wholly applicable to the states by the Fourteenth Amendment. . . . *Cantwell* v. *Connecticut,* 310 U.S. 296, 303. . . . In a series of cases since *Cantwell* the Court has repeatedly reaffirmed that doctrine, and we do so now. . . .

Second, this Court has rejected unequivocally the contention that the establishment clause forbids only governmental preference of one religion over another. * * *

MR. JUSTICE RUTLEDGE . . . declared:
"The [First] Amendment's purpose . . . was to create a complete and permanent separation of the spheres of religious activity and civil authority by comprehensively forbidding every form of public aid or support for religion." 330 U.S., at 31–32.

The same conclusion has been firmly maintained ever since that time. * * *

Finally, in *Engel* v. *Vitale,* only last year, these principles were so universally recognized that the Court without the citation of a single case and over the sole dissent of Mr. Justice Stewart reaffirmed them. . . .

. . . As we have indicated, . . . this Court . . . has consistently held that the clause withdrew all legislative power respecting religious belief or the expression thereof. The test may be stated as follows: what are the purpose and the primary effect of the enactment? If either is the advancement or inhibition of religion then the enactment exceeds the scope of legislative power as circumscribed by the Constitution. That is to say that to withstand the strictures of the Establishment Clause there must be a secular legislative purpose and a primary effect that neither advances nor inhibits religion. . . . The Free Exercise Clause, likewise considered many times here, withdraws from legislative power, state and federal, the exertion of any restraint on the free exercise of religion. Its purpose is to secure religious liberty in the individual by prohibiting any invasions thereof by civil authority. Hence it is necessary in a free exercise case for one to show the coercive effect of the enactment as it operates against him in the practice of his religion. The distinction between the two clauses is apparent—a violation of the Free Exercise Clause is predicated on coercion while the Establishment Clause violation need not be so attended.

Applying the Establishment Clause principles to the cases at bar. . . . [t]he trial court in No. 142 has found that such an opening exercise is a religious ceremony and was intended by the State to be so. We agree. . . .

. . . [I]n No. 119 . . . [t]he case came up on demurrer, of course, to a petition which alleged that . . . the exercise was sectarian. The short answer, therefore, is that the religious character of the exercise was admitted by the State. . . .

The conclusion follows that in both cases the laws require religious exercises and such exercises are being conducted in direct violation of the rights of the appellees and petitioners. . . .

. . . Nothing we have said here indicates that such study of the Bible or of religion, when presented objectively as part of a secular program of education, may not be effected consistently with the First Amendment. But the exercises here do not fall into those categories. . . .

Finally, we cannot accept that the concept of neutrality, which does not permit a State to require a religious exercise even with the consent of the majority of those affected, collides with the majority's right to free exercise of religion. While the Free Exercise Clause clearly prohibits the use of state action to deny the rights of free exercise to *anyone,* it has never meant that a majority could use the machinery of the State to practice its beliefs. . . .

. . . In the relationship between man and religion, the State is firmly committed to a position of neutrality. Though the application of that rule requires interpretation of a delicate sort, the rule itself is clearly and concisely stated in the words of the First Amendment. Applying that rule to the facts of these cases, we affirm the judgment in No. 142. In No. 119, the judgment is reversed and the cause remanded to the Maryland Court of Appeals for further proceedings consistent with this opinion.   *It is so ordered.* . . .

MR. JUSTICE DOUGLAS, concurring. . . .

The vice of . . . such arrangements under the Establishment Clause is that the state is lending its assistance to a church's efforts to gain and keep adherents. . . .

Such contributions may not be made by the State even in a minor degree without violating the Establishment Clause. . . .

MR. JUSTICE BRENNAN, concurring. . . .

. . . The fact is that the line which separates the secular from the sectarian in American life is elusive. . . .

I join fully in the opinion and the judgment of the Court. ° ° °

[A]n awareness of history and an appreciation of the aims of the Founding Fathers do not always resolve concrete problems. . . .

A more fruitful inquiry, it seems to me, is whether the practices here challenged threaten those consequences which the Framers deeply feared; whether, in short, they tend to promote that type of interdependence between religion and state which the First Amendment was designed to prevent. . . .

A too literal quest for the advice of the Founding Fathers upon the issues of these cases seems to me futile and misdirected for several reasons:

First, on our precise problem the historical record is at best ambiguous. . . .

Second, the structure of American education has greatly changed since the First Amendment was adopted. . . .

Third, our religious composition makes us a vastly more diverse people than were our forefathers. . . .

Fourth, the American experiment in free public education available to all children has been guided in large measure by the dramatic evolution of the religious diversity among the population which our public schools serve. * * *

[A]lmost from the beginning religious exercises in the public schools have been the subject of intense criticism, vigorous debate, and judicial or administrative prohibition. Significantly, educators and school boards early entertained doubts about both the legality and the soundness of opening the school day with compulsory prayer or Bible reading. * * *

[T]he panorama of history permits no other conclusion than that daily prayers and Bible readings in the public schools have always been designed to be, and have been regarded as, essentially religious exercises. . . .

. . . The limited province of the courts is to determine whether the means which the educators have chosen to achieve legitimate pedagogical ends infringe the constitutional freedoms of the First Amendment. * * *

While I do not question the judgment of experienced educators that the challenged practices may well achieve valuable secular ends, it seems to me that the State acts unconstitutionally if it either sets about to attain even indirectly religious ends by religious means, or if is uses religious means to serve secular ends where secular means would suffice. * * *

. . . [T]he availability of excusal or exemption simply has no relevance to the establishment question, if it is once found that these practices are essentially religious exercises designed at least in part to achieve religious aims through the use of public school facilities during the school day. . . .

. . . [T]he excusal procedure itself necessarily operates in such a way as to infringe the rights of free exercise of those children who wish to be excused. * * *

. . . What the Framers meant to foreclose, and what our decisions under the Establishment Clause have forbidden, are those involvements of religious with secular institutions which (a) serve the essentially religious activities of religious institutions; (b) employ the organs of government for essentially religious purposes; or (c) use essentially religious means to serve governmental ends, where secular means would suffice. . . .

The holding of the Court today plainly does not foreclose teaching *about* the Holy Scriptures or about the differences between religious sects in classes in literature or history. . . .

MR. JUSTICE STEWART, dissenting.

I think the records in the two cases before us are so fundamentally deficient as to make impossible an informed or responsible determination of the constitutional issues presented. Specifically, I cannot agree that on these records we can say that the Establishment Clause has necessarily been violated. But I think there exist serious questions under both that provision and the Free Exercise Clause — insofar as each is imbedded in the Fourteenth Amendment — which require the remand of these cases for the taking of additional evidence. . . .

. . . We err in the first place if we do not recognize, as a matter of history and as a matter of the imperatives of our free society, that religion and government must necessarily interact in countless ways. Secondly, the fact is that while in many contexts the Establishment Clause and the Free Exercise Clause fully complement each other, there are areas in which a doctrinaire reading of the Establishment Clause leads to irreconcilable conflict with the Free Exercise Clause.* * *

. . . Unlike the other First Amendment guarantees, there is an inherent limitation upon the applicability of the Establishment Clause's ban on state support to religion. That limitation was succinctly put in *Everson* v. *Board of Education,* 330 U.S. 1, 18. . . . "State power is no more to be used so as to handicap religions, than it is to favor them." * * *[T]here is involved in these cases a substantial free exercise claim on the part of those who affirmatively desire to have their children's school day open with the reading of passages from the Bible. * * *

What seems to me to be of paramount importance, then, is recognition of the fact that the claim advanced here in favor of Bible reading is sufficiently substantial to make simple reference to the constitutional phrase "establishment of religion" as inadequate an analysis of the cases before us as the ritualistic invocation of the nonconstitutional phrase "separation of church and state." What these cases compel, rather, is an analysis of just what the "neutrality" is which is required by the interplay of the Establishment and Free Exercise Clauses of the First Amendment, as imbedded in the Fourteenth. Our decisions make clear that there is no constitutional bar to the use of government property for religious purposes. * * *

. . . In the *Schempp* case there is evidence which indicates that variations were in fact permitted by the very school there involved, and that further variations were not introduced only because of the absence of requests from parents. And in the *Murray* case the Baltimore rule itself contains a provision permitting another version of the Bible to be substituted for the King James version.

. . . In the absence of coercion upon those who do not wish to participate . . . such provisions cannot, in my view, be held to represent the type of support of religion barred by the Establishment Clause. . . .

[I]t is important to stress that, strictly speaking, what is at issue here is a privilege rather than a right. In other words, the question presented is not whether exercises such as those at issue here are constitutionally compelled, but rather whether they are constitutionally invalid. And that issue, in my view, turns on the question of coercion. . . .

The governmental neutrality which the First and Fourteenth Amendments require in the cases before us, in other words, is the extension of even-handed treatment to all who believe, doubt or disbelieve—a refusal on the part of the State to weight the scales of private choice. In these cases, therefore, what is involved is not state action based on impermissible categories, but rather an attempt by the State to accommodate those differences which the existence in our society of a variety of religious beliefs make inevitable. The Constitution requires that such efforts be struck down only if they are proven to entail the use of the secular authority of government to coerce a preference among such beliefs. * * *

Viewed in this light, it seems to me clear that the records in both of the cases before us are wholly inadequate to support an informed or responsible decision. . . .

What our Constitution indispensably protects is the freedom of each of us . . . to believe or disbelieve, to worship or not worship, to pray or keep silent, according to his own conscience, uncoerced and unrestrained by government. It is conceivable that these school boards . . . might eventually find it impossible to administer a system of religious exercises during school hours in such à way as to meet this constitutional standard. . . . But I think we must not assume that school boards so lack the qualities of inventiveness and good will as to make possible the achievement of that goal.

I would remand both cases for further hearing.

Not all recent cases involving religious freedom have been concerned with public school policy. *Torcaso* v. *Watkins*, 367 U.S. 488, 81 S. Ct. 1680 (1961), questioned the validity of a section of the constitution of the state of Maryland. Mr. Torcaso, who had been appointed to the office of Notary Public by the Governor, was not given a commission to serve because he failed to qualify under Article 37 of the Declaration of Rights of the Maryland constitution. That article provides:

[N]o religious test ought ever to be required as a qualification for any office of profit or trust in this State, other than a declaration of belief in the existence of God. * * *

Refusing to declare such a belief, Mr. Torcaso charged that the requirement of a declaration of belief in God violated the First and Fourteenth Amendments to the United States Constitution. Mr. Justice Black, for the Court, said,

* * * We repeat and again reaffirm that neither a State nor the Federal Government can constitutionally force a person "to profess a belief or disbelief in any religion." Neither can constitutionally pass laws nor impose requirements which aid all religions as against non-believers, and neither can aid those religions based on a belief in the existence of God as against those religions founded on different beliefs.

In upholding the State's religious test for public office the highest court of Maryland said [223 Md. 49]:

"The petitioner is not compelled to believe or disbelieve, under threat of punishment or other compulsion. True, unless he makes the declaration of belief he cannot hold public office in Maryland, but he is not compelled to hold office."

The fact, however, that a person is not compelled to hold public office cannot possibly be an excuse for barring him from office by state-imposed criteria forbidden by the Constitution. This was settled by our holding in *Wieman* v. *Updegraff*, 344 U.S. 183. We there pointed out that whether or not "an abstract right to public employment exists," Congress could not pass a law providing " ' * * * that no federal employee shall attend Mass or take any active part in missionary work.' ".

This Maryland religious test for public office unconstitutionally invades the appellant's freedom of belief and religion and therefore cannot be enforced against him. . . . *Reversed and remanded.*

MR. JUSTICE FRANKFURTER and MR. JUSTICE HARLAN concur in the result.

Some three weeks before the *Torcaso* decision came the decisions on the validity of the Sunday closing laws. These decisions have had a much wider and more practical impact, because the Court classified these laws not as restrictions upon the practice of religion, but as exercises of the police power of the state to establish a common day of rest. The fact that the day of rest was Sunday, a day of religious significance to most Christians, was an historical convenience and not an attempt to discriminate against those whose day of worship was on Saturday. The four cases were *McGowan* v. *Maryland* (366 U.S. 420, 81 S. Ct. 1101; 1961), *Gallagher* v. *Crown Kosher Super Market* (366 U.S. 620, 81 S. Ct. 1122) from Massachusetts, and two cases from Pennsylvania: *Two Guys from Harrison-Allentown* v. *McGinley* (366 U.S. 582, 81 S. Ct. 1135) and *Braunfeld* v. *Brown* (366 U.S. 599, 81 S. Ct. 1144). All four cases raised First and Fourteenth Amendment questions concerning the equal protection of the laws, or laws respecting the establishment of religion, or unnecessarily infringing upon the First Amendment, or interfering with the free exercise of religion. All four involved stores, of which two (*Gallagher* and *Braunfeld*) were kosher food markets. The owners and many of their customers were members of the

Orthodox Jewish faith, which requires that they eat kosher food, and forbids them to shop on the Sabbath. In the *Gallagher* case, the owners of the store did not take advantage of the Massachusetts statute which allowed them to keep their stores open until 10 A.M. on Sunday, because it was not economically feasible to be open those few hours, or after sundown on Saturday. In the *Braunfeld* case, the appellants, members of the Orthodox Jewish faith, had kept their stores open on Sunday, during which time they had done a substantial amount of business. All alleged that the Sunday closing would impair their ability to earn a living, and *Braunfeld* also alleged he would be unable to continue in business, thereby losing his capital investment. In all four cases the statutes were upheld as within the power of the state to establish a common day of rest. There were, however, numerous dissents.

Abraham Braunfeld et al. v. *Albert N. Brown, Commissioner of Police, et al.,* 366 U.S. 599, 81 S. Ct. 1144 (1961)

MR. CHIEF JUSTICE WARREN announced the judgment of the Court and an opinion in which MR. JUSTICE BLACK, MR. JUSTICE CLARK, and MR. JUSTICE WHITTAKER concur.

This case concerns the constitutional validity of the application to appellants of the Pennsylvania criminal statute, enacted in 1959, which proscribes the Sunday retail sale of certain enumerated commodities. Among the questions presented are whether the statute is a law respecting an establishment of religion and whether the statute violates equal protection. Since both of these questions, in reference to this very statute, have already been answered in the negative, *Two Guys from Harrison-Allentown, Inc.,* v. *McGinley,* 366 U.S. 582, and since appellants present nothing new regarding them, they need not be considered here. Thus the only question for consideration is whether the statute interferes with the free exercise of appellants' religion.

Appellants are merchants in Philadelphia who engage in the retail sale of clothing and home furnishings within the proscription of the statute in issue. Each of the appellants is a member of the Orthodox Jewish faith. . . . Their complaint, as amended, alleged . . . that Sunday closing will result in impairing the ability of all apellants to earn a livelihood and will render appellant Braunfeld unable to continue in his business, thereby losing his capital investment. . . .

Appellants contend that the enforcement against them of the Pennsylvania statute will . . . either compel appellants to give up their Sabbath observance, a basic tenet of the Orthodox Jewish faith, or will put appellants at a serious economic disadvantage if they continue to adhere to their Sabbath. . . .

In *McGowan* v. *Maryland,* 366 U.S. 420 . . . we noted the significance that this Court has attributed to the development of religious freedom in Virginia in determining the scope of the First Amendment's protection. . . .

We also took cognizance, in *McGowan,* of the evolution of Sunday Closing Laws from wholly religious sanctions to legislation concerned with the establishment of a day of community tranquillity, respite and recreation, a day when the atmosphere is one of calm and relaxation rather than one of commercialism, as it is during the other six days of the week. We reviewed the still growing state preoccupation with improving the health, safety, morals and general well-being of our citizens.

Concededly, appellants and all other persons who wish to work on Sunday will be burdened economically by the State's day of rest mandate; and appellants point out that their religion requires them to refrain from work on Saturday as well. Our inquiry then is whether, in these circumstances, the First and Fourteenth Amendments forbid application of the Sunday Closing Law to appellants.

Certain aspects of religious exercise cannot, in any way, be restricted or burdened by either federal or state legislation. . . . The freedom to hold religious beliefs and opinions is absolute.

However, the freedom to act, even when the action is in accord with one's religious convictions, is not totally free from legislative restrictions. * * *

Thus, in *Reynolds* v. *United States,* this Court upheld the polygamy conviction of a member of the Mormon faith despite the fact that an accepted doctrine of his church then imposed upon its male members the *duty* to practice polygamy. . . .

But . . . the statute at bar does not make unlawful any religious practices of appellants; the Sunday law simply regulates a secular activity and, as applied to appellants, operates so as to make the practice of their religious beliefs more expensive. Furthermore, the law's effect does not inconvenience all members of the Orthodox Jewish faith but only those who believe it necessary to work on Sunday. And even these are not faced with as serious a choice as forsaking their religious practices or subjecting themselves to criminal prosecution. Fully recognizing that the alternatives open to appellants and others similarly situated—retaining their present occupations and incurring economic disadvantage or engaging in some other commercial activity which does not call for either Saturday or Sunday labor—may well result in some financial sacrifice in order to observe their religious beliefs, still the option is wholly different than when the legislation attempts to make a religious practice itself unlawful.

To strike down, without the most critical scrutiny, legislation which imposes only an indirect burden on the exercise of religion, i.e., legislation which does not make unlawful the religious practice itself, would radically restrict the operating latitude of the legislature. . . .

Needless to say, when entering the area of religious freedom, we must be fully cognizant of the particular protection that the Constitution has accorded it. Abhorrence of religious persecution and intolerance is a basic part of our heritage. But we are a cosmopolitan nation made up of people of almost every conceivable religious preference. . . . Consequently, it cannot be expected, much less required, that legislators enact no law regulating conduct that may in some way result in an economic disadvantage to some religious sects and not to others because of the special practices of the various religions. We do not believe that such an effect is an absolute test for determining whether the legislation violates the freedom of religion protected by the First Amendment.

Of course, to hold unassailable all legislation regulating conduct which imposes solely an indirect burden on the observance of religion would be a gross oversimplification. . . . But if the State regulates conduct by enacting a general law within its power, the purpose and effect of which is to advance the State's secular goals, the statute is valid despite its indirect burden on religious observance unless the State may accomplish its purpose by means which do not impose such a burden. . .

As we pointed out in *McGowan* v. *Maryland, supra,* we cannot find a State without power to provide a weekly respite from all labor and, at the same time, to set one day of the week apart from the others as a day of rest, repose, recreation and tranquillity. . . . However, appellants advance yet another means at the State's disposal which they would find unobjectionable. They contend that the State should cut an exception from the Sunday labor proscription for those people who, because of religious conviction, observe a day of rest other than Sunday. By such regulation, appellants contend, the economic disadvantages imposed by the present system would be removed and the State's interest in having all people rest one day would be satisfied.

A number of States provide such an exemption, and this may well be the wiser solution to the problem. But our concern is not with the wisdom of legislation but with its constitutional limitation. * * * For all of these reasons, we cannot say that the Pennsylvania statute before us in invalid, either on its face or as applied.

MR. JUSTICE HARLAN concurs in the judgment. MR. JUSTICE BRENNAN and MR. JUSTICE STEWART concur in our disposition of appellants' claims under the Establishment Clause and the Equal Protection Clause. MR. JUSTICE FRANKFURTER and MR. JUSTICE HARLAN have rejected appellants' claim under the Free Exercise Clause in a separate opinion.

Accordingly, the decision is affirmed.   *Affirmed.*

MR. JUSTICE BRENNAN, concurring and dissenting.

I agree with the THE CHIEF JUSTICE that there is no merit in appellants' establishment and equal-protection claims. I dissent, however, as to the claim that Pennsylvania has prohibited the free exercise of appellants' religion. . . .

I would approach this case differently, from the point of view of the individuals whose liberty is—concededly—curtailed by these enactments. For the values of the First Amendment, as embodied in the Fourteenth, look primarily towards the preservation of personal liberty, rather than towards the fulfillment of collective goals.

The appellants . . . allege—and the allegation must be taken as true, since the case comes to us on a motion to dismiss the complaint —that "* * * one who does not observe the Sabbath [by refraining from labor] * * * cannot be an Orthodox Jew." . . . .

Consequences even more drastic are alleged: "Plaintiff, Abraham Braunfeld, will be unable to continue in his business if he may not stay open on Sunday and he will thereby lose his capital invest-ment." In other words, the issue in this case—and we do not under-stand either appellees or the Court to contend otherwise—is whether a State may put an individual to a choice between his business and his religion. The Court today holds that it may. But I dissent, be-lieving that such a law prohibits the free exercise of religion.

The first question to be resolved, however, is somewhat broader than the facts of this case. That question concerns the appropriate standard of constitutional adjudication in cases in which a statute is assertedly in conflict with the First Amendment, whether that limi-tation applies of its own force, or as absorbed through the less definite words of the Fourteenth Amendment. The Court in such cases is not confined to the narrow inquiry whether the challenged law is rationally related to some legitimate legislative end. Nor is the case decided by a finding that the State's interest is substantial and important, as well as rationally justifiable. This canon of adjudication was clearly stated by Mr. Justice Jackson, speaking for the Court in *West Virginia State Board of Education* v. *Barnette*, 1943, 319 U.S. 624, 639: ". . . The test of legislation which collides with the Four-teenth Amendment, because it also collides with the principles of the First, is much more definite than the test when only the Four-teenth is involved. Much of the vagueness of the due process clause disappears when the specific prohibitions of the First become its standard. . . . [F]reedoms of speech and of press, of assembly, and of worship . . . are susceptible of restriction only to prevent grave and immediate danger to interests which the state may lawfully protect. It is important to note that while it is the Fourteenth Amendment which bears directly upon the state it is the more specific limiting principles of the First Amendment that finally govern this case."

This exacting standard has been consistently applied by this Court as the test of legislation under all clauses of the First Amendment, not only those specifically dealing with freedom of speech and of the press. For religous freedom—the freedom to believe and to practice strange and, it may be, foreign creeds—has classically been one of the highest values of our society. . . .

The honored place of religious freeedom in our constitutional hierarchy . . . must now be taken to be settled. Or at least so it appeared until today. For in this case the Court seems to say, without so much as a deferential nod towards that high place which we have accorded religious freedom in the past, that any substantial state interest will justify encroachments on religious practice, at least if those encroachments are cloaked in the guise of some nonreligious public purpose.

Admittedly, these laws do not compel overt affirmation of a repugnant belief, as in *Barnette,* nor do they prohibit outright any of appellants' religious practices. . . . But their effect is that appellants may not simultaneously practice their religion and their trade, without being hampered by a substantial competitive disadvantage. Their effect is that no one may at one and the same time be an Orthodox Jew and compete effectively with his Sunday-observing fellow tradesmen. . . .

What, then, is the compelling state interest which impels the Commonwealth of Pennsylvania to impede appellants' freedom of worship? What overbalancing need is so weighty in the constitutional scale that it justifies this substantial, though indirect, limitation of appellants' freedom? . . . It is the mere convenience of having everyone rest on the same day. It is to defend this interest that the Court holds that a State need not follow the alternative route of granting an exemption for those who in good faith observe a day of rest other than Sunday. . . .

In fine, the Court, in my view, has exalted administrative convenience to a constitutional level high enough to justify making one religion economically disadvantageous. The Court would justify this result on the ground that the effect on religion, though substantial, is indirect. The Court forgets, I think, a warning uttered during the congressional discussion of the First Amendment itself: "* * * the rights of conscience are, in their nature, of peculiar delicacy, and will little bear the gentlest touch of governmental hand * * *."

I would reverse this judgment and remand for a trial of appellants' allegations, limited to the free-exercise-of-religion issue.

MR. JUSTICE STEWART, dissenting.

I agree with substantially all that MR. JUSTICE BRENNAN has written. Pennsylvania has passed a law which compels an Orthodox Jew to choose between his religious faith and his economic survival. That is a cruel choice. It is a choice which I think no State can constitutionally demand. For me this is not something that can be swept under the rug and forgotten in the interest of enforced Sunday togetherness. I think the impact of this law upon these appellants grossly violates their constitutional right to the free exercise of their religion.

Although the Court upheld the Sunday closing laws, thus penalizing the Sabbatarians in fact, if not in the eyes of the law, it did not sanction South Carolina's interpretation of the eligibility provisions of an unemployment compensation statute as applied to a Sabbatarian. In *Sherbert* v. *Verner* the appellant, a member of the Seventh-Day Adventist Church, was discharged by her employer because she refused to work on Saturday. Unable to find work because of her unwillingness to work on that day, she filed a claim for unemployment benefits under the South Carolina Unemployment Compensation Act. As many similar statutes provide, eligibility for benefits requires that the applicant be able to work, and available for it. If the claimant has failed to accept suitable work, without good cause, he is not entitled to benefits. After a hearing, the Commission concluded that the claimant had so failed. That decision was upheld by the state court despite her claim of abridgment of her right to the free exercise of her religion under the First Amendment. The United States Supreme Court held that her disqualification for the reason stated did impose a burden on the free exercise of her religion, and that there was no compelling state interest in the enforcement of the eligibility provisions of the statute to justify the "substantial infringement of the appellant's First Amendment right." Justices Douglas and Stewart concurred, but called attention to the conflicts, as they saw them, between this decision and others.

Sherbert v. *Verner,* 374 U.S. 398, 83 S. Ct. 1790 (1963)

° ° ° In holding as we do, plainly we are not fostering the "establishment" of the Seventh-day Adventist religion in South Carolina, for the extension of unemployment benefits to Sabbatarians in common with Sunday worshippers reflects nothing more than the governmental obligation of neutrality in the face of religious differences, and does not represent that involvement of religious with secular institutions which it is the object of the Establishment Clause to forestall. . . .

Our holding today is only that South Carolina may not constitutionally apply the eligibility provisions so as to constrain a worker to abandon his religious convictions respecting the day of rest. This holding but reaffirms a principle that we announced a decade and a half ago, namely that no State may "exclude individual Catholics, Lutherans, Mohammedans, Baptists, Jews, Methodists, Non-believers, Presbyterians, or the members of any other faith, *because of their faith, or lack of it,* from receiving the benefits of public welfare legislation." *Everson* v. *Board of Education* 330 U.S. 1, 16. . . .

Reversed and remanded.

MR. JUSTICE DOUGLAS, concurring. . . .

The question is whether the South Carolina law . . . is a law "prohibiting the free exercise" of religion as those words are used in the First Amendment. It seems obvious to me that this law does run afoul of that clause. . . .

Some have thought that a majority of a community can, through state action, compel a minority to observe their particular religious scruples so long as the majority's rule can be said to perform some valid secular function. That was the essence of the Court's decision in the Sunday Blue Law Cases. . . , a ruling from which I then dissented (*McGowan* v. *Maryland, supra,* 366 U.S. pp. 575–576) and still dissent. . . .

That ruling of the Court travels part of the distance that South Carolina asks us to go now. . . .

The result turns not on the degree of injury, which may indeed be nonexistent by ordinary standards. The harm is the interference with the individual's scruples or conscience—an important area of privacy which the First Amendment fences off from government. . . .

This case is resolvable not in terms of what an individual can demand of government, but solely in terms of what government may not do to an individual in violation of his religious scruples. . . . For the Free Exercise Clause is written in terms of what the government cannot do to the individual, not in terms of what the individual can exact from the government.

. . . If appellant is otherwise qualified for unemployment benefits, payments will be made to her not as a Seventh-day Adventist, but as an unemployed worker. . . Thus, this case does not involve the problems of direct or indirect state assistance to a religious organization—matters relevant to the Establishment Clause, not in issue here.

MR. JUSTICE STEWART, concurring.

Although fully agreeing with the result which the Court reaches in this case, I cannot join the Court's opinion. This case presents a double-barreled dilemma, which in all candor I think the Court's opinion has not succeeded in papering over. The dilemma ought to be resolved. . . .

Twenty-three years ago in *Cantwell* v. *Connecticut,* 310 U.S. 296, 303, the Court said that both the Establishment Clause and the Free Exercise Clause of the First Amendment were made wholly applicable to the States by the Fourteenth Amendment. . . .

I am convinced that no liberty is more essential to the continued vitality of the free society which our Constitution guarantees than is the religious liberty protected by the Free Exercise Clause explicit in the First Amendment and imbedded in the Fourteenth. And I regret that on occasion, and specifically in *Braunfeld* v. *Brown, supra,* the Court has shown what has seemed to me a distressing insensitivity to the appropriate demands of this constitutional guarantee. By contrast I think that the Court's approach to the Establishment Clause has on occasion, and specifically in *Engel, Schempp* and *Murray,* been not only insensitive, but positively wooden, and that the Court has accorded to the Establishment Clause a meaning which neither the words, the history, nor the intention of the authors of that specific constitutional provision even remotely suggests.

But my views as to the correctness of the Court's decisions in these cases are beside the point here. The point is that the decisions are on the books. And the result is that there are many situations where legitimate claims under the Free Exercise Clause will run into head-on collision with the Court's insensitive and sterile construction of the Establishment Clause. The controversy now before us is clearly such a case. . . .

[T]he Establishment Clause as construed by this Court not only *permits* but affirmatively *requires* South Carolina equally to deny the appellant's claim for unemployment compensation when her refusal to work on Saturdays is based upon her religious creed. . . .

To require South Carolina to so administer its laws as to pay public money to the appellant under the circumstances of this case is thus clearly to require the State to violate the Establishment Clause as construed by this Court. This poses no problem for me, because I think the Court's mechanistic concept of the Establishment Clause is historically unsound and constitutionally wrong. . . .

I think our Constitution commands the positive protection by government of religious freedom—not only for a minority, however small—not only for the majority, however large—but for each of us. . . .

With all respect, I think it is the Court's duty to face up to the dilemma posed by the conflict between the Free Exercise Clause of the Constitution and the Establishment Clause as interpreted by the Court. It is a duty, I submit, which we owe to the people, the States, and the Nation, and a duty which we owe to ourselves. . . .

My second difference with the Court's opinion is that I cannot agree that today's decision can stand consistently with *Braunfeld* v. *Brown, supra.* . . .

I agree with the Court that the possiblity of that denial is enough to infringe upon the appellant's constitutional right to the free exercise of her religion. But it is clear to me that in order to reach this conclusion the court must explicitly reject the reasoning of *Braunfeld* v. *Brown.* I think the *Braunfeld* case was wrongly decided and should be overruled, and accordingly I concur in the result reached by the Court in the case before us.

MR. JUSTICE HARLAN, whom MR. JUSTICE WHITE joins, dissenting.

Today's decision is disturbing both in its rejection of existing precedent and in its implications for the future. * * *

[I]n no proper sense can it be said that the State discriminated against the appellant on the basis of her religious beliefs or that she was denied benefits *because* she was a Seventh-day Adventist. She was denied benefits just as any other claimant would be denied benefits who was not "available for work" for personal reasons.

With this background, this Court's decision comes into clearer focus. What the Court is holding is that if the State chooses to condition unemployment compensation on the applicant's availability for work, it is constitutionally compelled to *carve out an exception*—and to provide benefits—for those whose unavailability is due to their religious convictions. Such a holding has particular significance in two respects.

First, despite the Court's protestations to the contrary, the decision necessarily overrules *Braunfeld* v. *Brown,* 366 U.S. 599, which held that it did not offend the "Free Exercise" Clause of the Constitution for a State to forbid a Sabbatarian to do business on Sunday. The secular purpose of the statute before us today is even clearer than that involved in *Braunfeld.* . . .

Second, the implications of the present decision are far more troublesome than its apparently narrow dimensions would indicate at first glance. The meaning of today's holding, as already noted, is that the State must furnish unemployment benefits to one who is unavailable for work if the unavailability stems from the exercise of religious convictions. The State, in other words, must *single out* for financial assistance those whose behavior is religiously motivated, even though it denies such assistance to others whose identical behavior (in this case, inability to work no Saturdays) is not religiously motivated.

It has been suggested that such singling out of religious conduct for special treatment may violate the constitutional limitations on state action. . . . My own view, however, is that at least under the circumstances of this case it would be a permissible accommodation of religion for the State, if it *chose* to do so, to create an exception to its eligibility requirements for persons like the appellant.

For very much the same reasons, however, I cannot subscribe to the conclusion that the State is constitutionally *compelled* to carve out an exception to its general rule of eligibility in the present case . . . such compulsion in the present case is particularly inappropriate in light of the indirect, remote, and insubstantial effect of the decision below on the exercise of appellant's religion and in light of the direct financial assistance to religion that today's decision requires.

For these reasons I respectfully dissent from the opinion and judgment of the Court.

In *U. S.* v. *Seeger,* 380 U.S. 163, 85 S. Ct. 850 (1965), the Court was obliged to determine what the Congress meant by the phrase "religious training and belief" as used in the Universal Military Training and Service Act, 50 U.S.C. App. § 456 (j) (1958 ed.). The section exempts from training for combat and service in the armed forces those who "by reason of their religious training and belief are conscientiously opposed to participation in war in any form." The statute defines "religious training and belief" as "an individual's belief in a relation to a Supreme Being involving duties superior to those arising from any human relation, but not including essentially political, sociological, or philosophical views or a merely personal moral code." Three men who had claimed exemption as conscientious objectors raised the questions.

We have concluded that Congress, in using the expression "Supreme Being" rather than the designation "God," was merely clarifying the meaning of religious training and belief so as to embrace all religions and to exclude essentially political, sociological, or philosophical views. We believe that under this construction, the test of belief "in relation to a Supreme Being" is whether a given belief that is sincere and meaningful occupies a place in the life of its possessor parallel to that filled by the orthodox belief in God of one who clearly qualifies for the exemption. Where such beliefs have parallel positions in the lives of their respective holders we cannot say that one is "in a relation to a Supreme Being" and the other is not. We have concluded that the beliefs of the objectors in these cases meet these criteria, and, accordingly, we affirm the judgments in Nos. 50 and 51 and reverse the judgment in No. 29.[2]

<hr/>

[2]*U.S.* v. *Seeger,* 380 U.S. 163, pp. 165–66.

CHAPTER FOUR

★ ★ ★

Speech, Silence, and Censorship

ATTITUDES TOWARD RELIGIOUS beliefs and practices are no less fraught with emotional overtones than are attitudes toward freedom of speech. Even if it were possible to eliminate the all-too-human willingness to forbid the expression of opinions contrary to one's own, there are still enormous problems, many of them centered around the right of the individual to speak, and the right of the hearer not to be compelled to listen.

In a form of government so dependent upon the knowledge and understanding of citizens as ours, language is peculiarly important and vulnerable. Even language used with care can arouse ire, suspicion, and violent action as easily as it can inform or express sympathy and agreement. With the development of radio and television as means of communication, with the vast increase in the circulation of reading matter, with the higher educational level of the population, language has crucial importance, for both speech and the written word can be manipulated more quickly for special ends.

Of course, not all language is protected under the First Amendment. "Bad language," for example, has long been subject to regulation, and "name calling," if sufficiently vituperative or earthy, may be a misdemeanor. "Obscenity" is not protected and has never been, but the definition of obscenity has varied with the individual and the era. "Slander" and "libel" may be prosecuted in the criminal courts under certain conditions, or may give rise to a civil action.

Even granting the primacy of freedom of speech, speech is subject to some control in appropriate circumstances. As Justice Holmes said, in *Schenck* v. *U.S.,* ". . . The most stringent protection of free speech would not protect a man in falsely shouting fire in a theatre and caus-

78

ing a panic."[1] The circumstances under which the words are uttered will also, therefore, be taken into account when the Court is considering a particular case.

We are, however, faced with more than the cases which come before the court. Although most instances of censorship do not reach the dignity and importance of a Supreme Court case, they are important not only to the participants, but also to the public. Censorship takes many forms. Private censors may agree not to make purchases at a particular store unless specified "literature" is removed from the shelves. By quiet censorship, police may "suggest" that certain items should be removed from public view. In police raids upon bookstores or storage warehouses, thousands of books are taken and their circulation prevented. Official censors, although untrained and unguided by laws, decide what motion pictures or plays may be shown in the community. Finally, and pervasively, the threat of legal action is a form of censorship. And, of course, statutes, many of which have not been interpreted by the courts, are often so broadly written that if they were enforced strictly, relatively few publications would be available to the community. Many other statutes seem to lack a clearly identifiable objective standard.

Perhaps the least controversial censorship occurs during time of war, when some control of expression is believed necessary to forward the war effort. But what standards are appropriate, even in war time? In the *Schenck* case (*Schenck* v. *U.S.*, 249 U.S. 47, 39 S. Ct. 247; 1919) Mr. Justice Holmes formulated the "clear and present danger" test. The defendants were charged with a conspiracy to violate the Espionage Act of 1917 by wilfully conspiring to have printed and circulated a document calculated to cause insubordination and obstruct recruitment during World War I. Schenck, who was general secretary of the Socialist Party, had printed some 15,000 leaflets, intended to obstruct the draft. Some copies were sent by mail to men who were to be inducted in the armed services. The defendant claimed the protection of the First Amendment.

Justice Holmes' formulation of the test was,

> The question in every case is whether the words used are used in such circumstances and are of such a nature as to create a clear and present danger that they will bring about the substantive evils that Congress has a right to prevent. It is a question of proximity and degree. . . .[2]

[1] P. 52. [2] P. 52.

This "clear and present danger" doctrine has been used by the Court as a standard in appropriate instances, explained, modified, and (depending somewhat on the point of view) altered to the point of extinction as a standard for limiting freedom of speech.

Six years later, in *Gitlow* v. *New York* (268 U.S. 652, 45 S. Ct. 625; 1925) the Court extended the First Amendment to the states, saying,

> For present purposes we may and do assume that freedom of speech and of the press—which are protected by the First Amendment from abridgment by Congress—are among the fundamental personal rights and "liberties" protected by the due process clause of the Fourteenth Amendment by the States. . . .[3]

The State of New York had enacted a statute which defined criminal anarchy and prohibited its advocacy. The particular question was whether the statute contravened the due process clause of the Fourteenth Amendment, for even when there was "no evidence of any concrete result flowing from the publication of the Manifesto, or of circumstances showing the likelihood of such result" the defendant could be penalized for

> the mere utterance, as such, of "doctrine" having no quality of incitement, without regard either to the circumstances of its utterance or to the likelihood of unlawful sequences; and that, as the exercise of the right of free expression with relation to government was "only punishable," in circumstances involving likelihood of "substantive evil."[4]

The Court held that this "mere utterance" could be prohibited. Although this case substantially widened the influence of the First Amendment on the one hand by making it applicable to the states, it also limited the First Amendment by penalizing certain forms of utterance whether or not the speech had any effect at all upon the listeners. Mr. Justice Holmes dissented:

Gitlow v. *New York*, 268 U. S. 652, 45 S. Ct. 625 (1925)

MR. JUSTICE BRANDEIS and I are of opinion that this judgment should be reversed. The general principle of free speech, it seems to me, must be taken to be included in the Fourteenth Amendment, in view of the scope that has been given to the word "liberty" as there used, although perhaps it may be accepted with a somewhat larger latitude of interpretation than is allowed to Congress by the sweeping language that governs or ought to govern the laws of the United States. If I am right, then I think that the criterion sanctioned by the full Court in *Schenck* v. *United States*, 249 U.S. 47, 52, applies. "The question in every case is whether the words used are used in such circumstances and are of such a nature as to create a clear and

[3]P. 666. [4]P. 664.

present danger that they will bring about the substantive evils that [the State] has a right to prevent." It is true that in my opinion this criterion was departed from in *Abrams* v. *United States,* 250 U.S. 616, but the convictions that I expressed in that case are too deep for it to be possible for me as yet to believe that it and *Schaefer* v. *United States,* 251 U.S. 466, have settled the law. If what I think the correct test is applied, it is manifest that there was no present danger of an attempt to overthrow the government by force on the part of the admittedly small minority who shared the defendant's views. It is said that this manifesto was more than a theory, that it was an incite-ment. Every idea is an incitement. It offers itself for belief and if believed it is acted on unless some other belief outweighs it or some failure of energy stifles the movement at its birth. The only difference between the expression of an opinion and an incitement in the narrower sense is the speaker's enthusiasm for the result. Eloquence may set fire to reason. But whatever may be thought of the redundant discourse before us it had no chance of starting a present conflagration. If in the long run the beliefs expressed in proletarian dictatorship are destined to be accepted by the dominant forces of the community, the only meaning of free speech is that they should be given their chance and have their way.

If the publication of this document had been laid as an attempt to induce an uprising against government at once and not at some indefinite time in the future it would have presented a different question. The object would have been one with which the law might deal, subject to the doubt whether there was any danger that the publication could produce any result, or in other words, whether it was not futile and too remote from possible consequences. But the indictment alleges the publication and nothing more.

The right of the government to protect itself from the "advocacy" of certain ideas, whether or not there is a clear and present danger that the ideas may be put into action, was elaborated in *Dennis* v. *U.S.,* 341 U.S. 494, 71 S. Ct. 857 (1951). The trial of 11 leaders of the Communist Party, held in New York before Judge Medina, was widely publicized. It lasted over nine months, six of them devoted to taking evidence, and produced a record for the U.S. Supreme Court some 16,000 pages long. In the lower court, the defendants were found guilty of criminal conspiracy. The Supreme Court decision was six to two against the defendants, with Justice Clark not participating, and Justices Black and Douglas dissenting. Both these justices tend to believe that the rights given under the First Amendment are absolute and cannot be abrogated either by the Court or the Congress. Aside from this, a 16,000-page record is so extensive that all justices are not likely to emerge from a study of it with identical views of the facts essential to understand or decide the case. The majority redefined the "clear and present danger" test; Justice Jackson, concurring, saw the case in terms of a conspiracy statute, a trial for violating that statute, and a conviction for that offense. Justice Black saw the case as "a virulent form of prior censorship of speech and press, which I believe the First Amendment forbids. . . ." Justice Douglas saw it as treating mere speech, not "speech *plus* acts of sabotage or unlawful conduct." In his opinion, there was no "immediate injury to society" likely, and no evidence of any clear and present danger.

Dennis v. *United States,* 341 U.S. 494, 71 S. Ct. 857 (1951)

MR. CHIEF JUSTICE VINSON announced the judgment of the Court and an opinion in which MR. JUSTICE REED, MR. JUSTICE BURTON and MR. JUSTICE MINTON join.

Petitioners were indicted in July, 1948, for violation of the conspiracy provisions of the Smith Act, 54 Stat. 671, 18 U.S.C. (1946 ed.) §11, during the period of April, 1945, to July, 1948. . . . A verdict of guilty as to all the petitioners was returned by the jury on October 14, 1949. . . . We granted certiorari . . . limited to the following two questions: (1) Whether either §2 or §3 of the Act, inherently or as construed and applied in the instant case, violates the First Amendment and other provisions of the Bill of Rights; (2) whether either §2 or §3 of the Act, inherently or as construed and applied in the instant case, violates the First and Fifth Amendments because of indefiniteness.

Sections 2 and 3 of the Smith Act, 54 Stat. 671, 18 U.S.C. (1946 ed.) 10, 11 (see present 18 U.S.C. 2385), provide as follows:

"Sec. 2.

"(a) It shall be unlawful for any person—

"(1) to knowingly or willfully advocate, abet, advise or teach the duty, necessity, desirability, or propriety of overthrowing or destroying any government in the United States by force or violence, or by the assassination of any officer of any such government . . .

"Sec. 3. It shall be unlawful for any person to attempt to commit, or to conspire to commit, any of the acts prohibited by the provisions of * * * this title."

The indictment charged the petitioners with wilfully and knowingly conspiring (1) to organize as the Communist Party of the United States of America a society, group and assembly of persons who teach and advocate the overthrow and destruction of the Government of the United States by force and violence, and (2) knowingly and wilfully to advocate and teach the duty and necessity of overthrowing and destroying the Government of the United States by force and violence. The indictment further alleged that §2 of the Smith Act proscribes these acts and that any conspiracy to take such action is a violation of §3 of the act . . .

Whether on this record petitioners did in fact advocate the overthrow of the Government by force and violence is not before us, and we must base any discussion of this point upon the conclusions stated in the opinion of the Court of Appeals, which treated the issue in great detail. That court held that the record in this case amply supports the necessary finding of the jury that petitioners, the leaders of the Communist Party in this country, were unwilling to work within our framework of democracy, but intended to initiate a violent revolution whenever the propitious occasion appeared. Petitioners dispute the meaning to be drawn from the evidence. . . .

But the Court of Appeals held that the record supports the following broad conclusions: By virtue of their control over the political apparatus of the Communist Political Association, petitioners were able to transform that organization into the Communist Party; that the policies of the Association were changed from peaceful cooperation with the United States and its economic and political structure to a policy which had existed before the United States and the Soviet Union were fighting a common enemy, namely a policy which worked for the overthrow of the Government by force and violence; that the Communist Party is a highly disciplined organization, adept at infiltration into strategic positions, use of aliases, and double-meaning language; that the Party is rigidly controlled; that Communists, unlike other political parties, tolerate no dissension from the policy laid down by the guiding forces, but that the approved program is slavishly followed by the members of the Party; that the literature of the Party and the statements and activities of its leaders, petitioners here, advocate, and the general goal of the Party was, during the period in question, to achieve a successful overthrow of the existing order by force and violence. . . .

. . . [T]he trial judge . . . charged that the jury could not find the petitioners guilty under the indictment unless they found that petitioners had the intent "to overthrow * * * the Government of the United States by force and violence as speedily as circumstances would permit." * * *

The obvious purpose of the statute is to protect existing Government, not from change by peaceable, lawful and constitutional means, but from change by violence, revolution and terrorism. That it is within the *power* of the Congress to protect the Government of the United States from the armed rebellion is a proposition which requires little discussion. . . . The question with which we are concerned here is not whether Congress has such *power* but whether the *means* which it has employed conflict with the First and Fifth Amendments to the Constitution. * * *

One of the bases for the contention that the means which Congress has employed are invalid takes the form of an attack on the face of the statute on the grounds that by its terms it prohibits academic discussion of the merits of Marxism-Leninism, that it stifles ideas and is contrary to all concepts of a free speech and a free press. . . .

The very language of the Smith Act . . . is directed at advocacy, not discussion. . . . Congress did not intend to eradicate the free discussion of political theories, to destroy the traditional rights of Americans to discuss and evaluate ideas without fear of governmental sanction. Rather Congress was concerned with the very kind of activity in which the evidence showed these petitioners engaged.

We pointed out in *Douds, supra,* that the basis of the First Amendment is the hypothesis that speech can rebut speech, propaganda will answer propaganda, free debate of ideas will result in the wisest governmental policies. It is for this reason that this Court has recognized the inherent value of free discourse. . . . This is not an unlimited, unqualified right, but . . . the societal value of speech must, on occasion, be subordinated to other values and considerations. . . .

* * * Speech is not an absolute, above and beyond control by the legislature when its judgment, subject to review here, is that certain kinds of speech are so undesirable as to warrant criminal sanction. . . .

In this case we are squarely presented with the application of the "clear and present danger" test, and must decide what that phrase imports. . . .

Overthrow of the Government by force and violence is certainly a substantial enough interest for the Government to limit speech. . . . If, then, this interest may be protected, the literal problem which is presented is what has been meant by the use of the phrase "clear and present danger" of the utterances bringing about the evil within the power of Congress to punish.

Obviously, the words cannot mean that before the Government may act, it must wait until the *putsch* is about to be executed, the plans have been laid and the signal is awaited. . . . In the instant case the trial judge charged the jury that they could not convict unless they found that petitioners intended to overthrow the Government "as speedily as circumstances would permit." . . . What was meant was that the revolutionists would strike when they thought the time was ripe. We must therefore reject the contention that success or probability of success is the criterion. . . .

The situation with which Justices Holmes and Brandeis were concerned in *Gitlow* was a comparatively isolated event, bearing little relation in their minds to any substantial threat to the safety of the community. . . . They were not confronted with any situation comparable to the instant one—the development of an apparatus designed and dedicated to the overthrow of the Government, in the context of world crisis after crisis.

Chief Judge Learned Hand, writing for the majority below, interpreted the phrase as follows: "In each case [courts] must ask whether the gravity of the 'evil,' discounted by its improbability, justifies such invasion of free speech as is necessary to avoid the danger." 183 F. 2d at 212. We adopt this statement of the rule. . . .

Likewise, we are in accord with the court below, which affirmed the trial court's finding that the requisite danger existed. The formation by petitioners of such a highly organized conspiracy, with rigidly disciplined members subject to call when the leaders, these petitioners, felt that the time had come for action, coupled with the inflammable nature of world conditions, similar uprisings in other countries, and the touch-and-go nature of our relations with countries with whom petitioners were in the very least ideologically attuned, convince us that their convictions were justified on this score. And this analysis disposes of the contention that a conspiracy to advocate, as distinguished from the advocacy itself, cannot be constitutionally restrained, because it comprises only the preparation. It is the existence of the conspiracy which creates the danger. . . . If the ingredients of the reaction are present, we cannot bind the Government to wait until the catalyst is added.

Although we have concluded that the finding that there was a sufficient danger to warrant the application of the statute was justified on the merits, there remains the problem of whether the trial judge's treatment of the issue was correct. . . .

He reserved the question of the existence of the danger for his own determination, and the question becomes whether the issue is of such a nature that it should have been submitted to the jury. . . . The argument that the action of the trial court is erroneous, in declaring as a matter of law that such violation shows sufficient danger to justify the punishment despite the First Amendment, rests on the theory that a jury must decide a question of the application of the First Amendment. We do not agree. * * * We hold that the statute may be applied where there is a "clear and present danger" of the substantive evil which the legislature had the right to prevent. Bearing, as it does, the marks of a "question of law," the issue is properly one for the judge to decide. . . .

There remains to be discussed the question of vagueness — whether the statute as we have interpreted it is too vague, not sufficiently advising those who would speak of the limitations upon their activity. It is urged that such vagueness contravenes the First and Fifth Amendments. This argument is   particularly nonpersuasive when presented by petitioner, who the jury found, intended to overthrow the Government as speedily as circumstances would permit. . . .

We hold that §§2 (a) (1), 2(a) (3) and 3 of the Smith Act, do not inherently, or as construed or applied in the instant case, violate the First Amendment and other provisions of the Bill of Rights, or the First and Fifth Amendments because of indefiniteness. Petitioners intended to overthrow the Government of the United States as speedily as the circumstances would permit. Their conspiracy to organize the Communist Party and to teach and advocate the overthrow of the Government of the United States by force and violence created a "clear and present danger" of an attempt to overthrow the Government by force and violence. They were properly and constitutionally convicted for violation of the Smith Act. The judgments of conviction are affirmed.

MR. JUSTICE FRANKFURTER, concurring in affirmance of the judgment, * * *

On the one hand is the interest in security. The Communist Party was not designed by these defendants as an ordinary political party. . . .

In finding that the defendants violated the statute, we may not treat as established fact that the Communist Party in this country is of significant size, well-organized, well-disciplined, conditioned to embark on unlawful activity when given the command. But in determining whether application of the statute to the defendants is within the constitutional powers of Congress, we are not limited to the facts found by the jury. We must view such a question in the light of whatever is relevant to a legislative judgment. We may take judicial notice that the Communist doctrines which these defendants have conspired to advocate are in the ascendency in powerful nations who cannot be acquitted of unfriendliness to the institutions of this country. We may take account of evidence brought forward at this trial and elsewhere, much of which has long been common knowledge. In sum, it would amply justify a legislature in concluding that recruitment of additional members for the Party would create a substantial danger to national security. . . .

On the other hand is the interest in free speech. The right to exert all governmental powers in aid of maintaining our institutions and resisting their physical overthrow does not include intolerance of opinions and speech that cannot do harm although opposed and perhaps alien to dominant, traditional opinion. . . .

We have enjoyed so much freedom for so long that we are perhaps in danger of forgetting how much blood it cost to establish the Bill of Rights.

Of course no government can recognize a "right" of revolution, or a "right" to incite revolution if the incitement has no other purpose or effect. But speech is seldom restricted to a single purpose, and its effects may be manifold. A public interest is not wanting in granting freedom to speak their minds even to those who advocate the overthrow of the Government by force. For, as the evidence in this case abundantly illustrates, coupled with such advocacy is criticism of defects in our society. Criticism is the spur to reform. . . . Suppressing advocates of overthrow inevitably will also silence critics who do not advocate overthrow but fear that their criticism may be so construed. No matter how clear we may be that the defendants now before us are preparing to overthrow our Government at the propitious moment, it is self-delusion to think that we can punish them for their advocacy without adding to the risks run by loyal citizens who honestly believe in some of the reforms these defendants advance. It is a sobering fact that in sustaining the convictions before us we can hardly escape restriction on the interchange of ideas.

We must not overlook the value of that interchange. Freedom of expression is the well-spring of our civilization — the civilization we seek to maintain and further by recognizing the right of Congress to put some limitation upon expression. . . . Liberty of thought soon shrivels without freedom of expression. Nor can truth be pursued in an atmosphere hostile to the endeavor or under dangers which are hazarded only by heroes. . . .

It is not for us to decide how we would adjust the clash of interests which this case presents were the primary responsibility for reconciling it ours. Congress has determined that the danger created by advocacy of overthrow justifies the ensuing restriction on freedom of speech. . . .

The wisdom of the assumptions underlying the legislation and prosecution is another matter. In finding that Congress has acted within its power, a judge does not remotely imply that he favors the implications that lie beneath the legal issues. . . . The legislation we are here considering is but a truncated aspect of a deeper issue. ✴ ✴ ✴

Civil liberties draw at best only limited strength from legal guaranties. Preoccupation by our people with the constitutionality, instead of with the wisdom, of legislation or of executive action is preoccupation with a false value. . . .

Focusing attention on constitutionality tends to make constitutionality synonymous with wisdom. When legislation touches freedom of thought and freedom of speech, such a tendency is a formidable enemy of the free spirit. Much that should be rejected as illiberal, because repressive and envenoming, may well be not unconstitutional. The ultimate reliance for the deepest needs of civilization must be found outside their vindication in courts of law; apart from all else, judges, howsoever they may conscientiously seek to discipline themselves against it, unconsciously are too apt to be moved by the deep undercurrents of public feeling. A persistent, positive translation of the liberating faith into the feelings and thoughts and action of men and women is the real protection against attempts to strait-jacket the human mind. Such temptations will have their way, if fear and hatred are not exorcised. The mark of a truly civilized man is confidence in the strength and security derived from the inquiring mind. We may be grateful for such honest comforts as it supports, but we must be unafraid of its incertitudes. Without open minds there can be no open society. And if society be not open the spirit of man is mutilated and becomes enslaved. . . .

MR. JUSTICE BLACK, dissenting.

Here again. . .my basic disagreement with the Court is not as to how we should explain or reconcile what was said in prior decisions but springs from a fundamental difference in constitutional approach. Consequently, it would serve no useful purpose to state my position at length.

At the outset I want to emphasize what the crime involved in this case is, and what it is not. These petitioners were not charged with an attempt to overthrow the Government. They were not charged with overt acts of any kind designed to overthrow the Government. They were not even charged with saying anything or writing anything designed to overthrow the Government. The charge was that they agreed to assemble and to talk and publish certain ideas at a later date: The indictment is that they conspired to organize the Communist Party and to use speech or newspapers and other publications in the future to teach and advocate the forcible overthrow of the Government. No matter how it is worded, this is a virulent form of prior censorship of speech and press, which I believe the First Amendment forbids. I would hold §3 of the Smith Act authorizing this prior restraint unconstitutional on its face and as applied. * * *

So long as this Court exercises the power of judicial review of legislation, I cannot agree that the First Amendment permits us to sustain laws suppressing freedom of speech and press on the basis of Congress' or our own notions of mere "reasonableness." Such a doctrine waters down the First Amendment so that it amounts to little more than an admonition to Congress. The Amendment as so construed is not likely to protect any but those "safe" or orthodox views which rarely need its protection. I must also express my objection to the holding because, as MR. JUSTICE DOUGLAS' dissent shows, it sanctions the determination of a crucial issue of fact by the judge rather than by the jury. * * *

MR. JUSTICE DOUGLAS, dissenting. . . .

. . . Petitioners. . . .were not charged with a "conspiracy to overthrow" the Government. They were charged with a conspiracy to form a party and groups and assemblies of people who teach and advocate the overthrow of our Government by force or violence and with a conspiracy to advocate and teach its overthrow by force and violence. . . .

So far as the present record is concerned, what petitioners did was to organize people to teach and themselves teach the Marxist-Leninist doctrine contained chiefly in four books: *Foundations of Leninism* by Stalin (1924); *The Communist Manifesto* by Marx and Engels (1848); *State and Revolution* by Lenin; *History of the Communist Party of the Soviet Union* (B.) (1939). . . .

The opinion of the Court does not outlaw these texts nor condemn them to the fire. . . . The crime then depends not on what is taught but on who the teacher is. That is to make freedom of speech turn not on *what is said,* but on the *intent* with which it is said. Once we start down that road we enter territory dangerous to the liberties of every citizen. . . .

Free speech has occupied an exalted position because of the high service it has given our society. Its protection is essential to the very existence of a democracy. . . .

Full and free discussion has indeed been the first article of our faith. * * *

Free speech is the rule, not the exception. The restraint to be constitutional must be based on more than fear, on more than passionate opposition against the speech, on more than a revolted dislike for its contents. There must be some immediate injury to society that is likely if speech is allowed. . . .

Free speech—the glory of our system of government—should not be sacrificed on anything less than plain and objective proof of danger that the evil advocated is imminent. On this record no one can say that petitioners and their converts are in such a strategic position as to have even the slightest chance of achieving their aims.

The First Amendment provides that "Congress shall make no law * * * abridging the freedom of speech." The Constitution provides no exception. . . . The command of the First Amendment is so clear that we should not allow Congress to call a halt to free speech except in the extreme case of peril from the speech itself. The First Amendment makes confidence in the common sense of our people and in their maturity of judgment the great postulate of our democracy. * * *

Our faith should be that our people will never give support to these advocates of revolution, so long as we remain loyal to the purposes for which our Nation was founded. . . .

Six years later the *Dennis* decision was explained in *Yates* v. *U.S.*, which also had a substantial record (14,000 pages). The opinion defined "advocacy" more clearly: ". . . those to whom advocacy is addressed must be urged to *do* something." The defendants had been convicted in California for a violation of the same sections of the Smith Act as had the defendants in the *Dennis* case. They were also charged with "organizing" the Communist Party of the U.S., which advocates and teaches "the duty and necessity of overthrowing the Government of the United States by force and violence." Justice Black, with Justice Douglas joining, concurred in part and dissented in part.

In 1961 these two justices dissented again, this time joined by Mr. Justice Brennan and Chief Justice Warren, in *Scales* v. *U.S.*, a third "advocacy" case under the Smith Act. As Mr. Justice Harlan remarked, "We decide the issues raised upon the fullest consideration, the case having had an unusually long history in this Court." Indeed it had. It was heard by the U.S. Supreme Court, then retried, and reargued. The decision was announced in 1961, some six years after the original trial. The Court held that there had been sufficient evidence "to make a case for the jury on the issue of illegal Party advocacy," and Mr. Scales' conviction was upheld.

Yates v. *United States*, 354 U.S. 298, 77 S. Ct. 1064 (1957)

MR. JUSTICE HARLAN delivered the opinion of the Court.
* * * [T]he trial court refused to charge that, in order to convict, the jury must find that the advocacy which the defendants conspired to promote was of a kind calculated to "incite" persons to action for the forcible overthrow of the Government. It is argued that advocacy of forcible overthrow as mere *abstract doctrine* is within the free speech protection of the First Amendment; that the Smith Act, consistently with that constitutional provision, must be taken as proscribing only the sort of advocacy which incites to illegal *action*; and that the trial court's charge, by permitting conviction for mere advocacy, unrelated to its tendency to produce forcible action, resulted in an unconstitutional application of the Smith Act. * * *

There can be no doubt from the record that in so instructing the jury the court regarded as immaterial, and intended to withdraw from the jury's consideration, any issue as to the character of the advocacy in terms of its capacity to stir listeners to forcible action. . . . The court made it clear in colloquy with counsel that in its view the illegal advocacy was made out simply by showing that what was said dealt with forcible overthrow and that it was uttered with a specific intent to accomplish that purpose, insisting that all such advocacy was punishable "whether in language of incitement or not.". . .

We are thus faced with the question whether the Smith Act prohibits advocacy and teaching of forcible overthrow as an abstract principle, divorced from any effort to instigate action to that end, so long as such advocacy or teaching is engaged in with evil intent. We hold that it does not.

The distinction between advocacy of abstract doctrine and advocacy directed at promoting unlawful action is one that has been consistently recognized in the opinions of the Court. . . . This distinction was heavily underscored in *Gitlow* v. *People of State of New York*, 268 U.S. 652, in which the statute involved was nearly identical with the one now before us. * * *

. . .The legislative history of the Smith Act and related bills shows beyond all question that Congress was aware of the distinction between the advocacy or teaching of abstract doctrine and the advocacy or teaching of action, and that it did not intend to disregard it. The statute was aimed at the advocacy and teaching of concrete action for the forcible overthrow of the Government, and not of principles divorced from action. . . .

In failing to distinguish between advocacy of forcible overthrow as an abstract doctrine and advocacy of action to that end, the District Court appears to have been led astray by holding in *Dennis* that advocacy of violent action to be taken at some future time was enough. . . . In other words, the District Court apparently thought that *Dennis* obliterated the traditional dividing line between advocacy of abstract doctrine and advocacy of action.

This misconceives the situation confronting the Court in *Dennis* and what was held there. . . . [T]he jury's verdict . . . did establish that the advocacy was aimed at building up a seditious group and maintaining it in readiness for action at a propitious time. In such circumstances, said Chief Justice Vinson, the Government need not hold its hand "until the putsch is about to be executed, the plans have been laid and the signal is awaited. . . . The essence of the *Dennis* holding was that indoctrination of a group in preparation for future violent action, as well as exhortation to immediate action, by advocacy found to be directed to "action for the accomplishment" of forcible overthrow, to violence as "a rule or principle of action," and employing "language of incitement," *id.*, 341 U.S. at pages 511–512, is not constitutionally protected when the group is of sufficient size and cohesiveness, is sufficiently oriented towards action, and other circumstances are such as reasonably to justify apprehension that action will occur. This is quite a different thing from the view of the District Court here that mere doctrinal justification of forcible overthrow, if engaged in with the intent to accomplish overthrow, is punishable *per se* under the Smith Act. That sort of advocacy, even though uttered with the hope that it may ultimately lead to violent revolution, is too remote from concrete action to be regarded as the kind of indoctrination preparatory to action which was condemned in *Dennis.* * * *

. . . The jury was never told that the Smith Act does not denounce advocacy in the sense of preaching abstractly the forcible overthrow of the Government. . . . The essential distinction is that those to whom the advocacy is addressed must be urged to *do* something, now or in the future, rather than merely to *believe* in something. . . . It was. . . incumbent on the court to make clear in some fashion that the advocacy must be of action and not merely abstract doctrine. * * *

We recognize that distinctions between advocacy or teaching of abstract doctrines with evil intent, and that which is directed to stirring people to action, are often subtle and difficult to grasp, for in a broad sense, as Mr. Justice Holmes said in his dissenting opinion in *Gitlow, supra,* 268 U.S. at page 673: "Every idea is an incitement." But the very subtlety of these distinctions required the most clear and explicit instructions with reference to them, for they concerned an issue which went to the very heart of the charges against these petitioners. The need for precise and understandable instructions on this issue is further emphasized by the equivocal character of the evidence in this record. . . . Instances of speech that could be considered to amount to "advocacy of action" are so few and far between as to be almost completely overshadowed by the hundreds of instances in the record in which overthrow, if mentioned at all, occurs in the course of doctrinal disputation so remote from action as to be almost wholly lacking in probative value. . . . We can not allow a conviction to stand on such "an equivocal direction to the jury on a basic issue." *Bollenbach* v. *United States,* 326 U.S. 607, 613. * * *

MR. JUSTICE BLACK, with whom MR. JUSTICE DOUGLAS joins, concurring in part and dissenting in part.

I would reverse every one of these convictions and direct that all the defendants be acquitted. In my judgment the statutory provisions on which these prosecutions are based abridge freedom of speech, press and assembly in violation of the First Amendment to the United States Constitution. . . .

The kind of trials conducted here are wholly dissimilar to normal criminal trials. Ordinarily these "Smith Act" trials are prolonged affairs lasting for months. In part this is attributable to the routine introduction in evidence of massive collections of books, tracts, pamphlets, newspapers, and manifestoes discussing Communism, Socialism, Capitalism, Feudalism and governmental institutions in general, which, it is not too much to say, are turgid, diffuse, abstruse, and just plain dull. Of course, no juror can or is expected to plow his way through this jungle of verbiage. The testimony of witnesses is comparatively insignificant. Guilt or innocence may turn on what Marx or Engels or someone else wrote or advocated as much as a hundred or more years ago. Elaborate, refined distinctions are drawn between "Communism," "Marxism," "Leninism," "Trotskyism, and "Stalinism." When the propriety of obnoxious or unorthodox views about government is in reality made the crucial issue, as it must be in cases of this kind, prejudice makes conviction inevitable except in the rarest circumstances. * * *

In essence, petitioners were tried upon the charge that they believe in and want to foist upon this country a different and to us a despicable form of authoritarian government in which voices criticizing the existing order are summarily silenced. I fear that the present type of prosecutions are more in line with the philosophy of authoritarian government than with that expressed by our First Amendment.

Doubtlessly, dictators have to stamp out causes and beliefs which they deem subversive to their evil regimes. But governmental suppression of causes and beliefs seems to me to be the very antithesis of what our Constitution stands for. . . . The first Amendment provides the only kind of security system that can preserve a free government—one that leaves the way wide open for people to favor, discuss, advocate, or incite causes and doctrines however obnoxious and antagonistic such views may be to the rest of us. * * *

Scales v. *U.S.*, 367 U.S. 279, 81 S. Ct. 1469 (1961)

MR. JUSTICE HARLAN delivered the opinion of the Court.

Our writ issued in this case to review a judgment of the Court of Appeals affirming petitioner's conviction under the so-called membership clause of the Smith Act. 18 U.S.C. § 2385, 18 U.S.C.A. § 2385. The Act, among other things, makes a felony the acquisition or holding of knowing membership in any organization which advocates the overthrow of the Government of the United States by force or violence. The indictment charged that from January 1946 to the date of its filing (November 18, 1954) the Communist Party of the United States was such an organization, and that petitioner throughout that period was a member thereof, with knowledge of the Party's illegal purpose and a specific intent to accomplish overthrow "as speedily as circumstances would permit."

The validity of this conviction is challenged on statutory, constitutional, and evidentiary grounds, and further on the basis of certain alleged trial and procedural errors. . . . For reasons given in this opinion we affirm the Court of Appeals. * * *

* * * We hold that the statute was correctly interpreted by the two lower courts, and now turn to petitioner's basic constitutional challenge.

Fifth Amendment.

In our jurisprudence guilt is personal, and when the imposition of punishment on a status or on conduct can only be justified by reference to the relationship of that status or conduct to other concededly criminal activity (here advocacy of violent overthrow), that relationship must be sufficiently substantial to satisfy the concept of personal guilt in order to withstand attack under the Due Process Clause of the Fifth Amendment. Membership, without more, in an organization engaged in illegal advocacy, it is now said, has not heretofore been recognized by this Court to be such a relationship. This claim stands, and we shall examine it, independently of the claim made under the First Amendment.

Any thought that due process puts beyond the reach of the criminal law all individual associational relationships, unless accompanied by the commission of specific acts of criminality, is dispelled by familiar concepts of the law of conspiracy and complicity. * * *

. . . .In this instance it is an organization which engages in criminal activity, and we can perceive no reason why one who actively and knowingly works in the ranks of that organization, intending to contribute to the success of those specifically illegal activities, should be any more immune from prosecution than he to whom the organization has assigned the task of carrying out the substantive criminal act. Nor should the fact that Congress has focussed here on "membership," the characteristic relationship between an individual and the type of conspiratorial quasi-political associations with the criminal aspect of whose activities Congress was concerned, of itself require the conclusion that the legislature has traveled outside the familiar and permissible bounds of criminal imputability. In truth, the specificity of the proscribed relationship is not necessarily a vice; it provides instruction and warning.

What must be met, then, is the argument that membership, even when accompanied by the elements of knowledge and specific intent, affords an insufficient quantum of participation in the organization's alleged criminal activity, that is, an insufficiently significant form of aid and encouragement to permit the imposition of criminal sanctions on that basis. It must indeed be recognized that a person who merely becomes a member of an illegal organization, by that "act" alone need be doing nothing more than signifying his assent to its purposes and activities on one hand, and providing, on the other, only the sort of moral encouragement which comes from the knowledge that others believe in what the organization is doing. It may indeed be argued that such assent and encouragement do fall short of the concrete, practical impetus given to a criminal enterprise which is lent for instance by a commitment on the part of a conspirator to act in furtherance of that enterprise. A member, as distinguished from a conspirator, may indicate his approval of a criminal enterprise by the very fact of his membership without thereby necessarily committing himself to further it by any act or course of conduct whatever.

In an area of the criminal law which this Court has indicated more than once demands its watchful scrutiny (see *Dennis, supra,* 341 U.S. at page 516) these factors have weight and must be found to be overborne in a total constitutional assessment of the statute. We think, however, they are duly met when the statute is found to reach only "active" members having also a guilty knowledge and intent, and which therefore prevents a conviction on what otherwise might be regarded as merely an expression of sympathy with the alleged criminal enterprise, unaccompanied by any significant action in its support or any commitment to undertake such action.

Thus, given the construction of the membership clause already discussed, we think the factors called for in rendering members criminally responsible for the illegal advocacy of the organization fall within established, and therefore presumably constitutional, standards of criminal imputability.

First Amendment.

Little remains to be said concerning the claim that the statute infringes First Amendment freedoms. It was settled in *Dennis* that the advocacy with which we are here concerned is not constitutionally protected speech, and it was further established that a combination to promote such advocacy, albeit under the aegis of what purports to be a political party, is not such association as is protected by the First Amendment. We can discern no reason why membership, when it constitutes a purposeful form of complicity in a group engaging in this same forbidden advocacy, should receive any greater degree of protection from the guarantees of that Amendment. . . . The clause does not make criminal all association with an organization which has been shown to engage in illegal advocacy. There must be clear proof that a defendant "specifically intend [s] to accomplish [the aims of the organization] by resort to violence." *Noto* v. *United States, post,* 367 U.S. 290, page 299. Thus the member for whom the organization is a vehicle for the advancement of legitimate aims and policies does not fall within the ban of the statute: he lacks the requisite specific intent "to bring about the overthrow of the government as speedily as circumstances would permit." Such a person may be foolish, deluded, or perhaps merely optimistic, but he is not by this statute made a criminal.

We conclude that petitioner's constitutional challenge must be overruled.

MR. JUSTICE BLACK, dissenting. . . .

. . . My reasons for dissenting from this decision are primarily those set out by MR. JUSTICE BRENNAN — that § 4 (f) of the Subversive Activities Control Act bars prosecutions under the membership clause of the Smith Act — and MR. JUSTICE DOUGLAS. . . . There are, however, two additional points that I think should also be mentioned.

In an attempt to bring the issue of the constitutionality of the membership clause of the Smith Act within the authority of the *Dennis* and *Yates* cases, the Court has practically rewritten the statute under which petitioner stands convicted by treating the requirements of "activity" and "specific intent" as implicit in words that plainly do not include them. Petitioner's conviction is upheld just as though the membership clause had always contained these requirements. It seems clear to me that neither petitioner nor anyone else could ever have guessed that this law would be held to mean what this Court now holds it does mean. For that reason, it appears that petitioner has been convicted under a law that is, at best, unconstitutionally vague and, at worst, *ex post facto.* He has therefore been deprived of his right to be tried under a clearly defined, pre-existing "law of the land" as guaranteed by the Due Process Clause and I think his conviction should be reversed on that ground.

Secondly, I think it is important to point out the manner in which this case re-emphasizes the freedom-destroying nature of the "balancing test" presently in use by the Court to justify its refusal to apply specific constitutional protections of the Bill of Rights. In some of the recent cases in which it has "balanced" away the protections of the First Amendment, the Court has suggested that it was justified in the application of this "test" because no direct abridgment of First Amendment freedoms was involved, the abridgment in each of these cases being, in the Court's opinion, nothing more than "an incident of the informed exercise of a valid governmental function." A possible implication of that suggestion was that if the Court were confronted with what it would call a direct abridgment of speech, it would not apply the "balancing test" but would enforce the protections of the First Amendment according to its own terms. This case causes me to doubt that such an implication is justified. Petitioner is being sent to jail for the express reason that he has associated with people who have entertained unlawful ideas and said unlawful things, and that of course is a *direct* abridgment of his freedoms of speech and assembly under any definition that has ever been used for that term. Nevertheless, even as to this admittedly direct abridgment, the Court relies upon its prior decisions to the effect that the Government has power to abridge speech and assembly if its interest in doing so is sufficient to outweigh the interest in protecting these First Amendment freedoms.

This, I think, demonstrates the unlimited breadth and danger of the "balancing test" as it is currently being applied by a majority of this Court. Under that "test," the question in every case in which a First Amendment right is asserted is . . . simply whether the Government has an interest in abridging the right involved and, if so, whether that interest is of sufficient importance, in the opinion of a majority of this Court, to justify the Government's action in doing so. This doctrine, to say the very least, is capable of being used to justify almost any action Government may wish to take to suppress First Amendment freedoms.

MR. JUSTICE DOUGLAS, dissenting.

When we allow petitioner to be sentenced to prison for six years for being a "member" of the Communist Party, we make a sharp break with traditional concepts of First Amendment rights and make serious Mark Twain's lighthearted comment that "It is by the goodness of God that in our country we have those three unspeakably precious things: freedom of speech, freedom of conscience, and the prudence never to practice either of them."

Even the Alien and Sedition Laws—shameful reminders of an early chapter in intolerance—never went so far as we go today. . . . There is here no charge of conspiracy, no charge of any overt act to overthrow the Government by force and violence, no charge of any other criminal act. The charge is being a "member" of the Communist Party, "well-knowing" that it advocated the overthrow of the Government by force and violence, said defendant intending to bring about such overthrow by force and violence as speedily as circumstances would permit." That falls far short of a charge of conspiracy. Conspiracy rests not in intention alone but in an agreement with one or more others to promote an unlawful project. *United States v. Falcone*, 311 U.S. 205, 210. . . . No charge of any kind or sort of agreement hitherto embraced in the concept of a conspiracy is made here.

We legalize today guilt by association, sending a man to prison when he committed no unlawful act. Today's break with tradition is a serious one. It borrows from the totalitarian philosophy. . . .

The case is not saved by showing that petitioner was an active member. None of the activity constitutes a crime. * * *

Not one single illegal act is charged to petitioner. That is why the essence of the crime covered by the indictment is merely belief— belief in the proletarian revolution, belief in Communist creed. . . . Our long and painful experience with the law of treason, wholly apart from the First Amendment, should be enough warning that we as a free people should not venture again into the field of prosecuting beliefs.

That was the philosophy behind *West Virginia State Board of Education* v. *Barnette*, 319 U.S. 624, 641-642. . . .

Nothing but beliefs is on trial in this case. They are unpopular and to most of us revolting. But they are nonetheless ideas or dogmas or faiths within the broad framework of the First Amendment.

Belief in the principle of revolution is deep in our traditions. The Declaration of Independence proclaims it:
"whenever any Form of Government becomes destructive of these Ends, it is the Right of the People to alter or to abolish it, and to institute new Government, laying its Foundation on such Principles, and organizing its Powers in such Form, as to them shall seem most likely to effect their Safety and Happiness."

This right of revolution has been and is a part of the fabric of our institutions. * * *

This does not mean the helplessness of the established government in the face of armed resistance, for that government has the duty of maintaining existing institutions. . . . But it does mean that the right of revolution is ultimately reserved to the people themselves, whatever formal, but useless, remedies the existing government may offer. This is shown in the history of our revolution. Legislatures and governments have the right to protect themselves. They may judge as to the appropriate means of meeting force directed against them, but as to the propriety of the exercise of the ultimate right of revolution, there, as John Locke says, "The people shall be judge." . . .

MR. JUSTICE BRENNAN, with whom THE CHIEF JUSTICE and MR. JUSTICE DOUGLAS join, dissenting.

I think that in §4 (f) of the Internal Security Act Congress legislated immunity from prosecution under the membership clause of the Smith Act. The first sentence of §4 (f) is: "Neither the holding of office nor membership in any Communist organization by any person shall constitute per se a violation of subsection (a) or subsection (c) of this section or of any other criminal statute." The immunity granted by that sentence is not in my view restricted, as the Court holds, to *mere* membership, that is to membership which is nominal, passive or theoretical. The immunity also extends to "active and purposive membership, purposive that is as to the organization's criminal ends," which is the character of membership to which the Court today restricts the application of the membership clause of the Smith Act. . . . I think the Court asks the wrong question. The question is not . . . "repeal" [of] the membership clause. . . . The grant of immunity from prosecution . . . merely suspends prosecution . . . so long as the immunity is not withdrawn. . . .

The Congress was faced with a dilemma in legislating the policy of compulsory registration of Communists into the Internal Security

Act. This statute represented, in the words of the late John W. Davis, a policy of "ventilation rather than prohibition." Communists were to be forced to expose themselves to public view in order that the menace they present might be dealt with more effectively. The registration provisions of the Act are the very vitals of that measure. But compulsory disclosure of membership would compel admission of a crime, or provide a link to proof of a crime. Communists then could invoke their constitutional right to silence and the registration provisions would be wrecked on the rock of the Self-Incrimination Clause of the Fifth Amendment. It is no disparagement of the Congress to say that their deliberations reflect great uncertainty how to resolve the dilemma. Congress wrote the Internal Security Act knowing that the privilege against self-incrimination was a solid barrier against compulsory self-incrimination by congressional fiat. The legislative history of § 4 (f) is murky but I think there clearly emerges a congressional decision to extend immunity from prosecution for any membership in a Communist organization in order to safeguard against constitutional frustration the policy of disclosure embodied in the registration provisions. ° ° °

Although problems concerning the right of the government to protect itself from violence have arisen over the years with the resultant establishment of certain restrictions on speech, other groups have had difficulty in having limitations upon their right to speak removed. Labor has had difficulty first in establishing the right to organize without being guilty of conspiracy, and then in securing the right to strike. There were many reasons for the opposition to the right of labor to organize, but certainly high on the list was the belief that organizing, picketing and striking interfered with the property rights of employers. Such action on the part of labor can reduce the profit of a business, and possibly threaten its very existence. To protect these property rights, many states exercised the police power to pass statutes which severely restricted what we now recognize as First Amendment rights. In a form not uncommon to the times, Alabama passed such a statute, which was tested in *Thornhill* v. *Alabama.*

The statute provided:

> Any person or persons, who, without a just cause or legal excuse therefor, go near to or loiter about the premises or place of business of any other person, firm, corporation or association of people, engaged in a lawful business, for the purpose . . . of influencing, or inducing other persons not to trade with, . . . have business dealings with, or be employed by such persons . . . or who picket the works or place of business of such other persons ˙. . . for the purpose of hindering . . . or interfering with . . . any lawful business of another, shall be guilty of a misdemeanor. . . .

The petitioner was seen with half a dozen other men on a picket line at the Brown Wood Preserving Company. Pickets had been on duty at the plant for several weeks. There was no violence, nor threat of violence by the petitioner, who was arrested, charged, and convicted.

Thornhill v. *Alabama,* 310 U.S. 88, 60 S. Ct. 736 (1940)

. . . *First.* The freedom of speech and of the press, which are secured by the First Amendment against abridgment by the United States, are among the fundamental personal rights and liberties which are secured to all persons by the Fourteenth Amendment against abridgment by a State.

The safeguarding of these rights to the ends that men may speak as they think on matters vital to them and that falsehoods may be exposed through the processes of education and discussion is essential to free government. Those who won our independence had confidence in the power of free and fearless reasoning and communication of ideas to discover and spread political and economic truth. Noxious doctrines in those fields may be refuted and their evil averted by the courageous exercise of the power of correction of error through the processes of popular government. Compare *United States* v. *Carolene Products Co.,* 304 U.S. 144, 152–153n. Mere legislative preference for one rather than another means for combatting substantive evils, therefore, may well prove an inadequate foundation on which to rest regulations which are aimed at or in their operation diminish the effective exercise of rights so necessary to the maintenance of democratic institutions. It is imperative that, when the effective exercise of these rights is claimed to be abridged, the courts should "weigh the circumstances" and "appraise the substantiality of the reasons advanced" in support of the challenged regulations. *Schneider* v. *State,* 308 U.S. 147, 161, 162.

Second. The section in question must be judged upon its face. . . .

Third. Section 3448 has been applied by the state courts so as to prohibit a single individual from walking slowly and peacefully back and forth on the public sidewalk in front of the premises of an employer, without speaking to anyone, carrying a sign or placard on a staff above his head stating only the fact that the employer did not employ union men affiliated with the American Federation of Labor; the purpose of the described activity was concededly to advise customers and prospective customers of the relationship existing between the employer and its employees and thereby to induce such customers not to patronize the employer. . . . The statute as thus authoritatively construed and applied leaves room for no exceptions based upon either the number of persons engaged in the proscribed activity, the peaceful character of their demeanor, the nature of their dispute with an employer, or the restrained character and the accurateness of the terminology used in notifying the public of the facts of the dispute.

. . . It is apparent that one or the other of the offenses comprehends every practicable method whereby the facts of a labor dispute may be publicized in the vicinity of the place of business of an employer. The phrase "without just cause or legal excuse" does not in any effective manner restrict the breadth of the regulation; the words themselves have no ascertainable meaning either inherent or historical. Compare *Lanzetta* v. *New Jersey,* 306 U.S. 451, 453–455. The courses of action, listed under the first offense, which an accused—including an employee—may not urge others to take, comprehend those which in many instances would normally result from merely publicizing, without annoyance or threat of any kind, the facts of a labor dispute. An intention to hinder, delay or interfere with a lawful business, which is an element of the second offense, likewise can be proved merely by showing that others reacted in a way normally expectable of some upon learning the facts of a dispute. The vague contours of the term "picket" are nowhere delineated. Employees or others, accordingly, may be found to be within the purview of the term and convicted for engaging in activities identical with those proscribed by the first offense. In sum, whatever the means used to publicize the facts of a labor dispute, whether by printed sign, by pamphlet, by word of mouth or otherwise, all such activity without exception is within the inclusive prohibition of the statute so long as it occurs in the vicinity of the scene of the dispute.

Fourth. We think that §3448 is invalid on its face.

The freedom of speech and of the press guaranteed by the Consitution embraces at the least the liberty to discuss publicly and truthfully all matters of public concern without previous restraint or fear of subsequent punishment. . . .

. . . Free discussion concerning the conditions in industry and the causes of labor disputes appears to us indispensable to the effective and intelligent use of the processes of popular government to shape the destiny of modern industrial society. . . .

. . . But the group in power at any moment may not impose penal sanctions on peaceful and truthful discussion of matters of public interest merely on a showing that others may thereby be persuaded to take action inconsistent with its interests.

The State urges that the purpose of the challenged statute is the protection of the community from the violence and breaches of the peace, which, it asserts, are the concomitants of picketing. The power and the duty of the State to take adequate steps to preserve the peace and to protect the privacy, the lives, and the property of its residents cannot be doubted. But no clear and present danger of destruction of life or property, or invasion of the right of privacy, or breach of the peace can be thought to be inherent in the activities of every person who approaches the premises of an employer and publicizes the facts of a labor dispute involving the latter. We are not now concerned with picketing *en masse* or otherwise conducted which might occasion such imminent and aggravated danger to these interests as to justify a statute narrowly drawn to cover the precise situation giving rise to the danger. Compare *American Foundries* v. *Tri-City Council,* 257 U.S. 184, 205. Section 3448 in question here does not aim specifically at serious encroachments on these interests and does not evidence any such care in balancing these interests against the interests of the community and that of the individual in freedom of discussion on matters of public concern. . . . The danger of breach of the peace or serious invasion of rights of property or privacy at the scene of a labor dispute is not sufficiently imminent in all cases to warrant the legislature in determining that such place is not appropriate for the range of activities outlawed by §3448.

Reversed.

There are, however, a variety of ways in which the rights of labor to express its views and to appeal for support of a labor organization have been restricted. For example, a Texas statute required all labor organizers when soliciting members to carry an organizer's card issued by the state. The term "labor organizer" was broadly defined and interpreted. For failure to obtain the card, or to exhibit it on request, the organizer could be enjoined and fined.

The statute was tested in *Thomas* v. *Collins,* 323 U.S. 516, 65 S. Ct. 315 (1945). An *ex parte* injunction was issued to prevent a speech by Mr. Thomas, a labor organizer who had gone to Texas for the particular purpose of making a speech, and who did not obtain the required card. Despite the injunction, he spoke to the meeting of workers and solicited a specific person there to join the union. Although he claimed the statute was an unconstitutional restriction of his right to speak, he was fined and sentenced. The Court held that the statute as applied imposed previous restraint upon Mr. Thomas' rights of free speech and free assembly, and reversed the judgment.

Excluding the problems raised by the Fifth Amendment and those raised by technicalities in the rules of evidence, under what conditions can the government, state or federal, *compel* speech? If there is a conflict between the speech required and the religious beliefs of the individual, is he subject to punishment for refusing to speak? The problem arose in *Minersville School District* v. *Gobitis* (310 U.S. 586, 60 S. Ct. 1010, 1940), a Pennsylvania case. The School Board had adopted a resolution requiring pupils to salute the flag, and provided for expulsion if they refused. Lillian Gobitis, twelve, and William, age ten, her brother, were expelled because they refused on religious grounds to salute the national flag. As members of the Jehovah's Witness sect, they believed that "such a gesture of respect for the flag was forbidden by command of Scripture." They relied on three of the Ten Commandments, found in Chapter 20 of Exodus. Since education was compulsory, the children were sent to private school, a heavy financial burden for their father. His action to enjoin enforcement of the rule was upheld in the lower courts. But the Supreme Court overruled the lower court, and upheld the School District's rule. Mr. Justice Frankfurter said, "We must decide whether the requirement of participation in such a ceremony, exacted from a child who refuses upon sincere religious grounds, infringes without due process of law, the liberty guaranteed by the Fourteenth Amendment."[5] Despite his statement that "every possible leeway should be given to the claims of religious faith," (p. 594,) he concluded that this was "a general law, not aimed at the promotion or restriction of religious beliefs."[6] It was one of "various means to evoke that unifying sentiment without which there can ultimately be no liberties, civil or religious."[7] The appropriateness of the means were to be determined by the legislature, not by the courts.

The *Gobitis* decision was severely criticized, and three years later was reversed in a case involving a similar factual situation, but coming from West Virginia.

West Virginia State Board of Education et al. v. Barnette et al., 319 U.S. 674, 63 S. Ct. 1178 (1943)

MR. JUSTICE JACKSON delivered the opinion of the Court.

Following the decision by this Court on June 3, 1940, in *Minersville School District* v. *Gobitis,* 310 U.S. 586, the West Virginia legislature amended its statutes to require all schools therein to conduct courses of instruction in history, civics, and the Constitutions of the United States and of the State "for the purpose of teaching, fostering and perpetuating the ideals, principles and spirit of Americanism, and increasing the knowledge of the organization and machinery of the government." Appellant Board of Education was directed, with advice of the State Superintendent of Schools, to "prescribe the courses of study covering these subjects" for public schools. The Act made it the duty of private, parochial and denominational schools to prescribe courses of study "similar to those required for the public schools."

The Board of Education on January 9, 1942, adopted a resolution containing recitals taken largely from the Court's *Gobitis* opinion and ordering that the salute to the flag become "a regular part of the program of activities in the public schools," that all teachers and pupils "shall be required to participate in the salute honoring the Nation represented by the Flag; provided, however, that refusal to salute the Flag be regarded as an act of insubordination, and shall be dealt with accordingly." . . .

[5]*Minersville School District* v. *Gobitis,* 310 U.S. 586, pp. 592, 593.
[6]*Ibid.,* 310 U.S. 586, p. 594.
[7]*Ibid.,* p. 597.

Failure to conform is "insubordination" dealt with by expulsion. Readmission is denied by statute until compliance. Meanwhile the expelled child is "unlawfully absent" and may be proceeded against as a delinquent. His parents or guardians are liable to prosecution, and if convicted are subject to fine not exceeding $50 and jail term not exceeding thirty days.

Appellees, citizens of the United States and of West Virginia, brought suit in the United States District Court for themselves and others similarly situated asking its injunction to restrain enforcement these laws and regulations against Jehovah's Witnesses. The Witnesses are an unincorporated body teaching that the obligation imposed by law of God is superior to that of laws enacted by temporal government. Their religious beliefs include a literal version of Exodus, Chapter 20, verses 4 and 5, which says: "Thou shalt not make unto thee any graven image, or any likeness of anything that is in heaven above, or that is in the earth beneath, or that is in the water under the earth; thou shalt not bow down thyself to them nor serve them." They consider that the flag is an "image" within this command. For this reason they refuse to salute it.

Children of this faith have been expelled from school and are threatened with exclusion for no other cause. Officials threaten to send them to reformatories maintained for criminally inclined juveniles. Parents of such children have been prosecuted and are threatened with prosecutions for causing delinquency. . . .

This case calls upon us to reconsider a precedent decision, as the Court throughout its history often has been required to do. Before turning to the *Gobitis* case, however, it is desirable to notice certain characteristics by which this controversy is distinguished.

The freedom asserted by these appellees does not bring them into collision with rights asserted by any other individual. It is such conflicts which most frequently require intervention of the State to determine where the rights of one end and those of another begin. But the refusal of these persons to participate in the ceremony does not interfere with or deny rights of others to do so. Nor is there any question in this case that their behavior is peaceable and orderly. The sole conflict is between authority and rights of the individual. The State asserts power to condition access to public education on making a prescribed sign and profession and at the same time to coerce attendance by punishing both parent and child. The latter stand on a right of self-determination in matters that touch individual opinion and personal attitude. . . .

Here. . . . we are dealing with a compulsion of students to declare a belief. . . . The issue here is whether this slow and easily neglected route to aroused loyalties constitutionally may be short-cut by substituting a compulsory salute and slogan. . . .

There is no doubt that, in connection with the pledges, the flag salute is a form of utterance. . . . The use of an emblem or flag to symbolize some system, idea, institution, or personality, is a short cut from mind to mind. Causes and nations, political parties, lodges and ecclesiastical groups seek to knit the loyalty of their followings to a flag or banner, a color or design. . . . A person gets from a symbol the meaning he puts into it, and what is one man's comfort and inspiration is another's jest and scorn. . . .

Here . . . the State . . . requires the individual to communicate by word and sign his acceptance of the political ideas it thus bespeaks. . . . .

It is also to be noted that the compulsory flag salute and pledge requires affirmation of a belief and an attitude of mind. . . . It is now a commonplace that censorship or suppression of expression of opinion is tolerated by our Constitution only when the expression presents a clear and present danger of action of a kind the State is. empowered to prevent and punish. . . . [H]ere the power of compulsion is invoked without any allegation that remaining passive during a flag salute ritual creates a clear and present danger that would justify an effort even to muffle expression. To sustain the compulsory flag salute we are required to say that a Bill of Rights which guards the individual's right to speak his own mind, left it open to public authorities to compel him to utter what is not in his mind.

Whether the First Amendment to the Constitution will permit officials to order observance of ritual of this nature does not depend upon whether as a voluntary exercise we would think it to be good, bad or merely innocuous. . . . [V]alidity of the asserted power to force an American citizen publicly to profess any statement of belief or to engage in any ceremony of assent to one, presents questions of power that must be considered independently of any idea we may have as to the utility of the ceremony in question.

Nor does the issue as we see it turn on one's possession of particular religious views or the sincerity with which they are held. . . . It is not necessary to inquire whether non-conformist beliefs will exempt from the duty to salute unless we first find power to make the salute a legal duty.

The *Gobitis* decision, however, *assumed,* as did the argument in that case and in this, that power exists in the State to impose the flag salute discipline upon school children in general. . . . The question which underlies the flag salute controversy is whether such a cere- mony so touching matters of opinion and political attitude may be imposed upon the individual by official authority under powers committed to any political organization under our Constitution. We examine rather than assume existence of this power and, against this broader definition of issues in this case, reexamine specific grounds assigned for the *Gobitis* decision. * * *

The very purpose of a Bill of Rights was to withdraw certain subjects from the vicissitudes of political controversy, to place them beyond the reach of majorities and officials and to establish them as legal principles to be applied by the courts. One's right to life, liberty, and property, to free speech, a free press, freedom of worship and assembly, and other fundamental rights may not be submitted to vote; they depend on the outcome of no elections. . . . It is important to note that while it is the Fourteenth Amendment which bears directly upon the State it is the more specific limiting principles of the First Amendment that finally govern this case. . . .

Lastly, and this is the very heart of the *Gobitis* opinion, it reasons that "National unity is the basis of national security," that the authorities have "the right to select appropriate means for its attainment," and hence reaches the conclusion that such compulsory measures toward "national unity" are constitutional. *Id.* at 595. Upon the verity of this assumption depends our answer in this case.

National unity as an end which officials may foster by persuasion and example is not in question. The problem is whether under our Constitution compulsion as here employed is a permissible means for its achievement. . . .

Those who begin coercive elimination of dissent soon find themselves exterminating dissenters. Compulsory unification of opinion achieves only the unanimity of the graveyard.

It seems trite but necessary to say that the First Amendment to our Constitution was designed to avoid these ends by avoiding these beginnings. . . .

The case is made difficult not because the principles of its decision are obscure but because the flag involved is our own. Nevertheless, we apply the limitations of the Constitution with no fear that freedom to be intellectually and spiritually diverse or even contrary will disintegrate the social organization. . . . We can have intellectual individualism and the rich cultural diversities that we owe to exceptional minds only at the price of occasional eccentricity and abnormal attitudes. . . . But freedom to differ is not limited to things that do not matter much. That would be a mere shadow of freedom. The test of its substance is the right to differ as to things that touch the heart of the existing order.

If there is any fixed star in our constitutional constellation, it is that no official, high or petty, can prescribe what shall be orthodox in politics, nationalism, religion, or other matters of opinion or force citizens to confess by word or act their faith therein. If there are any circumstances which permit an exception, they do not now occur to us.

We think the action of the local authorities in compelling the flag salute and pledge transcends constitutional limitations on their power and invades the sphere of intellect and spirit which it is the purpose of the First Amendment to our Constitution to reserve from all official control.

The decision of this Court in *Minersville School District* v. *Gobitis* and the holdings of those few *per curiam* decisions which preceded and foreshadowed it are overruled, and the judgment enjoining enforcement of the West Virginia Regulation is *Affirmed.*

MR. JUSTICE ROBERTS and MR. JUSTICE REED adhere to the views

U.S. 586, and are of the opinion that the judgment below should be reversed.

MR. JUSTICE BLACK and MR. JUSTICE DOUGLAS, concurring.

We are substantially in agreement with the opinion just read, but since we originally joined with the Court in the *Gobitis* case, it is appropriate that we make a brief statement of reasons for our change of view.

Reluctance to make the Federal Constitution a rigid bar against state regulation of conduct thought inimical to the public welfare was the controlling influence which moved us to consent to the *Gobitis* decision. Long reflection convinced us that although the principle is sound, its application in the particular case was wrong. . . . *Jones* v. *Opelika*, 316 U.S. 584, 623. We believe that the statute before us fails to accord full scope to the freedom of religion secured to the appellees by the First and Fourteenth Amendments. ° ° °

MR. JUSTICE MURPHY, concurring.

° ° ° I agree with the opinion of the Court and join in it.

MR. JUSTICE FRANKFURTER, dissenting.

One who belongs to the most vilified and persecuted minority in history is not likely to be insensible to the freedoms guaranteed by our Constitution. Were my purely personal attitude relevant I should wholeheartedly associate myself with the general libertarian views in the Court's opinion, representing as they do the thought and action of a lifetime. But as judges we are neither Jew nor Gentile, neither Catholic nor agnostic. We owe equal attachment to the Constitution and are equally bound by our judicial obligations whether we derive our citizenship from the earliest or latest immigrants to these shores. As a member of this Court I am not justified in writing my private notions of policy into the Constitution, no matter how deeply I may cherish them or how mischievous I may deem their disregard. The duty of a judge who must decide which of two claims before the Court shall prevail, that of a State to enact and enforce laws within its general competence or that of an individual to refuse obedience because of the demands of his conscience, is not that of the ordinary person. It can never be emphasized too much that one's own opinion about the wisdom or evil of a law should be excluded altogether when one is doing one's duty on the bench. The only opinion about looking in that direction that is material is our opinion whether legislators could in reason have enacted such a law. In the light of all the circumstances, including the history of this question in this Court, it would require more daring than I possess to deny that reasonable legislators could have taken the action which is before us for review. Most unwillingly, therefore, I must differ from my brethren with regard to legislation like this. I cannot bring my mind to believe that the "liberty" secured by the Due Process Clause gives this Court authority to deny to the State of West Virginia the attainment of that which we all recognize as a legitimate legislative end, namely, the promotion of good citizenship, by employment of the means here chosen. . . .

The admonition that judicial self-restraint alone limits arbitrary exercise of our authority is relevant every time we are asked to nullify legislation. . . .

There is no warrant in the constitutional basis of this Court's authority for attributing different roles to it depending upon the nature of the challenge to the legislation. Our power does not vary according to the particular provision of the Bill of Rights which is invoked. . . . In no instance is this Court the primary protector of the particular liberty that is invoked. . . .

When Mr. Justice Holmes, speaking for this Court, wrote that "it must be remembered that legislatures are ultimate guardians of the liberties and welfare of the people in quite as great a degree as the courts," *Missouri, K. & T. Ry. Co.* v. *May*, 194 U.S. 267, 270, he went to the very essence of our constitutional system and the democratic conception of our society. He was stating the comprehensive judicial duty of this Court in our constitutional scheme whenever legislation is sought to be nullified on any ground, namely, that responsibility for legislation lies with legislatures, answerable as they are directly to the people and this Court's only and very narrow function is to determine whether within the broad grant of authority vested in legislatures they have exercised a judgment for which reasonable justification can be offered. . . .

The precise scope of the question before us defines the limits of the constitutional power that is in issue. . . . All that is in question is the right of the State to compel participation in this exercise by those who choose to attend the public schools.

We are not reviewing merely the action of a local school board. . . . We are in fact passing judgment on "the power of the State as a whole." *Rippey* v. *Texas*, 193 U.S. 504, 509. . . . Practically we are passing upon the political power of each of the forty-eight states. Moreover, since the First Amendment has been read into the Fourteenth, our problem is precisely the same as it would be if we had before us an Act of Congress for the District of Columbia. . . .

Under our constitutional system the legislature is charged solely with civil concerns of society. . . . But it by no means follows that legislative power is wanting whenever a general non-discriminatory civil regulation in fact touches conscientious scruples or religious beliefs of an individual or a group. . . .

This is no dry, technical matter. It cuts deep into one's conception of the democratic process — it concerns no less the practical differences between the means for making these accomodations that are open to courts and to legislatures. A court can only strike down. It can only say "This or that law is void." It cannot modify or qualify, it cannot make exceptions to a general requirement. And it strikes down not merely for a day. At least the finding of unconstitutionality ought not to have ephemeral significance unless the Constitution is to be reduced to the fugitive importance of mere legislation. When we are dealing with the Constitution of the United States, and more particularly with the great safeguards of the Bill of Rights, we are dealing with principles of liberty and justice "so rooted in the traditions and conscience of our people as to be ranked as fundamental" — something without which "a fair and enlightened system of justice would be impossible." *Palko* v. *Connecticut,* 302 U.S. 319, 325. . . . Judges should be very diffident in setting their judgment against that of a state in determining what is and what is not a major concern, what means are appropriate to proper ends, and what is the total social cost in striking the balance of imponderables. * * *

The essence of the religious freedom guaranteed by our Constitution is therefore this: no religion shall either receive the state's support or incur its hostility. Religion is outside the sphere of political government. This does not mean that all matters on which religious organizations or beliefs may pronounce are outside the sphere of government. . . .

An act compelling profession of allegiance to a religion, no matter how subtly or tenuously promoted, is bad. But an act promoting good citizenship and national allegiance is within the domain of governmental authority and is therefore to be judged by the same considerations of power and of constitutionality as those involved in the many claims of immunity from civil obedience because of religious scruples. * * *

Law is concerned with external behavior and not with the inner life of man. It rests in large measure upon compulsion. . . .

The state is not shut out from a domain because the individual conscience may deny the state's claim. The individual conscience may profess what faith it chooses. . . .

One may have the right to practice one's religion and at the same time owe the duty of formal obedience to laws that run counter to one's beliefs. * * *

If speech would violate the right of an individual to remain silent, for reasons of religious belief, are there conditions under which he can be compelled to stop speaking? For example, although an individual has the right to speak, even within the broadest limits of the First Amendment speech may be stopped in order to prevent a riot. A decision must be made in each situation, often in the face of hostility, the threat of mob action, or the realization that violence may lead to murder. The situation is one with which the police must contend on numerous occasions and, as a practical matter, the easiest solution is to stop the speaker before there is any violence. But at least technically what should be prevented is violence by the audience. As a matter of fact, the easier course of action (and sometimes the only possible course) is to stop the speaker, and thus avoid a riot which may be beyond the power of the police to control.

Such a situation arose in the *Terminiello* case, decided in 1949. The case is also an excellent example of how the Justices can read the same record and find "essential" facts which are irreconcilable with "essential" facts found by other readers of the same record. If the names were not mentioned, it would be virtually impossible to recognize the majority and minority opinions as being from the same case.

Terminiello v. *City of Chicago,* 337 U.S. 1, 69 S. Ct. 894 (1949)

MR. JUSTICE DOUGLAS delivered the opinion of the Court.

Petitioner after jury trial was found guilty of disorderly conduct in violation of a city ordinance of Chicago and fined. The case grew out of an address he delivered in an auditorium in Chicago under the auspices of the Christian Veterans of America. The meeting commanded considerable public attention. The auditorium was filled to capacity with over eight hundred persons present. Others were turned away. Outside of the auditorium a crowd of about one thousand persons gathered to protest against the meeting. A cordon of policemen was assigned to the meeting to maintain order; but they were not able to prevent several disturbances. The crowd outside was angry and turbulent.

Petitioner in his speech condemned the conduct of the crowd outside and vigorously, if not viciously, criticized various political and racial groups whose activities he denounced as inimical to the nation's welfare.

The trial court charged that "breach of the peace" consists of any "misbehavior which violates the public peace and decorum"; and that the "misbehavior may constitute a breach of the peace if it stirs the public to anger, invites dispute, brings about a condition of unrest, or creates a disturbance, or if it molests the inhabitants in the enjoyment of peace and quiet by arousing alarm." Petitioner did not take exception to that instruction. But he maintained at all times that the ordinance as applied to his conduct violated his right of free speech under the Federal Constitution, U.S. Const. Amend. 1. . . . The case is here on a petition for certiorari which we granted because of the importance of the question presented.

The argument here has been focused on the issue of whether the content of petitioner's speech was composed of derisive, fighting words, which carried it outside the scope of the constitutional guarantees. See *Chaplinksy* v. *New Hampshire,* 315 U.S. 568; *Cantwell* v. *Connecticut,* 310 U.S. 296, 310. We do not reach that question, for there is a preliminary question that is dispositive of the case.

As we have noted, the statutory words "breach of the peace" were defined in instructions to the jury to include speech which "stirs the public to anger, invites dispute, brings about a condition of unrest, or creates a disturbance. * * *" That construction of the ordinance is a ruling on a question of state law that is as binding on us as though the precise words had been written into the ordinance. See *Herbert* v. *Louisiana,* 272 U.S. 312, 317. . . .

The vitality of civil and political institutions in our society depends on free discussion. As Chief Justice Hughes wrote in *De Jonge* v.

Oregon, 299 U.S. 353, 365, it is only through free debate and free exchange of ideas that government remains responsive to the will of the people and peaceful change is effected. The right to speak freely and to promote diversity of ideas and programs is therefore one of the chief distinctions that sets us apart from totalitarian regimes.

Accordingly a function of free speech under our system of government is to invite dispute. It may indeed best serve its high purpose when it induces a condition of unrest, creates dissatisfaction with conditions as they are, or even stirs people to anger. Speech is often provocative and challenging. It may strike at prejudices and preconceptions and have profound unsettling effects as it presses for acceptance of an idea. That is why freedom of speech, though not absolute, *Chaplinsky* v. *New Hampshire, supra*, 315 U.S. at pages 571-572, is nevertheless protected against censorship or punishment, unless shown likely to produce a clear and present danger of a serious substantive evil that rises far above public inconvenience, annoyance, or unrest. See *Bridges* v. *California*, 314 U.S. 252, 262. There is no room under our Constitution for a more restrictive view. For the alternative would lead to standardization of ideas either by legislatures, courts, or dominant political or community groups.

The ordinance as construed by the trial court seriously invaded this province. It permitted conviction of petitioner if his speech stirred people to anger, invited public dispute, or brought about a condition of unrest. A conviction resting on any of those grounds may not stand. . . .

As construed and applied it at least contains parts that are unconstitutional. The verdict was a general one; and we do not know on this record but what it may rest on the invalid clauses. . . .

But it is said that throughout the appellate proceedings the Illinois courts assumed that the only conduct punishable and punished under the ordinance was conduct constituting "fighting words." . . . We cannot avoid that issue by saying that all Illinois did was to measure petitioner's conduct, not the ordinance, against the Constitution. Petitioner raised both points—that his speech was protected by the Constitution; that the inclusion of his speech within the ordinance was a violation of the Constitution. We would, therefore, strain at technicalities to conclude that the constitutionality of the ordinance as construed and applied to petitioner was not before the Illinois courts. The record makes clear that petitioner at all times challenged the constitutionality of the ordinance as construed and applied to him.

Reversed

MR. CHIEF JUSTICE VINSON, dissenting.

I dissent. The Court today reverses the Supreme Court of Illinois because it discovers in the record one sentence in the trial court's instructions which permitted the jury to convict on an unconstitutional basis. The offending sentence had heretofore gone completely undetected. It apparently was not even noticed, much less excepted to, by the petitioner's counsel at the trial. No objection was made to it in the two Illinois appellate tribunals which reviewed the case. . . . In short, the offending sentence in the charge to the jury was no part of the case until this Court's independent research ferreted it out of a lengthy and somewhat confused record. I think it too plain for argument that a reversal on such a basis does not accord with any principle governing review of state court decisions heretofore announced by this Court. . . . The fact is that the Illinois courts construed the ordinance as punishing only the use of "fighting words." Their opinions plainly show that they affirmed because they thought that the petitioner's speech had been found by the jury to come within that category. Their action was not, and cannot here be taken to be, an approval of the ordinance "as construed" by the instruction because the record clearly shows that the case was treated on appeal, both by counsel and by the courts, as if no such instruction existed. This Court can reverse the conviction because of the instruction only if we are to say that every time a state court affirms a conviction it necessarily must approve of every unnoticed and unobjected to error which we may discover in the record. If such is the doctrine of this case, I feel compelled to register my emphatic dissent. * * *

MR. JUSTICE FRANKFURTER, dissenting.

For the first time in the course of the 130 years in which State prosecutions have come here for review, this Court is today reversing a sentence imposed by a State court on a ground that was urged neither here nor below and that was explicitly disclaimed on behalf of the petitioner at the bar of this Court.

The impropriety of that part of the charge which is now made the basis of reversal was not raised at the trial nor before the Appellate Court of Illinois. . . . Thus an objection, not raised by counsel in the Illinois courts, not made the basis of the petition for certiorari here — not included in the "questions presented," nor in the "reasons relied on for the allowance of the writ" — and explicitly disavowed at the bar of this Court, is used to upset a conviction which has been sustained by three courts of Illinois.

Reliance on *Stromberg* v. *California*, 283 U.S. 359, for what is done today is wholly misplaced. Neither expressly nor by implication has that decision any bearing upon the issue which the Court's opinion in this case raises, namely, whether it is open for this Court to reverse the highest court of a State on a point which was not brought before that court, did not enter into the judgment rendered by that court, and at no stage of the proceedings in this Court was invoked as error by the State court whose reversal is here sought. * * *

Only the uninformed will deride as a merely technical point objection to what the Court is doing in this case. The matter touches the very basis of this Court's authority in reviewing the judgments of State courts. We have no authority to meddle with such a judgment unless some claim under the Constitution or the laws of the United States has been made before the State court whose judgment we are reviewing and unless the claim has been denied by that court. . . . The relation of the United States and the courts of the United States to the States and the courts of the States is a very delicate matter. It is too delicate to permit silence when a judgment of a State court is reversed in disregard of the duty of this Court to leave untouched an adjudication of a State unless that adjudication is based upon a claim of a federal right which the State has had an opportunity to meet and to recognize. . . . This is a court of review, not a tribunal unbounded by rules. We do not sit like a kadi under a tree dispensing justice according to considerations of individual expediency. * * *

On the merits of the issue reached by the Court I share MR. JUSTICE JACKSON'S views. . . .

MR. JUSTICE JACKSON and MR. JUSTICE BURTON join this dissent.

MR. JUSTICE JACKSON, dissenting.

The Court reverses this conviction by reiterating generalized approbations of freedom of speech with which, in the abstract, no one will disagree. Doubts as to their applicability are lulled by avoidance of more than passing reference to the circumstances of Terminiello's speech and judging it as if he had spoken to persons as dispassionate as empty benches, or like a modern Demosthenes practicing his Philippics on a lonely seashore.

But the local court that tried Terminiello was not indulging in theory. It was dealing with a riot and with a speech that provoked a hostile mob and incited a friendly one, and threatened violence between the two. When the trial judge instructed the jury that it might find Terminiello guilty of inducing a breach of the peace if his behavior stirred the public to anger, invited dispute, brought about unrest, created a disturbance or molested peace and quiet by arousing alarm, he was not speaking of these as harmless or abstract conditions. He was addressing his words to the concrete behavior and specific consequences disclosed by the evidence. He was saying to the jury, in effect, that if this particular speech added fuel to the situation already so inflamed as to threaten to get beyond police control, it could be punished as inducing a breach of peace. When the light of the evidence not recited by the Court is thrown upon the Court's opinion, it discloses that underneath a little issue of Terminiello and his hundred-dollar fine lurk some of the most far-reaching constitutional questions that can confront a people who value both liberty and order. This Court seems to regard these as enemies of each other and to be of the view that we must forego order to achieve liberty. So it fixes its eyes on a conception of freedom of speech so rigid as to tolerate no concession to society's need for public order. . . .

Terminiello, advertised as a Catholic Priest, but revealed at the trial to be under suspension by his Bishop, was brought to Chicago from Birmingham, Alabama, to address a gathering that assembled in response to a call signed by Gerald L. K. Smith, which, among other things, said:

"* * * The same people who hate Father Coughlin hate Father Terminiello. They have persecuted him, hounded him, threatened him, but he has remained unaffected by their anti-Christian campaign against him. You will hear all sorts of reports concerning Father Terminiello. But remember that he is a Priest in good standing and a fearless lover of Christ and America."

The jury may have considered that this call attempted to capitalize the hatreds this man has stirred and foreshadowed, if it did not intend to invite, the kind of demonstration that followed.

Terminiello's own testimony shows the conditions under which he spoke. So far as material it follows: . . . "When we got there the pickets were not marching; they were body to body and covered the sidewalk completely, some on the steps so that we had to form a flying wedge to get through. Police escorted us to the building, and I noticed four or five others there.

"They called us 'God damned Fascists, Nazis, ought to hang the so and sos'. When I entered the building I heard the howls of the people outside. * * * There were four or five plain clothes officers standing at the entrance to the stage and three or four at the entrance to the back door.

"The officers threatened that if they broke the door again they would arrest them and every time they opened the door a little to look out something was thrown at the officers, including ice-picks and rocks.

"A number of times the door was broken, was partly broken through. . . .

"I saw a number of windows broken by stones or missiles. I saw the back door being forced open, pushed open.

"The front door was broken partly open after the doors were closed. . . . I saw rocks being thrown through windows and that continued throughout at least the first half of the meeting, probably longer, and again attempts were made to force the front door, rather the front door was forced partly. The howling continued on the outside, cursing could be heard audibly in the hall at times. Police were rushing in and out of the front door protecting the front door, and there was a general commotion, all kinds of noises and violence—all from the outside.

"Between the time the first speaker spoke and I spoke, stones and bricks were thrown in all the time. I started to speak about 35 or 40 minutes after the meeting started, a little later than nine o'clock.* * *"

The court below, in addition to this recital, heard other evidence, that the crowd reached an estimated number of 1,500. . . . The crowd constituted "a surging, howling mob hurling epithets at those who would enter and tried to tear their clothes off." One young woman's coat was torn off and she had to be assisted into the meeting by policemen. . . . Bricks were thrown through the windowpanes before and during the speaking. About 28 windows were broken. The street was black with people on both sides for at least a block either way; bottles, stink bombs and brickbats were thrown. Police were unable to control the mob, which kept breaking the windows at the meeting hall, drowning out the speaker's voice at times and breaking in through the back door of the auditorium. About 17 of the group outside were arrested by the police.

Knowing of this environment, Terminiello made a long speech, from the stenographic record of which I omit relatively innocuous passages and add emphasis to what seems especially provocative:

"Father Terminiello: Now, I am going to whisper my greetings to you, Fellow Christians. I will interpret it. I said, 'Fellow *Christians,*' and I suppose there are *some of the scum got in by mistake,* so I want to tell a story about *the scum:* . . . Now, I am talking about the fifty-seven varieties that we have in America, and we have fifty-seven varieties of pinks and reds and pastel shades in this country; and all of it can be traced back to the twelve years we spent under the New Deal, because that was the build-up for what is going on in the world today.

"Now, my friends, they are planning another ruse; and if it ever happens to this cou-try [sic], God help America. They are going to try to put into Mr. Edgar Hoover's position a man by the name of *George Swarzwald.* I think even those who were uneducated on so-called sedition charges, that the majority of the individuals in this department, that Christ-like men and women who realize today what is going on in this country, men who are in this audience today, who want *to know the names of those people, before they are outside, they want to know the names if any. Did you hear any tonight that you recognize? Most of them probably are imported. They are imported from Russia, certainly. If you know the names, please send them to me immediately. * * *

"* * * Didn't you ever read the Morgenthau plan for the starvation of little babies and pregnant women in Germany? Whatever could a child that is born have to do with Hitler or anyone else at the beginning of the war? Why should every child in Germany today not live to be more than two or three months of age? Because Morgenthau wants it that way, and so did F. D. R. * * * You will know who is behind it when I tell you the story* of a doctor in Akron, Ohio. He boasted to a friend of mine within the last few days, while he was in the service of this country as a doctor, he and others of his kind made it a practice—now, this was not only one man—made it a practice to amputate the limbs of every German they came in contact with whenever they could get away with it; so, that they could never carry a gun. Imagine men of that caliber, sworn to serve this beautiful country of ours, *why should we tolerate them?*" . . .

Such was the speech. Evidence showed that it stirred the audience not only to cheer and applaud but to expressions of immediate anger, unrest and alarm. One called the speaker a "God damned liar" and was taken out by the police. Another said that "Jews, niggers and Catholics would have to be gotten rid of." One response was,"Yes, the Jews are all killers, murderers. If we don't kill them first, they will kill us." . . .

Terminiello, of course, disclaims being a fascist. Doubtless many of the indoor audience were not consciously such. His speech, however, followed, with fidelity that is more than coincidental, the pattern of European fascist leaders. . . .

As this case declares a nation-wide rule that disables local and state authorities from punishing conduct which produces conflicts of this kind, it is unrealistic not to take account of the nature, methods and objectives of the forces involved. This was not an isolated, spontaneous and unintended collision of political, racial or ideological adversaries. It was a local manifestation of a world-wide and standing conflict between two organized groups of revolutionary fanatics, each of which has imported to this country the strong-arm technique developed in the struggle by which their kind has devastated Europe. Increasingly, American cities have to cope with it. . . . We need not resort to speculation as to the purposes for which these tactics are calculated nor as to their consequences. Recent European history demonstrates both. * * *

The present obstacle to mastery of the streets by either radical or reactionary mob movements is not the opposing minority. It is the authority of local governments which represent the free choice of democratic and law-abiding elements, of all shades of opinion but who, whatever their differences, submit them to free elections which register the results of their free discussion. The fascist and communist groups, on the contrary, resort to these terror tactics to confuse, bully and discredit those freely chosen governments.

This drive by totalitarian groups to undermine the prestige and effectiveness of local democratic governments is advanced whenever either of them can win from this Court a ruling which paralyzes the power of these officials. . . . This is such a case. Terminiello's victory today certainly fulfills the most extravagant hopes of both right and left totalitarian groups, who want nothing so much as to paralyze and discredit the only democratic authority that can curb them in their battle for the streets.

I am unable to see that the local authorities have transgressed the Federal Constitution. * * *

A trial court and jury has found only that in the context of violence and disorder in which it was made, this speech was a provocation to immediate breach of the peace and therefore cannot claim constitutional immunity from punishment. . . .

Rioting is a substantive evil, which I take it no one will deny that the State and the City have the right and the duty to prevent and punish. Where an offense is induced by speech, the Court has laid down and often reiterated a test of the power of the authorities to deal with the speaking as also an offense. "The question in every case is whether the words *used are used in such circumstances* and are of *such a nature* as to create a *clear and present danger* that they will bring about the substantive evils that Congress [or the State or City] has a right to prevent." [Emphasis supplied.] Mr. Justice Holmes in *Schenck* v. *United States*, 249 U.S. 47, 52. * * *

This absence from the Constitution of any expressed power to deal with abuse of freedom of speech has enabled the Court to soar aloof from any consideration of the abuses which create problems for the states and to indulge in denials of local authority, some of which seem to me improvident in the light of functions which local governments must be relied on to perform for our free society. Quite apart from any other merits or defects, recent decisions have almost completely immunized this battle for the streets from any form of control. * * *

I do not think we should carry this handicap further, as we do today, but should adhere to the principles heretofore announced to safeguard our liberties against abuse as well as against invasion. It should not be necessary to recall these elementary principles, but it has been a long time since some of them were even mentioned in this Court's writing on the subject and results indicate they may have been overlooked.

I begin with the oft-forgotten principle which this case demonstrates, that freedom of speech exists only under law and not independently of it. . . .

No one will disagree that the fundamental, permanent and overriding policy of police and courts should be to permit and encourage utmost freedom of utterance. It is the legal right of any American citizen to advocate peaceful adoption of fascism or communism, socialism or capitalism. He may go far in expressing sentiments whether pro-semitic or anti-semitic, pro-negro or anti-negro, pro-Catholic or anti-Catholic. He is legally free to argue for some anti-American system of government to supersede by constitutional methods the one we have. It is our philosophy that the course of government should be controlled by a consensus of the governed. This process of reaching intelligent popular decisions requires free discussion. Hence we should tolerate no law or custom of censorship or suppression.

But we must bear in mind also that no serious outbreak of mob violence, race rioting, lynching or public disorder is likely to get going without help of some speech-making to some mass of people. . . . Unity of purpose, passion and hatred, which merges the many minds of a crowd into the mindlessness of a mob, almost invariably is supplied by speeches.* * *

Invocation of constitutional liberties as part of the strategy for overthrowing them presents a dilemma to a free people which may not be soluble by constitutional logic alone.

But I would not be understood as suggesting that the United

States can or should meet this dilemma by suppression of free, open
and public speaking on the part of any group or ideology. . . .

My confidence in American institutions and in the sound sense
of the American people is such that if with a stroke of the pen I could
silence every fascist and communist speaker, I would not do it. . . .
In the long run, maintenance of free speech will be more endangered
if the population can have no protection from the abuses which lead
to violence. . . . No liberty is made more secure by holding that
its abuses are inseparable from its enjoyment. We must not forget
that it is the free democratic communities that ask us to trust them to
maintain peace with liberty and that the factions engaged in this
battle are not interested permanently in either. . . .

This Court has gone far toward accepting the doctrine that civil
liberty means the removal of all restraints from these crowds and that
all local attempts to maintain order are impairments of the liberty of
the citizen. The choice is not between order and liberty. It is between liberty with order and anarchy without either. There is danger
that, if the court does not temper its doctrinairie logic with a little
practical wisdom, it will convert the constitutional Bill of Rights into
a suicide pact. I would affirm the conviction.

MR. JUSTICE BURTON joins in this opinion.

Mr. Justice Frankfurter's dissent was based, in part, on technical
grounds: the majority's reversal of the lower court decision was on "a
ground that was urged neither here nor below and that was explicitly
disclaimed on behalf of the petitioner at the bar of this Court."

This objection raises another point: how far are the Justices bound
by the record as they receive it, and how far are they entitled to go
beyond it? Many rules which are considered binding on the Justices
are court-made rules, not laws. But under what circumstances, if any,
should they avoid the application of rules they themselves — or their
predecessors in office — have made?

Until the advent of radio and television, it was possible to argue that
spoken words, because they reached fewer people, could be used more
freely than the same words put in writing. The speaker's audience was
smaller, and if there were damage, it was more localized. But publication in a newspaper, book, or magazine gave the words wider circulation, as well as permanent form. The argument ran, therefore, that more
stringent standards were required of writings, because the potential for
damage was greater.

In the hurly-burly of pursuit for public office, many scurrilous remarks are made, many defamatory words written, but the courts have
been more lenient in their interpretation of what is actionable when
such words are used in the heat of a political campaign.

Punishment for excesses is always possible in a criminal action, or damages may be assessed in a civil suit. But punishment after the event is quite different from the prevention of publication. "Prior restraint" on publication has been protested at least since the day of John Milton. "Prior restraint" may mean that a license is required before publication, or a statute may be passed which is so severe in its penalties and so unclear in its definition of the permissible that few are willing to risk publication.

Minnesota passed a statute which provided, in part, that any person who

> shall be engaged in the business of regularly or customarily producing, publishing or circulating, having in possession, selling or giving away. . . a malicious, scandalous and defamatory newspaper, magazine or other periodical, is guilty of a nuisance, and all persons guilty of such nuisance may be enjoined, as hereafter provided.[8]

Under the statute action was brought to enjoin publication of a "malicious, scandalous and defamatory newspaper, magazine and periodical" called *The Saturday Press*. There was no doubt that the articles published made extremely serious charges against certain public officers and others. MR. CHIEF JUSTICE HUGHES spoke for the Court.

Near v. *Minnesota*, 283 U.S. 697, 51 S. Ct. 625 (1931)

* * * This statute, for the suppression as a public nuisance of a newspaper or periodical, is unusual, if not unique, and raises questions of grave importance transcending the local interests involved in the particular action. It is no longer open to doubt that the liberty of the press, and of speech, is within the liberty safeguarded by the due process clause of the Fourteenth Amendment from invasion by state action. It was found impossible to conclude that this essential personal liberty of the citizen was left unprotected by the general guaranty of person and property. * * *

First. The statute is not aimed at the redress of individual or private wrongs. Remedies for libel remain available and unaffected. . . . The judgment in this case proceeded upon the mere proof of publication. The statute permits the defense, not of the truth alone, but only that the truth was published with good motives and for justifiable ends. . . .

Second. The statute is directed . . . at the continued publication by newspapers and periodicals of charges against public officers of corruption, malfeasance in office, or serious neglect of duty. Such charges by their very nature create a public scandal. . . .

Third. The object of the statute is not punishment, in the ordinary sense, but suppression of the offending newspaper or periodical. . . .

Fourth. The statute not only operates to suppress the offending

---

[8]As quoted in *Near* v. *Minnesota*, 283 U.S. 697, p. 702.

newspaper or periodical but to put the publisher under an effective censorship. . . .

If we cut through mere details of procedure, . . . unless the owner or publisher is able and disposed to bring competent evidence to satisfy the judge that the charges are true and are published with good motives and for justifiable ends, his newspaper or periodical is suppressed and further publication is made punishable as a contempt. This is of the essence of censorship. * * *

. . . As has been noted, the statute in question does not deal with punishments; it provides for no punishment, except in case of contempt for violation of the court's order, but for suppression and injunction, that is, for restraint upon publication. * * *

. . . Characterizing the publication as a business, and the business as a nuisance, does not permit an invasion of the constitutional immunity against restraint. Similarly, it does not matter that the newspaper or periodical is found to be "largely" or "chiefly" devoted to the publication of such derelictions. * * *

Equally unavailing is the insistence that the statute is designed to prevent the circulation of scandal which tends to disturb the public peace and to provoke assaults and the commission of crime. Charges of reprehensible conduct, and in particular of official malfeasance, unquestionably create a public scandal, but the theory of the constitutional guaranty is that even a more serious public evil would be caused by authority to prevent publication. * * *

For these reasons we hold the statute, so far as it authorized the proceedings in this action under clause (b) of section one, to be an infringement of the liberty of the press guaranteed by the Fourteenth Amendment. . . .   *Judgment reversed.*

Another possible method of preventing publication is through fear of a large judgment in a suit for libel. In *New York Times Co.* v. *Sullivan*, action had been brought by an individual for damages for an alleged libel.

New York Times Company v. *Sullivan*, 376 U. S. 254, 84 S. Ct. 710 (1964)

MR. JUSTICE BRENNAN delivered the opinion of the Court.

We are required for the first time in this case to determine the extent to which the constitutional protections for speech and press limit a State's power to award damages in a libel action brought by a public official against critics of his official conduct.

Respondent L. B. Sullivan is one of the three elected Commissioners of the City of Montgomery, Alabama. . . . He brought this civil libel action against four individual petitioners, who are Negroes and Alabama clergymen, and against petitioner the New York Times Company, a New York corporation which publishes the *New York Times*, a daily newspaper. A jury in the Circuit Court of Montgomery County awarded him damages of $500,000, the full amount claimed, against all the petitioners, and the Supreme Court of Alabama affirmed. 273 Ala. 656. . . .

Respondent's complaint alleged that he had been libeled by statements in a full-page advertisement that was carried in the *New York Times* on March 29, 1960. . . .

The text appeared over the names of 64 persons, many widely known for their activities in public affairs, religion, trade unions, and the performing arts. Below these names, and under a line reading "We in the south who are struggling daily for dignity and freedom warmly endorse this appeal," appeared the names of the four individual petitioners and of 16 other persons, all but two of whom were identified as clergymen in various Southern cities. The advertisement was signed at the bottom of the page by the "Committee to Defend Martin Luther King and the Struggle for Freedom in the South," and the officers of the Committee were listed. * * *

It is uncontroverted that some of the statements contained in the two paragraphs were not accurate descriptions of events which occurred in Montgomery. * * *

On the premise that the charges in the sixth paragraph could be read as referring to him, respondent was allowed to prove that he had not participated in the events described. . . .

Respondent made no effort to prove that he suffered actual pecuniary loss as a result of the alleged libel. One of his witnesses, a former employer, testified that if he had believed the statements . . . he would not re-employ respondent if he believed "that he allowed the Police Department to do the things that the paper say he did." But neither this witness nor any of the others testified that he had actually believed the statements in their supposed reference to respondent. . . .

[T]he advertisement . . . was published by the *Times* upon an order from a New York advertising agency acting for the signatory Committee. The agency submitted the advertisement with a letter from A. Philip Randolph, Chairman of the Committee, certifying that the persons whose names appeared on the advertisement had given their permission. Mr. Randolph was known to the *Times'* Advertising Acceptability Department as a responsible person, and in accepting the letter as sufficient proof of authorization it followed its established practice. There was testimony that the copy of the advertisement which accompanied the letter listed only sixty-four names appearing under the text, and that the statement, "We in the south * * * warmly endorse this appeal" and the list of names thereunder, which included those of the individual petitioners, were subsequently added when the first proof of the advertisement was received. Each of the individual petitioners testified that he had not authorized the use of his name, and that he had been unaware of its use until receipt of respondent's demand for a retraction. The manager of the Advertising Acceptability Department testified that he had approved the advertisement for publication because he knew nothing to cause him to believe that anything in it was false, and because it bore the endorsement of "a number of people who are well known and whose reputation" he "had no reason to question." Neither he nor anyone else at the *Times* made an effort to confirm the accuracy of the advertisement, either by checking it against recent *Times* news stories relating to some of the described events or by some other means.

Alabama law denies a public officer recovery of punitive damages in a libel action brought on account of a publication concerning his official conduct unless he first makes a written demand for a public retraction and the defendant fails or refuses to comply. Alabama Code, Tit. 7, §914. Respondent served such a demand upon each of the petitioners. None of the individual petitioners responded to the demand, primarily because each took the position that he had not authorized the use of his name on the advertisement and therefore had not published the statements that respondent alleged to have libeled him. The *Times* did not publish a retraction in response to the demand, but wrote respondent a letter stating, among other things, that "we * * * are somewhat puzzled as to how you think the statements in any way reflect on you," and "you might, if you desire, let us know in what respect you claim that the statements in the advertisement reflect on you." Respondent filed this suit a few days later without answering the letter. . . .

The trial judge submitted the case to the jury under instructions that the statements in the advertisement were "libelous per se" and were not privileged, so that petitioners might be held liable if the jury found that they had published the advertisement and that the statements were made "of and concerning" respondent. The jury was instructed that, because the statements were libelous *per se,* "the law * * * implies legal injury from the bare fact of publication itself," "falsity and malice are presumed," "general damages need not be alleged or proved but are presumed," and "punitive damages may be awarded by the jury even though the amount of actual damages is neither found nor shown." . . . He refused to charge . . . that the jury must be "convinced" of malice, in the sense of "actual intent" to harm or "gross negligence and recklessness," to make such an award, and he also refused to require that a verdict for respondent differentiate between compensatory and punitive damages. The judge rejected petitioners' contention that his rulings abridged the freedoms of speech and of the press that are guaranteed by the First and Fourteenth Amendments.

In affirming the judgment, the Supreme Court of Alabama sustained the trial judge's rulings and instructions in all respects. * * *

Because of the importance of the constitutional issues involved, we granted the separate petitions for certiorari of the individual petitioners and of the *Times*, 371 U.S. 946. We reverse the judgment. We hold that the rule of law applied by the Alabama courts is constitutionally deficient for failure to provide the safeguards for freedom of speech and of the press that are required by the First and Fourteenth Amendments in a libel action brought by a public official against critics of his official conduct.[4] We further hold that under the proper safeguards the evidence presented in this case is constitutionally insufficient to support the judgment for respondent.

We may dispose at the outset of two grounds asserted to insulate the judgment of the Alabama courts from constitutional scrutiny. The first is the proposition relied on by the State Supreme Court—that "The Fourteenth Amendment is directed against State action and not private action." That proposition has no application to this case. . . . It matters not that that law has been applied in a civil action and that it is common law only, though supplemented by statute. . . . The test is not the form in which state power has been applied but, whatever the form, whether such power has in fact been exercised. . . .

The second contention is that the constitutional guarantees of freedom of speech and of the press are inapplicable here, at least so far as the *Times* is concerned, because the allegedly libelous statements were published as part of a paid, "commercial" advertisement. The argument relies on *Valentine* v. *Chrestensen,* 316 U.S. 52. . . .

. . . That the *Times* was paid for publishing the advertisement is as immaterial in this connection as is the fact that newspapers and books are sold. *Smith* v. *California*, 361 U.S. 147, 150. Any other conclusion would discourage newspapers from carrying "editorial advertisements" of this type, and so might shut off an important outlet for the promulgation of information and ideas by persons who do not themselves have access to publishing facilities—who wish to exercise their freedom of speech even though they are not members of the press. Cf. *Lovell* v. *City of Griffin*, 303 U. S. 444. The effect would be to shackle the First Amendment in its attempt to secure "the widest possible dissemination of information from diverse and antagonistic sources." *Associated Press* v. *United States*, 326 U.S. 1, 20. To avoid placing such a handicap upon the freedoms of expression, we hold that if the allegedly libelous statements would otherwise be constitutionally protected from the present judgment, they do not forfeit that protection because they were published in the form of a paid advertisement.

Under Alabama law as applied in this case, a publication is "libelous per se" if the words "tend to injure a person * * * in his reputation" or to "bring [him] into public contempt"; the trial court stated that the standard was met if the words are such as to "injure him in his public office, or impute misconduct to him in his office, or want of official integrity, or want of fidelity to a public trust * * * ." The jury must find that the words were published "of and concerning" the plaintiff, but where the plaintiff is a public official his place

---

[4]Since we sustain the contentions of all the petitioners under the First Amendment's guarantees of freedom of speech and of the press as applied to the States by the Fourteenth Amendment, we do not decide the questions presented by the other claims of violation of the Fourteenth Amendment. . . . [This footnote is part of the opinion. — ED.]

in the governmental hierarchy is sufficient evidence to support a finding that his reputation has been affected by statements that reflect upon the agency of which he is in charge. Once "libel per se" has been established, the defendant has no defense as to stated facts unless he can persuade the jury that they were true in all their particulars. . . . Unless he can discharge the burden of proving the truth, general damages are presumed, and may be awarded without proof of pecuniary injury. A showing of actual malice is apparently a prerequisite to recovery of punitive damages, and the defendant may in any event forestall these by a retraction meeting the statutory requirements. Good motives and belief in truth do not negate an inference of malice, but are relevant only in mitigation of punitive damages if the jury chooses to accord them weight. . . .

The question before us is whether this rule of liability, as applied to an action brought by a public official against critics of his official conduct, abridges the freedom of speech and of the press that is guaranteed by the First and Fourteenth Amendments.

Respondent relies heavily, as did the Alabama courts, on statements of this Court to the effect that the Constitution does not protect libelous publications. Those statements do not foreclose our inquiry here. None of the cases sustained the use of libel laws to impose sanctions upon expression critical of the official conduct of public officials. * * *

The general proposition that freedom of expression upon public questions is secured by the First Amendment has long been settled by our decisions. * * *

Thus we consider this case against the background of a profound national commitment to the principle that debate on public issues should be uninhibited, robust, and wide-open, and that it may well include vehement, caustic, and sometimes unpleasantly sharp attacks on government and public officials. See *Terminiello* v. *Chicago*, 337 U.S. 1, 4. The present advertisement, as an expression of grievance and protest on one of the major public issues of our time, would seem clearly to qualify for the constitutional protection. The question is whether it forfeits that protection by the falsity of some of its facttual statements and by its alleged defamation of respondent.

Authoritative interpretations of the First Amendment guarantees have consistently refused to recognize an exception for any test of truth, whether administered by judges, juries, or administrative officials — and especially not one that puts the burden of proving truth on the speaker. * * *

[E]rroneous statement is inevitable in free debate, and . . . it must be protected if the freedoms of expression are to have the "breathing space" that they "need * * * to survive," *N.A.A.C.P.* v. *Button*, 371 U.S. 415, 433. * * *

Just as factual error affords no warrant for repressing speech that would be free, the same is true of injury to official reputation. . . . This is true even though the utterance contains "half-truths" and "misinformation." *Pennekamp* v. *Florida,* 328 U.S. 331, 342, 343. * * *

If neither factual error nor defamatory content suffices to remove the constitutional shield from criticism of official conduct, the combination of the two elements is no less inadequate. * * *

What a State may not constitutionally bring about by means of a criminal statute is likewise beyond the reach of its civil law of libel. . . . And since there is no double-jeopardy limitation applicable to civil lawsuits, this is not the only judgment that may be awarded against petitioners for the same publication. Whether or not a newspaper can survive a succession of such judgments, the pall of fear and timidity imposed upon those who would give voice to public criticism is an atmosphere in which the First Amendment freedoms cannot survive. . . .

The state rule of law is not saved by its allowance of the defense of truth. * * *

A rule compelling the critic of official conduct to guarantee the truth of all his factual assertions—and to do so on pain of libel judgments virtually unlimited in amount—leads to a comparable "self-censorship." Allowance of the defense of truth, with the burden of proving it on the defendant, does not mean that only false speech will be deterred. . . . Under such a rule, would-be critics of official conduct may be deterred from voicing their criticism, even though it is believed to be true and even though it is in fact true, because of doubt whether it can be proved in court or fear of the expense of having to do so. . . . The rule thus dampens the vigor and limits the variety of public debate. It is inconsistent with the First and Fourteenth Amendments.

The constitutional guarantees require, we think, a federal rule that prohibits a public official from recovering damages for a defamatory falsehood relating to his official conduct unless he proves that the statement was made with "actual malice"—that is, with knowledge that it was false or with reckless disregard of whether it was false or not. * * *

[A] privilege for criticism of official conduct is appropriately analogous to the protection accorded a public official when *he* is sued for libel by a private citizen . . .It would give public servants an unjustified preference over the public they serve, if critics of official conduct did not have a fair equivalent of the immunity granted to the officials themselves.

We conclude that such a privilege is required by the First and Fourteenth Amendments.

We hold today that the Constitution delimits a State's power to award damages for libel in actions brought by public officials against critics of their official conduct. Since this is such an action, the rule requiring proof of actual malice is applicable. While Alabama law apparently requires proof of actual malice for an award of punitive damages, where general damages are concerned malice is "presumed." Such a presumption is inconsistent with the federal rule. . . .

Since respondent may seek a new trial, we deem that considerations of effective judicial administration require us to review the evidence in the present record to determine whether it could constitutionally support a judgment for respondent. This Court's duty is not limited to the elaboration of constitutional principles; we must also in proper cases review the evidence to make certain that those principles have been constitutionally applied. This is such a case, particularly since the question is one of alleged trespass across "the line between speech unconditionally guaranteed and speech which may legitimately be regulated." *Speiser* v. *Randall,* 357 U.S. 513, 525. In cases where that line must be drawn, the rule is that we "examine for ourselves the statements in issue and the circumstances under which they were made to see * * * whether they are of a character which the principles of the First Amendment, as adopted by the Due Process Clause of the Fourteenth Amendment, protect." *Pennekamp* v. *Florida,* 328 U.S. 331, 335. We must "make an independent examination of the while record," *Edwards* v. *South Carolina,* 372 U.S. 229, 235, so as to assure ourselves that the judgment does not constitute a forbidden intrusion on the field of free expression.

Applying these standards, we consider that the proof presented to show actual malice lacks the convincing clarity which the constitutional standard demands, and hence that it would not constitutionally sustain the judgment for respondent under the proper rule of law. The case of the individual petitioners requires little discussion. . . .

As to the *Times,* we similarly conclude that the facts do not support a finding of actual malice. * * *

We also think the evidence was constitutionally defective in another respect: it was incapable of supporting the jury's finding that the allegedly libelous statements were made "of and concerning" respondent. . . . There was no reference to respondent in the advertisement, either by name or official position. . . . The statements upon which respondent principally relies as referring to him are the two allegations that did concern the police or police functions. . . . Although the statements may be taken as referring to the police, they did not on their face make even an oblique reference to respondent as an individual. Support for the asserted reference must, therefore, be sought in the testimony of respondent's witnesses. But none of them suggested any basis for the belief that respondent himself was attacked in the advertisement beyond the bare fact that he was in overall charge of the Police Department and thus bore official responsibility for police conduct. . . . This reliance on the bare fact of respondent's official position was made explicit by the Supreme Court of Alabama. . . .

This proposition has disquieting implications for criticism of governmental conduct. For good reason, "no court of last resort in this country has ever held, or even suggested, that prosecutions for libel on government have any place in the American system of jurisprudence." *City of Chicago* v. *Tribune Co.*, 307 Ill. 595, 601. The present proposition would sidestep this obstacle by transmuting criticism of government, however impersonal it may seem on its face, into personal criticism, and hence potential libel, of the officials of whom the government is composed. . . . We hold that such a proposition may not constitutionally be utilized to establish that an otherwise impersonal attack on governmental operations was a libel of an official responsible for those operations. Since it was relied on exclusively here, and there was no other evidence to connect the statements with respondent, the evidence was constitutionally insufficient to support a finding that the statements referred to respondent. ·

The judgment of the Supreme Court of Alabama is reversed and the case is remanded to that court for further proceedings not inconsistent with this opinion. *Reversed and remanded.*

MR. JUSTICE BLACK, with whom MR. JUSTICE DOUGLAS joins (concurring).

I concur in reversing this half-million-dollar judgment against the *New York Times* and the four individual defendants. . . . I base my vote to reverse on the belief that the First and Fourteenth Amendments not merely "delimit" a State's power to award damages to "a public official against critics of his official conduct" but completely prohibit a State from exercising such a power. . . . Unlike the Court . . . I vote to reverse exclusively on the ground that the *Times* and the individual defendants had an absolute, unconditional constitutional right to publish in the *Times* advertisement their criticisms of the Montgomery agencies and officials. * * *

We would, I think, more faithfully interpret the First Amendment by holding that at the very least it leaves the people and the press free to criticize officials and discuss public affairs with impunity. * * *

I regret that the Court has stopped short of this holding indispensable to preserve our free press from destruction.

MR. JUSTICE GOLDBERG, with whom MR. JUSTICE DOUGLAS joins (concurring in the result). . . .

In my view, the First and Fourteenth Amendments to the Constitution afford to the citizen and to the press an absolute, unconditional privilege to criticize official conduct despite the harm which may flow from excesses and abuses. * * *

We must recognize that we are writing upon a clean slate. To impose liability, * * * for critical, albeit erroneous or even malicious, comments on official conduct would effectively resurrect "the obsolete doctrine that the governed must not criticize their governors." * * *

I strongly believe that the Constitution accords citizens and press an unconditional freedom to criticize official conduct. It necessarily follows that in a case such as this, where all agree that the allegedly defamatory statements related to official conduct, the judgments for libel cannot constitutionally be sustained.

Publication is, of course, not synonymous with distribution, but as the Court has pointed out, distribution is a part of the right to speak. It is a futile gesture to publish a pamphlet and then be denied the right to circulate it. In exercising the police power of the states a number of efforts have been made to restrict or forbid distribution. Sometimes the restriction appears in the form of an ordinance forbidding littering the streets, or the requirement that one who wishes to distribute literature must obtain a license for that purpose, or refrain from entering upon the property of another without a special invitation. In *Lovell* v. *Griffin* (303 U.S. 444, 1938) the Court struck down an ordinance which required that written permission be obtained from the city manager for the distribution "either by hand or otherwise, [of] circulars, handbooks, advertising, or literature of any kind, whether said articles are being delivered free, or whether the same are being sold. . . ."[9] The Court specifically included distribution within the protection of the First Amendment as applied to the States by the Fourteenth Amendment. Quoting from an earlier case, the Court said, "Liberty of circulating is as essential to that freedom as liberty of publishing; indeed, without the circulation, the publication would be of little value."[10]

Included in "speech" are motion pictures, but the Court did not so include them until 1952, in the "Miracle" case: *Burstyn* v. *Wilson* (343 U.S. 495). Motion pictures enjoy the same freedoms and are subject to the same restrictions imposed upon other forms of expression. Standards for censorship were outlined in *Freedman* v. *Maryland*.

Freedman v. *State of Maryland*, 380 U.S. 51, 85 S. Ct. 734 (1965)

* * * Applying the settled rule of our cases, we hold that a noncriminal process which requires the prior submission of a film to a censor avoids constitutional infirmity only if it takes place under procedural safeguards designed to obviate the dangers of a censorship system. First, the burden of proving that the film is unprotected expression must rest on the censor. . . . Second, while the State may require advance submission of all films, in order to proceed effectively to bar all showings of unprotected films, the requirement cannot be administered in a manner which would lend an effect of finality to the censor's determination whether a film constitutes protected expression. The teaching of our cases is that, because only a judicial determination in an adversary proceeding ensures the necessary sensitivity to freedom of expression, only a procedure

[9]p. 447. [10]*Ex parte Jackson*, 96 U.S. 727, p. 733.

requiring a judicial determination suffices to impose a valid final restraint. . . . To this end, the exhibitor must be assured, by statute or authoritative judicial construction, that the censor will, within a specified brief period, either issue a license or go to court to restrain showing the film. Any restraint imposed in advance of a final judicial determination on the merits must similarly be limited to preservation of the status quo for the shortest fixed period compatible with sound judicial resolution. Moreover, we are well aware that, even after expiration of a temporary restraint, an administrative refusal to license, signifying the censor's view that the film is unprotected, may have a discouraging effect on the exhibitor. See *Bantam Books, Inc.* v. *Sullivan, supra.* Therefore, the procedure must also assure a prompt final judicial decision, to minimize the deterrent effect of an interim and possibly erroneous denial of a license.

Without these safeguards, it may prove too burdensome to seek review of the censor's determination. . . .

It is readily apparent that the Maryland procedural scheme does not satisfy these criteria. . . . We hold, therefore, that appellant's conviction must be reversed. The Maryland scheme fails to provide adequate safeguards against undue inhibition of protected expression, and this renders the §2 requirement of prior submission of films to the Board an invalid previous restraint. ° ° °

Reversed.

As previously mentioned, obscenity is not within the protection of freedom of speech under the First or Fourteenth Amendment. Difficulties in this area arise because there is no agreement about the meaning of the word, which has always been difficult to define since it depends in part upon a subjective viewpoint: what is obscene to one person is not to another. The difference may be one of the time, the upbringing, the culture of the individuals who must define the term. Everyday experience suggests that perfectly acceptable language in one person's judgment is questionable, if not positively obscene, in the view of another. The legal problem is to develop and express a standard against which particular utterances can be measured.

In fact, local communities apply their own standards—or, to be more precise, those persons in local communities who are interested in "protecting" others apply their personal standards and all too often their personal prejudices as well. "Banned in Boston," where standards have been more puritanical than those in many other communities, for a number of years virtually guaranteed a book's brisk sale in other states.

Development of a meaningful standard has taken time, and basic ideas have been variously expressed: no "dirt for dirt's sake," no treatment of sex in a manner appealing to "prurient interests"—a definititon which seems to have given another word common usage, but does little to clarify the problem. "Ideas having even the slightest redeeming social importance" is another vague phrase which helps expand the boundaries of freedom of speech somewhat. A difficulty in dealing with limitations on "obscenity" is the common definition of the word: "inciting lustful thoughts, or arousing lustful desires." Many people are of the opinion that the mere incitement of thoughts or desires, unaccompanied by action, is beyond the power of law to reach. But the definition does seem to leave the decision to the private reaction of the censor, whose "lustful thoughts" may be more easily aroused than those of other readers or hearers. The censor himself may not qualify as a judge to say "whether to the average person, applying contemporary community standards, the dominant theme of the material taken as a whole appeals to prurient interest. . . ." But it was not until the *Jacobellis* case, in 1964, that the word "community" was defined.

Roth v. *United States; Alberts* v. *California,* 354 U.S. 476, 77 S. Ct. 1304 (1957)

MR. JUSTICE BRENNAN delivered the opinion of the Court.

The constitutionality of a criminal obscenity statute is the question in each of these cases. In *Roth,* the primary constitutional question is whether the federal obscenity statute violates the provision of the First Amendment. . . . In *Alberts,* the primary constitutional question is whether the obscenity provisions of the California Penal Code invade the freedoms of speech and press as they may be incorporated in the liberty protected from state action by the Due Process Clause of the Fourteenth Amendment.

Other constitutional questions are: whether these statutes violate due process, because too vague to support conviction for crime; whether power to punish speech and press offensive to decency and morality is in the States alone, so that the federal obscenity statute violates the Ninth and Tenth Amendments (raised in *Roth*); and whether Congress, by enacting the federal obscenity statute, under the power delegated by Art. I, § 8 cl. 7, to establish post offices and post roads, pre-empted the regulation of the subject matter (raised in *Alberts*).

Roth conducted a business in New York in the publication and sale of books, photographs and magazines. He used circulars and advertising matter to solicit sales. He was convicted . . . upon 4 counts of a[n] . . . indictment charging him with mailing obscene circulars and advertising, and an obscene book, in violation of the federal obscenity statute. . . .

Alberts conducted a mail-order business from Los Angeles. He was convicted . . . under a misdemeanor complaint which charged him with lewdly keeping for sale obscene and indecent books, and with writing, composing and publishing an obscene advertisement of them, in violation of the California Penal Code. . . .

The dispositive question is whether obscenity is utterance within the area of protected speech and press. Although this is the first time the question has been squarely presented to this Court, either under the First Amendment or under the Fourteenth Amendment, expressions found in numerous opinions indicate that this Court has always assumed that obscenity is not protected by the freedoms of speech and press. . . .

The protection given speech and press was fashioned to assure unfettered interchange of ideas for the bringing about of political and social changes desired by the people. . . .

All ideas having even the slightest redeeming social import-ance — unorthodox ideas, controversial ideas, even ideas hateful to the prevailing climate of opinion — have the full protection of the guaranties, unless excludable because they encroach upon the limited area of more important interests. But implicit in the history of the First Amendment is the rejection of obscenity as utterly without redeeming social importance. . . . We hold that obscenity is not within the area of constitutionally protected speech or press.

It is strenuously urged that these obscenity statutes offend the constitutional guaranties because they punish incitation to impure sexual *thoughts*, not shown to be related to any overt antisocial conduct which is or may be incited in the persons stimulated to such *thoughts*. . . . In *Roth* the trial judge instructed the jury: "The words 'obscene, lewd and lascivious' as used in the law, signify that form of immorality which has relation to sexual impurity and has a ten-dency to excite lustful *thoughts*." [Emphasis added.] In *Alberts*, the trial judge applied the test laid down in *People* v. *Wepplo*, 78 Cal. App. 2d Supp. 959, . . . namely, whether the material has "a sub-stantial tendency to deprave or corrupt its readers by inciting lasciv-ious *thoughts* or arousing lustful desires." [Emphasis added.] It is in-sisted that the constitutional guaranties are violated because con-victions may be had without proof either that obscene material will perceptibly create a clear and present danger of antisocial conduct, or will probably induce its recipients to such conduct. But, in light of our holding that obscenity is not protected speech, the complete answer to this argument is in the holding of this Court in *Beauharnais* v. *People of State of Illinois, supra,* 343 U.S. at page 266. . . .

However, sex and obscenity are not synonymous. Obscene mate-rial is material which deals with sex in a manner appealing to prurient interest. The portrayal of sex, e.g., in art, literature and scientific works, is not itself sufficient reason to deny material the constitutional protection of freedom of speech and press. * * *

The early leading standard of obscenity allowed material to be judged merely by the effect of an isolated excerpt upon particularly susceptible persons. . . . [L]ater decisions . . . substituted this test: whether to the average person, applying contemporary com-munity standards, the dominant theme of the material taken as a whole appeals to prurient interest. . . .

Both trial courts below . . . used the proper definition of obscen-ity. * * *

We therefore hold that the federal obscenity statute punishing the use of the mails for obscene material is a proper exercise of the postal power delegated to Congress by Art I, § 8, cl. 7 . . . .

Alberts argues that because his was a mail-order business, the California statute is repugnant to Art. 1, § 8, cl. 7, under which the Congress allegedly preempted the regulatory field by enacting the federal obscenity statute punishing the mailing or advertising by mail of obscene material. The federal statute deals only with actual mailing; it does not eliminate the power of the state to punish "keeping for sale" or "advertising" obscene material. . . .

MR. CHIEF JUSTICE WARREN, concurring in the result.

I agree with the result reached by the Court in these cases, but, because we are operating in a field of expression and because broad language used here may eventually be applied to the arts and sciences and freedom of communication generally, I would limit our decision to the facts before us and to the validity of the statutes in question as applied.

Appellant Alberts was charged with wilfully, unlawfully and lewdly disseminating obscene matter. Obscenity has been construed by the California courts to mean having a substantial tendency to corrupt by arousing lustful desires. * * *

The line dividing the salacious or pornographic from literature or science is not straight and unwavering. . . . The conduct of the defendant is the central issue, not the obscenity of a book or picture. . . .

The personal element in these cases is seen most strongly in the requirement of *scienter*. . . . The defendants . . . were plainly engaged in the commercial exploitation of the morbid and shameful craving for materials with prurient effect. I believe that the State and Federal Governments can constitutionally punish such conduct. That is all that these cases present to us, and that is all we need to decide. . . .

MR. JUSTICE HARLAN, concurring in the result in No. 61, and dissenting in No. 582.

I regret not to be able to join the Court's opinion. I cannot do so because I find lurking beneath its disarming generalizations a number of problems which not only leave me with serious misgivings as to the future effect of today's decisions, but which also, in my view, call for different results in these two cases.

My basic difficulties with the Court's opinion are threefold. First, the opinion paints with such a broad brush that I fear it may result in a loosening of the tight reins which state and federal courts should hold upon the enforcement of obscenity statutes. Second, the Court fails to discriminate between the different factors which, in my opinion, are involved in the constitutional adjudication of state and federal obscenity cases. Third, relevant distinctions between the two obscenity statutes here involved, and the Court's own definition of "obscenity," are ignored.

In final analysis, the problem presented by these cases is how far, and on what terms, the state and federal governments have power to punish individuals for disseminating books considered to be undesirable because of their nature or supposed deleterious effect upon human conduct. . . . The Court seems to assume that "obscenity" is a peculiar *genus* of "speech and press," which is as distinct, recognizable, and classifiable as poison ivy is among other plants. . . . [T]he question whether a *particular* book may be suppressed becomes a mere matter of classification, of "fact," to be entrusted to a factfinder and insulated from independent constitutional judgment. But surely the problem cannot be solved in such a generalized fashion. . . .

[I]f "obscenity" is to be suppressed, the question whether a particular work is of that character involves not really an issue of fact but a question of constitutional *judgment* of the most sensitive and delicate kind. . . . I am very much afraid that the broad manner in which the Court has decided these cases will tend to obscure the peculiar responsibilities resting on state and federal courts in this field and encourage them to rely on easy labeling and jury verdicts as a substitute for facing up to the tough individual problems of constitutional judgment involved in every obscenity case.

My second reason for dissatisfaction with the Court's opinion is that . . . [i]t does not seem to matter to the Court that in one case we balance the power of a State in this field against the restrictions of the Fourteenth Amendment, and in the other the power of the Federal Government against the limitations of the First Amendment. . . .

Thirdly, the Court has not been bothered by the fact that the two cases involve different statutes. In California the book must have a "tendency to deprave or corrupt its readers"; under the federal statute it must tend "to stir sexual impulses and lead to sexually impure thoughts." The two statutes do not seem to me to present the same problems. . . .

We likewise reject the common definition of obscene as that which "tends to corrupt or debase." If this means anything different from tendency to arouse lustful thought and desire, it suggests that change of character or actual misbehavior follows from contact with obscenity. Evidence of such consequences is lacking. * * * On the other hand, "appeal to prurient interest" refers to qualities of the material itself: the capacity to attract individuals eager for a forbidden look. . . .

I concur in the judgment of the Court in No. 61, *Alberts* v. *People of State of California.* * * *

[O]ur function in reviewing state judgments under the Fourteenth Amendment is a narrow one. . . . We can inquire only whether the state action so subverts the fundamental liberties inplicit in the Due Process Clause that it cannot be sustained as a rational exercise of power. * * *

. . . It seems to me clear that it is not irrational, in our present state of knowledge, to consider that pornography can induce a type of sexual conduct which a State may deem obnoxious to the moral fabric of society. . . .

Nothing in the broad and flexible command of the Due Process Clause forbids California to prosecute one who sells books whose dominant tendency might be to "deprave or corrupt" a reader. I agree with the Court, of course, that the books must be judged as a whole and in relation to the normal adult reader. . . .

I concur in the judgment. . . .

I dissent in No. 582, *Roth* v. *United States.*

We are faced here with the question whether the federal obscenity statute, as construed and applied in this case, violates the First Amendment to the Constitution. . . .

Congress has no substantive power over sexual morality. Such powers as the Federal Government has in this field are but incidental to its other powers, here the postal power. * * *

[T]he dangers of federal censorship in this field are far greater than anything the States may do. * * *

I judge this case, then, in view of what I think is the attenuated federal interest in this field, in view of the very real danger of a deadening uniformity which can result from nation-wide federal censorship, and in view of the fact that the constitutionality of this conviction must be weighed against the First and not the Fourteenth Amendment. So viewed, I do not think that this conviction can be upheld. . . . I cannot agree that any book which tends to stir sexual impulses and lead to sexually impure thoughts necessarily is "utterly without redeeming social importance.". . . . [M]uch of the great literature of the world could lead to conviction under such a view of the statute. Moreover, in no event do I think that the limited federal interest in this area can extend to mere "thoughts". . . .

It is no answer to say, as the Court does, that obscenity is not protected speech. The point is that this statute, as here construed, defines obscenity so widely that it encompasses matters which might very well be protected speech. I do not think that the federal statute can be constitutionally construed to reach other than what the Government has termed as "hard-core" pornography. . . .

I would reverse this case. . . .

MR. JUSTICE DOUGLAS, with whom MR. JUSTICE BLACK concurs, dissenting.

When we sustain these convictions, we make the legality of a publication turn on the purity of thought which a book or tract instills in the mind of the reader. I do not think we can approve that standard and be faithful to the command of the First Amendment, which by its terms is a restraint on Congress and which by the Fourteenth is a restraint on the States. * * *

. . . Even the ill-starred *Dennis* case conceded that speech to be punishable must have some relation to action which could be penalized by government. . . .

The tests by which these convictions were obtained require only the arousing of sexual thoughts. Yet the arousing of sexual thoughts and desires happens every day in normal life in dozens of ways. Nearly 30 years ago a questionnaire sent to college and normal school women graduates asked what things were most stimulating sexually. Of 409 replies, 9 said "music"; 18 said "pictures"; 29 said "dancing"; 40 said "drama"; 95 said "books"; and 218 said "man." Alpert, *Judicial Censorship of Obscene Literature*, 52 *Harv. L. Rev.* 40, 73.

The test of obscenity the Court endorses today gives the censor free range over a vast domain. * * *

The absence of dependable information of the effect of obscene literature on human conduct should make us wary. . . .

The standard of what offends "the common conscience of the community" conflicts, in my judgment, with the command of the First Amendment that "Congress shall make no law * * * abridging the freedom of speech, or press." . . .

Any test that turns on what is offensive to the community's standards is too loose, too capricious, too destructive of freedom of expression to be squared with the First Amendment. Under that test, juries can censor, suppress, and punish what they don't like, provided the matter relates to "sexual impurity" or has a tendency "to excite lustful thoughts." This is community censorship in one of its worst forms. * * *

Government should be concerned with antisocial conduct, not with utterances. . . .

The Court today suggests a third standard. It defines obscene material as that "which deals with sex in a manner appealing to prurient interest." . . . Under the First Amendment, that standard is no more valid than those which the courts below adopted.

I do not think that the problem can be resolved by the Court's statement that "obscenity is not expression protected by the First Amendment." . . . I reject too the implication that problems of freedom of speech and of the press are to be resolved by weighing against the values of free expression, the judgment of the Court that a particular form of that expression has "no redeeming social importance." The First Amendment, its prohibition in terms absolute, was designed to preclude courts as well as legislatures from weighing the values of speech against silence. The First Amendment puts free speech in the preferred position.

Freedom of expression can be suppressed if, and to the extent that, it is so closely brigaded with illegal action as to be an inseparable part of it. . . . As a people, we cannot afford to relax that standard. For the test that suppresses a cheap tract today can suppress a literary gem tomorrow. All it need do is to incite a lascivious thought or arouse a lustful desire. The list of books that judges or juries can place in that category is endless.

I would give the broad sweep of the First Amendment full support. I have the same confidence in the ability of our people to reject noxious literature as I have in their capacity to sort out the true from the false in theology, economics, politics, or any other field.

Jacobellis v. *State of Ohio,* 378 U.S. 184, 84 S. Ct. 1676 (1964)

MR. JUSTICE BRENNAN announced the judgment of the Court and delivered an opinion in which MR. JUSTICE GOLDBERG joins.

Appellant, Nico Jacobellis, manager of a motion picture theater in Cleveland Heights, Ohio, was convicted on two counts for possessing and exhibiting an obscene film in violation of Ohio Revised Code § 2905.34. He was fined . . . and was sentenced to the workhouse if the fines were not paid. His conviction . . . was affirmed. . . . The dispositive question is whether the state courts properly found that the motion picture involved, a French film called *"Les Amants"* ("The Lovers"), was obscene and hence not entitled to the protection for free expression that is guaranteed by the First and Fourteenth Amendments. We conclude that the film is not obscene and that the judgment must accordingly be reversed.

Motion pictures are within the ambit of the constitutional guarantees of freedom of speech and of the press. *Joseph Burstyn, Inc.* v. *Wilson,* 343 U.S. 495. But in *Roth* v. *United States* and *Alberts* v. *California,* 354 U.S. 476, we held that obscenity is not subject to those guarantees. Application of an obscenity law to suppress a motion picture thus requires ascertainment of the "dim and uncertain line" that often separates obscenity from constitutionally protected expression. *Bantam Books, Inc.* v. *Sullivan,* 372 U.S. 58, 66. . . . It has been suggested that this is a task in which our Court need not involve itself. . . . Such an abnegation of judicial supervision in this field would be inconsistent with our duty to uphold the constitutional guarantees. Since it is only "obscenity" that is excluded from the constitutional protection, the question whether a particular work is obscene necessarily implicates an issue of constitutional law. See *Roth* v. *United States, supra,* 354 U.S., at 497–498, (separate opinion). Such an issue, we think, must ultimately be decided by this Court. . . .

In other areas involving constitutional rights under the Due Process Clause, the Court has consistently recognized its duty to apply the applicable rules of law upon the basis of an independent review of the facts of each case. . . . And this has been particularly true where rights have been asserted under the First Amendment guarantees of free expression. . . . We cannot understand why the Court's duty should be any different in the present case, where Jacobellis has been subjected to a criminal conviction for disseminating a work of expression and is challenging that conviction as a deprivation of rights guaranteed by the First and Fourteenth Amendments. Nor can we understand why the Court's performance of its constitutional and judicial function in this sort of case should be denigrated by such epithets as "censor" or "super-censor." . . . Hence we reaffirm the principle that, in "obscenity" cases as in all others involving rights derived from the First Amendment guarantees of free expression, this Court cannot avoid making an independent constitutional judgment on the facts of the case as to whether the material involved is constitutionally protected.

The question of the proper standard for making this determination has been the subject of much discussion and controversy since our decision in *Roth-Alberts* seven years ago. Recognizing that the test for obscenity enunciated there—"whether to the average person, applying contemporary community standards, the dominant theme of the material taken as a whole appeals to prurient interest," 354 U.S., at 489, is not perfect, we think any substitute would raise equally difficult problems, and we therefore adhere to that standard. . . . Nor may the constitutional status of the material be made to turn on a "weighing" of its social importance against its prurient appeal, for a work cannot be proscribed unless it is "utterly" without social importance. . . . It should also be recognized that the *Roth* standard requires in the first instance a finding that the material "goes substantially beyond customary limits of candor in description or representation of such matters." . . .

It has been suggested that the "contemporary community standards" aspect of the *Roth* test implies a determination of the constitutional question of obscenity in each case by the standards of the particular local community from which the case arises. This is an incorrect reading of *Roth*. . . .

We do not see how any "local" definition of the "community" could properly be employed in delineating the area of expression that is protected by the Federal Constitution. . . .

It is true that local communities throughout the land are in fact diverse, . . . and that in cases such as this one the Court is confronted with the task of reconciling the rights of such communities with the rights of individuals. Communities vary, however, in many respects other than their toleration of alleged obscenity, and such variances have never been considered to require or justify a varying standard for application of the Federal Constitution. Such a task is admittedly difficult and delicate, but it is inherent in the Court's duty of determining whether a particular conviction worked a deprivation of rights guaranteed by the Federal Constitution. The Court has not shrunk from discharging that duty in other areas, and we see no reason why it should do so here. . . . We thus reaffirm the position taken in *Roth* to the effect that the constitutional status of an allegedly obscene work must be determined on the basis of a national standard. It is, after all, a national Constitution we are expounding. . . . Since the present conviction is based upon exhibition of the film to the public at large and not upon its exhibition to children, the judgment must be reviewed under the strict standard applicable in determining the scope of the expression that is protected by the Constitution.

We have applied that standard to the motion picture in question. . . . We have viewed the film, in the light of the record made in the trial court, and we conclude that it is not obscene within the standards enunciated in *Alberts* v. *California* and *Roth* v. *United States*, which we reaffirm here.   *Reversed.* * * *

THE CHIEF JUSTICE, with whom MR. JUSTICE CLARK joins, dissenting.

In this and other cases in this area of the law, which are coming to us in ever-increasing numbers, we are faced with the resolution of rights basic both to individuals and to society as a whole. Specifically, we are called upon to reconcile the right of the Nation and of the States to maintain a decent society and, on the other hand, the right of individuals to express themselves freely in accordance with the guarantees of the First and Fourteenth Amendments. . . . [N]either courts nor legislatures have been able to evolve a truly satisfactory definition of obscenity. . . . The obscenity problem . . . is aggravated by the fact that it involves the area of public expression, an area in which a broad range of freedom is vital to our society and is constitutionally protected. . . .

For all the sound and fury that the *Roth* test has generated, it has not been proved unsound, and I believe that we should try to live with it—at least until a more satisfactory definition is evolved. . . . There must be a rule of reason in this as in other areas of the law and we have attempted in the *Roth* case to provide such a rule.

It is my belief that when the Court said in *Roth* that obscenity is to be defined by reference to "community standards," it meant community standards—not a national standard, as is sometimes argued. I believe that there is no provable "national standard" and perhaps there should be none. . . .

We are told that only "hard core pornography" should be denied the protection of the First Amendment. But who can define "hard core pornography" with any greater clarity than "obscenity"? . . .

In my opinion, the use to which various materials are put—not just the words and pictures themselves—must be considered in determining whether or not the materials are obscene. . . .

Finally, material which is in fact obscene under the *Roth* test may be proscribed in a number of ways . . . If the proceeding involved is criminal, there must be a right to a jury trial, a right to counsel, and all the other safeguards necessary to assure due process of law. If the proceeding is civil in nature, the constitutional requirements applicable in such a case must also be observed. . . .

In light of the foregoing, I would reiterate my acceptance of the rule of the *Roth* case: Material is obscene and not constitutionally protected against regulation and proscription if "to the average person, applying contemporary community standards, the dominant theme of the material taken as a whole appeals to prurient interest." 354 U.S., at 489. I would commit the enforcement of this rule to the appropriate state and federal courts, and I would accept their judgments made pursuant to the *Roth* rule, limiting myself to a consideration only of whether there is sufficient evidence in the record upon which a finding of obscenity could be made. If there is no evidence in the record upon which such a finding could be made, obviously the material involved cannot be held obscene. Cf. *Thompson* v. *City of Louisville*, 362 U.S. 199. But since a mere modicum of evidence may satisfy a "no evidence" standard, I am unwilling to give the important constitutional right of free expression such limited protection. . . . Therefore, once a finding of obscenity has been made below under a proper application of the *Roth* test, I would apply a "sufficient evidence" standard of review — requiring something more than merely any evidence but something less than "substantial evidence on the record [including the allegedly obscene material] as a whole." . . . This is the only reasonable way I can see to obviate the necessity of this Court's sitting as the Super Censor of all the obscenity purveyed throughout the Nation. . . .

MR. JUSTICE HARLAN, dissenting.

While agreeing with my Brother BRENNAN'S opinion that the responsibilities of the Court in this area are no different than those which attend the adjudication of kindred constitutional questions, I have heretofore expressed the view that the States are constitutionally permitted greater latitude in determining what is bannable on the score of obscenity than is so with the Federal Government. See my opinion in *Roth* v. *United States*, 354 U.S. 476, 496. . . .

The more I see of these obscenity cases the more convinced I become that in permitting the States wide, but not federally unrestricted, scope in this field, while holding the Federal Government with a tight rein, lies the best promise for achieving a sensible accommodation between the public interest sought to be served by obscenity laws. . . . I would apply to the Federal Government the *Roth* standards as amplified in my opinion in *Manual Enterprises, supra*. As to the States, I would make the federal test one of rationality. I would not prohibit them from banning any material which, taken as a whole, has been reasonably found in state judicial proceedings to treat with sex in a fundamentally offensive manner, under rationally established criteria for judging such material.

On this basis, having viewed the motion picture in question, I think the State acted within permissible limits in condemning the film and would affirm the judgment of the Ohio Supreme Court.

As the Court pointed out in *Bantam Books* v. *Sullivan*, 372 U.S. 60, 83 S. Ct. 631 (1963), a state may not censor by indirection in an area in which direct censorship is forbidden. The Rhode Island legislature established a "Rhode Island Commission to Encourage Morality in Youth," with

Bantam Books v. *Sullivan*

* * * the duty to educate the public concerning any book, picture, pamphlet, ballad, printed paper or other thing containing obscene,

indecent or impure language, or manifestly tending to the corruption of youth as defined in sections 13, 47, 48 and 49 of chapter 610 of the general laws, as amended, and to investigate and recommend the prosecution of all violations of said sections   * * *.[11]

The Commission reviewed books and magazines and then notified distributors that the material designated had been reviewed, and "declared by a majority if its members to be objectionable for sale, distribution or display to youths under 18 years of age."[12] There was also a reminder of the Commission's duty to recommend prosecution of "purveyors of obscenity." The distributor then refused to fill orders, withdrew books from sale, and refused new orders, all, he testified, rather than face some sort of court action "against ourselves, as well as the people that we supply." The result of the Commission's actions was, of course, to prevent the sale of books it listed, even though it was admitted that several listed were not obscene within the Supreme Court's definition of obscenity. The Court said,

> . . . But though the Commission is limited to informal sanctions . . . the record amply demonstrates that the Commission deliberately set about to achieve the suppression of publications deemed "objectionable" and succeeded in its aim. We are not the first court to look through forms to the substance and recognize that informal censorship may sufficiently inhibit the circulation of publications to warrant injunctive relief. . . .
>
> It would be naive to credit the state's assertion that these blacklists are in the nature of mere legal advice, when they plainly serve as instruments of regulation independent of the laws against obscenity. . . .
>
> Herein lies the vice of the system. . . . In thus obviating the need to employ criminal sanctions, the State has at the same time eliminated the safeguards of the criminal process. . . .
>
> What Rhode Island has done, in fact, has been to subject the distribution of publications to a system of prior administrative restraints. . . .[13]

Rhode Island has not been alone in subjecting the distribution of publications to a system of prior administrative restraints. In the *Lamont* case the issue was not obscenity, but the dissemination of political ideas.

Lamont v. *Postmaster General of United States,* 381 U.S. 301, 85 S. Ct. 1493 (1965)

MR. JUSTICE DOUGLAS delivered the opinion of the Court.
These appeals present the same question: is § 305(a) of the Postal

[11]As quoted in *Bantam Books, Inc.* v. *Sullivan,* 372 U.S. 58, pp. 59–60.
[12]*Ibid.,* p. 61.   [13]*Ibid.,* pp. 67, 68.

Service and Federal Employees Salary Act of 1962, 76 Stat. 840, constitutional as construed and applied? The statute provides in part: "Mail matter, except sealed letters, which originates or which is printed or otherwise prepared in a foreign country and which is determined by the Secretary of the Treasury pursuant to rules and regulations to be promulgated by him to be 'communist political propaganda', shall be detained by the Postmaster General upon its arrival for delivery in the United States, or upon its subsequent deposit in the United States domestic mails, and the addressee shall be notified that such matter has been received and will be delivered only upon the addressee's request, except that such detention shall not be required in the case of any matter which is furnished pursuant to subscription or which is otherwise ascertained by the Postmaster General to be desired by the addressee." 39 U.S.C. § 4008(a).

The statute defines "communist political propaganda" as political propaganda (as that term is defined in § 1(j) of the Foreign Agents Registration Act of 1938[1] which is issued by or on behalf of any country with respect to which there is in effect a suspension or withdrawal of tariff concessions or from which foreign assistance is withheld pursuant to certain specified statutes. 39 U.S.C. § 4008(b). The statute contains an exemption from its provisions for mail addressed to government agencies and educational institutions, or officials thereof, and for mail sent pursuant to a reciprocal cultural international agreement. 39 U.S.C. § 4008(c).

To implement the statute the Post office maintains 10 or 11 screening points through which is routed all unsealed mail from the designated foreign countries. At these points the nonexempt mail is examined by Customs authorities. When it is determined that a piece of mail is "communist political propaganda," the addressee is mailed a notice identifying the mail being detained and advising that it will be destroyed unless the addressee requests delivery by returning an attached reply card within 20 days.

Prior to March 1, 1965, the reply card contained a space in which the addressee could request delivery of any "similar publication" in the future. A list of the persons thus manifesting a desire to receive "communist political propaganda" was maintained by the Post Office. The Government in its brief informs us that the keeping of

[1]"The term 'political propaganda' includes any oral, visual, graphic, written, pictoria, or other communication or expression by any person (1) which is reasonably adapted to, or which the person disseminating the same believes will, or which he intends to, prevail upon, indoctrinate, convert, induce, or in any other way influence a recipient or any section of the public within the United States with reference to the political or public interests, policies, or relations of a government of a foreign country or a foreign political party or with reference to the foreign policies of the United States or promote in the United States racial, religious, or social dissensions, or (2) which advocates, advises, instigates, or promotes any racial, social, political, or religious disorder, civil riot, or other conflict involving the use of force or violence in any other American republic or the overthrow of any government or political subdivision of any other American republic by any means involving the use of force or violence." 22 U.S.C. § 611(j). [Footnote included in opinion.—ED.]

this list was terminated, effective March 15, 1965. Thus, under the new practice, a notice is sent and must be returned for each individual piece of mail desired. The only standing instruction which it is now possible to leave with the Post Office is *not* to deliver any "communist political propaganda." And the Solicitor General advises us that the Post Office Department "intends to retain its assumption that those who do not return the card want neither the identified publication nor any similar one arriving subsequently."

No. 491 arose out of the Post Office's detention in 1963 of a copy of the *Peking Review* #12 addressed to appellant, Dr. Corliss Lamont, who is engaged in the publishing and distributing of pamphlets. Lamont did not respond to the notice of detention which was sent to him but instead instituted this suit to enjoin enforcement of the statute, alleging that it infringed his rights under the First and Fifth Amendments. The Post Office thereupon notified Lamont that it considered his institution of the suit to be an expression of his desire to receive "communist political propaganda" and therefore none of his mail would be detained. Lamont amended his complaint to challenge on constitutional grounds the placement of his name on the list of those desiring to receive "communist political propaganda." The majority of the three-judge District Court nonetheless dismissed the complaint as moot, 229 F. Supp. 913, because Lamont would now receive his mail unimpeded. . . .

Like Lamont, appellee Heilberg in No. 848, when his mail was detained refused to return the reply card and instead filed a complaint in the District Court for an injunction against enforcement of the statute. The Post Office reacted to this complaint in the same manner as it had to Lamont's complaint, but the District Court declined to hold that Heilberg's action was thereby mooted. Instead the District Court reached the merits and unanimously held that the statute was unconstitutional under the First Amendment. . . .

There is no longer even a colorable question of mootness in these cases, for the new procedure, as described above, requires the postal authorities to send a separate notice for each item as it is received and the addressee to make a separate request for each item. . . . The Government concedes that the changed procedure entirely precludes any claim of mootness and leaves for our consideration the sole question of the constitutionality of the statute.

We conclude that the Act as construed and applied is unconstitutional because it requires an official act (viz. returning the reply card) as a limitation on the unfettered exercise of the addressee's First Amendment rights. As stated by Mr. Justice Holmes in *United States ex rel. Milwaukee Social Democratic Pub. Co. v. Burleson*, 255 U.S. 407, 437, (dissenting): "The United States may give up the postoffice when it sees fit, but while it carries it on, the use of the mails is almost as much a part of free speech as the right to use our tongues * * *." . . .

Here the Congress—expressly restrained by the First Amendment from "abridging" freedom of speech and of press—is the actor. The

Act sets administrative officials astride the flow of mail to inspect it, appraise it, write the addressee about it, and await a response before dispatching the mail. . . . We rest on the narrow ground that the addressee in order to receive his mail must request in writing that it be delivered. This amounts in our judgment to an unconstitutional abridgment of the addressee's First Amendment rights. The addressee carries an affirmative obligation which we do not think the Government may impose on him. This requirement is almost certain to have a deterrent effect, especially as respects those who have sensitive positions. Their livelihood may be dependent on a security clearance. Public officials like schoolteachers who have no tenure, might think they would invite disaster if they read what the Federal Government says contains the seeds of treason. Apart from them, any addressee is likely to feel some inhibition in sending for literature which federal officials have condemned as "communist political propaganda. The regime of this Act is at war with the "uninhibited, robust, and wide-open" debate and discussion that are contemplated by the First Amendment. *New York Times Co.* v. *Sullivan,* 376 U.S. 254, 270. . . .

We reverse the judgment in No. 491 and affirm that in No. 848.

It is so ordered. . . .

MR. JUSTICE BRENNAN, with whom MR. JUSTICE GOLDBERG joins, concurring. . . .

It is true that the First Amendment contains no specific guarantee of access to publications. However, the protection of the Bill of Rights goes beyond the specific guarantees to protect from congressional abridgment those equally fundamental personal rights necessary to make the express guarantees fully meaningful. . . . I think the right to receive publications is such a fundamental right. The dissemination of ideas can accomplish nothing if otherwise willing addressees are not free to receive and consider them. It would be a barren market place of ideas that had only sellers and no buyers.

Even if we were to accept the characterization of this statute as a regulation not intended to control the content of speech, but only incidentally limiting its unfettered exercise, . . . we "have consistently held that only a compelling [governmental] interest in the regulation of a subject within [governmental] constitutional power to regulate can justify limiting First Amendment freedoms." *N.A.A.C.P.* v. *Button,* 371 U.S. 415, 438. . . . [T]he Government argues that . . . only inconvenience and not an abridgment is involved. But inhibition as well as prohibition against the exercise of precious First Amendment rights is a power denied to government. . . . Moreover, the addressees' failure to return this form results not only in nondelivery of the particular publication but also of all similar publications or material. . . . In any event, we cannot sustain an intrusion on First Amendment rights on the ground that the intrusion is only a minor one. . . .

In the area of First Amendment freedoms, government has the duty to confine itself to the least intrusive regulations which are adequate for the purpose. . . . If the Government wishes to withdraw a subsidy or a privilege, it must do so by means and on terms which do not endanger First Amendment rights. . . .

The *Griswold* case is difficult to classify, except as one implicating the Due Process Clause of the Fourteenth Amendment. "Zones of privacy," the right of association, and the effort of the state of Connecticut to "contract the spectrum of available knowledge" were all discussed.

Griswold v. *State of Connecticut*, 381 U.S. 479, 85 S. Ct. 1678 (1965)

MR. JUSTICE DOUGLAS delivered the opinion of the Court.

Appellant Griswold is Executive Director of the Planned Parenthood League of Connecticut. Appellant Buxton is a licensed physician and a professor at the Yale Medical School who served as Medical Director for the League at its Center in New Haven—a center open and operating from November 1 to November 10, 1961, when appellants were arrested.

They gave information, instruction, and medical advice to *married persons* as to the means of preventing conception. They examined the wife and prescribed the best contraceptive device or material for her use. Fees were usually charged, although some couples were serviced free.

The statutes whose constitutionality is involved in this appeal are §§ 53–32 and 54–196 of the General Statutes of Connecticut (1938). The former provides:

"Any person who uses any drug, medicinal article or instrument for the purpose of preventing conception shall be fined not less than fifty dollars or imprisoned not less than sixty days nor more than one year or be both fined and imprisoned."

Section 54–196 provides:

"Any person who assists, abets, counsels, cause, hires or commands another to commit any offense may be prosecuted and punished as if he were the principal offender."

The appellants were found guilty as accessories and fined $100 each, against the claim that the accessory statute as so applied violated the Fourteenth Amendment. . . .

We think that appellants have standing to raise the constitutional rights of the married people with whom they had a professional relationship. . . . Certainly the accessory should have standing to assert that the offense which he is charged with assisting is not, or cannot constitutionally be a crime. . . .

The rights of husband and wife, pressed here, are likely to be diluted or adversely affected unless those rights are considered in a suit involving those who have this kind of confidential relation to them.

Coming to the merits, we are met with a wide range of questions that implicate the Due Process Clause of the Fourteenth Amendment. . . . We do not sit as a super-legislature to determine the wisdom, need, and propriety of laws that touch economic problems, business affairs, or social conditions. This law, however, operates directly on an intimate relation of husband and wife and their physician's role in one aspect of that relation.

The association of people is not mentioned in the Constitution nor in the Bill of Rights. The right to educate a child in a school of the parents' choice—whether public or private or parochial—is also not mentioned. Nor is the right to study any particular subject or any foreign language. Yet the First Amendment has been construed to include certain of those rights. . . .

In other words, the State may not, consistently with the spirit of the First Amendment, contract the spectrum of available knowledge. The right of freedom of speech and press includes not only the right to utter or to print, but the right to distribute, the right to receive, the right to read (*Martin* v. *City of Struthers,* 319 U.S. 141, 143), and freedom of inquiry, freedom of thought, and freedom to teach (see *Wieman* v. *Updegraff,* 344 U.S. 183, 195), indeed the freedom of the entire university community. *Sweezy* v. *State of New Hampshire,* 354 U.S. 234, *Baggett* v. *Bullitt,* 377 U.S. 360, 369. Without those peripheral rights the specific rights would be less secure. . . .

In *N.A.A.C.P.* v. *State of Alabama,* 357 U.S. 449, 462, we protected the "freedom to associate and privacy in one's associations," noting that freedom of association was a peripheral First Amendment right. . . . [T]he First Amendment has a penumbra where privacy is protected from governmental intrusion. In like context, we have protected forms of "association" that are not political in the customary sense but pertain to the social, legal, and economic benefit of the members. . . .

Those cases involved more than the "right of assembly"—a right that extends to all irrespective of their race or ideology. *DeJonge* v. *State of Oregon,* 299 U.S. 353. The right of "association," like the right of belief (*West Virginia State Board of Education* v. *Barnette,* 319 U.S. 624), is more than the right to attend a meeting; it includes the right to express one's attitude or philosophies by membership in a group or by affiliation with it or by other lawful means. Association in that context is a form of expression of opinion; and while it is not expressly included in the First Amendment its existence is necessary in making the express guarantees fully meaningful.

The foregoing cases suggest that specific guarantees in the Bill of Rights have penumbras, formed by emanations from those guarantees that help give them life and substance. . . . Various guarantees create zones of privacy. The right of association contained in the penumbra of the First Amendment is one, as we have seen. . . . The Fourth Amendment explicitly affirms the "right of the people to be secure in their persons, houses, papers, and effects, against unreasonable searches and seizures." The Fifth Amendment in its Self-Incrimination Clause enables the citizen to create a zone of privacy which government may not force him to surrender to his detriment. The Ninth Amendment provides: "The enumeration in the Constitution, of certain rights, shall not be construed to deny or disparage others retained by the people." . . . .

The present case, then, concerns a relationship lying within the zone of privacy created by several fundamental constitutional guarantees. And it concerns a law which, in forbidding the *use* of contraceptives rather than regulating their manufacture or sale, seeks to achieve its goals by means having a maximum destructive impact upon that relationship. Such a law cannot stand in light of the familiar principle, so often applied by this Court, that a "governmental purpose to control or prevent activities constitutionally subject to state regulation may not be achieved by means which sweep unnecessarily broadly and thereby invade the area of protected freedoms." *N.A.A.C.P.* v. *Alabama,* 357 U.S. 288, 307. Would we allow the police to search the sacred precincts of marital bedrooms for telltale signs of the use of contraceptives? The very idea is repulsive to the notions of privacy surrounding the marriage relationship.

We deal with a right of privacy older than the Bill of Rights—older than our political parties, older than our school system. Marriage is a coming together for better or for worse, hopefully enduring and intimate to the degree of being sacred. It is an association that promotes a way of life, not causes; a harmony in living, not political faiths; a bilateral loyalty, not commercial or social projects. Yet it is an association for as noble a purpose as any involved in our prior decisions.   *Reversed.*

MR. JUSTICE GOLDBERG, whom THE CHIEF JUSTICE and MR. JUSTICE BRENNAN join, concurring.

I agree with the Court that Connecticut's birth control law unconstitutionally intrudes upon the right of marital privacy, and I join in its opinion and judgment. Although I have not accepted the view that " 'due process' as used in the Fourteenth Amendment includes all of the first eight Amendments," *id.,* 367 U.S. at 516, I do agree that the concept of liberty protects those personal rights that are fundamental, and is not confined to the specific terms of the Bill of Rights. My conclusion that the concept of liberty is not so restricted and that it embraces the right of marital privacy though that right is not mentioned explicitly in the Constitution is supported both by numerous decisions of this Court, referred to in the Court's opinion, and by the language and history of the Ninth Amendment. In reaching the conclusion that the right of marital privacy is protected, as being within the protected penumbra of specific guarantees of the Bill of Rights, the Court refers to the Ninth Amendment, *ante.* . . . I add these words to emphasize the relevance of that Amendment to the Court's holding. . . .

. . . The language and history of the Ninth Amendment reveal that the Framers of the Constitution believed that there are additional fundamental rights, protected from governmental infringement, which exist alongside those fundamental rights specifically mentioned in the first eight constitutional amendments. . . .

It was proffered to quiet expressed fears that a bill of specifically enumerated rights could not be sufficiently broad to cover all essential rights and that the specific mention of certain rights would be interpreted as a denial that others were protected. . . .

While this Court has had little occasion to interpret the Ninth Amendment, "[i]t cannot be presumed that any clause in the constitution is intended to be without effect." *Marbury* v. *Madison,* 1 Cranch 137, 174. . . . The Ninth Amendment to the Constitution may be regarded by some as a recent discovery but since 1791 it has been a basic part of the Constitution which we are sworn to uphold. To hold that a right so basic and fundamental and so deep-rooted in our society as the right of privacy in marriage may be infringed because that right is not guaranteed in so many words by the first eight amendments to the Constitution is to ignore the Ninth Amendment and to give it no effect whatsoever. Moreover, a judicial construction that this fundamental right is not protected by the Constitution because it is not mentioned in explicit terms by one of the first eight amendments or elsewhere in the Constitution would violate the Ninth Amendment, which specifically states that "[t]he enumeration in the Constitution, of certain rights shall not be *construed* to deny or disparage others retained by the people." [Emphasis added.]

A dissenting opinion suggests that my interpretation of the Ninth Amendment somehow "broaden[s] the powers of this Court." . . . . With all due respect, I believe that it misses the import of what I am saying. . . .

Nor am I turning somersaults with history in arguing that the Ninth Amendment is relevant in a case dealing with a *State's* refringement of a fundamental right. . . . In sum, the Ninth Amendment simply lends strong support to the view that the "liberty" protected by the Fifth and Fourteenth Amendments from infringement by the Federal Government or the States is not restricted to rights specifically mentioned in the first eight amendments. . . .

In determining which rights are fundamental, . . . [t]he inquiry is whether a right involved "is of such a character that it cannot be denied without violating those "fundamental principles of liberty and justice which lie at the base of all our civil and political institutions" * * *." *Powell* v. *State of Alabama,* 287 U.S. 45, 67. . . .

I agree fully with the Court that, applying these tests, the right of privacy is a fundamental personal right, "emanat[ing] from the totality of the constitutional scheme under which we live." *Id.,* at 521. . . .

The Connecticut statutes here involved deal with a particularly important and sensitive area of privacy—that of the marital relation and the marital home. . . .

The entire fabric of the Constitution and the purposes that clearly underlie its specific guarantees demonstrate that the rights to marital privacy and to marry and raise a family are of similar order and magnitude as the fundamental rights specifically protected. . . .

Although the Connecticut birth-control law obviously encroaches upon a fundamental personal liberty, the State does not show that the law serves any "subordinating state interest which is compelling" or that it is "necessary ° ° ° to the accomplishment of a permissible state policy." . . . It is clear that the State interest in safeguarding marital fidelity can be served by a more discriminately tailored statute. . . .

In sum, I believe that the right of privacy in the marital relation is fundamental and basic—a personal right "retained by the people" within the meaning of the Ninth Amendment. Connecticut cannot constitutionally abridge this fundamental right, which is protected by the Fourteenth Amendment from infringement by the States. I agree with the Court that petitioners' convictions must therefore be reversed.

MR. JUSTICE HARLAN, concurring in the judgment.

I fully agree with the judgment of reversal, but find myself unable to join the Court's opinion. . . .

[W]hat I find implicit in the Court's opinion is that the "incorporation" doctrine may be used to *restrict* the reach of Fourteenth Amendment Due Process. For me this is just as unacceptable constitutional doctrine as is the use of the "incorporation" approach to *impose* upon the States all the requirements of the Bill of Rights as found in the provisions of the first eight amendments and in the decisions of this Court interpreting them. . . .

In my view, the proper constitutional inquiry in this case is whether this Connecticut statute infringes the Due Process Clause of the Fourteenth Amendment because the enactment violates basic values "implicit in the concept of ordered liberty," *Palko* v. *State of Connecticut,* 302 U.S. 319, 325. . . . For reasons stated at length in my dissenting opinion in *Poe* v. *Ullman, supra,* I believe that it does. . . .

MR. JUSTICE WHITE, concurring in the judgment.

In my view this Connecticut law as applied to married couples deprives them of "liberty" without due process of law, as that concept is used in the Fourteenth Amendment. I therefore concur in the judgment of the Court reversing these convictions under Connecticut's aiding and abetting statute. . . .

I wholly fail to see how the ban on the use of contraceptives by married couples in any way reinforces the State's ban on illicit sexual relationships. . . . Connecticut does not bar the importation or possession of contraceptive devices . . . and their availability in that State is not seriously disputed. . . . Moreover, it would appear that the sale of contraceptives to prevent disease is plainly legal under Connecticut law. . . .

I find nothing in this record justifying the sweeping scope of this statute, with its telling effect on the freedoms of married persons, and therefore conclude that it deprives such persons of liberty without due process of law.

MR. JUSTICE BLACK, with whom MR. JUSTICE STEWART joins, dissenting.

I agree with my Brother STEWART's dissenting opinion. And like him I do not to any extent whatever base my view that this Connecticut law is constitutional on a belief that the law is wise or that its policy is a good one. In order that there may be no room at all to doubt why I vote as I do, I feel constrained to add that the law is every bit as offensive to me as it is my Brethren of the majority and my Brothers HARLAN, WHITE and GOLDBERG who, reciting reasons why it is offensive to them, hold it unconstitutional. There is no single one of the graphic and eloquent strictures and criticisms fired at the policy of this Connecticut law either by the Court's opinion or by those of my concurring Brethren to which I cannot subscribe— except their conclusion that the evil qualities they see in the law make it unconstitutional. . . .

. . . . Strongly as I desire to protect all First Amendment freedoms, I am unable to stretch the Amendment so as to afford protection to the conduct of these defendants in violating the Connecticut law. . . .

One of the most effective ways of diluting or expanding a constitutionally guaranteed right is to substitute for the crucial word or words of a constitutional guarantee another word, more or less flexible and more or less restricted in its meaning. This fact is well illustrated by the use of the term "right of privacy" as a comprehensive substitute for the Fourth Amendment's guarantee against "unreasonable searches and seizures. . . . I get nowhere in this case by talk about a constitutional "right of privacy" as an emanation from one or more constitutional provisions. I like my privacy as well as the next one, but I am nevertheless compelled to admit that government has a right to invade it unless prohibited by some specific constitutional provision. For these reasons I cannot agree with the Court's judgment and the reasons it gives for holding this Connecticut law unconstitutional. . . .

My disagreement with the Court's opinion holding that there is such a violation here is a narrow one, relating to the application of the First Amendment to the facts and circumstances of this particular case. But my disagreement with Brothers HARLAN, WHITE and GOLDBERG is more basic. I think that if properly construed neither the Due Process Clause nor the Ninth Amendment, nor both together, could under any circumstances be a proper basis for invalidating the Connecticut law. I discuss the due process and Ninth Amendment arguments together because on analysis they turn out to be the same thing—merely using different words to claim for this

Court and the federal judiciary power to invalidate any legislative act which the judges find irrational, unreasonable or offensive. . . .

. . . I do not believe that we are granted power by the Due Process Clause or any other constitutional provision or provisions to measure constitutionality by our belief that legislation is arbitrary, capricious or unreasonable or accomplishes no justifiable purpose, or is offense to our own notions of "civilized standards of conduct." . . . The use by federal courts of such a formula or doctrine or whatnot to veto federal or state laws simply takes away from Congress and States the power to make laws based on their own judgment of fairness and wisdom and transfers that power to this Court for ultimate determination—a power which was specifically denied to federal courts by the convention that framed the Constitution. . . .

One would certainly have to look far beyond the language of the Ninth Amendment to find that the Framers vested in this Court any such awesome veto powers over lawmaking, either by the States or by the Congress. Nor does anything in the history of the Amendment offer any support for such a shocking doctrine. The whole history of the adoption of the Constitution and Bill of Rights points the other way. . . . That Amendment was passed, not to broaden the powers of this Court or any other department of "the General Government," but, as every student of history knows, to assure the people that the Constitution in all its provisions was intended to limit the Federal Government to the powers granted expressly or by necessary implication. . . .

My point is that there is no provision of the Constitution which either expressly or impliedly vests power in this Court to sit as a supervisory agency over acts of duly constituted legislative bodies and set aside their laws because of the Court's belief that the legislative policies adopted are unreasonable, unwise, arbitrary, capricious or irrational. . . .

I cannot rely on the Due Process Clause or the Ninth Amendment or any mysterious and uncertain natural law concept as a reason for striking down this state law. The Due Process Clause with an "arbitrary and capricious" or "shocking to the conscience" formula. . . . is no less dangerous when used to enforce this Court's views about personal rights than those about economic rights. I had thought that we had laid that formula, as a means for striking down state legislation, to rest once and for all in cases like *West Coast Hotel Co.* v. *Parrish*, 300 U.S. 379, and many other opinions. . . .

So far as I am concerned, Connecticut's law as applied here is not forbidden by any provision of the Federal Constitution as that Constitution was written, and I am therefore to affirm.

MR. JUSTICE STEWART, whom MR. JUSTICE BLACK joins, dissenting.

Since 1879 Connecticut has had on its books a law which forbids the use of contraceptives by anyone. I think this is an uncommonly silly law. . . . But we are not asked in this case to say whether we think this law is unwise, or even asinine. We are asked to hold that it violates the United States Constitution. And that I cannot do.

In the course of its opinion the Court refers to no less than six Amendments to the Constitution: the First, the Third, the Fourth, the Fifth, the Ninth, and the Fourteenth. But the Court does not say which of these Amendments, if any, it thinks is infringed by this Connecticut law.

We *are* told that the Due Process Clause of the Fourteenth Amendment is not, as such, the "guide" in this case. With that much I agree. There is no claim that this law, duly enacted by the Connecticut Legislature, is unconstitutionally vague. There is no claim that the appellants were denied any of the elements of procedural due process at their trial, so as to make their convictions constitutionally invalid. . . .

As to the First, Third, Fourth, and Fifth Amendments, I can find nothing in any of them to invalidate this Connecticut law, even assuming that all those Amendments are fully applicable against the States. . . .

The Court also quotes the Ninth Amendment, and my Brother GOLDBERG'S concurring opinion relies heavily upon it. But to say that the Ninth Amendment has anything to do with this case is to turn somersaults with history. . . .

What provision of the Constitution, then, does make this state law invalid? The Court says it is the right of privacy "created by several fundamental constitutional guarantees." With all deference, I can find no such general right of privacy in the Bill of Rights, in any other part of the Constitution, or in any case ever before decided by this Court. . . .

CHAPTER FIVE

Loyalty and Security: Investigations and Oaths

The Power of Congress to Investigate

SINCE CONGRESS HAS the power to legislate, it must also have the power to investigate in order to determine if legislation is necessary, or if legislation enacted has been effective. This investigatory power, although not specifically mentioned in the Constitution, has long been treated as an attribute of the power to legislate. In 1927, however, the question was raised directly in *McGrain v. Daugherty*, 273 U.S. 135, 47 S. Ct. 319. In that case a Senate Committee, which was investigating the actions of Attorney General Harry M. Daugherty and the Justice Department, issued a subpoena to require the appearance of the Attorney General's brother, ordering him to produce specified records in his possession. When he refused to appear, he was arrested by a deputy of the Senate Sergeant-at-Arms, to compel his attendance.

On a petition for habeas corpus, Mally Daugherty was released, and the Sergeant-at-Arms, McGrain, appealed. The Supreme Court reviewed the history of the power of Congress to investigate, and held that "the object of the investigation and of the efforts to secure the witness's testimony was to obtain information for legislative purposes."[1] The final order was therefore reversed, for the witness was subject to the subpoena power of the Congress.

But the power of the Congress to investigate is not without limit, even though the Congress is pursuing a proper legislative purpose. Basic constitutional rights of witnesses must be protected. Since the guidelines for such protection are determined on the basis of individual cases as they come before the courts, it has taken the courts a number of years to spell out the following requirements. The authorization

[1]*McGrain* v. *Daugherty*, 273 U.S. 135, p. 177.

creating the committee and giving it power must have been given by the Congress in such terms that the purposes of the investigation can be determined with reasonable clarity and specificity; and the investigation must have some relationship to a legislative purpose. If the committee has established rules for its own conduct, and for the examination of witnesses, it must follow them. It must also act as a committee, or at least as a subcommittee of more than one member, if it is to hear witnesses who may be cited for contempt. When witnesses appear before it, the committee must explain the purpose of the investigation, and what the committee believes the witness can contribute. It must also make clear to the witness the relevancy of the questions asked to the purpose of the investigation.

With such broad powers at the command of Congress, and with the felt necessity to legislate in areas which may impinge upon the individual's rights under the Bill of Rights, there are frequent conflicts between congressional committees and the witnesses who appear before them. Most common sources of conflict, perhaps, have been those hearings in which the House Un-American Activities Committee, as it is commonly called, has purported to study the possible need for, or success of, legislation directed toward control of "subversive" activities. The witness has, of course, certain protections: freedom of speech and association under the First Amendment and the right not to incriminate himself under the Fifth. But one constitutional problem has been to define the moment he surrenders those rights. If a witness gives more than his name, has he given up his right to invoke the Fifth Amendment? It is quite possible that a revelation of his address would be as incriminating as an admission of guilt in a criminal trial. Witnesses are obligated to answer appropriate questions, but the problem still remains: how can the witness be cooperative, and yet not lose his rights under the First and Fifth Amendments? An unjustified refusal to answer can result in a citation for contempt, a trial, and punishment if the witness is found guilty.

John T. Watkins, who had been a labor union official and organizer, was a cooperative witness — up to a point — when he was questioned by a Subcommittee of the House Committee on Un-American Activities. He answered freely and in detail questions relating to his own activities, but he refused to answer those concerning certain others whose names were read to him. His reason for refusing was that information about persons who might have been members of the Communist Party in the past but had long since dissociated themselves from it was not relevant to the work of the Committee. He was cited for contempt, tried, found guilty, and appealed.

A basic requirement for finding an accused person guilty is that the alleged crime be defined with enough clarity for him to have known that his action was proscribed. The *Watkins* case turned upon the fact that in the Court's opinion Mr. Watkins could not have known that in refusing to answer certain of the questions he was committing contempt. The reasoning of Chief Justice Warren's opinion has given guidance both to Congressional committees and to witnesses.

Watkins v. *United States,* 354 U.S. 178, 77 S. Ct. 1173 (1957)

MR. CHIEF JUSTICE WARREN delivered the opinion of the Court. * * *

We start with several basic premises on which there is general agreement. The power of the Congress to conduct investigations is inherent in the legislative process. That power is broad. * * * But, broad as is this power of inquiry, it is not unlimited. There is no general authority to expose the private affairs of individuals without justification in terms of the functions of the Congress. This was freely conceded by the Solicitor General in his argument of this case. Nor is the Congress a law enforcement or trial agency. These are functions of the executive and judicial departments of government. No inquiry is an end in itself; it must be related to and in furtherance of a legitimate task of the Congress. Investigations conducted solely for the personal aggrandizement of the investigators or to "punish" those investigated are indefensible.

It is unquestionably the duty of all citizens to cooperate with the Congress in its efforts to obtain the facts needed for intelligent legislative action. It is their unremitting obligation to respond to subpoenas, to respect the dignity of the Congress and its committees and to testify fully with respect to matters within the province of proper investigation. This, of course, assumes that the constitutional rights of witnesses will be respected by the Congress as they are in a court of justice. The Bill of Rights is applicable to investigations as to all forms of governmental action. Witnesses cannot be compelled to give evidence against themselves. They cannot be subjected to unreasonable search and seizure. Nor can the First Amendment freedoms of speech, press, religion, or political belief and association be abridged. * * *

In the decade following World War II, there appeared a new kind of congressional inquiry unknown in prior periods of American history. Principally this was the result of the various investigations into the threat of subversion of the United States Government, but other subjects of congressional interest also contributed to the changed scene. This new phase of legislative inquiry involved a broad-scale intrusion into the lives and affairs of private citizens. It brought before the courts novel questions of the appropriate limits of congressional inquiry. Prior cases like *Kilbourn, McGrain* and *Sinclair,* had defined the scope of investigative power in terms of the inherent limitations of the sources of that power. In the more recent cases, the emphasis shifted to problems of accommodating the interest of the Government with the rights and privileges of individuals. The central theme was the application of the Bill of Rights as a restraint upon the assertion of governmental power in this form.

It was during this period that the Fifth Amendment privilege against self-incrimination was frequently invoked and recognized as a legal limit upon the authority of a committee to require that a witness answer its questions. Some early doubts as to the applicability of that privilege before a legislative committee never matured. When the matter reached this Court, the Government did not challenge in any way that the Fifth Amendment protection was available to the witness, and such a challenge could not have prevailed. * * *

A far more difficult task evolved from the claim by witnesses that the committees' interrogations were infringements upon the freedoms of the First Amendment. Clearly, an investigation is subject to the command that the Congress shall make no law abridging freedom of speech or press or assembly. While it is true that there is no statute to be reviewed, and that an investigation is not a law, nevertheless an investigation is part of lawmaking. It is justified solely as an adjunct to the legislative process. The First Amendment may be invoked against infringement of the protected freedoms by law or by lawmaking.

Abuses of the investigative process may imperceptibly lead to abridgment of protected freedoms. The mere summoning of a witness and compelling him to testify, against his will, about his beliefs, expressions or associations is a measure of governmental interference. And when those forced revelations concern matters that are unorthodox, unpopular, or even hateful to the general public, the reaction in the life of the witness may be disastrous. This effect is even more harsh when it is past beliefs, expressions or associations that are disclosed and judged by current standards rather than those contemporary with the matters exposed. Nor does the witness alone suffer the consequences. Those who are identified by witnesses and thereby placed in the same glare of publicity are equally subject to public stigma, scorn and obloquy. Beyond that, there is the more subtle and immeasurable effect upon those who tend to adhere to the most orthodox and uncontroversial views and associations in order to avoid a similar fate at some future time. That this impact is partly the result of non-governmental activity by private persons cannot relieve the investigators of their responsibility for initiating the reaction.

The Court recognized the restraints of the Bill of Rights upon congressional investigations in *United States* v. *Rumely*, 345 U.S.41. The magnitude and complexity of the problem of applying the First Amendment to that case led the Court to construe narrowly the resolution describing the committee's authority. It was concluded that, when First Amendment rights are threatened, the delegation of power to the committee must be clearly revealed in its charter.

Accommodation of the congressional need for particular information with the individual and personal interest in privacy is an arduous and delicate task for any court. We do not underestimate the difficulties that would attend such an undertaking. It is manifest that despite the adverse effects which follow upon compelled disclosure of private matters, not all such inquiries are barred. *Kilbourn* v. *Thompson* teaches that such an investigation into individual affairs is invalid if unrelated to any legislative purpose. That is beyond the powers conferred upon the Congress in the Constitution. *United States* v. *Rumely* makes it plain that the mere semblance of legislative purpose would not justify an inquiry in the face of the Bill of Rights. The critical element is the existence of, and the weight to be ascribed to, the interest of the Congress in demanding disclosures from an unwilling witness. We cannot simply assume, however, that every congressional investigation is justified by a public need that overbalances any private rights affected. To do so would be to abdicate the responsibility placed by the Constitution upon the judiciary to insure that the Congress does not unjustifiably encroach upon an individual's right to privacy nor abridge his liberty of speech, press, religion or assembly. ° ° °

We have no doubt that there is no congressional power to expose for the sake of exposure. The public is, of course, entitled to be informed concerning the workings of its government. That cannot be inflated into a general power to expose where the predominant result can only be an invasion of the private rights of individuals. ° ° °

. . . The theory of a committee inquiry is that the committee members are serving as the representatives of the parent assembly in collecting information for a legislative purpose. Their function is to act as the eyes and ears of the Congress in obtaining facts upon which the full legislature can act. ° ° °

An essential premise in this situation is that the House or Senate shall have instructed the committee members on what they are to do with the power delegated to them. It is the responsibility of the Congress, in the first instance, to insure that compulsory process is used only in furtherance of a legislative purpose. That requires that the instructions to an investigating committee spell out that group's jurisdiction and purpose with sufficient particularity. Those instructions are embodied in the authorizing resolution. That document is the committee's charter. Broadly drafted and loosely worded, however, such resolutions can leave tremendous latitude to the discretion of the investigators. The more vague the committee's charter is, the greater becomes the possibility that the committee's specific actions are not in conformity with the will of the parent House of Congress.

The authorizing resolution of the Un-American Activities Committee was adopted in 1938 when a select committee, under the chairmanship of Representative Dies, was created. Several years later, the Committee was made a standing organ of the House with the same mandate. It defines the Committee's authority as follows:

"The Committee on Un-American Activities, as a whole or by sub-committee, is authorized to make from time to time investigations of (i) the extent, character, and objects of un-American propaganda activities in the United States, (ii) the diffusion within the United States of subversive and un-American propaganda that is instigated from foreign countries or of a domestic origin and attacks the principle of the form of government as guaranteed by our Constitution, and (iii) all other questions in relation thereto that would aid Congress in any necessary remedial legislation."

It would be difficult to imagine a less explicit authorizing resolution. Who can define the meaning of "un-American"? What is that single, solitary "principle of the form of government as guaranteed by our Constitution"? There is no need to dwell upon the language, however. At one time, perhaps, the resolution might have been read narrowly to confine the Committee to the subject of propaganda. The events that have transpired in the fifteen years before the interrogation of petitioner make such a construction impossible at this date.

The members of the Committee have clearly demonstrated that they did not feel themselves restricted in any way to propaganda in the narrow sense of the word. Unquestionably the Committee conceived of its task in the grand view of its name. Un-American activities were its target, no matter how or where manifested. * * *

Combining the language of the resolution with the construction it has been given, it is evident that the preliminary control of the Committee exercised by the House of Representatives is slight or non-existent. No one could reasonably deduce from the charter the kind of investigation that the Committee was directed to make. As a result, we are asked to engage in a process of retroactive rationalization. Looking backward from the events that transpired, we are asked to uphold the Committee's actions unless it appears that they were clearly not authorized by the charter. . . . No doubt every reasonable indulgence of legality must be accorded to the actions of a coordinate branch of our Government. But such deference cannot yield to an unnecessary and unreasonable dissipation of precious constitutional freedoms. * * *

The Government contends that the public interest at the core of the investigations of the Un-American Activities Committee is the need by the Congress to be informed of efforts to overthrow the Government by force and violence so that adequate legislative safeguards can be erected. From this core, however, the Committee can radiate outward infinitely to any topic thought to be related in some way to armed insurrection. The outer reaches of this domain are known only by the content of "un-American activities." Remoteness of subject can be aggravated by a probe for a depth of detail even farther removed from any basis of legislative action. A third dimension is added when the investigators turn their attention to the past to collect minutiae on remote topics, on the hypothesis that the past may reflect upon the present.

The consequences that flow from this situation are manifold. In the first place a reviewing court is unable to make the kind of judgment made by the Court in *United States* v. *Rumely, supra*. The Committee is allowed, in essence, to define its own authority, to choose the direction and focus of its activities. * * *

More important and more fundamental than that, however, it insulates the House that has authorized the investigation from the witnesses who are subjected to the sanctions of compulsory process. There is a wide gulf between the responsibility for the use of investigative power and the actual exercise of that power. This is an especially vital consideration in assuring respect for constitutional liberties. Protected freedoms should not be placed in danger in the absence of a clear determination by the House or the Senate that a particular inquiry is justified by a specific legislative need.

It is, of course, not the function of this Court to prescribe rigid rules for the Congress to follow in drafting resolutions establishing investigating committees. That is a matter peculiarly within the realm of the legislature, and its decisions will be accepted by the courts up to the point where their own duty to enforce the constitutionally protected rights of individuals is affected. An excessively broad charter, like that of the House Un-American Activities Committee, places the courts in an untenable position if they are to strike a balance between the public need for a particular interrogation and the right of citizens to carry on their affairs free from unnecessary governmental interference. It is impossible in such a situation to ascertain whether any legislative purpose justifies the disclosures sought and, if so, the importance of that information to the Congress in furtherance of its legislative function. The reason no court can make this critical judgment is that the House of Representatives itself has never mde it. Only the legislative assembly initiating an investigation can assay the relative necessity of specific disclosures.

Absence of the qualitative consideration of petitioner's questioning by the House of Representatives aggravates a serious problem, revealed in this case, in the relationship of congressional investigating committees and the witnesses who appear before them. Plainly these committees are restricted to the missions delegated to them. . . . No witness can be compelled to make disclosures on matters outside that area. This is a jurisdictional concept of pertinency drawn from the nature of a congressional committee's source of authority. . . . When the definition of jurisdictional pertinency is as uncertain and wavering as in the case of the Un-American Activities Committee, it becomes extremely difficult for the Committee to limit its inquiries to statutory pertinency.

Since World War II, the Congress has practically abandoned its original practice of utilizing the coercive sanction of contempt proceedings at the bar of the House. . . . The Congress has instead invoked the aid of the federal judicial system in protecting itself against contumacious conduct. It has become customary to refer these matters to the United States Attorneys for prosecution under criminal law. . . .

In fulfillment of their obligation under this statute, the courts must accord to the defendants every right which is guaranteed to defendants in all other criminal cases. Among these is the right to have available, through a sufficiently precise statute, information revealing the standard of criminality before the commission of the alleged offense. Applied to persons prosecuted under 192, this raises a special problem in that the statute defines the crime as refusal to answer "any question pertinent to the question under inquiry." Part of the standard of criminality, therefore, is the pertinency of the questions propounded to the witness.

The problem attains proportion when viewed from the standpoint of the witness who appears before a congressional committee. He must decide at the time the questions are propounded whether or not to answer.

It is obvious that a person compelled to make this choice is entitled to have knowledge of the subject to which the interrogation is deemed pertinent. That knowledge must be available with the same degree of explicitness and clarity that the Due Process Clause requires in the expression of any element of a criminal offense. The "vice of vagueness" must be avoided here as in all other crimes. There are several sources that can outline the "question under inquiry" in such a way that the rules against vagueness are satisfied. The authorizing resolution, the remarks of the chairman or members of the committee, or even the nature of the proceedings themselves might sometimes make the topic clear. This case demonstrates, however, that these sources often leave the matter in grave doubt. * * *

The Government believes that the topic of inquiry before the Subcommittee concerned Communist infiltration in labor. * * * Looking at the entire hearings, however, there is strong reason to doubt that the subject revolved about labor matters. . . .

The most serious doubts as to the Subcommittee's "question under inquiry," however, stem from the precise questions that petitioner has been charged with refusing to answer. Under the terms of the statute, after all, it is these which must be proved pertinent. Petitioner is charged with refusing to tell the Subcommittee whether or not he knew that certain named persons had been members of the Communist Party in the past. * * *

The final source of evidence as to the "question under inquiry" is the Chairman's response when petitioner objected to the questions on the grounds of lack of pertinency. The Chairman then announced that the Subcommittee was investigating "subversion and subversive propaganda." This is a subject at least as broad and indefinite as the authorizing resolution of the Committee, if not more so. . . .

The statement of the Committee Chairman in this case, in response to petitioner's protest, was woefully inadequate to convey sufficient information as to the pertinency of the questions to the subject under inquiry. Petitioner was thus not accorded a fair opportunity to determine whether he was within his rights in refusing to answer, and his conviction is necessarily invalid under the Due Process Clause of the Fifth Amendment. . . .

The conclusions we have reached in this case will not prevent the Congress, through its committees, from obtaining any information it needs for the proper fulfillment of its role in our scheme of government. The legislature is free to determine the kinds of data that should be collected. It is only those investigations that are conducted by use of compulsory process that give rise to a need to protect the rights of individuals against illegal encroachment. That protection can be readily achieved through procedures which prevent the separation of power from responsibility and which provide the constitutional requisites of fairness for witnesses. A measure of added care on the part of the House and the Senate in authorizing the use of compulsory process and by their committees in exercising that power would suffice. That is a small price to pay if it serves to uphold the principles of limited, constitutional government without constricting the power of the Congress to inform itself.

The judgment of the Court of Appeals is reversed, and the case is remanded to the District Court with instructions to dismiss the indictment.   *It is so ordered.* . . .

MR. JUSTICE FRANKFURTER, concurring. * * *
While implied authority for the questioning by the Committee, sweeping as was its inquiry, may be squeezed out of the repeated acquiescence by Congress in the Committee's inquiries, the basis for determining petitioner's guilt is not thereby laid. Prosecution for contempt of Congress presupposes an adequate opportunity for the defendant to have awareness of the pertinency of the information that he has denied to Congress. And the basis of such awareness must be contemporaneous with the witness' refusal to answer and not at the trial for it. Accordingly, the actual scope of the inquiry that the Committee was authorized to conduct and the relevance of the questions to that inquiry must be shown to have been luminous at the time when asked and not left, at best, in cloudiness. The circumstances of this case were wanting in these essentials.

MR. JUSTICE CLARK, dissenting.
As I see it the chief fault in the majority opinion is its mischievous curbing of the informing function of the Congress. While I am not versed in its procedures, my experience in the executive branch of the Government leads me to believe that the requirements laid down in the opinion for the operation of the committee system of inquiry are both unnecessary and unworkable. . . .

It may be that at times the House Committee on Un-American Activities has, as the Court says, "conceived of its task in the grand view of its name." And, perhaps, as the Court indicates, the rules of conduct placed upon the Committee by the House admit of individual abuse and unfairness. But that is none of our affair. So long as the object of legislative inquiry is legitimate and the questions propounded are pertinent thereto, it is not for the courts to interfere with the committee system of inquiry. To hold otherwise would be an infringement on the power given the Congress to inform itself, and thus a trespass upon the fundamental American principle of separation of powers. The majority has substituted the judiciary as the grand inquisitor and supervisor of congressional investigations. It has never been so. * * *

I think the Committee here was acting entirely within its scope and that the purpose of its inquiry was set out with "undisputable clarity." In the first place, the authorizing language of the Reorganization Act must be read as a whole, not dissected. It authorized investigation into subversive activity, its extent, character, objects, and diffusion. While the language might have been more explicit than using such words as "un-American," or phrases like "principle of the form of government," still these are fairly well understood terms. We must construe them to give them meaning if we can. * * *

The Court condemns the long-established and long-recognized committee system of inquiry of the House because it raises serious questions concerning the protection it affords to constitutional rights. . . . There is nothing in the First Amendment that provides the guarantees Watkins claims. That Amendment was designed to prevent attempts by law to curtail freedom of speech. . . . Watkins sought to vindicate the rights, if any, of his associates. It is settled that one cannot invoke the constitutional rights of another. . . .

While there may be no restraint by the Government of one's beliefs, the right of free belief has never been extended to include the withholding of knowledge of past events or transactions. . . .The First Amendment does not make speech or silence permissible to a person in such measure as he chooses. Watkins has here exercised his own choice as to when he talks, what questions he answers, and when he remains silent. A witness is not given such a choice by the Amendment. Remote and indirect disadvantages such as "public stigma, scorn and obloquy" may be related to the First Amendment, but they are not enough to block investigation. * * *

. . . This inquiry is far different from the cases relied upon by the Court. * * * We should afford to Congress the presumption that it takes every precaution possible to avoid unnecessary damage to reputations. . . .The record in this case shows no conduct on the part of the Un-American Activities Committee that justifies condemnation. That there may have been such occasions is not for us to consider here. . . . To carry on its heavy responsibility the compulsion of truth that does not incriminate is not only necessary to the Congress but is permitted within the limits of the Constitution.

The opinion in the *Watkins* case was received with enthusiasm by the many who had been deeply concerned by what they believed to be the House Committee's disregard to certain fundamental rights of witnesses, and with something akin to despair by those who either saw no violation of the Bill of Rights, or believed that a violation was necessary to save the United States from communism. Two years later, with the decision in *Barenblatt* v. *U.S.*, both reactions were modified.

The majority of the Court rarely considers a question identical with one recently decided, although perception of such an identity may be the basis for a dissenting opinion. In the majority opinion, therefore, the problem in the *Barenblatt* case was not identical with that presented in the *Watkins* case, but certain pronouncements of the the Court did reverse some of the points of view set forth in the *Watkins* case. Mr. Barenblatt's case was before the U.S. Supreme Court for the second time; his original conviction had been affirmed by the Court of Appeals, but the Supreme Court vacated the judgment and sent the case back for consideration in the light of the *Watkins* case. The case reached the Supreme Court again.

Barenblatt v. *United States of America*, 360 U.S. 109, 79 S. Ct. 1081, (1959)

MR. JUSTICE HARLAN delivered the opinion of the Court.

Once more the Court is required to resolve the conflicting constitutional claims of congressional power and of an individual's right to resist its exercise. The Congressional power in question concerns the internal process of Congress in moving within its legislative domain; it involves the utilization of its committees to secure "testimony needed to enable it efficiently to exercise a legislative function belonging to it under the Constitution." *McGrain* v. *Daugherty*, 273 U.S. 135, 160. The scope of the power of inquiry, in short, is as penetrating and far-reaching as the potential power to enact and appropriate under the Constitution.

Broad as it is, the power is not, however, without limitations. Since Congress may only investigate into those areas in which it may potentially legislate or appropriate, it cannot inquire into matters which are within the exclusive province of one of the other branches of the Government. . . .

The congressional power of inquiry, its range and scope, and an individual's duty in relation to it, must be viewed in proper perspective. . . . The power and the right of resistance to it are to be judged in the concrete, not on the basis of abstractions. In the present case congressional efforts to learn the extent of a nation-wide, indeed worldwide, problem have brought one of its investigating committees into the field of education. Of course, broadly viewed, inquiries cannot be made into the teaching that is pursued in any of our educational institutions. When academic teaching-freedom and its corollary learning-freedom, so essential to the well-being of the Nation, are claimed, this Court will always be on the alert against intrusion by Congress into this constitutionally protected domain. But this does not mean that the Congress is precluded from interrogating a witness merely because he is a teacher. . . .

We here review petitioner's conviction . . . for contempt of Congress, arising from his refusal to answer certain questions put to him by a Subcommittee of the House Committee on Un-American Activities during the course of an inquiry concerning alleged Communist infiltration into the field of education. . . .

Pursuant to a subpoena, and accompanied by counsel, petitioner on June 28, 1954 appeared as a witness before this congressional Subcommittee. After answering a few preliminary questions and testifying that he had been a graduate student and teaching fellow at the University of Michigan from 1947 to 1950 and an instructor in psychology at Vassar College from 1950 to shortly before his appearance before the Subcommittee, petitioner objected generally to the right of the Subcommittee to inquire into his "political" and "religious" beliefs or any "other personal and private affairs" or "associational activities," upon grounds set forth in a previously prepared memorandum which he was allowed to file with the Subcommittee. Thereafter petitioner specifically declined to answer . . . five questions. . . .

In each instance the grounds of refusal were those set forth in the prepared statement. Petitioner expressly disclaimed reliance upon "the Fifth Amendment." * * *

Petitioner's various contentions resolve themselves into three propositions: First, the compelling of testimony by the Subcommittee was neither legislatively authorized nor constitutionally permissible because of the vagueness of Rule XI of the House of Representatives, Eighty-Third Congress, the charter of authority of the parent Committee. Second, petitioner was not adequately apprised of the pertinency of the Subcommittee's questions to the subject matter of the inquiry. Third, the questions petitioner refused to answer infringed rights protected by the First Amendment. . . .

At the outset it should be noted that Rule XI authorized this Subcommittee to compel testimony within the framework of the investigative authority conferred on the Un-American Activities Committee. . . . A principal contention in Watkins was that the refusals to answer were justified because the requirement of 2 U.S.C. § 192, that the questions asked be "pertinent to the question under inquiry" had not been satisfied. 354 U.S. at pages 208–209. This Court reversed the conviction solely on that ground. . . . In short, while Watkins was critical of Rule XI, it did not involve the broad and inflexible holding petitioner now attributes to it.

Petitioner also contends, independently of *Watkins,* that the vagueness of Rule XI deprived the Subcommittee of the right to compel testimony in this investigation into Communist activity. We cannot agree with this contention. . . . Granting the vagueness of the Rule, we may not read it in isolation from its long history in the House of Representatives . . . The Rule comes to us with a "persuasive gloss of legislative history," *United States* v. *Witkovich*, 353 U.S.194, 199, which shows beyond doubt that in pursuance of its legislative concerns in the domain of "national security" the House has clothed the Un-American Activities Committee with pervasive authority to investigate Communist activities in this country. * * *

We are urged, however, to construe Rule XI so as at least to exclude the field of education from the Committee's compulsory authority. . . .

To the contrary, the legislative gloss on Rule XI is again compelling. Not only is there no indication that the House ever viewed the field of education as being outside the Committee's authority under Rule XI, but the legislative history affirmatively evinces House approval of this phase of the Committee's work. * * *

Undeniably a conviction for contempt under 2 U.S.C. §192 cannot stand unless the questions asked are pertinent to the subject matter of the investigation. *Watkins* v. *United States, supra,* 354 U.S. at pages 214-215. But the factors which led us to rest decision on this ground in *Watkins* were very different from those involved here.

In *Watkins* the petitioner had made specific objection to the Subcommittee's questions on the ground of pertinency; the question under inquiry had not been disclosed in any illuminating manner; and the questions asked the petitioner were not only amorphous on their face, but in some instances clearly foreign to the alleged subject matter of the investigation—"Communism in labor." *Id.,* 354 U.S. at pages 185, 209-215.

In contrast, petitioner in the case before us raised no objection on the ground of pertinency at the time any of the questions were put to him. * * *

We need not, however, rest decision on petitioner's failure to object on this score, for here "pertinency" was made to appear "with undisputable clarity," *Id.,* 354 U.S. at page 214. . . . What we deal with here is whether petitioner was sufficiently apprised of "the topic under inquiry" thus authorized "and the connective reasoning whereby the precise questions asked related to it." *Id.* 354 U.S. at page 215. . . .

The subject matter of the inquiry had been identified at the commencement of the investigation as Communist infiltration into the field of education . . . [U]nlike *Watkins,* 354 U.S. at pages 182–185, petitioner refused to answer questions as to his own Communist Party affiliations, whose pertinency of course was clear beyond doubt. * * *

The precise constitutional issue confronting us is whether the Subcommittee's inquiry into petitioner's past or present membership in the Communist Party transgressed the provisions of the First Amendment, which of course reach and limit congressional investigations. *Watkins, supra,* 354 U.S. at page 197.

The Court's past cases establish sure guides to decision. . . . Where First Amendment rights are asserted to bar governmental interrogation resolution of the issue always involves a balancing by the courts of the competing private and public interests at stake in the particular circumstances shown. These principles were recognized in the *Watkins* case. * * *

The first question is whether this investigation was related to a valid legislative purpose, for Congress may not constitutionally require an individual to disclose his political relationships or other private affairs except in relation to such a purpose. . . .

That Congress has wide power to legislate in the field of Communist activity in this Country, and to conduct appropriate investigations in aid thereof, is hardly debatable. . . . In the last analysis this power rests on the right of self-preservation, "the ultimate value of any society," *Dennis* v. *United States,* 341 U.S. 494,509. Justification for its exercise in turn rests on the long and widely accepted view that the tenets of the Communist Party include the ultimate overthrow of the Government of the United States by force and violence, a view which has been given formal expression by the Congress.

On these premises, this Court in its constitutional adjudications has consistently refused to view the Communist Party as an ordinary political party, and has upheld federal legislation aimed at the Communist problem which in a different context would certainly have raised constitutional issues of the gravest character. * * *

We think that investigatory power in this domain is not to be denied Congress solely because the field of education is involved. * * *

An investigation of advocacy of or preparation for overthrow certainly embraces the right to identify a witness as a member of the Communist Party (see *Barsky* v. *United States,* 83 U.S. App. D.C. 127), and to inquire into the various manifestations of the Party's tenets. . . .

Nor can we accept the further contention that this investigation should not be deemed to have been in furtherance of a legislative purpose because the true objective of the Committee and of the Congress was purely "exposure." So long as Congress acts in pursuance of its constitutional power, the judiciary lacks authority to intervene on the basis of the motives which spurred the exercise of that power. * * *

Finally, the record is barren of other factors which in themselves might sometimes lead to the conclusion that the individual interests at stake were not subordinate to those of the state. There is no indication in this record that the Subcommittee was attempting to pillory witnesses. * * *

Affirmed.

MR. JUSTICE BLACK, with whom THE CHIEF JUSTICE, and MR. JUSTICE DOUGLAS concur, dissenting.

On May 28, 1954, petitioner Lloyd Barenblatt, then 31 years old, and a teacher of psychology at Vassar College, was summoned to appear before a Subcommittee of the House Committee on Un-American Activities. . . . [B]efore Barenblatt appeared on June 28, his four-year contract with Vassar expired and was not renewed. He, therefore, came to the Committee as a private citizen without a job. . . . He asserted that the Committee was violating the Constitution by abridging freedom of speech, thought, press, and association, and by conducting legislative trials of known or suspected Communists which trespassed on the exclusive power of the judiciary. . . .

The Court today affirms, and thereby sanctions the use of the contempt power to enforce questioning by congressional committees in the realm of speech and association. I cannot agree with this disposition of the case for I believe that the resolution establishing the House Un-American Activities Committee and the questions that Committee asked Barenblatt violate the Constitution in several respects. (1) Rule XI creating the Committee authorizes such a sweeping, unlimited, all-inclusive and undiscriminating compulsory examination of witnesses in the field of speech, press, petition and assembly that it violates the procedural requirements of the Due Process Clause of the Fifth Amendment. (2) Compelling an answer to the questions asked Barenblatt abridges freedom of speech and association in contravention of the First Amendment. (3) The Committee proceedings were part of a legislative program to stigmatize and punish by public identification and exposure all witnesses considered by the Committee to be guilty of Communist affiliations, as well as all witnesses who refused to answer Committee questions on constitutional grounds; the Committee was thus improperly seeking to try, convict, and punish suspects, a task which the Constitution expressly denies to Congress and grants exclusively to the courts, to be exercised by them only after indictment and in full compliance with all the safeguards provided by the Bill of Rights.

It goes without saying that a law to be valid must be clear enough to make its commands understandable. For obvious reasons, the standard of certainty required in criminal statutes is more exacting than in noncriminal statutes. . . . For a statute broad enough to support infringement of speech, writings, thoughts and public assemblies, against the unequivocal command of the First Amendment necessarily leaves all persons to guess just what the law really means to cover, and fear of a wrong guess inevitably leads people to forego the very rights the Constitution sought to protect above all others. Vagueness becomes even more intolerable in this area if one accepts, as the Court today does, a balancing test to decide if First Amendment rights shall be protected. . . .

Measured by the foregoing standards, Rule XI cannot support any conviction for refusal to testify. In substance it authorizes the Committee to compel witnesses to give evidence about all "un-American propaganda," whether instigated in this country or abroad. The word "propaganda" seems to mean anything that people say, write, think or associate together about. The term "un-American" is equally vague. * * *

On the Court's own test, the issue is whether Barenblatt can know with sufficient certainty, at the time of his interrogation, that there is so compelling a need for his replies that infringement of his rights of free association is justified. The record does not disclose where Barenblatt can find what that need is. . . .

But even if Barenblatt could evaluate the importance to the Government of the information sought, Rule XI would still be too broad to support his conviction. For we are dealing here with governmental procedures which the Court itself admits reach to the very fringes of congressional power. In such cases more is required of legislatures than a vague delegation to be filled in later by mute acquiescence. If Congress wants ideas investigated, if it even wants them investigated in the field of education, it must be prepared to say so expressly and unequivocally. And it is not enough that a court through exhaustive research can establish, even conclusively, that Congress wished to allow the investigation. I can find no such unequivocal statement here.

For all these reasons, I would hold that Rule XI is too broad to be meaningful and cannot support petitioner's conviction. . . .

I do not agree that laws directly abridging First Amendment freedoms can be justified by a congressional or judicial balancing process. * * * Rule XI, on its face and as here applied, since it attempts inquiry into beliefs, not action—ideas and associations, not conduct—does just that. . . .

But even assuming what I cannot assume, that some balancing is proper in this case, I feel that the Court after stating the test ignores it completely. At most it balances the right of the Government to preserve itself, against Barenblatt's right to refrain from revealing Communist affiliations. Such a balance, however, mistakes the factors to be weighed. In the first place, it completely leaves out the real interest in Barenblatt's silence, the interest of the people as a whole in being able to join organizations, advocate causes and make political "mistakes" without later being subjected to governmental penalties for having dared to think for themselves. It is this right, the right to err politically, which keeps us strong as a Nation. * * * It is admitted that this Committee can only seek information for the purpose of suggesting laws, and that Congress' power to make laws in the realm of speech and association is quite limited, even on the Court's test. Its interest in making such laws in the field of education, primarily a state function, is clearly narrower still. Yet the Court styles this attenuated interest self-preservation and allows it to overcome the need our country has to let us all think, speak, and associate politically as we like and without fear of reprisal. . . .

Moreover, I cannot agree with the Court's notion that First Amendment freedoms must be abridged in order to "preserve" our country. That notion rests on the unarticulated premise that this Nation's security hangs upon its power to punish people because of what they think, speak or write about, or because of those with whom they associate for political purposes. The Government, in its brief, virtually admits this position when it speaks of the "communication of unlawful ideas." I challenge this premise, and deny that ideas can be proscribed under our Constitution. . . . Our Constitution assumes that the common sense of the people and their attachment to our country will enable them, after free discussion, to withstand ideas that are wrong. . . .

The Court implies, however, that the ordinary rules and requirements of the Constitution do not apply because the Committee is merely after Communists and they do not constitute a political party but only a criminal gang. * * *

The fact is that once we allow any group which has some political aims or ideas to be driven from the ballot and from the battle for men's minds because some of its members are bad and some of its tenets are illegal, no group is safe. * * *

It is, sadly, no answer to say that this Court will not allow the trend to overwhelm us; that today's holding will be strictly confined to "Communists," as the Court's language implies. This decision can no more be contained than could the holding in *American Communications Ass'n., C.I.O.* v. *Douds*, 339 U.S. 382.

* * * Today, Communists or suspected Communists have been denied an opportunity to work as government employees, lawyers, doctors, teachers, pharmacists, veterinarians, subway conductors, industrial workers and in just about any other job. . . . In today's holding they are singled out and, as a class, are subjected to inquisitions which the Court suggests would be unconstitutional but for the fact of "Communism." Nevertheless, this Court still sits! . . .

Finally, I think Barenblatt's conviction violates the Constitution because the chief aim, purpose and practice of the House Un-American Activities Committee, as disclosed by its many reports, is to try witnesses and punish them because they are or have been Communists or because they refuse to admit or deny Communist affiliations. The punishment imposed is generally punishment by humiliation and public shame. * * *

The same intent to expose and punish is manifest in the Committee's investigation which led to Barenblatt's conviction. The declared purpose of the invetigation was to identify to the people of Michigan the individuals responsible for the, alleged, Communist success there. * * *

. . . Such publicity is clearly punishment, and the Constitution allows only one way in which people can be convicted and punished. . . . Thus if communism is to be made a crime, and Communists are to be subjected to "pains and penalties," I would still hold this conviction bad, for the crime of communism like all others, can be punished only by court and jury after a trial with all judicial safeguards. * * *

Ultimately all the questions in this case really boil down to one— whether we as a people will try fearfully and futilely to preserve democracy by adopting totalitarian methods, or whether in accordance with our traditions and our Constitution we will have the confidence and courage to be free.

I would reverse this conviction. . . .

MR. JUSTICE BRENNAN, dissenting.

I would reverse this conviction. . . . An investigation in which the processes of law-making and law-evaluating are submerged entirely in exposure of individual behavior—in adjudication, of a sort, through the exposure process—is outside the constitutional pale of congressional inquiry. . . .

Loyalty and Security

Within the framework of our constitutional guarantees of freedom of speech and association, and the other protections of the Bill of Rights, there are many legal difficulties inherent in a "loyalty" program that tries to weed out "disloyal" persons employed by the government. One basic dilemma is the difficulty of defining the word itself in concrete and constitutional terms. Despite the intricacies inherent in such programs, they have been set up for those in the civil service, the armed services, the Atomic Energy Commission, port security, and most recently, industrial security. This last addition was made because in *Greene* v. *McElroy*, (360 U.S. 474, 79 S. Ct. 1400; 1959), the Court determined that there was no Presidential or Congressional authorization for the elaborate clearance program, "which embodies procedures traditionally believed to be inadequate to protect affected persons."[2]

Beyond identifying those who are secretly employed by foreign powers, standards must be evolved. Does adherence to unpopular political views indicate disloyalty? How much can the free expression of ideas be curbed? As a practical matter, should there be an investigation of those who may be subject to conflicts which might make them disloyal under special circumstances? Is not the best defense against possible disloyalty an investigation to reveal the individual's background, ideas, and personal weaknesses? Is it not better to discharge, or to refuse to employ, those whose weaknesses might make them a target for blackmail by an enemy of the country? Should the individual investigated be informed of the derogatory remarks made about him? Should

[2] *Greene* v. *McElroy*, 360 U.S. 474, p. 504.

the person who made them be identified, so that the circumstances in which the remarks were made could be explained, or prejudice pointed out? How can the rights of the employee, or prospective employee, be protected? What rights does the employee have? Does not such a program abridge the rights of freedom of speech and association? Is there a violation of the due process clause of the Fifth or Fourteenth Amendments? Is dismissal punishment? These constitutional questions have not yet been resolved.

The program was first established by President Truman who issued Executive Order 9835, establishing the procedure to be followed in such investigations. The two basic problems were stating the criteria to be used in determining loyalty, and establishing procedural rights to be given the employee.

The program has had three successive criteria for use in determining the individual's loyalty. The first standard was, "on all the evidence reasonable grounds exist for belief that the person involved is disloyal to the Government." In 1951, the standard was tightened, and became "on all the evidence there is reasonable doubt as to the loyalty of the person involved to the Government of the United States." The third standard, adopted in 1953, was that employment was not "clearly consistent with the interests of national security." The Supreme Court has never passed upon the constitutionality of these criteria, nor of the program. Cases have, however, touched certain peripheral matters.

Under Executive Order 9835 the Attorney General was given power to compile a list of foreign or domestic organizations which were "totalitarian, fascist, communist, or subversive." "Membership in, affiliation with or sympathetic association with" any of these organization was a factor to be considered in determining whether "on all the evidence reasonable grounds exist for belief that the person involved is disloyal to the Government." There was no requirement that the organization be given a hearing before being listed as subversive. Three organizations so listed brought action against the Attorney General for declaratory and injunctive relief. The three cases were reviewed together by the Supreme Court.

These cases also illustrate the hazards inherent in technical pleadings. The Attorney General filed a motion to dismiss each case, on the grounds that the complainants had no justiciable case. But such a motion has a special meaning: the party filing the motion says, in effect, that *taking the facts alleged in the complaint as true,* the complainant has no justiciable case. For purposes of argument, therefore, the Supreme Court was bound to take the facts alleged in the complaints as true, even though there was no evidence offered in the trial court to sustain or controvert those alleged facts. Indeed there was no trial: the whole case was based upon pleadings, and not upon the proof commonly offered in a trial. But even though the decision was based on such technicalities, unencumbered by evidence, there was no unanimity among the Justices, who were not even in agreement about what were "facts" in the complaints. After this decision, organizations which seemed to come within the purview of the statute were given an opportunity for a hearing before being listed. But the constitutional issue was not reached in this case, nor in any subsequent case.

> *Joint Anti-Fascist Refugee Committee* v. *McGrath, Atty. Gen. of the United States, et al.;*
> *National Council of American-Soviet Friendship, Inc., et al.* v. *McGrath, Atty. Gen. of the United States, et al.;*
> *International Workers Order, Inc., et al.* v. *McGrath, Atty. Gen. of the United States, et al.,*
> 341 U.S. 123, 71 S. Ct. 624 (1951)

MR. JUSTICE BURTON announced the judgment of the Court and delivered the following opinion, in which MR. JUSTICE DOUGLAS joins.

In each of these cases the same issue is raised by the dismissal of a complaint for its failure to state a claim upon which relief can be granted. That issue is whether, in the face of the facts alleged in the complaint and therefore admitted by the motion to dismiss, the Attorney General of the United States has authority to include the complaining organization in a list of organizations designated by him as Communist and furnished by him to the Loyalty Review Board of the United States Civil Service Commission. He claims to derive authority to do this from provisions in Part III, § 3, of Executive Order No. 9835, issued by the President, March 21, 1947, 5 U.S.C.A. § 631 note:

"Part III—Responsibilities of Civil Service Commission

✿   ✿   ✿

"3. The Loyalty Review Board shall currently be furnished by the Department of Justice the name of each foreign or domestic organization, association, movement, group or combination of persons which the Attorney General, after appropriate investigation and determination, designates as totalitarian, fascist, communist or subversive, or as having adopted a policy of advocating or approving the commission of acts of force or violence to deny others their rights under the Constitution of the United States, or as seeking to alter the form of government of the United States by unconstitutional means.

"a. The Loyalty Review Board shall disseminate such information to all departments and agencies."

The respective complaints describe the complaining organizations as engaged in charitable or civic activities or in the business of fraternal insurance. Each implies an attitude of cooperation and helpfulness, rather than one of hostility or disloyalty, on the part of the organization toward the United States. Two of the complaints deny expressly that the organization is within any classification specified in Part III, § 3, of the order.

For the reasons hereinafter stated, we conclude that, *if the allegations of the complaints are taken as true* (as they must be on the motions to dismiss), the Executive Order does not authorize the Attorney General to furnish the Loyalty Review Board with a list containing such a designation as he gave to each of these organizations without other justification. Under such circumstances his own admissions render his designations patently arbitrary because they are contrary to the alleged and uncontroverted facts constituting the entire record before us. The complaining organizations have not been afforded any opportunity to substantiate their allegations, but at this stage of the proceedings the Attorney General has chosen not to deny their allegations and has not otherwise placed them in issue.

Whatever may be his authority to designate these organizations as Communist upon undisclosed facts in his possession, he has not chosen to limit himself to that authorization. By his present procedure he has claimed authority so to designate them upon the very facts alleged by them in their own complaints. Self-serving or not, those allegations do not state facts from which alone a reasonable determination can be derived that the organizations are Communist. To defend such a designation of them, on the basis of the complaints alone, is an assertion of Presidential authority so to designate an organization at the option of the Attorney General without reliance upon either disclosed or undisclosed facts supplying a reasonable basis for the determination. It is that, and only that outer limit of the authority of the Attorney General that is now before us. . . . Executive Order No. 9835 . . . announced the President's Employees Loyalty Program in the Executive Branch of the Government. . . . It provides for the Loyalty Review Board and sets up a standard for refusals of and removals from employment on grounds relating to loyalty. It outlines the use to be made in that connection of the list of organizations to be furnished by the Attorney General. The organizations to be designated on that list are not limited to those having federal employees in their memberships. They may even exclude such employees from membership. Accordingly, the impact of the Attorney General's list is by no means limited to persons who are subject to the Employees Loyalty Program.

The Attorney General included each of the complaining organizations in the list he furnished to the Loyalty Review Board November 24, 1947. That list was disseminated by the Board to all departments and agencies of the United States December 4, 1947. 13 Fed. Reg. 1473. The complaints allege that such action resulted in nationwide publicity and caused the injuries to the complaining organizations which are detailed later. . . . We granted certiorari because of the importance of the issues and their relation to the Employees Loyalty Program. . . .

No. 8. – The Refugee Committee Case

The complainant is the Joint Anti-Fascist Refugee Committee, an unincorporated association in the City and State of New York. It is the petitioner here. The . . . Attorney General, . . . and the members of the Loyalty Review Board . . . are the respondents here.

The following statement, based on the allegations of the complaint, summarizes the situation before us: The complainant is "a charitable organization engaged in relief work" which carried on its relief activities from 1942 to 1946 under a license from the President's War Relief Control Board. Thereafter, it voluntarily submitted its program, budgets and audits for inspection by the Advisory Committee on Voluntary Foreign Aid of the United States Government. Since its inception, it has, through voluntary contributions, raised and disbursed funds for the benefit of anti-Fascist refugees who assisted the Government of Spain against its overthrow by force and violence. The organization's aims and purposes "are to raise, administer and distribute funds for the relief and rehabilitation of Spanish Republicans in exile and other anti-fascist refugees who fought in the war against Franco."

It has disbursed $1,011,448 in cash, and $217,903 in kind, for the relief of anti-fascist refugees and their families. . . . The acts of the Attorney General and the Loyalty Review Board, purporting to be taken by them under authority of the Executive Order, have seriously and irreparably impaired, and will continue to so impair, the reputation of the organization and the moral support and good will of the American people necessary for the continuance of its charitable activities. Upon information and belief, these acts have caused many contributors, especially present and prospective civil servants, to reduce or discontinue their contributions to the organization; members and participants in its activities have been "vilified and subjected to public shame, disgrace, ridicule and obloquy * * *" thereby inflicting upon it economic injury and discouraging participation in its activities. . . .

This complaint does not contain an express denial that the complaining organization is within the classifications named in Part III, § 3, of Executive Order No. 9835. It does, however, state that the actions of the Attorney General and the Loyalty Review Board which are complained of are unauthorized and without warrant in law and amount to a deprivation of the complainant's rights in violation of the Constitution; that Executive Order No. 9835, on its face and as construed and applied, violates the First, Fifth, Ninth and Tenth Amendments to the Constitution of the United States. . . .

No. 7. – The National Council Case

In this case the court below relied upon its decision in the Refugee Committee case and reached the same result, *per curiam* (unreported). Except as indicated below in our summary of the facts alleged, this case, for our purposes, is like the first. . . . The complaint alleges that all of the complainants are seriously and irreparably injured in their capacity to conduct the National Council's educational, cultural and fund-raising program, and that the individual complainants have suffered personal losses such as the removal of one from an assistant rectorship of a church, . . . The complaint expressly states that—"In all its activities the National Council has sought to further the best interests of the American people by lawful, peaceful and constitutional means. It has never in any way engaged in any conduct or activity which provides any basis for it to be designated as 'totalitarian, fascist, communist or subversive, or as having adopted a policy of advocating or approving the commission of acts of force or violence to deny others their rights under the Constitution of the United States, or as seeking to alter the form of government of the United States by unconstitutional means.'"

No. 71.—The International Workers Case

The complaining organization, which is the petitioner here, is a fraternal benefit society, organized in 1930 as a corporation under the Insurance Law of the State of New York, McK.Consol.Laws, c. 28, operating for the mutual benefit of its members and their beneficiaries and not for profit. . . . Among the allegations of damage, made upon information and belief, the complaint states that, solely as a result of the respondents' acts, there have been instituted against the order and its members a multiplicity of administrative proceedings, including those to rescind licenses, franchises, or tax exemptions, or to impede the naturalization of its members. . . . If, upon the allegations in any of these complaints, it had appeared that the acts of the respondents, from which relief was sought, were authorized by the President under his Executive Order No. 9835, the case would have bristled with constitutional issues. . . . It is our obligation, however, not to reach those issues unless the allegations before us squarely present them. See *United States* v. *Lovett,* 328 U.S. 303, 320.

The Executive Order contains no express or implied attempt to confer power on anyone to act arbitrarily or capriciously—even assuming a constitutional power to do so. The order includes in the purposes of the President's program not only the protection of the United States against disloyal employees but the "equal protection" of loyal employees against unfounded accusations of disloyalty. . . . The standards stated for refusal of and removal from employment require that "on all the evidence, reasonable grounds [shall] exist for belief that the person involved is disloyal * * *." . . . The order contains the express requirement that each designation of an organization by the Attorney General on such a list shall be made only after an "appropriate * * * determination" as prescribed. . . . An "appropriate" governmental "determination" must be the result of a process of reasoning. It cannot be an arbitrary fiat contrary to the known facts. This is inherent in the meaning of "determination." It is implicit in a government of laws and not of men. Where an act of an official plainly falls outside of the scope of his authority, he does not make that act legal by doing it and then invoking the doctrine of administrative construction to cover it. It remains, therefore, for us to decide whether, *on the face of these complaints,* the Attorney General is acting within his authority in furnishing the Loyalty Review Board with a designation of the complaining organizations either as "Communist" or as within any other classification of Part III, § 3, of the order. . . . The inclusion of any of the complaining organizations in the designated list solely on the facts alleged in the respective complaints, which must be the basis for our decision here, is therefore an arbitrary and unauthorized act. In the two cases where the complaint specifically alleges the factual absence of any basis for the designation, and the respondents' motion admits that allegation, the designation is necessarily contrary to the record. . . .

Since we find that the conduct ascribed to the Attorney General by the complaints is patently arbitrary, the deference ordinarily due administrative construction of an administrative order is not sufficient to bring his alleged conduct within the authority conferred by Executive Order No. 9835. . . .

When the acts of the Attorney General and of the members of the Loyalty Review Board are stripped of the Presidential authorization claimed for them by the respondents, they stand, on the face of these complaints, as unauthorized publications of admittedly unfounded designations of the complaining organizations as "Communist." Their effect is to cripple the functioning and damage the reputation of those organizations in their respective communities and in the nation. The complaints, on that basis, sufficiently charge that such acts violate each complaining organization's common-law right to be free from defamation. . . .

. . . These complaints ask only for declaratory and injunctive relief striking the names of the designated organizations from the Attorney General's published list and, as far as practicable, correcting the public records.

The respondents are not immune from such a proceeding. . . .

Finally, the standing of the petitioners to bring these suits is clear. The touchstone to justiciability is injury to a legally protected right and the right of a bona fide charitable organization to carry on its work, free from defamatory statements of the kind discussed, is such a right. . . . We long have granted relief to parties whose legal rights have been violated by unlawful public action, although such action made no direct demands upon them. *Columbia Broadcasting System* v. *United States,* 316 U.S. 407. . . . The complaints here amply allege past and impending serious damages caused by the actions of which the petitioners complain.

Nothing we have said purports to adjudicate the truth of petitioners' allegations that they are not in fact communistic. We have assumed that the designations made by the Attorney General are arbitrary because we are compelled to make that assumption by his motions to dismiss the complaints. Whether the complaining organizations are in fact communistic or whether the Attorney General possesses information from which he could reasonably find them to be so must await determination by the District Court upon remand. . . .   *Reversed and remanded.* . . .

MR. JUSTICE BLACK, concurring. . . .
. . . In the present climate of public opinion it appears certain that the Attorney General's much publicized findings, regardless of their truth or falsity, are the practical equivalents of confiscation and death sentences for any blacklisted organization not possessing extraordinary financial, political or religious prestige and influence. ✻ ✻ ✻

More fundamentally, however, in my judgment the executive has no constitutional authority, with or without a hearing, officially to prepare and publish the lists challenged by petitioners. In the first place, the system adopted effectively punishes many organizations and their members merely because of their political beliefs and utterances, and to this extent smacks of a most evil type of censorship. This cannot be reconciled with the First Amendment as I interpret it. See my dissent in *American Communications Ass'n, C. I. O.* v. *Douds,* 339 U.S. 382, 445. Moreover, officially prepared and proclaimed governmental blacklists possess almost every quality of bills of attainder, the use of which was from the beginning forbidden to both national and state governments. U.S. Const. Art. I, §§ 9, 10. It is true that the classic bill of attainder was a condemnation by the legislature following investigation by that body, see *United States* v. *Lovett,* 328 U.S. 303, while in the present case the Attorney General performed the official tasks. But I cannot believe that the authors of the Constitution, who outlawed the bill of attainder, inadvertently endowed the executive with power to engage in the same tyrannical practices that had made the bill such an odious institution. ✻ ✻ ✻

A number of fundamental problems presented by the loyalty program must be faced. The first is that the person investigated is not on trial; at most, he is entitled to an administrative hearing, in which the basic protections of the trial process do not apply. Second, there is no presumption of innocence; in fact, the burden of proving himself worthy of maintaining his position is upon the employee. Third, there is no right to summons records of the investigatory agency. Fourth, the names of those who have given the information upon which the case is based are unknown. That information is also withheld from those whose responsibility it is to give the individual a hearing. Fifth, there is no right of confrontation, and a virtual certainty that the informers were not under oath. There are, in other words, none of the procedural protections worked out by courts over the centuries in England and the United States.

There are other hazards, less obvious, but nonetheless real. There is no way of testing the attitude of the person who gave derogatory information; since that person is not at the hearing, it is not possible to cross-examine him to reveal bias, mistakes, or inaccuracies. Since the information actually given to the investigator is unknown, there is no way of explaining it or putting it in context. There is no certainty that the investigator has the skills an experienced attorney has developed to ascertain the facts of the matters at hand. Hearings have been conducted by persons untrained in the law, untrained in legal procedure, or in recognizing relevant testimony. Moreover, each change in standards has required a new investigation and reassessment of the employee.

Finally, there is the problem of expense. Excluding expense to the government, the total of which is not known, there is expense to the worker. He may be represented by an attorney, he may have witnesses, and he may present other information for the consideration of the board. But while he is awaiting hearing he is suspended from his work, without pay, and is reinstated only when he is cleared. That may take as long as two years. There are probably relatively few government employees who can wait for clearance; a quiet resignation, without a hearing, is sometimes the only course open.

Because of the sensitivity of the area, the strong possibility of uncorrectable unfairness to the employee, and because due process procedures as they are known to the courts are not available, the Supreme Court has been careful to protect whatever procedural rights the employee may have. Justices Douglas and Black have consistently held that the constitutional questions should be reached.

In *Cole* v. *Young* (351 U.S. 536, 76 S. Ct. 861; 1956), the Court defined the term "national security" as that term was used in 5 U.S.C.A. s §§22– 1, 22– 3. Certain department and agency heads of the government were given summary suspension and dismissal powers when deemed necessary "in the interest of the national security of the United States." Mr. Cole was a preference-eligible veteran under the Veteran's Preference Act of 1944, holding a position as a food and drug inspector for New York. He was suspended, and appealed. The Court spelled out the meaning of "national security":

> (1) . . . the term "national security" is used in the Act in a definite and limited sense and relates only to those activities which are directly concerned with the Nation's safety, as distinguished from the general welfare; and (2) that no determination has been made that petitioner's position was affected with the "national security," as that term is used in the Act.[3]

[3]*Cole* v. *Young*, 351 U.S. 536, p. 543.

CHAPTER SIX

Assembly and Association; Travel; Desegregation

Assembly and Association

BECAUSE OF THE close association in everyday life between freedom of speech, press, and religion on one hand, and freedom of assembly on the other, as a practical matter it is sometimes difficult to separate the two areas. But the First Amendment makes a distinction. That amendment reads:

> Congress shall make no law respecting an establishment of religion, or prohibiting the free exercise thereof; or abridging the freedom of speech, or of the press; or the right of the people peaceably to assemble, and to petition the Government for a redress of grievances.

Does the last clause mean that the right of the people peaceably to assemble is limited to the purpose of petitioning the Government for a redress of grievances? In *U.S.* v. *Cruikshank,* 92 U.S. 542 (1876), it was so interpreted. Not until sixty-one years later was this restriction removed and the right to assemble recognized to be as basic and as applicable to the states under the Fourteenth Amendment as freedom of speech and press.

De Jonge v. *Oregon,* 299 U.S. 353, 57 S. Ct. 255 (1937)

> . . . We are concerned with but one of the described offenses and with the validity of the statute in this particular application. The charge is that appellant assisted in the conduct of a meeting which was called under the auspices of the Communist Party, an organization advocating criminal syndicalism. The defense was that the meeting was public and orderly and was held for a lawful purpose. . . . Appellant moved for a direction of acquittal, contending that the statute as applied to him, for merely assisting at a meeting called by the Communist Party at which nothing unlawful was done or advocated, violated the due process clause of the Fourteenth Amendment of the Constitution of the United States.

This contention was overruled. Appellant was found guilty as charged. * * *

On the theory that this was a charge that criminal syndicalism and sabotage were advocated at the meeting in question, defendant moved for acquittal insisting that the evidence was insufficient to warrant his conviction. * * *

We must take the indictment as thus construed. . . . His sole offense as charged, and for which he was convicted and sentenced to imprisonment for seven years, was that he had assisted in the conduct of a public meeting, albeit otherwise lawful, which was held under the auspices of the Communist Party.

The broad reach of the statute as thus applied is plain. * * * Thus if the Communist Party had called a public meeting in Portland to discuss the tariff, or the foreign policy of the Government, or taxation, or relief, . . . every speaker who assisted in the conduct of the meeting would be equally guilty with the defendant in this case, upon the charge as here defined and sustained. . . .

While the States are entitled to protect themselves from the abuse of the privileges of our institutions through an attempted substitution of force and violence in the place of peaceful political action in order to effect revolutionary changes in government, none of our decisions go to the length of sustaining such a curtailment of the right of free speech and assembly as the Oregon statute demands in its present application. . . .

Freedom of speech and of the press are fundamental rights which are safeguarded by the due process clause of the Fourteenth Amendment of the Federal Constitution. *Gitlow* v. *New York, supra*, p. 666. . . . The right of peaceable assembly is a right cognate to those of free speech and free press and is equally fundamental. The First Amendment of the Federal Constitution expressly guarantees that right against abridgment by Congress. But explicit mention there does not argue exclusion elsewhere. For the right is one that cannot be denied without violating those fundamental principles of liberty and justice which lie at the base of all civil and political institutions, — principles which the Fourteenth Amendment embodies in the general terms of its due process clause. *Hebert* v. *Louisiana*, 272 U.S. 312, 316. . . .

. . . But the legislative intervention can find constitutional justification only by dealing with the abuse. The rights themselves must not be curtailed. The greater the importance of safeguarding the community from incitements to the overthrow of our institutions by force and violence, the more imperative is the need to preserve inviolate the constitutional rights of free speech, free press and free assembly in order to maintain the opportunity for free political discussion, to the end that government may be responsive to the will of the people and that changes, if desired, may be obtained by peaceful means. Therein lies the security of the Republic, the very foundation of constitutional government.

It follows from these considerations that, consistently with the Federal Constitution, peaceable assembly for lawful discussion cannot be made a crime. The holding of meetings for peaceable political action cannot be proscribed. Those who assist in the conduct of such meetings cannot be branded as criminals on that score. The question, if the rights of free speech and peaceable assembly are to be preserved, is not as to the auspices under which the meeting is held but as to its purpose; not as to the relations of the speakers, but whether their utterances transcend the bounds of the freedom of speech which the Constitution protects. . . .

The defendant was none the less entitled to discuss the public issues of the day and thus in a lawful manner, without incitement to violence or crime, to seek redress of alleged grievances. That was of the essence of his guaranteed personal liberty.

We hold that the Oregon statute as applied to the particular charge as defined by the state court is repugnant to the due process clause of the Fourteenth Amendment. The judgment of conviction is reversed. . . .

The exercise of freedom of speech and religion so often involves a gathering of people that conflicts often affect more than one right under the First Amendment. Because freedom of speech and religion occupy a "preferred position," in the words of the Court, many decisions are made on the basis of these rights, although the freedom to assemble is also in question.

When the rights of one individual conflict with those of another, the problem is to preserve the rights of both. Public safety may provide an answer, by requiring a license if public facilities are to be used. But reaching a solution is sometimes handicapped by the majority's preference for one right over another, or one viewpoint over another. Nonetheless, in the interests of orderly government there must be a solution to the conflict. When the state does intervene, by exercising the police power or adopting a statute defining that power, the issue is the exact point at which exercise of the police power must stop in order not to encroach upon the constitutional rights of individuals. However exactly the power is defined, it may still be applied with partiality. Such an application in itself may raise a constitutional issue.

Edwards v. *South Carolina*, 372 U.S. 229, 83 S. Ct. 680 (1963)

MR. JUSTICE STEWART delivered the opinion of the Court.

The petitioners, 187 in number, were convicted in a magistrate's court in Columbia, South Carolina, of the common-law crime of breach of the peace. Their convictions were ultimately affirmed by the South Carolina Supreme Court. . . . We granted certiorari . . .

to consider the claim that these convictions cannot be squared with the Fourteenth Amendment of the United States Constitution.

There was no substantial conflict in the trial evidence. Late in the morning of March 2, 1961, the petitioners, high school and college students of the Negro race, met at the Zion Baptist Church in Columbia. From there, at about noon, they walked in separate groups of about 15 to the South Carolina State House grounds, an area of two city blocks open to the general public. Their purpose was "to submit a protest to the citizens of South Carolina . . . , our feelings and our dissatisfaction with the present condition of discriminatory actions against Negroes, in general, and to let them know that we were dissatisfied and that we would like for the laws which prohibited Negro privileges in this State to be removed."

Already on the State House grounds when the petitioners arrived were 30 or more law enforcement officers. . . . Each group of petitioners entered the grounds through a driveway and parking area known in the record as the "horseshoe." As they entered, they were told by the law enforcement officials that "they had a right, as a citizen, to go through the State House grounds, as any other citizen has, as long as they were peaceful." During the next half hour or 45 minutes, the petitioners, in the same small groups, walked single file or two abreast in an orderly way through the grounds, each group carrying placards bearing such messages as "I am proud to be a Negro," and "Down with segregation."

During this time a crowd of some 200 to 300 onlookers had collected in the horseshoe area and on the adjacent sidewalks. There was no evidence to suggest that these onlookers were anything but curious, and no evidence at all of any threatening remarks, hostile gestures, or offensive language on the part of any member of the crowd. The City Manager testified that he recognized some of the onlookers, whom he did not identify, as "possible trouble makers," but his subsequent testimony made clear that nobody among the crowd actually caused or threatened any trouble. There was no obstruction of pedestrian or vehicular traffic within the State House grounds. . . .

In the situation and under the circumstances thus described, the police authorities advised the petitioners that they would be arrested if they did not disperse within 15 minutes. Instead of dispersing, the petitioners engaged in what the City Manager described as "boisterous," "loud," and "flamboyant" conduct, which, as his later testimony made clear, consisted of listening to a "religious harangue" by one of their leaders, and loudly singing "The Star Spangled Banner" and other patriotic and religious songs, while stamping their feet and clapping their hands. After 15 minutes had passed, the police arrested the petitioners and marched them off to jail.

Upon this evidence the state trial court convicted the petitioners of breach of the peace. . . .

The state courts have held that the petitioners' conduct constituted breach of the peace under state law, and we may accept their decision as binding upon us to that extent. But it nevertheless remains our duty in a case such as this to make an independent examination of the whole record. . . . And it is clear to us that in arresting, convicting, and punishing the petitioners under the circumstances disclosed by this record, South Carolina infringed the petitioners' constitutionally protected rights of free speech, free assembly, and freedom to petition for redress of their grievances.

It has long been established that these First Amendment freedoms are protected by the Fourteenth Amendment from invasion by the States. . . . The circumstances in this case reflect an exercise of these basic constitutional rights in their most pristine and classic form. The petitioners . . . peaceably assembled at the site of the State Government and there peaceably expressed their grievances "to the citizens of South Carolina, along with the Legislative Bodies of South Carolina." Not until they were told by police officials that they must disperse on pain of arrest did they do more. . . . There was no violence or threat of violence on their part, or on the part of any member of the crowd watching them. Police protection was "ample." ° ° °

. . . These petitioners were convicted of an offense so generalized as to be, in the words of the South Carolina Supreme Court, "not susceptible of exact definition." And they were convicted upon evidence which showed no more than that the opinions which they were peaceably expressing were sufficiently opposed to the views of the majority of the community to attract a crowd and necessitate police protection.

The Fourteenth Amendment does not permit a State to make criminal the peaceful expression of unpopular views. . . . Speech is often provocative and challenging. . . . *Terminiello* v. *Chicago*, 337 U.S. 1, 4–5, . . .

As Chief Justice Hughes wrote in *Stromberg* v. *California*, "The maintenance of the opportunity for free political discussion to the end that government may be responsive to the will of the people and that changes may be obtained by lawful means, an opportunity essential to the security of the Republic, is a fundamental principle of our constitutional system. A statute which upon its face, and as authoritatively construed, is so vague and indefinite as to permit the punishment of the fair use of this opportunity is repugnant to the guaranty of liberty contained in the Fourteenth Amendment. ° ° °" 283 U.S. 359, 369.

For these reasons we conclude that these criminal convictions cannot stand.   *Reversed.*

MR. JUSTICE CLARK, dissenting.

. . . Petitioners, of course, had a right to peaceable assembly, to espouse their cause and to petition, but in my view the manner in which they exercised those rights was by no means the passive demonstration which this Court relates; rather, as the City Manager of Columbia testified, "a dangerous situation was building up" which

South Carolina's courts expressly found had created "an actual interference with traffic and an imminently threatened disturbance of the peace of the community." Since the Court does not attack the state courts' findings and accepts the convictions as "binding" to the extent that the petitioners' conduct constituted a breach of the peace, it is difficult for me to understand its understatement of the facts and reversal of the convictions.

The priceless character of First Amendment freedoms cannot be gainsaid, but it does not follow that they are absolutes immune from necessary state action, reasonably designed for the protection of society. . . . For that reason it is our duty to consider the context in which the arrests here were made. . . . It is undisputed that the city officials specifically granted petitioners permission to assemble, imposing only the requirement that they be "peaceful." Petitioners then gathered on the State House grounds, during a General Assembly session, in a large number of almost 200, marching and carrying placards with slogans such as "Down with segregation" and "You may jail our bodies but not our souls." Some of them were singing.

The activity continued for approximately 45 minutes, during the busy noon-hour period, while a crowd of some 300 persons congregated in front of the State House and around the area directly in front of its entrance. . . . It was only after the large crowd had gathered, among which the City Manager and Chief of Police recognized potential troublemakers, and which together with the students had become massed on and around the "horseshoe" so closely that vehicular and pedestrian traffic was materially impeded, that any action against the petitioners was taken. Then the City Manager in . . . the utmost good faith, decided that danger to peace and safety was imminent. . . . He approached the recognized leader of the petitioners and requested him to tell the various groups of petitioners to disperse within 15 minutes, failing which they would be arrested. . . .

Ultimately, the petitioners were arrested, as they apparently planned from the beginning, and convicted on evidence the sufficiency of which the Court does not challenge. The question thus seems to me whether a State is constitutionally prohibited from enforcing laws to prevent breach of the peace in a situation where city officials in good faith believe, and the record shows, that disorder and violence are imminent, merely because the activities constituting that breach contain claimed elements of constitutionally protected speech and assembly. To me the answer under our cases is clearly in the negative. * * *

The gravity of the danger here surely needs no further explication. . . . This record . . . shows no steps backward from a standard of "clear and present danger." But to say that the police may not intervene until the riot had occurred is like keeping out the doctor until the patient dies. I cannot subscribe to such a doctrine. * * *

I would affirm the convictions.

There are many other ways to interfere with the right of assembly and association, as shown by the lengthy litigation involving various branches of the National Association for the Advancement of Colored People. Because of the Association's activity in behalf of what it believes are the individual's constitutional rights, it has naturally aroused opposition among those who believe that those constitutional rights are adequately protected. The most effective way to control or eliminate the organization and its activities would seem to be by use of the state's power over corporations.

A corporation is an artificial entity with limited powers, created by the state or federal government. The entity has certain attributes of a person, but because it is not in fact a person, it has limitations a person does not have. A state may restrict the types of corporations it will charter, or limit the purposes for which a corporation may be organized. A state need not, for instance, grant a charter to an organization planning to conduct a gambling establishment when gambling is against the state's public policy. Nor need it allow a corporation organized in another state to conduct a gambling business within its borders. If there is no conflict with public policy, foreign corporations (that is, corporations organized in some other state) are commonly admitted to do business within a state, but at the time of admittance the state may place special restrictions upon them.

The state may not prevent a corporation from exercising such rights as a "person" which judicial interpretation has given it under the federal constitution. On the other hand, not being a "citizen" of a state, it is not entitled to the privileges and immunities enjoyed by citizens.

Commonly, state statutes apply to various types of corporations: perhaps a special statute on corporations organized for commercial banking, one on those organized for educational and charitable purposes, and such others as the state may deem appropriate. A statute on general regulations applies to all corporations: such matters as filing the names of the corporation officers in a place specified, requirements on annual reports, and similar matters. These statutes can be amended as needed. Such an amendment was the reason for the appeal in *National Association for the Advancement of Colored People* v. *Alabama*. The initial decision in this case was only the beginning of litigation.

> *National Association for the Advancement of Colored People* v.
> *Alabama,* 357 U.S. 449, 78 S. Ct. 1163 (1958)
> MR. JUSTICE HARLAN delivered the opinion of the Court.
> . . . The question presented is whether Alabama, consistently

with the Due Process Clause of the Fourteenth Amendment, can compel petitioner to reveal to the State's Attorney General the names and addresses of all its Alabama members and agents, without regard to their positions or functions in the Association. The judgment of contempt was based upon petitioner's refusal to comply fully with a court order requiring in part the production of membership lists. Petitioner's claim is that the order, in the circumstances shown by this record, violated rights assured to petitioner and its members under the Constitution.

Alabama has a statute similar to those of many other States which requires foreign corporations, except as exempted, to qualify before doing business by filing the corporate charter with the Secretary of State and designating a place of business and an agent to receive service of process. The statute imposes a fine on a corporation transacting intrastate business before qualifying and provides for criminal prosecution of officers of such a corporation. The National Association for the Advancement of Colored People is a nonprofit membership corporation organized under the laws of New York. Its purposes, fostered on a nationwide basis, are those indicated by its name,* and it operates through chartered affiliates which are independent unincorporated associations, with membership therein equivalent to membership in petitioner. The first Alabama affiliates were chartered in 1918. Since that time the aims of the Association have been advanced through activities of its affiliates, and in 1951 the Association itself opened a regional office in Alabama. . . . The Association has never complied with the qualification statute, from which it considered itself exempt.

In 1956 the Attorney General of Alabama brought an equity suit in the State Circuit Court, Montgomery County, to enjoin the Association from conducting further activities within, and to oust it from, the State. Among other things the bill in equity alleged that the Association had opened a regional office and had organized various affiliates in Alabama; had recruited members and solicited contributions within the State; had given financial support and furnished legal assistance to Negro students seeking admission to the state university; and had supported a Negro boycott of the bus lines in Montgomery to compel the seating of passengers without regard to race. . . . On the day the complaint was filed, the Circuit Court issued *ex parte* an order restraining the Association, *pendente lite,* from engaging in further activities within the State and forbidding it to take any steps to qualify itself to do business therein.

Petitioner demurred to the allegations of the bill and moved to dissolve the restraining order. It contended that its activities did not subject it to the qualification requirements of the statute and that in any event what the State sought to accomplish by its suit would violate rights to freedom of speech and assembly guaranteed under the Fourteenth Amendment to the Constitution of the United States. Before the date set for a hearing on this motion, the State moved for the production of a large number of the Association's records and papers, including bank statements, leases, deeds, and records containing the names and addresses of all Alabama "members" and "agents" of the Association. It alleged that all such documents were necessary for adequate preparation for the hearing. . . . Over petitioner's objections, the court ordered the production of a substantial part of the requested records, including the membership lists. . . .

Thereafter petitioner filed its answer to the bill in equity. It admitted its Alabama activities substantially as alleged in the complaint and that it had not qualified to do business in the State. Although still disclaiming the statute's application to it, petitioner offered to qualify. . . . However petitioner did not comply with the production order, and for this failure was adjudged in civil contempt and fined $10,000. The contempt judgment provided that the fine would be subject to reduction or remission if compliance were forthcoming within five days but otherwise would be increased to $100,000.

At the end of the five-day period petitioner produced substantially all the data called for by the production order except its membership lists, as to which it contended that Alabama could not constitutionally compel disclosure. . . . While a similar stay application, which was later denied, was pending before the Supreme Court of Alabama, the Circuit Court made a further order adjudging petitioner in continuing contempt and increasing the fine already imposed to $100,000. Under Alabama law, . . . the effect of the contempt adjudication was to foreclose petitioner from obtaining a hearing on the merits of the underlying ouster action, or from taking any steps to dissolve the temporary restraining order which had been issued *ex parte,* until it purged itself of contempt. . . .

The State Supreme Court thereafter twice dismissed petitions for certiorari to review this final contempt judgment. . . .

We granted certiorari because of the importance of the constitutional questions presented. ° ° °

We are unable to reconcile the procedural holding of the Alabama Supreme Court in the present case with its past unambiguous holdings as to the scope of review available upon a writ of certiorari addressed to a contempt judgment. ° ° °

We hold that this Court has jurisdiction to entertain petitioner's federal claims. . . .

The Association both urges that it is constitutionally entitled to resist official inquiry into its membership lists, and that it may assert, on behalf of its members, a right personal to them to be protected from compelled disclosure by the State of their affiliation with the Association as revealed by the membership lists. We think that petitioner argues more appropriately the rights of its members, and that its nexus with them is sufficient to permit that it act as their representative before this Court. In so concluding, we reject respondent's argument that the Association lacks standing to assert here constitutional rights pertaining to the members, who are not of course parties to the litigation.

To limit the breadth of issues which must be dealt with in particular litigation, this Court has generally insisted that parties rely only on constitutional rights which are personal to themselves. . . . The principle is not disrespected where constitutional rights of persons who are not immediately before the Court could not be effectively vindicated except through an appropriate representative before the Court. . . .

If petitioner's rank-and-file members are constitutionally entitled to withhold their connection with the Association despite the production order, it is manifest that this right is properly assertable by the Association. To require that it be claimed by the members themselves would result in nullification of the right at the very moment of its assertion. Petitioner is the appropriate party to assert these rights, because it and its members are in every practical sense identical. The Association, which provides in its constitution that "[a]ny person who is in accordance with [its] principles and policies * * *" may become a member, is but the medium through which its individual members seek to make more effective the expression of their own views. The reasonable likelihood that the Association itself through diminished financial support and membership may be adversely affected if production is compelled is a further factor pointing towards our holding that petitioner has standing to complain of the production order on behalf of its members. . . .

We thus reach petitioner's claim that the production order in the state litigation trespasses upon fundamental freedoms protected by the Due Process Clause of the Fourteenth Amendment. Petitioner argues that in view of the facts and circumstances shown in the record, the effect of compelled disclosure of the membership lists will be to abridge the rights of its rank-and-file members to engage in lawful association in support of their common beliefs. It contends that governmental action which, although not directly suppressing association, nevertheless carries this consequence, can be justified only upon some overriding valid interest of the State.

Effective advocacy of both public and private points of view, particularly controversial ones, is undeniably enhanced by group association, as this Court has more than once recognized by remarking upon the close nexus between the freedoms of speech and assembly. *De Jonge* v. *Oregon*, 299 U.S. 353, 364.

It is beyond debate that freedom to engage in association for the advancement of beliefs and ideas is an inseparable aspect of the "liberty" assured by the Due Process Clause of the Fourteenth Amendment, which embraces freedom of speech. See *Gitlow* v. *New York*, 268 U.S. 652, 666. . . . Of course, it is immaterial whether the beliefs sought to be advanced by association pertain to political, economic, religious or cultural matters, and state action which may have the effect of curtailing the freedom to associate is subject to the closest scrutiny.

The fact that Alabama, so far as is relevant to the validity of the contempt judgment presently under review, has taken no direct action . . . to restrict the right of petitioner's members to associate freely, does not end inquiry into the effect of the production order. . . . In the domain of these indispensable liberties, whether of speech, press, or association, the decisions of this Court recognize that abridgment of such rights, even though unintended, may inevitably follow from varied forms of governmental action. . . . The governmental action challenged may appear to be totally unrelated to protected liberties. . . .

It is hardly a novel perception that compelled disclosure of affiliation with groups engaged in advocacy may constitute as effective a restraint on freedom of association as the forms of governmental action in the cases above were thought likely to produce upon the particular constitutional rights there involved. This Court has recognized the vital relationship between freedom to associate and privacy in one's associations. . . . Compelled disclosure of membership in an organization engaged in advocacy of particular beliefs is of the same order. Inviolability of privacy in group association may in many circumstances be indispensable to preservation of freedom of association, particularly where a group espouses dissident beliefs. . . .

We think that the production order, in the respects here drawn in question, must be regarded as entailing the likelihood of a substantial restraint upon the exercise by petitioner's members of their right to freedom of association. Petitioner has made an uncontroverted showing that on past occasions revelation of the identity of its rank-and-file members has exposed these members to economic reprisal, loss of employment, threat of physical coercion, and other manifestations of public hostility. Under these circumstances, we think it apparent that compelled disclosure of petitioner's Alabama membership is likely to affect adversely the ability of petitioner and its members to pursue their collective effort to foster beliefs which they admittedly have the right to advocate, in that it may induce members to withdraw from the Association and dissuade others from joining it because of fear of exposure of their beliefs shown through their associations and of the consequences of this exposure.

It is not sufficient to answer, as the State does here, that whatever repressive effect compulsory disclosure of names of petitioner's members may have upon participation by Alabama citizens in petitioner's activities follows not from *state* action but from *private* community pressures. The crucial factor is the interplay of governmental and private action, for it is only after the initial exertion of state power represented by the production order that private action takes hold.

We turn to the final question whether Alabama has demonstrated an interest in obtaining the disclosures it seeks from petitioner which is sufficient to justify the deterrent effect which we have concluded these disclosures may well have on the free exercise by petitioner's members of their constitutionally protected right of association. . . . Such a " * * * subordinating interest of the State must be compelling," *Sweezy* v. *New Hampshire,* 354 U.S. 234, 265. . . .

Whether there was "justification" in this instance turns solely on the substantiality of Alabama's interest in obtaining the membership lists. * * *

[W]hatever interest the State may have in obtaining names of ordinary members has not been shown to be sufficient to overcome petitioner's constitutional objections to the production order. * * *

We hold that the immunity from state scrutiny of membership lists which the Association claims on behalf of its members is here so related to the right of the members to pursue their lawful private interest privately and to associate freely with others in so doing as to come within the protection of the Fourteenth Amendment. And we conclude that Alabama has fallen short of showing a controlling justification for the deterrent effect on the free enjoyment of the right to associate which disclosure of membership lists is likely to have. Accordingly, the judgment of civil contempt and the $100,000 fine which resulted from petitioner's refusal to comply with the production order in this respect must fall. . . .

For the reasons stated, the judgment of the Supreme Court of Alabama must be reversed and the case remanded for proceedings not inconsistent with this opinion.   *Reversed.*

Following this reversal, the state Supreme Court reenacted the judgment for contempt, and on appeal to the United States Supreme Court in 1959, the judgment was again reversed. When, after a year, Alabama granted no further hearing, the Association filed a petition in the federal district court to enjoin enforcement of the state court order. That court dismissed the action, "because it would not assume that the executive and judicial officers of Alabama involved in the litigation would fail to protect 'the constitutional rights of all citizens.'"[1] Appealing from this dismissal, the Association reached the Supreme Court a third time. The District Court was instructed to proceed with a hearing unless the Alabama courts granted a hearing no later than January 2, 1962. In December, 1961, the Alabama court finally acted on the temporary order of 1956. Four days before the date set by the U.S. Supreme Court for a trial on the merits if Alabama had not granted a hearing, the Circuit Court of Montgomery County "permanently enjoined the Association and those affiliated with it from doing 'any further business of any description or kind' in Alabama and from attempting to qualify to do business there."[2] The Alabama Supreme Court affirmed the judgment on procedural grounds. The case reached the U.S. Supreme Court again,

[1]377 U.S. 288, 291. [2]*Ibid*, p. 292.

and after a careful consideration of the procedural points raised by the Alabama Supreme Court, the judgment of that Court was reversed.

National Association for the Advancement of Colored People v. *Alabama* ex. rel. *Flowers*, 377 U.S. 288, 84 S. Ct. 1302 (1964)

* * * There is nothing in these sections [of the statute] which attaches the consequence of permanent ouster to a foreign corporation which fails to register. . . .

Alabama cases confirm that the registration requirements are what they appear on their face to be: provisions ensuring that foreign corporations will be amenable to suit in Alabama courts. * * *

This Court has repeatedly held that a governmental purpose to control or prevent activities constitutionally subject to state regulation may not be achieved by means which sweep unnecessarily broadly and thereby invade the area of protected freedoms.* * *

In the first proceedings in this case, we held that the compelled disclosure of the names of the petitioner's members would entail "the likelihood of a substantial restraint upon the exercise by petitioner's members of their right to freedom of association." 357 U.S., at 462. It is obvious that the complete suppression of the Association's activities in Alabama which was accomplished by the order below is an even more serious abridgment of that right. The allegations of illegal conduct contained in the third charge against the petitioner suggest no legitimate governmental objective which requires such restraint. * * *

There is no occasion in this case for us to consider how much survives of the principle that a State can impose such conditions as it chooses on the right of a foreign corporation to do business within the State, or can exclude it from the State altogether. . . . This case, in truth, involves not the privilege of a corporation to do business in a State, but rather the freedom of individuals to associate for the collective advocacy of ideas. "Freedoms such as * * * [this] are protected not only against heavy-handed frontal attack, but also from being stifled by more subtle governmental interference." *Bates* v. *City of Little Rock*, 361 U.S. 516, 523.

The judgment below must be reversed. * * * Should we unhappily be mistaken in our belief that the Supreme Court of Alabama will promptly implement this disposition, leave is given the Association to apply to this Court for further appropriate relief.

Another method to limit or prevent freedom of association may be found in the right of an owner to control his property. The argument in favor of a property owner's power has a long and honorable history, going back through the years to the time when the right to own and control real property was limited by the feudal system. The rights of the real property owner include the right to exclude others from it, and to

control the use to which it is put. The state, of course, has an overriding right to take real property by eminent domain, or to restrict its
use under the police power. But, on the whole, control of real property
lies with the owner. This is one argument, much simplified, employed
to exclude Negroes and other racial groups from restaurants, lunch
counters, and stores.

This right to control one's property was the basis of the argument in
Shelley v. *Kraemer*, which was concerned with an agreement restricting
the use of certain property. Such agreements are not uncommon; they
may be written into the deed, or made separately, for the purpose of
protecting the property, the owner's investment, and other property
in the neighborhood. Racial restrictions were by no means uncommon.

In the *Shelley* case, 30 of 39 property owners in a particular section
of St. Louis, Missouri, had signed a contract to restrict "use and occupancy" of the property for a term of fifty years; specifically excluded
were "people of the Negro or Mongolian Race." The Shelleys, who
were Negroes, purchased property so restricted, although they had no
actual knowledge of the restrictive agreement at that time.

Shelley v. *Kraemer,* 334 U.S. 1, 67 S. Ct. 836 (1948)

* * * . . . Here the particular patterns of discrimination and the
areas in which the restrictions are to operate, are determined, in
the first instance, by the terms of agreements among private individuals. Participation of the State consists in the enforcement of the
restrictions so defined. The crucial issue with which we are here
confronted is whether this distinction removes these cases from
the operation of the prohibitory provisions of the Fourteenth
Amendment.
. . . That Amendment erects no shield against merely private
conduct, however discriminatory or wrongful. . . .
But here there was more. These are cases in which the purposes of
the agreements were secured only by judicial enforcement by state
courts of the restrictive terms of the agreements. * * *
The short of the matter is that from the time of the adoption of
the Fourteenth Amendment until the present, it has been the consistent ruling of this Court that the action of the States to which the
Amendment has reference includes action of state courts and state
judicial officials. . . .
We have no doubt that there has been state action in these cases
in the full and complete sense of the phrase. The undisputed facts
disclose that petitioners were willing purchasers of properties upon
which they desired to establish homes. The owners of the properties
were willing sellers; and contracts of sale were accordingly consum-
mated. It is clear that but for the active intervention of the state courts,

supported by the full panoply of state power, petitioners would have been free to occupy the properties in question without restraint. . . .

The enforcement of the restrictive agreements by the state courts in these cases was directed pursuant to the common-law policy of the States as formulated by those courts in earlier decisions. . . . The judicial action in each case bears the clear and unmistakable imprimatur of the State. We have noted that previous decisions of this Court have established the proposition that judicial action is not immunized from the operation of the Fourteenth Amendment simply because it is taken pursuant to the state's common-law policy. Nor is the Amendment ineffective simply because the particular pattern of discrimination, which the State has enforced, was defined initially by the terms of a private agreement. State action, as that phrase is understood for the purposes of the Fourteenth Amendment, refers to exertions of state power in all forms. And when the effect of that action is to deny rights subject to the protection of the Fourteenth Amendment, it is the obligation of this Court to enforce the constitutional commands.

We hold that in granting judicial enforcement for the restrictive agreements in these cases, the States have denied petitioners the equal protection of the laws and that, therefore, the action of the state courts cannot stand. We have noted that freedom from discrimination by the States in the enjoyment of property rights was among the basic objectives sought to be effectuated by the framers of the Fourteenth Amendment. That such discrimination has occurred in these cases is clear. Because of the race or color of these petitioners they have been denied rights of ownership or occupancy enjoyed as a matter of course by other citizens of different race or color. * * *

The problem of defining the scope of the restrictions which the Federal Constitution imposes upon exertions of power by the States has given rise to many of the most persistent and fundamental issues which this Court has been called upon to consider. . . .

The historical context in which the Fourteenth Amendment became a part of the Constitution should not be forgotten. Whatever else the framers sought to achieve, it is clear that the matter of primary concern was the establishment of equality in the enjoyment of basic civil and political rights and the preservation of those rights from discriminatory action on the part of the States based on considerations of race or color. . . . Upon full consideration, we have concluded that in these cases the States have acted to deny petitioners the equal protection of the laws guaranteed by the Fourteenth Amendment. . . .

For the reasons stated, the judgment . . . must be reversed.

For the same reasons, no damages for the breach of such an agreement can be awarded (*Barrows* v. *Jackson*, 346 U.S. 249, 73 S. Ct. 1931; 1953). Such contracts not only limit the right to convey property freely, but also restrict the right of association.

It is commonly recognized that people with special responsibilities toward others may have special burdens or restrictions placed upon them. No one, for instance, may practice medicine without the requisite education and examinations required by the state. Lawyers are in a similar category and, in a more variable fashion, so are public school teachers. But with the power to require a certain uniformity of educational standards, is there also the power to require a conformity of beliefs, or to condition practice of a profession upon revelation of beliefs or associations, or even to compel associations? The basis for such restrictions is, of course, the assumption that the individual has the power to influence the beliefs and actions of others.

Because of the assumption that teachers exert a strong influence upon their students, teachers have been subject to public scrutiny and held to standards of conduct which would, in other professions, seem somewhat unreasonable. Tenure systems help public school teachers achieve a reasonable degree of freedom and privacy, but not all school systems have provisions for tenure. Even where tenure systems exist, the right of the state to inquire into the loyalty of the teacher, or to require an oath in which loyalty is professed, has been upheld by the United States Supreme Court. But professing loyalty is not identical with revealing one's associates, either past or present.

In 1949 the New York legislature enacted the Feinberg law, which required a teacher to reveal membership in organizations that "advocate, advise, teach or embrace" the doctrine of violent or other unlawful overthrow of the government. The organizations so characterized could not be listed until there had been notice and a full hearing. Teachers who were members of such organizations could, after hearing, be removed from their positions in the public schools. In *Adler* v. *Board of Education* the provision was attacked as an abridgment of freedom of speech and association. The case also illustrates the conflicting viewpoints of the members of the Court. The majority held that the law was carefully drawn, protected the rights of the teachers, and did not deny the appellant freedom of speech or assembly. Mr. Justice Minton delivered the opinion.

Adler v. *Board of Education of the City of New York*, 342 U.S. 485, 72 S. Ct. 380 (1952)

. . . A teacher works in a sensitive area in a schoolroom. There he shapes the attitude of young minds towards the society in which they live. In this, the state has a vital concern. It must preserve the integrity of the schools. That the school authorities have the right and the duty to screen the officials, teachers, and employees as to their fitness to maintain the integrity of the schools as a part of ordered society, cannot be doubted. One's associates, past and present, as well as one's conduct, may properly be considered in determining fitness and loyalty. From time immemorial, one's reputation has been determined in part by the company he keeps. In the employment of officials and teachers of the school system, the state may very properly inquire into the company they keep, and we know of no rule, constitutional or otherwise, that prevents the state, when determining the fitness and loyalty of such persons, from considering the organizations and persons with whom they associate.

If, under the procedure set up in the New York law, a person is found to be unfit and is disqualified from employment in the public school system because of membership in a listed organization, he is not thereby denied the right of free speech and assembly. His freedom of choice between membership in the organization and employment in the school system might be limited, but not his freedom of speech or assembly, except in the remote sense that limitation is inherent in every choice. Certainly such limitation is not one the state may not make in the exercise of its police power to protect the schools from pollution and thereby to defend its own existence. . . .[3]

Neither Justice Black nor Justice Douglas agreed, because both were of the opinion that the law deprived teachers of their right to freedom of thought, expression, and association. Mr. Justice Frankfurter's dissent was more technical: the case was not ripe for decision because the plan had not actually been put into operation. The Court, he said, "should avoid constitutional adjudications on merely abstract or speculative issues. . . ."[4]

Eight years later, in 1960, a bare majority of the Court refused to uphold the State of Arkansas' requirement of an annual affidavit from its public school and college teachers, who were not protected by tenure.

Shelton v. *Tucker et al.*, 364 U.S. 479, 81 S. Ct. 247 (1960)

MR. JUSTICE STEWART delivered the opinion of the Court.

I.

It is urged here, as it was unsuccessfully urged throughout the proceedings in both the federal and state courts, that Act 10 deprives teachers in Arkansas of their rights to personal, associational, and academic liberty, protected by the Due Process Clause of the Fourteenth Amendment from invasion by state action. In considering this contention, we deal with two basic postulates.

First. There can be no doubt of the right of a State to investigate the competence and fitness of those whom it hires to teach in its

[3]*Ibid.*, p. 385.
[4]*Ibid.*, p. 407.

schools, as this Court before now has had occasion to recognize. . . .
. . . Here . . . there can be no question of the relevance of a
State's inquiry into the fitness and competence of its teachers.

Second. It is not disputed that to compel a teacher to disclose his
every associational tie is to impair that teacher's right of free association, a right closely allied to freedom of speech and a right which,
like free speech, lies at the foundation of a free society. *De Jonge* v.
Oregon, 299 U.S. 353, 364; *Bates* v. *Little Rock, supra,* 361 U.S. at
pages 522–523. Such interference with personal freedom is con-
spicuously accented when the teacher serves at the absolute will of
those to whom the disclosure must be made – those who any year can
terminate the teacher's employment without bringing charges, without notice, without a hearing, without affording an opportunity to
explain.

The statute does not provide that the information it requires be
kept confidential. Each school board is left free to deal with the
information as it wishes. The record contains evidence to indicate
that fear of public disclosure is neither theoretical nor groundless.
Even if there were no disclosure to the general public, the pressure
upon a teacher to avoid any ties which might displease those who
control his professional destiny would be constant and heavy. Public
exposure, bringing with it the possibility of public pressures upon
school boards to discharge teachers who belong to unpopular or
minority organizations, would simply operate to widen and aggravate
the impairment of constitutional liberty.

The vigilant protection of constitutional freedoms is nowhere
more vital than in the community of American schools. . . . "Schol-
arship cannot flourish in an atmosphere of suspicion and distrust.
Teachers and students must always remain free to inquire, to study
and to evaluate * * *." *Sweezy* v. *New Hampshire,* 354 U.S. 234,
250.

II.

The question to be decided here is . . . whether the State can ask
every one of its teachers to disclose every single organization with
which he has been associated over a five-year period. The scope of
the inquiry required by Act 10 is completely unlimited. The statute
requires a teacher to reveal the church to which he belongs, or to
which he has given financial support. It requires him to disclose his
political party, and every political organization to which he may have
contributed over a five-year period. It requires him to list, without
number, every conceivable kind of associational tie – social, professional, political, avocational, or religious. Many such relationships
could have no possible bearing upon the teacher's occupational
competence or fitness.

In a series of decisions this Court has held that, even though the
governmental purpose be legitimate and substantial, that purpose
cannot be pursued by means that broadly stifle fundamental personal
liberties when the end can be more narrowly achieved. The breadth

of legislative abridgment must be viewed in the light of less drastic means for achieving the same basic purpose. * * *

The unlimited and indiscriminate sweep of the statute now before us brings it within the ban of our prior cases. The statute's comprehensive interference with associational freedom goes far beyond what might be justified in the exercise of the State's legitimate inquiry into the fitness and competency of its teachers. The judgments in both cases must be reversed. . . .   It is so ordered.

MR. JUSTICE FRANKFURTER, dissenting.

As one who has strong views against crude intrusions by the state into the atmosphere of creative freedom in which alone the spirit and mind of a teacher can fruitfully function, I may find displeasure with the Arkansas legislation now under review. But in maintaining the distinction between private views and constitutional restrictions, I am constrained to find that it does not exceed the permissible range of state action limited by the Fourteenth Amendment. * * *

Where state assertions of authority are attacked as impermissibly restrictive upon thought, expression, or association, the existence *vel non* of other possible less restrictive means of achieving the object which the State seeks is, of course, a constitutionally relevant consideration. This is not because some novel, particular rule of law obtains in cases of this kind. Whenever the reasonableness and fairness of a measure are at issue — as they are in every case in which this Court must apply the standards of reason and fairness, with the appropriate scope to be given those concepts, in enforcing the Due Process Clause of the Fourteenth Amendment as a limitation upon state action — the availability or unavailability of alternative methods of proceeding is germane. * * *

Consideration of alternatives may focus the precise exercise of state legislative authority which is tested in this Court by the standard of reasonableness, but it does not alter or displace that standard. The issue remains whether, in light of the particular kind of restriction upon individual liberty which a regulation entails, it is reasonable for a legislature to choose that form of regulation rather than others less restrictive. To that determination, the range of judgment easily open to a legislature in considering the relative degrees of efficiency of alternative means in achieving the end it seeks is pertinent.

In the present case the Court strikes down an Arkansas statute requiring that teachers disclose to school officials all of their organizational relationships, on the ground that "Many such relationships could have no possible bearing upon the teacher's occupational competence or fitness." Granted that a given teacher's membership in the First Street Congregation is, standing alone, of little relevance to what may rightly be expected of a teacher, is that membership equally irrelevant when it is discovered that the teacher is in fact a member of the First Street Congregation *and* the Second Street Congregation *and* the Third Street Congregation *and* the 4-H Club *and* the 3-H Club *and* half a dozen other groups? Presumably, a teacher may have so many divers associations, so many divers commitments, that they consume his time and energy and interest at the expense of his work or even of his professional dedication. . . . Surely, a school board is entitled to inquire whether any of its teachers has placed himself, or is placing himself, in a condition where his work may suffer. * * *

If I dissent from the Court's disposition in these cases, it is not that I put a low value on academic freedom. . . . It is because that very freedom in its most creative reaches, is dependent in no small part upon the careful and discriminating selection of teachers. This process of selection is an intricate affair, a matter of fine judgment, and if it is to be informed, it must be based upon a comprehensive range of information. I am unable to say, on the face of this statute, that Arkansas could not reasonably find that the information which the statute requires — and which may not be otherwise acquired than by asking the question which it asks — is germane to that selection. Nor, on this record, can I attribute to the State a purpose to employ the enactment as a device for the accomplishment of what is constitutionally forbidden. . . . Because I do not find the disclosure of teachers' associations to their school boards is, without more, such a restriction upon their liberty, or upon that of the community, as to overbalance the State's interest in asking the question, I would affirm the judgments below.

I am authorized to say that MR. JUSTICE CLARK, MR. JUSTICE HARLAN and MR. JUSTICE WHITTAKER agree with this opinion.

MR. JUSTICE HARLAN, whom MR. JUSTICE FRANKFURTER, MR. JUSTICE CLARK and MR. JUSTICE WHITTAKER join, dissenting.
. . . It must be emphasized that neither of these cases actually presents an issue of racial discrimination. . . .

The issue is whether, consistently with the Fourteenth Amendment, a State may require teachers in its public schools or colleges to disclose, as a condition precedent to their initial or continued employment, all organizations to which they have belonged, paid dues, or contributed within the past five years. . . .

I believe it impossible to determine *a priori* the place where the line should be drawn between what would be permissible inquiry and over-broad inquiry in a situation like this. Certainly the Court does not point that place out. * * *

. . . All that is now here is the validity of the statute on its face, and I am unable to agree that in this posture of things the enactment can be said to be unconstitutional.

I would affirm in both cases.

As a part of its police power, a state may also enact statutes to control the practice of law. It determines what educational requirements are necessary, what examinations may be required of aspirants, and it may prevent the unauthorized practice of law. Virginia enacted a statute which, according to the Virginia Supreme Court of Appeals, was designed "to strengthen the existing statutes to further control the evils of solicitation of legal business . . . "[5] — a worthy object. But worthy ends must be supported by constitutional means. Whether the state used means within its power was the question in the following case.

National Association for the Advancement of Colored People v. Button, 371 U.S. 415, 83 S. Ct. 328 (1963)

MR. JUSTICE BRENNAN delivered the opinion of the Court.

This case originated in companion suits by the National Association for the Advancement of Colored People, Inc. (N.A.A.C.P.) and the N.A.A.C.P. Legal Defense and Educational Fund, Inc. (Defense Fund), brought in 1957. . . . The suits sought to restrain the enforcement of Chapters 31, 32, 33, 35, and 36 of the Virginia Acts of Assembly, 1956 Extra Session, on the ground that the statutes, as applied to the activities of the plaintiffs, violated the Fourteenth Amendment. . . . [T]he N.A.A.C.P. filed the instant petition. . . . [T]he only issue before us is the constitutionality of Chapter 33 as applied to the activities of the N.A.A.C.P.

There is no substantial dispute as to the facts; the dispute centers about the constitutionality under the Fourteenth Amendment of Chapter 33, as construed and applied by the Virginia Supreme Court of Appeals to include N.A.A.C.P.'s activities within the statute's ban against "the improper solicitation of any legal or professional business."

The N.A.A.C.P. . . . is licensed to do business in Virginia, and has 89 branches there. The Virginia branches are organized into the Virginia State Conference of N.A.A.C.P. Branches (the Conference), an unincorporated association, which in 1957 had some 13,500 members. The activities of the Conference are financed jointly by the national organization and the local branches from contributions and membership dues. N.A.A.C.P. policy, binding upon local branches and conferences, is set by the annual national convention.

The basic aims and purposes of N.A.A.C.P. are to secure the elimination of all racial barriers which deprive Negro citizens of the privileges and burdens of equal citizenship rights in the United States. To this end the Association . . . devotes much of its funds and energies to an extensive program of assisting certain kinds of litigation on behalf of its declared purposes. For more than 10 years, the Virginia Conference has concentrated upon financing litigation aimed at ending racial segregation in the public schools of the Common wealth.

The Conference ordinarily will finance only cases in which the assisted litigant retains an N.A.A.C.P. staff lawyer to represent him. The Conference maintains a legal staff of 15 attorneys, all of whom are Negroes and members of the N.A.A.C.P. . . . Each legal staff

[5]N.A.A.C.P. v. Button, 371 U.S. 415, 424.

member must agree to abide by the policies of the N.A.A.C.P., which . . . limit the kinds of litigation which the N.A.A.C.P. will assist. . . . The Conference defrays all expenses of litigation in an assisted case, and usually, although not always, pays each lawyer on the case a per diem fee not to exceed $60, plus out-of-pocket expenses. . . . None of the staff receives a salary or retainer from the N.A.A.C.P. . . . The actual conduct of assisted litigation is under the control of the attorney.

In litigation involving public school segregation . . . [t]ypically, a local N.A.A.C.P. branch will invite a member of the legal staff to explain to a meeting of parents and children the legal steps necessary to achieve desegregation. The staff member will bring forms to the meeting authorizing him, and other N.A.A.C.P. or Defense Fund attorneys of his designation, to represent the signers in legal proceedings to achieve desegregation. . . . It is usual, after obtaining authorization, for the staff lawyer to bring into the case the other staff members in the area where suit is to be brought. . . . In effect, then, the prospective litigant retains not so much a particular attorney as the "firm" of N.A.A.C.P. and Defense Fund lawyers, which has a corporate reputation for expertness in presenting and arguing the difficult questions of law that frequently arise in civil rights litigation. . . .

. . . While the Conference . . . encourages the bringing of lawsuits, the plaintiffs in particular actions, so far as appears, make their own decisions to become such.

Statutory regulation of unethical and nonprofessional conduct by attorneys has been in force in Virginia since 1849. . . . Prior to 1956, however, no attempt was made to proscribe under such regulations the activities of the N.A.A.C.P., which had been carried on openly for many years in substantially the manner described. In 1956, however, the legislature amended, by the addition of Chapter 33, the provisions of the Virginia Code forbidding solicitation of legal business by . . . an agent for an individual or organization which retains a lawyer in connection with an action to which it is not a party and in which it has no pecuniary right or liability. . . . The Virginia Supreme Court of Appeals held that the chapter's purpose "was to strengthen the existing statutes to further control the evils of solicitation of legal business ° ° °." . . . The court held that the activities of N.A.A.C.P., the Virginia Conference, the Defense Fund, and the lawyers furnished by them, fell within, and could constitutionally be proscribed by, the chapter's expanded definition of improper solicitation of legal business, and also violated Canons 35 and 47 of the American Bar Association's Canons of Professional Ethics, which the court had adopted in 1938. . . .

Petitioner challenges the decision of the Supreme Court of Appeals on many grounds. But we reach only one: that Chapter 33 as construed and applied abridges the freedoms of the First Amendment, protected against state action by the Fourteenth. More specifically, petitioner claims that the chapter infringes the right of the N.A.A.C.P. and its members and lawyers to associate for the purpose of assisting persons who seek legal redress for infringements of their constitutionally guaranteed and other rights. We think petitioner may assert this right on its own behalf because, though a corporation, it is directly engaged in those activities, claimed to be constitutionally protected, which the statute would curtail. . . . We also think petitioner has standing to assert the corresponding rights of its members. . . .

We reverse the judgment of the Virginia Supreme Court of Appeals. We hold that the activities of the N.A.A.C.P., its affiliates and legal staff shown on this record are modes of expression and association protected by the First and Fourteenth Amendments which Virginia may not prohibit, under its power to regulate the legal profession, as improper solicitation of legal business violative of Chapter 33 and the Canons of Professional Ethics.

We meet at the outset the contention that "solicitation" is wholly outside the area of freedoms protected by the First Amendment. To this contention there are two answers. The first is that a State cannot foreclose the exercise of constitutional rights by mere labels. The second is that abstract discussion is not the only species of communication which the Constitution protects; the First Amendment also protects vigorous advocacy, certainly of lawful ends, against governmental intrusion. *Thomas* v. *Collins*, 323 U.S. 516, 537. . . . In the context of N.A.A.C.P. objectives, litigation is not a technique of resolving private differences; it is a means for achieving the lawful objectives of equality of treatment by all government, federal, state and local, for the members of the Negro community in this country. It is thus a form of political expression. Groups which find themselves unable to achieve their objectives through the ballot frequently turn to the courts. . . .

[T]here is no longer any doubt that the First and Fourteenth Amendments protect certain forms of orderly group activity. . . .

Our concern is with the impact of enforcement of Chapter 33 upon First Amendment freedoms. . . . We have no doubt that the opinion of the Supreme Court of Appeals in the instant case was intended as a full and authoritative construction of Chapter 33 as applied in a detailed factual context. That construction binds us. . . .

But it does not follow that this Court now has only a clear-cut task to decide whether the activities of the petitioner deemed unlawful by the Supreme Court of Appeals are constitutionally privileged. . . . [T]he instant decree may be invalid if it prohibits privileged exercises of First Amendment rights whether or not the record discloses that the petitioner has engaged in privileged conduct. . . . The objectionable quality of vagueness and overbreadth . . . depend[s] upon . . . the danger of tolerating, in the area of First Amendment freedoms, the existence of a penal statute susceptible of sweeping and improper application. . . . These freedoms are delicate and vulnerable, as well as supremely precious in our society. The threat of sanctions may deter their exercise almost as potently as the actual application of sanctions. . . .

We conclude that under Chapter 33, as authoritatively construed by the Supreme Court of Appeals, a person who advises another that his legal rights have been infringed and refers him to a particular attorney or group of attorneys (for example, to the Virginia Conference's legal staff) for assistance has committed a crime, as has the attorney who knowingly renders assistance under such circumstances. * * *

It makes no difference whether such prosecutions or proceedings would actually be commenced. It is enough that a vague and broad statute lends itself to selective enforcement against unpopular causes. . . . [A] statute broadly curtailing group activity leading to litigation may easily become a weapon of oppression, however evenhanded its terms appear. . . . * * *

We hold that Chapter 33 as construed violates the Fourteenth Amendment by unduly inhibiting protected freedoms of expression and association. In so holding, we reject two further contentions of respondents. The first is that the Virginia Supreme Court of Appeals has guaranteed free expression by expressly confirming petitioner's right to continue its advocacy of civil-rights litigation. . . .

The second contention is that Virginia has a subordinating interest in the regulation of the legal profession, embodied in Chapter 33, which justifies limiting petitioner's First Amendment rights. . . . [A] State may not, under the guise of prohibiting professional misconduct, ignore constitutional rights. * * *

We conclude that although the petitioner has amply shown that its activities fall within the First Amendment's protections, the State has failed to advance any substantial regulatory interest, in the form of substantive evils flowing from petitioner's activities, which can justify the broad prohibitions which it has imposed. Nothing that this record shows as to the nature and purpose of N.A.A.C.P. activities permits an inference of any injurious intervention in or control of litigation which would constitutionally authorize the application of Chapter 33 to those activities. A *fortiori*, nothing in this record justifies the breadth and vagueness of the Virginia Supreme Court of Appeals' decree.

A final observation is in order. Because our disposition is rested on the First Amendment as absorbed in the Fourteenth, we do not reach the considerations of race or racial discrimination which are the predicate of petitioner's challenge to the statute under the Equal Protection Clause. That the petitioner happens to be engaged in activities of expression and association on behalf of the rights of Negro children to equal opportunity is constitutionally irrelevant to the ground of our decision. . . . The Constitution protects expression and association without regard to the race, creed, or political or religious affiliation of the members of the group which invokes its shield, or to the truth, popularity, or social utility of the ideas and beliefs which are offered. . . .   *Reversed.*

MR. JUSTICE DOUGLAS, concurring. * * *

MR. JUSTICE WHITE, concurring in part and dissenting in part. * * *

MR. JUSTICE HARLAN, whom MR. JUSTICE CLARK and MR. JUSTICE STEWART join, dissenting.

No member of this Court would disagree that the validity of state action claimed to infringe rights assured by the Fourteenth Amendment is to be judged by the same basic constitutional standards whether or not racial problems are involved. . . . With all respect, I believe that the striking down of this Virginia statute cannot be squared with accepted constitutional doctrine in the domain of state regulatory power over the legal profession. . . .

At the outset the factual premises on which the Virginia Supreme Court of Appeals upheld the application of Chapter 33 to the activities of the N.A.A.C.P. in the area of litigation, as well as the scope of that court's holding, should be delineated.

First, the lawyers who participate in litigation sponsored by petitioner are, almost without exception, members of the legal staff of the N.A.A.C.P. Virginia State Conference. . . .

Second, it is equally clear that the N.A.A.C.P.'s directions, or those of its officers and divisions, to staff lawyers cover many subjects relating to the form and substance of litigation. . . .

Third, contrary to the conclusion of the Federal District Court in the original federal proceeding, *N.A.A.C.P.* v. *Patty,* 159 F. Supp. 503, 508–509, the present record establishes that the petitioner does a great deal more than to advocate litigation and to wait for prospective litigants to come forward. . . .

Fourth, there is substantial evidence indicating that the normal incidents of the attorney-client relationship were often absent in litigation handled by staff lawyers and financed by petitioner. . . .

On these factual premises, amply supported by the evidence, the Virginia Supreme Court of Appeals held that petitioner and those associated with it

"solicit prospective litigants to authorize the filing of suits by N.A.A.C.P. and Fund [Educational Defense Fund] lawyers, who are paid by the Conference and controlled by N.A.A.C.P. policies * * *" . . .

and concluded that this conduct violated Chapter 33 as well as Canons 35 and 47 of the Canons of Professional Ethics of the American Bar Association, which had been adopted by the Virginia courts more than 20 years ago. * * *

In my opinion the litigation program of the N.A.A.C.P., as shown by this record, falls within an area of activity which a State may constitutionally regulate. * * *

[H]ere, the question is whether the particular regulation of conduct concerning litigation has a reasonable relation to the furtherance of a proper state interest, and whether that interest outweighs any foreseeable harm to the furtherance of protected freedoms. . . .

The interest which Virginia has here asserted is that of maintaining high professional standards among those who practice law within its borders. This Court has consistently recognized the broad range of judgments that a State may properly make in regulating any profession. . . .

First, with regard to the claimed absence of the pecuniary element, it cannot well be suggested that the attorneys here are donating their services, since they are in fact compensated for their work. Nor can it tenably be argued that petitioner's litigating activities fall into the accepted category of aid to indigent litigants. * * *

Second, . . . [I]n a particular litigation, it is not impossible that after authorizing action in his behalf, a Negro parent, concerned that a continued frontal attack could result in schools closed for years, might prefer to wait. . . . The parent, of course, is free to withdraw his authorization, but is his lawyer, retained and paid by petitioner and subject to its directions on matters of policy, able to advise the parent with that undivided allegiance that is the hallmark of the attorney-client relation? I am afraid not. . . .

Third, . . . The true question is whether the State has taken action which unreasonably obstructs the assertion of federal rights. Here, it cannot be said that the underlying state policy is inevitably inconsistent with federal interests. * * *

Of cardinal importance, this regulatory enactment as construed . . . prevents only the solicitation of business for attorneys subject to petitioner's control, and as so limited, should be sustained. . . .

The Court's remaining line of reasoning is that Chapter 33 as construed . . . must be struck down on the score of vagueness and ambiguity. . . . The cardinal difficulty with this argument is that there simply is no real uncertainty in the statute, as the state court found, 202 Va., at 154 . . . or in that court's construction of it. . . . The test is whether the law in question has established standards of guilt sufficiently ascertainable that men of common intelligence need not guess at its meaning. . . . No such language is to be found here.

Ambiguity in the present statute can be made to appear only at the price of strained reading of the state court's opinion. . . . Nor do I think it may reasonably be concluded that the state court meant to preclude the N.A.A.C.P. from recommending "outside" attorneys to prospective litigants, so long as it retained no power of direction over such lawyers. . . . Indeed the ambiguity which this Court now finds quite evidently escaped the notice of both petitioner and its counsel for they did not so much as suggest such an argument in their briefs. . . . The due process claim is disposed of once it appears that this statute falls within the range of permissible state regulation in pursuance of a legitimate goal. . . .

As to equal protection, this position is premised on the claim that the law was directed solely at petitioner's activities on behalf of Negro litigants. But Chapter 33 as it comes to us, with a narrowing construction by the state court that anchors the statute firmly to the common law and to the court's own independently existing supervisory powers over the Virginia legal profession, leaves no room for any finding of discriminatory purpose. Petitioner is merely one of a variety of organizations that may come within the scope of the long-standing prohibitions against solicitation and unauthorized practice. . . . [T]he present precord is barren of any evidence suggesting . . . unequal application, and we may not presume that it will occur. . . .

I would affirm.

Travel

The right to travel is closely related to the freedom of association. As a practical matter, the right to travel abroad must be seen in a larger context, for citizens who are detained in foreign lands expect assistance from their government. It would seem logical, therefore, to prohibit travel to areas where the United States cannot offer such assistance through its diplomatic staff. It would also seem proper to detain in this country persons whose purpose in traveling may be to foster efforts to overthrow the U.S. government by force or violence. The difficulties with the latter reason for refusing a passport are many, because such a purpose must be determined, as a practical matter, on the basis of past utterances and actions of the person concerned. That determination raises an immediate conflict with the right to freedom of speech and association. Most difficulties center around speech or association involving the Communist Party, its members, or activities and organizations it has sponsored. It is frequently forgotten that the Communist Party was for a number of years as "legal" a party as the Democratic, Republican, Socialist, or Prohibition parties, with candidates on the ballot. Membership in the party was not illegal, nor was working for the party proscribed.

Although the Internal Security Act of 1950 forbade Communists to apply for passports when a Communist organization was registered under the Act, or when there was in effect "a final order of the Board requiring an organization to register," no such registration or order was in effect at the time Mr. Kent applied for a passport. His application was denied, on the basis that he was a Communist, and that he had consistently followed the Communist Party line. Mr. Kent neither asked for a hearing, nor filed the affidavit required, but did reapply for a passport, taking the position that questions concerning his political beliefs were unrelated to the issuance of a passport. When he was told that no passport would be issued until he had met the requirements of the State Department, he brought action. On appeal, the Court held that

Congress had not delegated to the Secretary of State the particular authority he had exercised in this case.

. . . We deal with beliefs, with associations, with ideological matters. We must remember that we are dealing here with citizens who have neither been accused of crimes nor found guilty. They are being denied their freedom of movement solely because of their refusal to be subject to inquiry into their beliefs and associations. They do not seek to escape the law nor to violate it. They may or may not be Communists. But assuming they are, the only law which Congress has passed expressly curtailing the movement of Communists across our borders has not yet become effective. . . .[6]

On the same day, the Court also reversed a lower court decision which had upheld the denial of a passport to Weldon Bruce Dayton. Mr. Dayton had executed the affidavit required by the Department of State, explained other associations, but was still denied a passport on the basis of information in the possession of the Department which it would not divulge.

The first test of the section concerning passports in the Subversive Activities Control Act of 1950 came in 1964, in *Aptheker* v. *Secretary of State.*

Aptheker v. *Secretary of State*, 378 U.S. 500, 84 S. Ct. 1659 (1964)

MR. JUSTICE GOLDBERG delivered the opinion of the Court.
This appeal involves a single question: the constitutionality of §6 of the Subversive Activities Control Act of 1950, 64 Stat. 993, 50 U.S.C. §785. Section 6 provides in pertinent part that:
"(a) When a Communist organization * * * is registered or there is in effect a final order of the Board requiring such organization to register, it shall be unlawful for any member of such organization, with knowledge or notice that such organization is so registered or that such order has become final—
"(1) to make application for a passport, or the renewal of a passport, to be issued or renewed by or under the authority of the United States; or
"(2) to use or attempt to use any such passport."
Section 6 became effective, with respect to appellants, on October 20, 1961, when a final order of the Subversive Activities Control Board issued directing the Communist Party of the United States to register under §7 of the Subversive Activities Control Act. The registration order had been upheld earlier in 1961 by this Court's decision in *Communist Party of the United States* v. *Subversive Activities Control Board*, 367 U.S. 1. . . . Subsequently, on January 22, 1962, the Acting Director of the Passport Office notified

[6]*Kent* v. *Dulles,* 357 U.S. 116, 130, 78 S. Ct. 1113, 1120, (1958)

appellants that their passports were revoked because the Department of State believed that their use of the passports would violate §6. . . .

Appellants requested and received hearings to review the revocations of their passports. The respective hearing examiners concluded that "the Department of State had reason to believe that [appellants are] within the purview of Sec. 6(a) (2) of the Subversive Activities Control Act, and as a result thereof * * *use of a passport would be in violation of the law." . . .

Appellants thereupon filed separate complaints seeking declaratory and injunctive relief . . . which have been considered together, asked that judgments be entered declaring §6 of the Subversive Activities Control Act unconstitutional and ordering the Secretary of State to issue passports to appellants. . . .

Appellants attack §6, both on its face and as applied, as an unconstitutional deprivation of the liberty guaranteed in the Bill of Rights. The Government, while conceding that the right to travel is protected by the Fifth Amendment, contends that the Due Process Clause does not prevent the reasonable regulation of liberty and that §6 is a reasonable regulation because of its relation to the danger the world Communist movement presents for our national security. Alternatively, the Government argues that "whether or not denial of passports to some members of the Communist Party might be deemed not reasonably related to national security, surely Section 6 was reasonable as applied to the top-ranking Party leaders involved here."

We hold for the reasons stated below, that §6 of the Control Act too broadly and indiscriminately restricts the right to travel and thereby abridges the liberty guaranteed by the Fifth Amendment.

In 1958 in *Kent* v. *Dulles*, 357 U.S. 116, 127, this Court declared that the right to travel abroad is "an important aspect of the citizen's 'liberty'" guaranteed in the Due Process Clause of the Fifth Amendment. . . .

In *Kent*, however, the Court concluded that Congress had not conferred authority upon the Secretary of State to deny passports because of alleged Communist beliefs and associations. . . .

The present case, therefore, is the first in which this Court has been called upon to consider the constitutionality of the restrictions which § 6 imposes on the right to travel.

The substantiality of the restrictions cannot be doubted. The denial of a passport, given existing domestic and foreign laws, is a severe restriction upon, and in effect a prohibition against, worldwide foreign travel. Present laws and regulations make it a crime for a United States citizen to travel outside the Western Hemisphere or to Cuba without a passport. By its plain import § 6 of the Control Act effectively prohibits travel anywhere in the world outside the Western Hemisphere by members of any "Communist organization"—including "Communist-action" and "Communist-front" organizations. . . . Since freedom of association is itself guaranteed in the First Amendment, restrictions imposed upon the right to travel cannot be dismissed by asserting that the right to travel could be fully exercised if the individual would first yield up his membership in a given association. . . .

It is a familiar and basic principle, recently reaffirmed in *N.A.A.C.P.* v. *Alabama*, 377 U.S. 88, 307, that "a governmental purpose to control or prevent activities constitutionally subject to state regulation may not be achieved by means which sweep unnecessarily broadly and thereby invade the area of protected freedoms.". . .

This principle requires that we consider the congressional purpose underlying § 6 of the Control Act. The Government emphasizes that the legislation in question flows, as the statute itself declares, from the congressional desire to protect our national security. That Congress under the Constitution has power to safeguard our Nation's security is obvious and unarguable. Cf. *Kennedy* v. *Mendoza-Martinez*, 372 U.S. 144, 159–160. As we said in *Mendoza-Martinez*, "while the Constitution protects against invasions of individual rights, it is not a suicide pact." *Id.*, 372 U.S., at 160. At the same time the Constitution requires that the powers of government "must be so exercised as not, in attaining a permissible end, unduly to infringe" a constitutionally protected freedom. *Cantwell* v. *Connecticut, supra,* 310 U.S., at 304.

Section 6 provides that any member of a Communist organization which has registered or has been ordered to register commits a crime if he attempts to use or obtain a United States passport. The section applies to members who act "with knowledge or notice" that the organization is under a final registration order. "Notice" is specifically defined in § 13 (k). That section provides that publication in the Federal Register of the fact of registration or of issuance of a final registration order "shall constitute notice to all members of such organization that such order has become final." Thus the terms of § 6 apply whether or not the member actually knows or believes that he is associated with what is deemed to be a "Communist-action" or a "Communist-front" organization. . . . The provision therefore sweeps within its prohibition both knowing and unknowing members. In related contexts this Court has had occasion to consider the substantiality of the relationship between an individual and a group where, as here, the fact of membership in that group has been made the sole criterion for limiting the individual's freedom. In *Wieman* v. *Updegraff*, 344 U.S. 183, the Court . . . concluded that: "Indiscriminate classification of innocent with knowing activity must fall as an assertion of arbitrary power." *Id.*, 344 U.S., at 191.

Section 6 also renders irrelevant the member's degree of activity in the organization and his commitment to its purpose. These factors, like knowledge, would bear on the likelihood that travel by such a person would be attended by the type of activity which Congress sought to control. . . . Section 6, however, establishes an irrebuttable presumption that individuals who are members of the specified organizations will, if given passports, engage in activities inimical to the security of the United States. . . .

In addition to the absence of criteria linking the bare fact of membership to the individual's knowledge, activity or commitment, § 6 also excludes other considerations which might more closely relate the denial of passports to the stated purpose of the legislation. The prohibition of § 6 applies regardless of the purposes for which an individual wishes to travel. . . . In determining whether there has been an abridgment of the Fifth Amendment's guarantee of liberty, this Court must recognize the danger of punishing a member of a Communist organization "for his adherence to lawful and constitutionally protected purposes, because of other and unprotected purposes which he does not necessarily share." *Noto* v. *United States,* 367 U.S. 290, 299–300. In addition it must be noted that § 6 applies to a member regardless of the security-sensitivity of the areas in which he wishes to travel. . . .

In determining the constitutionality of § 6, it is also important to consider that Congress has within its power "less drastic" means of achieving the congressional objective of safeguarding our national security. . . .

In our view, the foregoing considerations compel the conclusion that § 6 of the Control Act is unconstitutional on its face. The section, judged by its plain import and by the substantive evil which Congress sought to control, sweeps too widely and too indiscriminately across the liberty guaranteed in the Fifth Amendment. The prohibition against travel is supported only by a tenuous relationship between the bare fact of organizational membership and the activity Congress sought to proscribe. The broad and enveloping prohibition indiscriminately excludes plainly relevant considerations such as the individual's knowledge, activity, commitment, and purposes in and places for travel. The section therefore is patently not a regulation "narrowly drawn to prevent the supposed evil," cf. *Cantwell* v. *Connecticut,* 310 U.S., at 307, yet here, as elsewhere, precision must be the touchstone of legislation so affecting basic freedoms, *N.A. A.C.P.* v. *Button,* 371 U.S., at 438.

The Government alternatively urges that if § 6 cannot be sustained on its face, the prohibition should nevertheless be held constitutional as applied to these particular appellants. . . .

This Court will not consider the abstract question of whether Congress might have enacted a valid statute but instead must ask whether the statute that Congress did enact will permissibly bear a construction rendering it free from constitutional defects.

The clarity and preciseness of the provision in question make it impossible to narrow its indiscriminately cast and overly broad scope without substantial rewriting. . . .

Since this case involves a personal liberty protected by the Bill of Rights, we believe that the proper approach to legislation curtailing that liberty must be that adopted by this Court in *N.A.A.C.P.* v. *Button,* 371 U.S. 413, and *Thornhill* v. *Alabama,* 310 U.S. 88. Similarly, since freedom of travel is a constitutional liberty closely related to rights of free speech and association, we believe that appellants in this case should not be required to assume the burden of demon-

strating that Congress could not have written a statute constitutionally prohibiting their travel.

Accordingly the judgment of the three-judge District Court is
reversed and the cause remanded for proceedings in conformity with
this opinion.

MR. JUSTICE BLACK, concurring.

I concur in the Court's holding that this section of the Act is unconstitutional, but not on the ground that the Due Process Clause of
the Fifth Amendment, standing alone, confers on all our people a
constitutional liberty to travel abroad at will. . . . For reasons stated
in my dissenting opinion in *Communist Party* v. *Subversieve Activities Control Board,* 367 U.S. I, 137, I think the whole Act, including
§ 6, is not a valid law, that it sets up a comprehensive statutory plan
which violates the Federal Constitution because (1) it constitutes a
"Bill of Attainder," which Art. I, § 9, of the Constitution forbids
Congress to pass; (2) it penalizes and punishes petitioners and restricts their liberty on legislative and administrative fact-findings that
they are subversives, and in effect traitors to their country, without
giving them the benefit of a trial according to due process, which
requires a trial by jury before an independent judge, after an indictment, and in accordance with all the other procedural protections of
the Fourth, Fifth, and Sixth Amendments; and (3) it denies petitioners the freedom of speech, press, and association which the First
Amendment guarantees. . . .

MR. JUSTICE DOUGLAS, concurring. . . .

Freedom of movement is kin to the right of assembly and to the
right of association. These rights may not be abridged, *De Jonge* v.
Oregon, 299 U.S. 353, *N.A.A.C.P.* v. *Alabama,* 357 U.S. 449,
460–462. . . .

MR. JUSTICE CLARK, whom MR. JUSTICE HARLAN joins and whom
MR. JUSTICE WHITE joins in part, dissenting.

The Court refuses to consider the constitutionality of § 6 of the
Subversive Activities Control Act as applied to the appellants in this
case, Elizabeth Gurley Flynn, the Chairman of the Communist Party
of the United States, and Herbert Aptheker, the editor of the Party's
"theoretical organ," *Political Affairs.* Instead, the Court declares the
section invalid on its face under the Fifth Amendment. This is contrary to the long, prevailing practice of this Court. . . .

As applied to the prosecution of the Communist Party's top digni-
taries, the section is clearly constitutional. . . .

(1) There is a finding here—not under attack—that Mrs. Flynn
"was an active, participating and continuous member of the Communist Party of the United States; was active in the Party's affairs and its
organization; and, indeed, was and still is one of its principal
officials." Likewise there is a finding—not under attack—as to Aptheker that he "[Aptheker] makes it quite clear in his own words that
he has been a member of the Communist Party since 1939 and that

he is very proud of his association and will do whatever he can to further the aims and goals of the Party." . . . In view of these circumstances, no one could say with truth that the petitioners did not know that they were associated with a Communist-action organization. In fact, neither petitioner claims lack of notice or knowledge of the requirements of the section.

(2) As to knowledge that the Communist Party is involved in a world Communist movement aimed at establishing a totalitarian Communist dictatorship in countries throughout the world, Congress made specific findings in the Subversive Activities Control Act of 1950 (the very statute under which the hearing was held at which petitioners testified for the Party) and in the Communist Control Act of 1954 that: "the Communist Party of the United States * * * is in fact an instrumentality of a conspiracy to overthrow the Government of the United States," 68 Stat. 775. . . . These findings of the Congress, like those of the Examiner which are not under attack here, are binding on this Court. *Communist Party* v. *Control Board, supra.* There we said: "It is not for the courts to reexamine the validity of these legislative findings and reject them. . . ."

How does the Court escape? It says that the section "sweeps within its prohibition both innocent and knowing members." But we have no "innocent members" before us. Neither petitioner contests these findings. . . .

Nor do I believe the section invalid "on its face." While the right to travel abroad is a part of the liberty protected by the Fifth Amendment, the Due Process clause does not prohibit reasonable regulation of life, liberty or property. Here the restriction is reasonably related to the national security . . . The right to travel is not absolute. Congress had ample evidence that use of passports by Americans belonging to the world Communist movement is a threat to our national security. . . . The denial is reasonably related to the national security. The degree of restraint upon travel is outweighed by the dangers to our very existence.

The remedy adopted by the Congress is reasonably tailored to accomplish the purpose. . . . The fact that all persons in a class may not engage in harmful conduct does not of itself make the classification invalid. *Westfall* v. *United States,* 274 U.S. 256, 259. . .

Nor do I subscribe to the loose generalization that individual guilt may be conclusively presumed from membership in the Party. One cannot consider the matter in isolation but must relate it to the subject matter involved and the legislative findings upon which the action is based. . . . The Act here does not prohibit membership, but merely restricts members in a field in which the Congress has found danger to our security. . . . Here proof of actual membership is necessary and notice of registration or entry of a final order directing registration under the Act is required. Finally, the member of the Party here can avoid the Act's sanctions by terminating his membership, which was not possible in *Wieman.* . . . The evidence before Congress as to the danger to national security was of such strength that it warranted the denial of passports, a much less onerous disability than loss of employment.

For these reasons, I would affirm.

In *Zemel* v. *Rusk,* 381 U.S. 1, 85 S. Ct. 1271 (1965), there was a direct challenge to the delegation of power to refuse to validate passports of citizens for travel in Cuba, and to the constitutionality of such authority. Mr. Zemel, who held a valid passport, asked to have it validated for travel in Cuba as a tourist, but the request was twice denied, because the request did not meet the standards established by the Secretary, who had limited validation to those whose travel was believed to be in the best interests of the United States, such as newsmen or businessmen. Mr. Zemel was neither. Despite dissents by Mr. Justice Black and Mr. Justice Goldberg, the delegation of authority and the constitutionality were both upheld.

Desegregation

A number of the cases considered in preceding sections arose as a result of efforts to oppose the consequences of the School Desegregation Cases of 1954. However unaware the average citizen might have been, the decisions were inevitable, and came as no surprise to the many who read with care the decisions of the United States Supreme Court. Over a period of years there had been attempts to have the "separate but equal" doctrine of *Plessy* v. *Ferguson* overturned, but in each case the Court had been able to point out that the school facilities, although separate, were not equal. But in each case, the standards of equality required were more carefully defined, less concerned with bricks and mortar and more concerned with "intangible" factors. In *Missouri ex rel. Gaines* v. *Canada* (305 U.S. 337, 59 S. Ct. 232; 1938), the Court found that Lloyd Gaines, a Negro graduate of a segregated university, was denied the equal protection of the laws because he was denied admission to the University of Missouri Law School because of his race, although he was otherwise qualified. Missouri had provided for the payment of "reasonable tuition fees" in universities in neighboring states where Negroes were admitted. That, however, was not sufficient to satisfy the requirements of equal protection. In *Sipuel* v. *University of Oklahoma* (332 U.S. 631, 68 S. Ct. 299; 1948), the Court held that the petitioner was

entitled to secure legal education afforded by a state institution. . . . The State must provide it for her in conformity with the equal protection clause of the Fourteenth Amendment, and provide it as soon as it does for applicants of any other group.[7]

In *McLaurin* v. *Oklahoma State Regents* (339 U.S. 637, 70 S. Ct. 851; 1950), the Court held that segregation within the graduate school to which Mr. McLaurin had been admitted was a violation of equal protection, even though it was a separation required by state statute. Mr. McLaurin was studying for an advanced degree in education, which was not possible to obtain in an institution "established for and/or used by the colored race," to quote the statute. He was assigned to a classroom seat in a row reserved for colored students; he was assigned to a special table in the library, and although he was allowed to eat in the lunch room at the same time as other students, he was assigned to a special table. As the Court said,

> There is a vast difference—a Constitutional difference—between restrictions imposed by the state which prohibit the intellectual commingling of students, and the refusal of individuals to commingle where the state presents no such bar.[8]

The final case, argued and decided the same day as the *McLaurin* case, was *Sweatt* v. *Painter,* 339 U.S. 629, 70 S. Ct. 848 (1950). Mr. Sweatt had been denied admission to the University of Texas Law School solely because of his race. A law school for Negroes was established while Mr. Sweatt was trying to enforce his rights by court action, but Mr. Sweatt refused to register in the new school. The trial court found that the new school offered the petitioner "'privileges, advantages, and opportunities for the study of law substantially equivalent to those offered by the State to white students at the University of Texas,'"[9] and denied mandamus. The Supreme Court compared, point by point, the facilities offered by the two institutions, and found the University of Texas Law School was clearly superior. Then the Court went on to say,

Sweatt v. *Painter,* 339 U.S. 629, 634–636 (1950)

> . . . What is more important, the University of Texas Law school possesses to a far greater degree those qualities which are incapable of objective measurement but which make for greatness in a law school. Such qualities, to name but a few, include reputation of the faculty, experience of the administration, position and influence of the alumni, standing in the community, traditions and prestige. It

[7]*Sipuel* v. *University of Oklahoma,* 332 U.S. 631, pp. 632, 633.
[8]*McLaurin* v. *Oklahoma State Regents,* 339 U.S. 637, p. 641.
[9]*Sweatt* v. *Painter,* 339 U.S. 629 p. 632.

is difficult to believe that one who had a free choice between these law schools would consider the question close.

Moreover, although the law is a highly learned profession, we are well aware that it is an intensely practical one. The law school, the proving ground for legal learning and practice, cannot be effective in isolation from the individuals and institutions with which the law interacts. Few students and no one who has practiced law would choose to study in an academic vacuum, removed from the interplay of ideas and the exchange of views with which the law is concerned. The law school to which Texas is willing to admit petitioner excludes from its student body members of the racial groups which number 85% of the population of the State and include most of the lawyers, witnesses, jurors, judges and other officials with whom petitioner will inevitably be dealing when he becomes a member of the Texas Bar. With such a substantial and significant segment of society excluded, we cannot conclude that the education offered petitioner is substantially equal to that which he would receive if admitted to the University of Texas Law School.

It may be argued that excluding petitioner from that school is no different from excluding white students from the new law school. This contention overlooks realities. It is unlikely that a member of a group so decisively in the majority, attending a school with rich traditions and prestige which only a history of consistently maintained excellence could command, would claim that the opportunities afforded him for legal education were unequal to those held open to petitioner. . . .

It is fundamental that these cases concern rights which are personal and present. This Court has stated unanimously that "The State must provide [legal education] for [petitioner] in conformity with the equal protection clause of the Fourteenth Amendment and provide it as soon as it does for applicants of any other group." *Sipuel* v. *Board of Regents,* 332 U.S. 631, 633, (1948). . .

In accordance with these cases, petitioner may claim his full constitutional right: legal education equivalent to that offered by the State to students of other races. Such education is not available to him in a separate law school as offered by the State. We cannot, therefore, agree with respondents that the doctrine of *Plessy* v. *Ferguson,* 163 U.S. 537 (1896), requires affirmance of the judgment below. Nor need we reach petitioner's contention that *Plessy* v. *Ferguson* should be reexamined in the light of contemporary knowledge respecting the purposes of the Fourteenth Amendment and the effects of racial segregation. See *supra,* 339 U.S. 631.

We hold that the Equal Protection Clause of the Fourteenth Amendment requires that petitioner be admitted to the University of Texas Law School. The judgment is reversed and the cause is remanded for proceedings not inconsistent with this opinion.

Reversed.

Other cases concerning admission to college or graduate school followed these decisions.

The logic which applied to admission to college was ultimately applied to the separate-but-equal claims at the public school level. In *Brown* v. *Topeka,* 347 U.S. 483 (1954), 349 U.S. 294 (1955), and the four companion cases the Court proceeded with great caution. First argued in 1952, they were reargued in the 1953 term. The attorneys-general of a number of states filed briefs as *amici curiae,* as did other organizations. After the initial decision in 1954, the Court itself requested answers to and viewpoints on a wide variety of questions, ranging from the original intent of Congress in proposing the Fourteenth Amendment, through the effect of "separate but equal" on Negro children, to ideas concerning the orders the Court should issue to implement the decision. The second decision came in 1955.

Brown v. *Board of Education,* 347 U.S. 483, 74 S. Ct. 686 (1954)

MR. CHIEF JUSTICE WARREN delivered the opinion of the Court.

These cases come to us from the States of Kansas, South Carolina, Virginia, and Delaware. They are premised on different fact and different local conditions, but a common legal question justifies their consideration together in this consolidated opinion.

In each of the cases, minors of the Negro race, through their legal representatives, seek the aid of the courts in obtaining admission to the public schools of their community on a nonsegregated basis. In each instance, they had been denied admission to schools attended by white children under laws requiring or permitting segregation according to race. This segregation was alleged to deprive the plaintiffs of the equal protection of the laws under the Fourteenth Amendment. In each of the cases other than the Delaware case, a three-judge federal district court denied relief to the plaintiffs on the so-called "separate but equal" doctrine announced by this Court in *Plessy* v. *Ferguson,* 163 U.S. 537. Under that doctrine, equality of treatment is accorded when the races are provided substantially equal facilities, even though these facilities be separate. In the Delaware case, the Supreme Court of Delaware adhered to that doctrine, but ordered that the plaintiffs be admitted to the white schools because of their superiority to the Negro schools.

The plaintiffs contend that segregated public schools are not "equal" and cannot be made "equal," and that hence they are deprived of the equal protection of the laws. Because of the obvious importance of the question presented, the Court took jurisdiction. Argument was heard in the 1952 Term, and reargument was heard this Term on certain questions propounded by the Court.

Reargument was largely devoted to the circumstances surrounding the adoption of the Fourteenth Amendment in 1868. It covered exhaustively consideration of the Amendment in Congress, ratification by the states, the existing practices in racial segregation, and the views of proponents and opponents of the Amendment. This discussion and our own investigation convince us that, although these sources cast some light, it is not enough to resolve the problem with which we are faced. At best, they are inconclusive. The most avid proponents of the post-War Amendments undoubtedly intended them to remove all legal distinctions among "all persons born or naturalized in the United States." Their opponents, just as certainly, were antagonistic to both the letter and the spirit of the Amendments and wished them to have the most limited effect. What others in Congress and the state legislatures had in mind cannot be determined with any degree of certainty.

An additional reason for the inconclusive nature of the Amendment's history, with respect to segregated schools, is the status of public education at that time. In the South, the movement toward free common schools, supported by general taxation had not yet taken hold. Education of white children was largely in the hands of private groups. Education of Negroes was almost non-existent, and practically all of the race were illiterate. In fact, any education of Negroes was forbidden by law in some states. Today, in contrast, many Negroes have achieved outstanding success in the arts and sciences as well as in the business and professional world. It is true that public school education at the time of the Amendment had advanced further in the North, but the effect of the Amendment on Northern States was generally ignored in the congressional debates. Even in the North, the conditions of public education did not approximate those existing today. The curriculum was usually rudimentary; ungraded schools were common in rural areas; the school term was but three months a year in many states; and compulsory school attendance was virtually unknown. As a consequence, it is not surprising that there should be so little in the history of the Fourteenth Amendment relating to its intended effect on public education.

In the first cases in this Court construing the Fourteenth Amendment, decided shortly after its adoption, the Court interpreted it as proscribing all state-imposed discriminations against the Negro race. The doctrine of "separate but equal" did not make its appearance in this Court until 1896 in the case of *Plessy* v. *Ferguson, supra,* involving not education but transportation. American courts have since labored with the doctrine for over half a century. In this Court, there have been six cases involving the "separate but equal" doctrine in the field of public education. In *Cumming* v. *County Board of Education,* 175 U.S. 528, and *Gong Lum* v. *Rice,* 275 U.S. 78, the validity of the doctrine itself was not challenged. In more recent cases, all on the graduate school level, inequality was found in that specific benefits enjoyed by white students were denied to Negro students of the same educational qualifications. *Missouri* ex rel. *Gaines* v. *Canada,* 305 U.S. 337; *Sipuel* v. *Board of Regents of University of Okla-*

homa, 332 U.S. 631; *Sweatt* v. *Painter,* 339 U.S. 629; *McLaurin* v. *Oklahoma State Regents,* 339 U.S. 637. In none of these cases was it necessary to re-examine the doctrine to grant relief to the Negro plaintiff. And in *Sweatt* v. *Painter, supra,* Court expressly reserved decision on the question whether *Plessy* v. *Ferguson* should be held inapplicable to public education.

In the instant cases, that question is directly presented. Here, unlike *Sweatt* v. *Painter,* there are findings below that the Negro and white schools involved have been equalized, or are being equalized, with respect to buildings, curricula, qualifications and salaries of teachers, and other "tangible" factors. Our decision, therefore, cannot turn on merely a comparison of these tangible factors in the Negro and white schools involved in each of the cases. We must look instead to the effect of segregation itself on public education.

In approaching this problem, we cannot turn the clock back to 1868 when the Amendment was adopted, or even to 1896 when *Plessy* v. *Ferguson* was written. We must consider public education in the light of its full development and its present place in American life throughout the Nation. Only in this way can it be determined if segregation in public schools deprives these plaintiffs of the equal protection of the laws.

Today, education is perhaps the most important function of state and local governments. Compulsory school attendance laws and the great expenditures for education both demonstrate our recognition of the importance of education to our democratic society. It is required in the performance of our most basic public responsibilities, even service in the armed forces. It is the very foundation of good citizenship. Today it is a principal instrument in awakening the child to cultural values, in preparing him for later professional training, and in helping him to adjust normally to his environment. In these days, it is doubtful that any child may reasonably be expected to succeed in life if he is denied the opportunity of an education. Such an opportunity, where the state has undertaken to provide it, is a right which must be made available to all on equal terms.

We come then to the question presented: Does segregation of children in public schools solely on the basis of race, even though the physical facilities and other "tangible" factors may be equal, deprive the children of the minority group of equal educational opportunities? We believe that it does.

In *Sweatt* v. *Painter, supra,* in finding that a segregated law school for Negroes could not provide them equal educational opportunities, this Court relied in large part on "those qualities which are incapable of objective measurement but which make for greatness in a law school." In *McLaurin* v. *Oklahoma State Regents, supra,* the Court, in requiring that a Negro admitted to a white graduate school be treated like all other students, again resorted to intangible considerations: ". . . his ability to study, to engage in discussions and exchange views with other students, and in general, to learn his profession." Such considerations apply with added force to children in grade and high schools. To separate them from others of similar age and qualifications solely because of their race generates a feeling of inferiority as to their status in the community that may affect their hearts and minds in a way unlikely ever to be undone. The effect of this separation of their educational opportunities was well stated by a finding in the Kansas case by a court which nevertheless felt compelled to rule against the Negro plaintiffs:

"Segregation of white and colored children in public schools has a detrimental effect upon the colored children. The impact is greater when it has the sanction of the law; for the policy of separating the races is usually interpreted as denoting the inferiority of the negro group. A sense of inferiority affects the motivation of a child to learn. Segregation with the sanction of law, therefore, has a tendency to [retard] the educational and mental development of negro children and to deprive them of some of the benefits they would receive in a racial[ly] integrated school system."

Whatever may have been the extent of psychological knowledge at the time of *Plessy* v. *Ferguson,* this finding is amply supported by modern authority. Any language in *Plessy* v. *Ferguson* contrary to this finding is rejected.

We conclude that in the field of public education the doctrine of "separate but equal" has no place. Separate educational facilities are inherently unequal. Therefore, we hold that the plaintiffs and others similarly situated for whom the actions have been brought are, by reason of the segregation complained of, deprived of the equal protection of the laws guaranteed by the Fourteenth Amendment. This disposition makes unnecessary any discussion whether such segregation also violates the Due Process Clause of the Fourteenth Amendment.

Because these are class actions, because of the wide applicability of this decision, and because of the great variety of local conditions, the formulation of decrees in these cases presents problems of considerable complexity. On reargument, the consideration of appropriate relief was necessarily subordinated to the primary question—the constitutionality of segregation in public education. We have now announced that such segregation is a denial of the equal protection of the laws. In order that we may have the full assistance of the parties in formulating decrees, the cases will be restored to the docket, and the parties are requested to present further argument on Questions 4 and 5 previously propounded by the Court for the reargument this Term. The Attorney General of the United States is again invited to participate. The Attorneys General of the states requiring or permitting segregation in public education will also be permitted to appear as *amici curiae* upon request to do so by September 15, 1954, and submission of briefs by October 1, 1954.

It is so ordered.

Brown v. Board of Education of Topeka, Kansas, 349 U.S. 294, 75 S. Ct. 753; 1955

MR. CHIEF JUSTICE WARREN delivered the opinion of the Court.

These cases were decided on May 17, 1954. The opinions of that date, declaring the fundamental principle that racial discrimination in public education is unconstitutional, are incorporated herein by reference. All provisions of federal, state, or local law requiring or permitting such discrimination must yield to this principle. There remains for consideration the manner in which relief is to be accorded.

Because these cases arose under different local conditions and their disposition will involve a variety of local problems, we requested further argument on the question of relief. In view of the nationwide importance of the decision, we invited the Attorney General of the United States and the Attorneys General of all states requiring or permitting racial discrimination in public education to present their views on that question. . . .

These presentations were informative and helpful to the Court in its consideration of the complexities arising from the transition to a system of public education freed of racial discrimination. The presentations also demonstrated that substantial steps to eliminate racial discrimination in public schools have already been taken. . . .

Full implementation of these constitutional principles may require solution of varied local school problems. School authorities have the primary responsibility for elucidating, assessing, and solving these problems; courts will have to consider whether the action of school authorities constitutes good faith implementation of the governing constitutional principles. Because of their proximity to local conditions and the possible need for further hearings, the courts which originally heard these cases can best perform this judicial appraisal. Accordingly, we believe it appropriate to remand the cases to those courts.

In fashioning and effectuating the decrees, the courts will be guided by equitable principles. . . . At stake is the personal interest of the plaintiffs in admission to public schools as soon as practicable on a nondiscriminatory basis. To effectuate this interest may call for elimination of a variety of obstacles in making the transition to school systems operated in accordance with the constitutional principles set forth in our May 17, 1954, decision. Courts of equity may properly take into account the public interest in the elimination of such obstacles in a systematic and effective manner. But it should go without saying that the vitality of these constitutional principles cannot be allowed to yield simply because of disagreement with them.

While giving weight to these public and private considerations, the courts will require that the defendants make a prompt and reasonable start toward full compliance with our May 17, 1954, ruling.

Once such a start has been made, the courts may find that additional time is necessary to carry out the ruling in an effective manner. The burden rests upon the defendants to establish that such time is necessary in the public interest and is consistent with good faith compliance at the earliest practicable date. To that end, the courts may consider problems related to administration arising from the physical condition of the school plant, the school transportation system, personnel, revision of school districts and attendance areas into compact units to achieve a system of determining admisssion to the public schools on a nonracial basis, and revision of local laws and regulations which may be necessary in solving the foregoing problems. They will also consider the adequacy of any plans the defendants may propose to meet these problems and to effectuate a transition to a racially nondiscriminatory school system. During this period of transition, the courts will retain jurisdiction of these cases.

The judgments below, except that in the Delaware case, are accordingly reversed and the cases are remanded to the District Courts to take such proceedings and enter such orders and decrees consistent with this opinion as are necessary and proper to admit to public schools on a racially nondiscriminatory basis with all deliberate speed the parties to these cases. The judgment in the Delaware case . . . is affirmed on the basis of the principles stated in our May 17, 1954, opinion. . . .   *It is so ordered.*

Bolling v. *Sharpe,* 347 U.S. 497, 74 S. Ct. 694 (1954), was decided separately, for it was the only case in which a federal district was involved. Such separate treatment was required because the

Fifth Amendment, applicable to the District of Columbia, does not contain an equal protection clause as does the Fourteenth Amendment which applies only to the states. But the concepts of equal protection and due process, both stemming from our American idea of fairness, are not mutually exclusive. The "equal protection of the laws" is a more explicit safeguard of prohibited unfairness than "due process of law," and, therefore, we do not imply that the two are always interchangeable phrases. But, as this Court has recognized, discrimination may be so unjustifiable as to be violative of due process.[10]

The caution of the Court in dealing with the school segregation cases was necessary, for millions of people would be affected by the decisions, many of them in a fashion they would consider adverse. In some 17 states and in the District of Columbia segregation was required by law; in four states, it was subject to local option. Over ten and a half million children, almost four-fifths of them white, would be affected by the decisions. With the attitude of some states toward desegregation on any level, open defiance of the Court's decree was possible, as was

[10]*Bolling* v. *Sharpe,* 347 U.S. 497, p. 499.

more subtle delay to prevent implementation of the Court's orders, even though time was allowed to work out the problems, both psychological and financial.

Desegregation of the public schools was only a part of the problem. If segregation in the public schools were a denial of equal protection of the law, it would be difficult, if not impossible, to defend in other public areas. According to the terms of the Fourteenth Amendment,

> No State shall make or enforce any law which shall abridge the privileges or immunities of citizens of the United States; nor shall any State deprive any person of life, liberty or property, without due process of law; nor deny to any person within its jurisdiction the equal protection of the law.

In *The Civil Rights Cases* (109 U.S. 3, 3 S. Ct. 18; 1883), the Court had held that the Amendment was a limitation upon the states, not upon the inhabitants of a state who might discriminate on the basis of race. But what is state action? Clearly the state could not pass a law depriving any person of "life, liberty, or property without due process of law," but neither could it use its legal processes to enforce private discrimination, as was apparent in *Shelley* v. *Kraemer*. Of course, a number of years passed before the Court made this point of view explicit, but by the time the School Desegregation cases were decided it seemed fairly clear that under the equal protection clause, state action could not be used to enforce segregation, although the limits of state power had to be tested in a number of cases. A state (or subdivisions of a state) may refuse to provide certain services, but if they are provided, segregation cannot be compelled by the law. Nor may segregation be continued by conveying property to individuals to operate on a segregated basis. As the Court said in *Johnson* v. *Virginia*, 373 U.S. 61, 83 S. Ct. 1053 (1963), a case in which a Negro had been convicted of contempt of the Traffic Court of Richmond because he sat in the section of the courtroom reserved for whites,

> It is no longer open to question that a State may not constitutionally require segregation of public facilities. . . . State-compelled segregation in a court of justice is a manifest violation of the State's duty to deny no one the equal protection of its laws. [11]

Although a number of communities made good-faith efforts to desegregate schools and other public facilities, others did not. The defiant, or those who suffer at their hands, reach the courts. The School Board of the City of Little Rock, Ark., worked out a careful plan for desegregation, but was unable to put it in effect, because of action by the Gover-

[11] *Johnson* v. *Virginia*, 373 U.S. 61, p. 62.

nor of the state who took the position that the state had no duty to obey federal court orders based on the Supreme Court's interpretation of the Constitution. On September 2, 1957, the day before nine Negro children were to enter Little Rock Central High School, the Governor ordered National Guard units to prevent effectuation of the School Board's integration plan, despite the lack of a request for such action by local authorities. Some three weeks later the President of the United States sent federal troops to assure admission of the Negro students to the high school. Federalized National Guardsmen replaced them, and remained for the rest of the school year. Because of local hostility, which seemed to have been encouraged by the Governor's action, the Board petitioned in February of 1958 to delay the desegregation program. A special August term upheld the Court of Appeals' decision denying the school board the right to delay.[12]

A less flamboyant way to evade desegregation was put into effect by the County Public School Board of Prince Edward County, Virginia, one of the parties in the original Desegregation Cases. Desegregation was avoided by closing the public schools and awarding tuition grants to enable pupils to attend private segregated schools. A 1964 decision (377 U.S. 218, 84 S. Ct. 1226), held the public schools in Prince Edward County

and meanwhile contributing to the support of the private segregated white schools that took their place denied the petitioners the equal protection of the laws.[13]

An effort to hasten desegregation in areas other than the public schools culminated in the passage of the Civil Rights Act of 1964, in which the power of Congress over interstate commerce was the vehicle. The first part to be tested was the public accommodations sections, which were sustained in two opinions based upon different factual situations. The opinions were announced on December 14, 1964.

Underlying these new decisions are many others which have over the years attempted to define "interstate commerce," the exact point at which that commerce loses its interstate charcter and is therefore no longer subject to federal control. In *U.S.* v. *E. C. Knight* (156 U.S. 1, 15 S. Ct. 249; 1895), the distinction made was between "external" and "internal" trade. Although contracts made within a state would have an indirect effect on interstate commerce, the indirect effect was not sufficient to bring the company's activities within the federal law. Mr.

[12] *Cooper* v. *Aaron*, 358 U.S. 14, 78 S. Ct. 1401 (1958).
[13] *Griffin* v. *County School Board of Prince Edward Co.*, 377 U.S. 218, p.232.

Justice Harlan, of *Plessy* v. *Ferguson* fame, dissented, going back to the principles of *Gibbons* v. *Ogden,* to which the Court has now returned. But that return did not come about quickly.

The right of Congress to impose certain controls on commerce was recognized in *Stafford* v. *Wallace,* 258 U.S. 495, 42 S. Ct. 397 (1922), where practices "obstructed" or "unduly burdened" interstate commerce. In *National Labor Relations Board* v. *Jones* & *Laughlin Steel Corporation* (301 U.S. 1, 57 S. Ct. 615; 1937), the Court recognized that activities

> . . . intrastate in character, when separately considered, if they have such a close and substantial relation to interstate commerce that their control is essential or appropriate to protect that commerce from burdens and obstructions, Congress cannot be denied the power to exercise that control. . . . The question is necessarily one of degree.[14]

In 1942, in *Wickard* v. *Filburn* (317 U.S. 111, 63 S. Ct. 72) the Court came back to the *Gibbons* v. *Ogden* case (9 Wheat. 1; 1824).

> The Court's recognition of the relevance of the economic effects in the application of the Commerce Clause . . . has made the mechanical application of legal formulas no longer feasible. . . .
> . . . But even if appellant's activity be local and though it may not be regarded as commerce, it may still, whatever its nature, be reached by Congress if it exerts a substantial economic effect on interstate commerce, and this irrespective of whether such effect is what might at some earlier time have been defined as "direct" or "indirect". . . .[15]

As early as 1946, in *Morgan* v. *Virginia* (328 U.S. 373, 66 S. Ct. 1050), the United States Supreme Court had determined that racial discrimination could be an undue burden on commerce "in matters where uniformity is necessary—necessary in the constitutional sense of useful in accomplishing a permitted purpose."[16]

This development of the meaning "commerce" explains the phraseology of Title II of the Civil Rights Act of 1964, and why the United States Supreme Court could find that both the Heart of Atlanta Motel and Ollie's Barbecue were subject to the Act.

> *Heart of Atlanta Motel, Inc.* v. *United States,* 379 U.S. 241, 85 S. Ct. 348 (1964)

MR. JUSTICE CLARK delivered the opinion of the Court.

This is a declaratory judgment action, 28 U.S.C. § 2201 and § 2202, attacking the constitutionality of Title II of the Civil Rights Act of

[14]*N.L.R.B.* v. *Jones and Laughlin Steel Corp.,* 301 U.S. 1, p. 37.
[15]*Gibbons* v. *Ogden,* 9 Wheat. 1 (1824). [16]*Morgan* v. *Virginia,* 328 U.S. 373 p. 377.

1964, 78 Stat. 241. . . . A three-judge court . . . sustained the validity of the Act and issued a permanent injunction on appellee's counterclaim restraining appellants from continuing to violate the Act. . . . We affirm the judgment. . . .

The case comes here on admissions and stipulated facts. Appellant owns and operates the Heart of Atlanta Motel which has 216 rooms available to transient guests. The motel is located on Courtland Street, two blocks from downtown Peachtree Street. It is readily accessible to interstate highways 75 and 85 and state highways 23 and 41. Appellant solicits patronage from outside the State of Georgia through various national advertising media, including magazines of national circulation; it maintains over 50 billboards and highway signs within the State, soliciting patronage for the motel; it accepts convention trade from outside Georgia and approximately 75% of its registered guests are from out of State. Prior to passage of the Act the motel had followed a practice of refusing to rent rooms to Negroes, and it alleged that it intended to continue to do so. In an effort to perpetuate that policy this suit was filed.

The appellant contends that Congress in passing this Act exceeded its power to regulate commerce under Art. I §8, cl. 3, of the Constitution of the United States; that the Act violates the Fifth Amendment because appellant is deprived of the right to choose its customers and operate its business as it wishes, resulting in a taking of its liberty and property without due process of law and a just compensation; and, finally, that by requiring appellant to rent available rooms to Negroes against its will, Congress is subjecting it to involuntary servitude in contravention of the Thirteenth Amendment.

The appellees counter that the unavailability to Negroes of adequate accommodations interferes significantly with interstate travel, and that Congress, under the Commerce Clause, has power to remove such obstructions and restraints; that the Fifth Amendment does not forbid reasonable regulation and that consequential damage does not constitute a "taking" within the meaning of that amendment; that the Thirteenth Amendment claim fails because it is entirely frivolous to say that an amendment directed to the abolition of human bondage and the removal of widespread disabilities associated with slavery places discrimination in public accommodations beyond the reach of both federal and state law.

At the trial the appellant offered no evidence, submitting the case on the pleadings, admissions and stipulations of facts; however, appellees proved the refusal of the motel to accept Negro transients after the passage of the Act. The District Court . . . issued a permanent injunction on the counterclaim of the appellees. It restrained the appellant from "refusing to accept Negroes as guests in the motel by reason of their race or color" and from "making any distinction whatever upon the basis of race or color in the availability of the goods, services, facilities, privileges, advantages or accommodations offered or made available to guests of the motel or to the general public, within or upon any of the premises of the Heart of Atlanta Motel, Inc.". . . .

Congress first evidenced its interest in civil rights legislation in the Civil Rights or Enforcement Act of April 9, 1866. There followed a series of six Acts, culminating in the Civil Rights Act of March 1, 1875. In 1883 this Court struck down the public accommodations sections of the 1875 Act in the *Civil Rights Cases*, 109 U.S.3. . . . No major legislation in this field had been enacted by Congress for 82 years when the Civil Rights Act of 1957 became law. It was followed by the Civil Rights Act of 1960. Three years later, on June 19, 1963, the late President Kennedy called for civil rights legislation in a message to Congress to which he attached a proposed bill. . . . However, it was not until July 2, 1964 that the Civil Rights Bill of 1964, here under attack, was finally passed. . . .

The Act as finally adopted was most comprehensive, undertaking to prevent through peaceful and voluntary settlement discrimination in voting, as well as in places of accommodation and public facilities, federally secured programs and in employment. Since Title II is the only portion under attack here, we confine our consideration to those public accommodation provisions. . . .

. . . Title [II] is divided into seven sections beginning with § 201 (a) which provides that:

"All persons shall be entitled to the full and equal enjoyment of the goods, services, facilities, privileges, advantages, and accommodations of any place of public accommodation, as defined in this section, without discrimination or segregation on the ground of race, color, religion, or national origin." * * *

It is admitted that the operation of the motel brings it within the provisions of §201(a) of the Act and that appellant refused to provide lodging for transient Negroes because of their race or color and that intends to continue that policy unless restrained.

The sole question posed is, therefore, the constitutionality of the Civil Rights Act of 1964 as applied to these facts. The legislative history of the Act indicates that Congress based the Act on § 5 and the Equal Protection Clause of the Fourteenth Amendment as well as its power to regulate interstate commerce under Art. I, §8, cl. 3 of the Constitution.

The Senate Commerce Committee made it quite clear that the fundamental object of Title II was to vindicate "the deprivation of personal dignity that surely accompanies denials of equal access to public establishments." At the same time, however, it noted that such an objective has been and could be readily achieved "by congressional action based on the commerce power of the Constitution." S.Rep. No 872, at 16–17. Our study of the legislative record, made in the light of prior cases, has brought us to the conclusion that Congress possessed ample power in this regard, and we have therefore not considered the other grounds relied upon. . . .

In light of our ground for decision, it might be well at the outset to discuss the *Civil Rights Cases, supra,* which declared provisions of the Civil Rights Act of 1875 unconstitutional. 18 Stat. 335, 336. We think that decision inapposite, and without precedential value in determining the constitutionality of the present Act. Unlike Title II of the present legislation, the 1875 Act broadly proscribed discrimination in "inns, public conveyances on land or water, theaters, and other places of public amusement," without limiting the categories of affected businesses to those impinging upon interstate commerce. ⁂ ⁂ ⁂

While the Act as adopted carried no congressional findings the record of its passage through each house is replete with evidence of the burdens that discrimination by race or color places upon interstate commerce. . . . This testimony included the fact . . . that Negroes in particular have been the subject of discrimination in transient accommodations . . . and that these conditions had become so acute as to require the listing of available lodging for Negroes in a special guidebook which was itself "dramatic testimony of the difficulties" Negroes encounter in travel. . . . These exclusionary practices were found to be nationwide. . . . This testimony indicated a qualitative as well as quantitive effect on interstate travel by Negroes. . . .

The power of Congress to deal with these obstructions depends on the meaning of the Commerce Clause. Its meaning was first enunciated 140 years ago by the great Chief Justice John Marshall in *Gibbons* v. *Ogden,* 9 Wheat. 1 (1824), in these words: . . .

". . . commerce . . . is intercourse ⁂ ⁂ ⁂ between nations, and parts of nations, in all its branches, and is regulated by prescribing rules for carrying on that intercourse [At 189–190.] ⁂ ⁂ ⁂

"To what commerce does this power extend? The constitution informs us, to commerce 'with foreign nations, and among the several States, and with the Indian tribes.' ⁂ ⁂ ⁂

"We are now arrived at the inquiry—What is this power?

"It is the power to regulate; that is, to prescribe the rule by which commerce is to be governed. This power, like all others vested in Congress, is complete in itself, may be exercised to its utmost extent, and acknowledges no limitations, other than are prescribed in the constitution ⁂ ⁂ ⁂ . . ."

In short, the determinative test of the exercise of power by the Congress under the Commerce Clause is simply whether the activity sought to be regulated is "commerce which concerns more than one state" and has a real and substantial relation to the national interest. Let us now turn to this facet of the problem. ⁂ ⁂ ⁂

. . . In framing Title II of this Act Congress was also dealing with what is considered a moral problem. But that fact does not detract from the overwhelming evidence of the disruptive effect that racial discrimination has had on commercial intercourse. It was this burden which empowered Congress to enact appropriate legislation, and, given this basis for the exercise of its power, Congress was not restricted by the fact that the particular obstruction to interstate commerce with which it was dealing was also deemed a moral and social wrong.

It is said that the operation of the motel here is of a purely local character. But, assuming this to be true, "if it is interstate commerce that feels the pinch, it does not matter how local the operation which applies the squeeze." *United States* v. *Women's Sportswear Mfg. Ass'n*, 336 U.S. 460, 464 (1949). Thus the power of Congress to promote interstate commerce also includes the power to regulate the local incidents thereof, including local activities in both the States of origin and destination, which might have a substantial and harmful effect upon that commerce. . . .

Nor does the Act deprive appellant of liberty or property under the Fifth Amendment. The commerce power invoked here by the Congress is a specific and plenary one authorized by the Constitution itself. The only questions are: (1) whether Congress had a rational basis for finding that racial discrimination by motels affected commerce, and (2) if it had such a basis, whether the means it selected to eliminate that evil are reasonable and appropriate. If they are, appellant has no "right" to select its guests as it sees fit, free from governmental regulation. * * *

We find no merit in the remainder of appellant's contentions, including that of "involuntary servitude." As we have seen, 32 States prohibit racial discrimination in public accommodations. These laws but codify the common-law innkeeper rule which long predated the Thirteenth Amendment. It is difficult to believe that the Amendment was intended to abrogate this principle. . . .

We, therefore, conclude that the action of the Congress in the adoption of the Act as applied here to a motel which concededly serves interstate travelers is within the power granted it by the Commerce Clause of the Constitution, as interpreted by this Court for 140 years. . . . How obstructions in commerce may be removed—what means are to be employed—is within the sound and exclusive discretion of the Congress. It is subject only to one *caveat* —that means chosen by it must be reasonably adapted to the end permitted by the Constitution. We cannot say that its choice here was not so adapted. The Constitution requires no more.   *Affirmed.*

APPENDIX omitted.

MR. JUSTICE BLACK, concurring.† * * *

The basic constitutional question . . . which this Court must now decide is whether Congress exceeded its powers to regulate interstate commerce and pass all laws necessary and proper to such

---

†This opinion applies also to No. 543, *Katzenbach* v. *McClung*, 379 U. S. 294, 85 S. Ct. 377. [Footnote included in opinion—ED.]

regulation in subjecting either this motel or this restaurant to Title II's commands that applicants for food and lodging be served without regard to their color. And if the regulation is otherwise within the congressional commerce power, the motel and the restaurant proprietors further contend that it would be a denial of due process under the Fifth Amendment to compel them to serve Negroes against their will. I agree that all these constitutional contentions must be rejected. . . .

It requires no novel or strained interpretation of the Commerce Clause to sustain Title II as applied in either of these cases. At least since *Gibbons* v. *Ogden,* 9 Wheat. 1, decided in 1824, . . . it has been uniformly accepted that the power of Congress to regulate commerce among the States is plenary. . . .

Furthermore, it has long been held that the Necessary and Proper Clause, Art. 1, § 8, cl. 18, adds to the commerce power of Congress the power to regulate local instrumentalities operating within a single state if their activities burden the flow of commerce among the States. . . . [S]ince the *Shreveport Case* this Court has steadfastly followed, and indeed has emphasized time and time again, that Congress has ample power to protect interstate commerce from activities adversely and injuriously affecting it, which but for this adverse effect on interstate commerce would be beyond the power of Congress to regulate. . . .

There can be no doubt that the operations of both the motel and the restaurant here fall squarely within the measure Congress chose to adopt in the Act and deemed adequate to show a constitutionally prohibitable adverse effect on commerce. The choice of policy is of course within the exclusive power of Congress; but whether particular operations affect interstate commerce sufficiently to come under the constitutional power of Congress to regulate them is ultimately a judicial rather than a legislative question, and can be settled finally only by this Court. . . . * * *

But in deciding the constitutional power of Congress in cases like the two before us we do not consider the effect on interstate commerce of only one isolated, individual, local event, without regard to the fact that this single local event when added to many others of a similar nature may impose a burden on interstate commerce by reducing its volume or distorting its flow. . . . And the flow of interstate commerce may be impeded or distorted substantially if local sellers of interstate food are permitted to exclude all Negro consumers. Measuring, as this Court has so often held is required, by the aggregate effect of a great number of such acts of discrimination, I am of the opinion that Congress has constitutional power under the Commerce and Necessary and Proper Clauses to protect interstate commerce from the injuries bound to befall it from these discriminatory practices. . . .

In view of the Commerce Clause it is not possible to deny that the aim of protecting interstate commerce from undue burdens is a legitimate end. In view of the Thirteenth, Fourteenth and Fifteenth Amendments, it is not possible to deny that the aim of protecting Negroes from discrimination is also a legitimate end. The means adopted to achieve these ends are also appropriate, plainly adopted to achieve them and not prohibited by the Constitution but consistent with both its letter and spirit. . . .

The restaurant and motel proprietors argue also however, that Congress violated the Due Process Clause of the Fifth Amendment by requiring that they serve Negroes if they serve others. This argument comes down to this: that the broad power of Congress to enact laws deemed necessary and proper to regulate and protect interstate commerce is practically nullified by the negative constitutional command that no person shall be deprived of "life, liberty, or property, without due process of law" and that private property shall not be "taken" for public use without just compensation. In the past this Court has consistently held that regulation of the use of property by the Federal Government or by the States does not violate either the Fifth or the Fourteenth Amendments. . . . Moreover, it would be highly ironical to use the guarantee of due process—a guarantee which plays so important a part in the Fourteenth Amendment, an amendment adopted with the predominant aim ot protecting Negroes from discrimination—in order to strip Congress of power to protect Negroes from discrimination. . . .

For the foregoing reasons I concur in holding that the anti-racial-discrimination provision of Title II of the Civil Rights Act of 1964 are valid as applied to this motel and restaurant. . . .

MR. JUSTICE DOUGLAS, concurring.* . . .

Though I join the Court's opinion, I am somewhat reluctant here, as I was in *Edwards* v. *People of State of California*, 314 U.S. 160, 177, to rest solely on the Commerce Clause. My reluctance is not due to any conviction that Congress lacks power to regulate commerce in the interests of human rights. It is rather my belief that the right of people to be free of state action that discriminates against them because of race, like the "right of persons to move freely from State to State" (*Edwards* v. *People of State of California, supra*, at 177) "occupies a more protected position in our constitutional system than does the movement of cattle, fruit, steel and coal across state lines." *Ibid.*

Hence I would prefer to rest on the assertion of legislative power contained in §5 of the Fourteenth Amendment which states: "The Congress shall have power to enforce, by appropriate legislation, the provisions of this article"—a power which the Court concedes was exercised at least in part in this Act.

A decision based on the Fourteenth Amendment would have a more settling effect, making unnecessary litigation over whether a

---

*This opinion applies also to No. 543, *Katzenbach* v. *McClung*, 379 U.S. 294, 85 S. Ct. 377. [Footnote included in opinion.—Ed.]

particular restaurant or inn is within the commerce definitions of the Act or whether a particular customer is an interstate traveler. Under my construction, the Act would apply to all customers in all the enumerated places of public accommodation. And that construction would put an end to all obstructionist strategies and finally close one door on a bitter chapter in American history. . . .

I think the Court is correct in concluding that the Act is not founded on the Commerce Clause to the exclusion of the Enforcement Clause of the Fourteenth Amendment. . . .

"State action" – the key to Fourteenth Amendment guarantees – is defined by § 201(d). . . .

That definition is within our decision of *Shelley* v. *Kraemer,* 334 U.S. 1, for the "discrimination" in the present cases is "enforced by officials of the State," i.e., by the state judiciary under the trespass laws. * * *

Thus while I agree with the Court that Congress in fashioning the present Act used the Commerce Clause to regulate racial segregation, it also used (and properly so) some of its power under §5 of the Fourteenth Amendment. . . .

MR. JUSTICE GOLDBERG, concurring.*

I join in the opinions and judgments of the Court, since I agree "that the action of the Congress in the adoption of the Act as applied here * * * is within the power granted it by the Commerce Clause of the Constitution, as interpreted by this Court for 140 years," *Heart of Atlanta Motel, Inc.* v. *United States,* at 360.

The primary purpose of the Civil Rights Act of 1964, however, as the Court recognizes, and as I would underscore, is the vindication of human dignity and not mere economics. The Senate Commerce Committee made this quite clear. . . .

Katzenbach v. *McClung* 379 U.S. 294, 85 S. Ct. 377 (1964)

MR. JUSTICE CLARK delivered the opinion of the Court.

This case was argued with No. 515, *Hear of Atlanta Motel* v. *United States et al.,* decided this date, in which we upheld the constitutional validity of Title II of the Civil Rights Act of 1964 against an attack by hotels, motels, and like establishments. This complaint for injunctive relief against appellants attacks the constitutionality of the Act as applied to a restaurant. . . . An injunction was issued restraining appellants from enforcing the Act against the restaurant. . . . We now reverse the judgment. . . .

Ollie's Barbecue is a family-owned restaurant in Birmingham, Alabama . . . with a seating capacity of 220 customers. . . . The restaurant caters to a family and white-collar trade with a take-out

---

*This opinion applies also to No. 543, *Katzenbach* v. *McClung* 379 U.S. 294. [Footnote in opinion. – ED.]

service for Negroes. It employs 36 persons, two-thirds of whom are Negroes. . . .

The District Court expressly found that a substantial portion of the food served in the restaurant had moved in interstate commerce. The restaurant has refused to serve Negroes in its dining accommodations since its original opening in 1927, and since July 2, 1964, it has been operating in violation of the Act. The court below concluded that if it were required to serve Negroes it would lose a substantial amount of business.

On the merits, the District Court held that the Act could not be applied under the Fourteenth Amendment because it was conceded that the State 'of Alabama was not involved in the refusal of the restaurant to serve Negroes. . . . The Court concluded, however, that the Congress . . . had legislated a conclusive presumption that a restaurant affects interstate commerce if it serves or offers to serve interstate travelers or if a substantial portion of the food which it serves had moved in commerce. This, the court held, it could not do because there was no demonstrable connection between food purchased in interstate commerce and sold in a restaurant and the conclusion of Congress that discrimination in the restaurant would affect that commerce.

The basic holding in *Heart of Atlanta Motel, supra,* answers many of the contentions made by the appellees. . . .[1]

Section . . . 201(b) defines establishments as places of public accommodation if their operations affect commerce or segregation by them is supported by state action. Sections 201(b) (2) and (c) place any "restaurant * * * principally engaged in selling food for consumption on the premises" under the Act "if * * * it serves or offers to serve interstate travelers or a substantial portion of the food which it serves * * * has moved in commerce. . . ."

As we noted in *Heart of Atlanta Motel* both Houses of Congress conducted prolonged hearings on the Act. . . . The record is replete with testimony of the burdens placed on interstate commerce by racial discrimination in restaurants. . . . In addition, the Attorney General testified that this type of discrimination imposed "an artificial restriction on the market" and interfered with the flow of merchandise. . . .

Moreover there was an impressive array of testimony that discrimination in restaurants had a direct and highly restrictive effect upon interstate travel by Negroes. This resulted, it was said, because discrimination practices prevent Negroes from buying prepared food served on the premises while on a trip, except in isolated and unkempt restaurants and under most unsatisfactory and often unpleasant conditions. This obviously discourages travel and obstructs interstate commerce for one can hardly travel without eating.

[1] That decision disposes of the challenges that the appellees base on the Fifth, Ninth, Tenth, and Thirteenth Amendments, and on the *Civil Rights Cases,* 109 U.S. 3 (1883). [Footnote in opinion.—ED.]

Likewise, . . . discrimination deterred professional, as well as skilled, people from moving into areas where such practices occurred and thereby caused industry to be reluctant to establish there. S. Rep. No. 872, at 18–19.

We believe that this testimony afforded ample basis for the conclusion that established restaurants in such areas sold less interstate goods because of the discrimination, that interstate travel was obstructed directly by it, that business in general suffered and that many new businesses refrained from establishing there as a result of it. Hence the District Court was in error in concluding that there was no connection between discrimination and the movement of interstate commerce. . . .

It goes without saying that, viewed in isolation, the volume of food purchased by Ollie's Barbecue from sources supplied from out of state was insignificant when compared with the total foodstuffs moving in commerce. But, as our late Brother Jackson said for the Court in *Wickard* v. *Filburn*, 317 U.S. 111 (1942):

"That appellee's own contribution to the demand for wheat may be trivial by itself is not enough to remove him from the scope of federal regulation where, as here, his contribution, taken together with that of many others similarly situated, is far from trivial." [At 127– 128] * * *

Article I, §8, cl. 3, confers upon Congress the power "To regulate Commerce * * * among the several States" and Clause 18 of the same Article grants it the power "To make all Laws which shall be necessary and proper for carrying into Execution the foregoing Powers * * *." . . . Much is said about a restaurant business being local but "even if appellee's activity be local and though it may not be regarded as commerce, it may still, whatever its nature, be reached by Congress if it exerts a substantial economic effect on interstate commerce * * *." *Wickard* v. *Filburn, supra,* 125. . . .

This Court has held time and again that this power extends to activities or retail establishments, including restaurants, which directly or indirectly burden or obstruct interstate commerce. . . .

The appellees contend that Congress has arbitrarily created a conclusive presumption that all restaurants meeting the criteria set out in the Act "affect commerce." . . .

But Congress' action in framing this Act was not unprecedented. . . .

. . . Congress has determined for itself that refusals of service to Negroes have imposed burdens both upon the interstate flow of food and upon the movement of products generally. Of course, the mere fact that Congress has said when particular activity shall be deemed to affect commerce does not preclude further examination by this Court. But where we find that the legislators, in light of the facts and testimony before them, have a rational basis for finding a chosen regulatory scheme necessary to the protection of commerce, our investigation is at an end. The only remaining question—one answered in the affirmative by the court below—is whether the particular restaurant either serves or offers to serve interstate travelers or serves food a substantial portion of which has moved in interstate commerce. * * *

The absence of direct evidence connecting discriminatory restaurant service with the flow of interstate food, a factor on which the appellees place much reliance, is not, given the evidence as to the effect of such practices on other aspects of commerce, a crucial matter.

The power of Congress in this field is broad and sweeping; where it keeps within its sphere and violates no express constitutional limitation it has been the rule of this Court, going back almost to the founding days of the Republic, not to interfere. The Civil Rights Act of 1964, as here applied, we find to be plainly appropriate in the resolution of what the Congress found to be a national commercial problem of the first magnitude. We find it in no violation of any express limitations of the Constitution and we therefore declare it valid.

The judgment is therefore reversed. . . .

There are many other situations in which racial discrimination has been the motivating factor of the conduct complained of, but these cases have been decided on other grounds. Many of them have been in criminal law, and have been decided by the Supreme Court on the issue of fair trial, due process of law, forced confessions, or similar violations of the rights of the individual. In these cases the fact of racial discrimination has been subordinated to the questions concerning the treatment to which the accused is entitled, whatever his race may be.

CHAPTER SEVEN

Search and Seizure; Self-Incrimination; Sixth Amendment Rights to Counsel and Confrontation

Search and Seizure

A NUMBER OF ambiguities in the Fourth Amendment have had to be resolved by judicial decree. The Amendment reads:

> The rights of the people to be secure in their persons, houses, papers, and effects, against unreasonable searches and seizures, shall not be violated, and no warrants shall issue, but upon probable cause, supported by Oath or affirmation, and particularly describing the place to be searched, and the persons or things to be seized.

The words "unreasonable," "probable cause," and "particularly describing" have all required judicial interpretation.

However, three other ambiguities are not apparent in the phraseology. The first is the close relationship between the Fourth Amendment and the Fifth Amendment's proscription against self-incrimination. The second is the fact that until *Mapp* v. *Ohio* in 1961, the strictures of the Fourth Amendment applied to the states only insofar as a particular search and seizure violated the due process standards of the Fourteenth Amendment. Part of the Court's assessment of these standards took into consideration the power of each state in our federal system to establish its own norms of justice, as long as those norms came within the somewhat uncertain boundaries of "due process of law." The third is the result of the advance of science, and involves issues which have been raised by the development of wiretapping and electronic listening devices.

If the Fourth Amendment is violated, either in a federal case or under "due process of law" in a state case, and evidence resulting from the search or seizure is wrongly admitted, the case may be reversed, perhaps leaving law enforcement officers without sufficient evidence for a second conviction. The Fourth Amendment has never been interpreted to forbid search or seizure before a warrant is procured. Search and seizure may be valid without a warrant, if there is reasonable cause to believe that a crime is about to be committed, is being committed, or has just been committed or if in fact a crime is being conmitted or has just been committed. The Fourth Amendment is commonly invoked by litigants who claim that search warrants could have been procured, but were not.

In 1886 the Supreme Court found the Fourth and Fifth Amendments interdependent in the *Boyd* case (*Boyd* v. *U.S.*, 116 U.S. 616, 6 S. Ct. 524). Under a statute of 1874, in all suits "other than criminal" arising under the revenue laws of the United States, the attorney for the government could ask the court to require a defendant to produce in court specified papers within his control. If the defendant failed to produce the papers, the allegations in the prosecuting attorney's motion to produce would be taken as confessed. If the papers were produced, the government was permitted to examine them, and could offer them in evidence "on behalf ot the United States." In other words, the defendant was required to produce evidence for the government and it could be used against him. If he refused to produce the papers, he was admitting the truth of the government's allegations. He could, therefore, lose the the case either way. Technically, however, this proceeding was "other than criminal," thus presumably avoiding entanglement with the Fifth Amendment's proscription against self-incrimination. The Supreme Court found that the proceedings under this section of the statute were criminal in nature, even though they were civil in form. In addition, the Court held that the requirement of producing the papers was not only the equivalent of a search and seizure, but was also an *unreasonable* search and seizure, because it was made for the purpose of compelling a person "in a criminal case to be a witness against himself." The Court looked beyond the form to the substance to protect the rights of the defendant.

The development of the telephone, wiretapping and electronic eavesdropping devices, and efforts to limit their use to invade the constitutional rights of individuals have resulted in a subdivision of problems revolving around search and seizure and self-incrimination. Some of the problems are old: the Supreme Court's recognition of the right of the states to control their judicial processes is one, and the old common law rule that even though evidence is obtained by illegal means it is still admissible is another. In addition to the application of old viewpoints to the use of these highly sophisticated electronic devices, statutes have been adopted by the federal government and by a number of states. All are directed toward at least the control of the use of the new devices, and some statutes forbid their use. A number of states have adopted statutes which allow particular officers to obtain special permission to use these tools for limited investigatory purposes. Of course, when a statute is adopted, there are also immediate questions concerning its meaning and application.

In *Olmstead* v. *U.S.*, 277 U.S. 438, 48 S. Ct. 564 (1928), the sole question considered was "whether the use of private telephone conversations between the defendants and others, intercepted by wire tapping, amounted to a violation of the Fourth and Fifth Amendments."[1] Three telephone companies were allowed to file briefs as *amici curiae*. Their interest, of course, was to protect the privacy of telephone conversations. By the use of evidence procured by means of tapping their telephone wires, Olmstead and others had been convicted of a conspiracy to violate the Prohibition Act. Since the wires had been tapped in the basement of a public building, there was no question of trespass because the agents had not gone upon the property of the defendants. There was, however, a state statute which made it a misdemeanor to "intercept, read, or in any way interrupt or delay the sending of a message over any telegraph or telephone line. . . ."[2]

Olmstead v. *United States*, 277 U.S. 438, 48 S. Ct. 564 (1928)

MR. CHIEF JUSTICE TAFT delivered the opinion of the Court. * * *

The well-known historical purpose of the Fourth Amendment, directed against general warrants and writs of assistance, was to prevent the use of governmental force to search a man's house, his person, his papers and his effects; and to prevent their seizure against his will. This phase of the misuse of governmental power of compulsion is the emphasis of the opinion of the Court in the *Boyd* case. This appears too in the *Weeks* case, in the *Silverthorne* case and in the *Amos* case. * * *

The Amendment itself shows that the search is to be of material things — the person, the house, his papers or his effects. The description of the warrant necessary to make the proceeding lawful, is that it

[1]*Olmstead* v. *U.S.*, 277 U.S. 438, p. 455.
[2]*Olmstead* v. *U.S.*, 277 U.S. 438, p. 468.

must specify the place to be searched and the person or *things* to be seized. * * *

The United States takes no such care of telegraph or telephone messages as of mailed sealed letters. The Amendment does not forbid what was done here. There was no searching. There was no seizure. The evidence was secured by the use of the sense of hearing and that only. There was no entry of the houses or offices of the defendants. * * *

Congress may of course protect the secrecy of telephone messages by making them, when intercepted, inadmissible in evidence in federal criminal trials, by direct legislation, and thus depart from the common law of evidence. But the courts may not adopt such a policy by attributing an enlarged and unusual meaning to the Fourth Amendment. . . .

Neither the cases we have cited nor any of the many federal decisions brought to our attention hold the Fourth Amendment to have been violated as against a defendant unless there has been an official search and seizure of his person, or such a seizure of his papers or his tangible material effects, or an actual physical invasion of his house "or curtilage" for the purpose of making a seizure.

We think, therefore, that the wire tapping here disclosed did not amount to a search or seizure within the meaning of the Fourth Amendment. * * *

A standard which would forbid the reception of evidence if obtained by other than nice ethical conduct by government officials would make society suffer and give criminals greater immunity than has been known heretofore. In the absence of controlling legislation by Congress, those who realize the difficulties in bringing offenders to justice may well deem it wise that the exclusion of evidence should be confined to cases where rights under the Constitution would be violated by admitting it. * * *

MR. JUSTICE HOLMES dissenting.

[W]e must consider the two objects of desire, both of which we cannot have, and make up our minds which to choose. It is desirable that criminals should be detected, and to that end that all available evidence should be used. It also is desirable that the Government should not itself foster and pay for other crimes, when they are the means by which the evidence is to be obtained. If it pays its officers for having got evidence by crime I do not see why it may not as well pay them for getting it in the same way, and I can attach no importance to protestations of disapproval if it knowingly accepts and pays and announces that in future it will pay for the fruits. We have to choose, and for my part I think it a less evil that some criminals should escape than that the Government should play an ignoble part.

For those who agree with me, no distinction can be taken between the Government as prosecutor and the Government as judge. If the existing code does not permit district attorneys to have a hand in such dirty business it does not permit the judge to allow such iniq-uities to succeed. . . . And if all that I have said so far be accepted it makes no difference that in this case wire tapping is made a crime by the law of the State, not by the law of the United States. . . . I hardly think that the United States would appear to greater advant-age when paying for an odious crime against State law than when inciting to the disregard of its own. * * *

MR. JUSTICE BRANDEIS, dissenting. * * *
. . . "We must never forget," said Mr. Chief Justice Marshall in *McCulloch* v. *Maryland,* 4 Wheat, 316, 407, "that it is a constitution we are expounding." Since then, this Court has repeatedly sustained the exercise of power by Congress, under various clauses of that instrument, over objects of which the Fathers could not have dreamed. . . . Clauses guaranteeing to the individual protection against specific abuses of power, must have a similar capacity of adaptation to a changing world. . . .
When the Fourth and Fifth Amendments were adopted, "the form that evil had theretofore taken," had been necessarily simple. Force and violence were then the only means known to man by which a Government could directly effect self-incrimination. . . . Subtler and more far-reaching means of invading privacy have become available to the Government. Discovery and invention have made it possible for the Government, by means far more effective than stretching upon the rack, to obtain disclosure in court of what is whispered in the closet.

With the adoption of the Federal Communications Act in 1934, the question of restrictions upon wiretapping at both state and federal levels became infinitely more complex. The meaning and applica-bility of Section 605 of that Act have been the subject of controversy ever since. In part, the section follows.

. . . no person not being authorized by the sender shall intercept any communication and divulge or publish the existence, contents, substance, purport, effect, or meaning of such intercepted communi-cation to any person; and no person not being entitled thereto shall receive or assist in receiving any interstate or foreign communication by wire or radio and use the same or any information therein con-tained for his own benefit or for the benefit of another not entitled thereto; and no person having received such intercepted communi-cation or having become acquainted with the contents, substance, purport, effect, or meaning of the same or any part thereof, knowing that such information was so obtained, shall divulge or publish the existence, contents, substance, purport, effect, or meaning of the same or any part thereof, or use the same or any information con-tained for his own benefit or for the benefit of another not entitled thereto: . . .

Problems concerning the meaning and application of the statute were considered in the two *Nardone* cases. The first, *Nardone* v. *U.S.*, 302 U.S. 379, 58 S. Ct. 275 (1937), questioned the applicability of the statute to the federal government as the sovereign. The Court, however applied the principle that "the sovereign is embraced by general words of a statute intended to prevent injury and wrong."[3] The statute, therefore, included federal agents in the ban against interception and communication, and testimony about the contents of a message was banned. In the second *Nardone* case (*Nardone* v. *U.S.* 308 U.S. 338, 60 S. Ct. 266; 1939), the Court held inadmissible "testimony which had become accessible by the use of" wiretapping.[4] Quoting another case, the Court found pertinent: "'The essence of a provision forbidding the acquisition of evidence in a certain way is that not merely evidence so acquired shall not be used before the court, but that it shall not be used at all.'"[5] Derivative or direct, the evidence obtained by the federal government in wire tapping cannot be used. The fact that the evidence is obtained by tapping an intrastate line does not make it admissible (*Weiss* v. *U.S.*, 308 U.S. 321, 60 S. Ct. 269; 1939). One step closer to protection against evidence procured by wiretapping was taken in *Benanti* v. *U.S.*, 355 U.S. 96, 78 S. Ct. 155 (1957), in which the Court held that "evidence obtained by means forbidden by Section 605, whether by state or federal agents, is inadmissible in federal court."[6] The case also seemed to interpret the statute as prohibiting wiretapping by state officers acting under authority of state law.

In state courts admissibility of evidence procured by illegal search and seizure was limited by the law of the state, and not the federal law. In affirming the State of Colorado Supreme Court's decision to allow the admission of evidence obtained by unreasonable search and seizure, in *Wolf* v. *Colorado* MR. JUSTICE FRANKFURTER delivered the opinion of the Court.

Wolf v. *Colorado*, 338 U.S. 25, 69 S. Ct. 1359 (1949)

The precise question for consideration is this: Does a conviction by a State court for a State offense deny the "due process of law" required by the Fourteenth Amendment, solely because evidence that was admitted at the trial was obtained under circumstances which would have rendered it inadmissible in a prosecution for violation of a federal law in a court of the United States because there deemed to be an infraction of the Fourth Amendment as applied in *Weeks* v. *United States*, 232 U.S. 383? . . . The notion that the "due process of

---

[3]*Nardone* v. *U.S.*, 302 U.S. 379, p. 384.   [4]*Nardone* v. *U.S.*, 308 U.S. 338, p. 339.
[5]*Ibid.*, p. 341.   [6]*Benanti* v. *U.S.*, 355 U.S. 96, p. 100.

law" guaranteed by the Fourteenth Amendment is shorthand for the first eight amendments of the Constitution and thereby incorporates them has been rejected by this Court again and again, after impressive consideration. . . .

This Clause exacts from the States for the lowliest and the most outcast all that is "implicit in the concept of ordered liberty." 302 U.S. at page 325.

Due process of law thus conveys neither formal nor fixed nor narrow requirements. It is the compendious expression for all those rights which the courts must enforce because they are basic to our free society. But basic rights do not become petrified as of any one time, even though, as a matter of human experience, some may not too rhetorically be called eternal verities. . . .

To rely on a tidy formula for the easy determination of what is a fundamental right for purposes of legal enforcement . . . belittles the scale of the conception of due process. The real clue to the problem . . . is not to ask where the line is once and for all to be drawn but to recognize that it is for the Court to draw it by the gradual and empiric process of "inclusion and exclusion." *Davidson* v. *New Orleans* 96 U.S. 97, 104. . . .

The security of one's privacy against arbitrary intrusion by the police — which is at the core of the Fourth Amendment — is basic to a free society. It is therefore implicit in "the concept of ordered liberty" and as such enforceable againt the States through the Due Process Clause. . . . But the ways of enforcing such a basic right raise questions of a different order. How such arbitrary conduct should be checked, what remedies against it should be afforded, the means by which the right should be made effective, are all questions that are not to be so dogmatically answered as to preclude the varying solutions which spring from an allowable range of judgment on issues not susceptible of quantitative solution. . . . But the immediate question is whether the basic right to protection against arbitrary intrusion by the police demands the exclusion of logically relevant evidence obtained by an unreasonable search and seizure because, in a federal prosecution for a federal crime, it would be excluded. . . . When we find that in fact most of the English-speaking world does not regard as vital to such protection the exclusion of evidence thus obtained, we must hesitate to treat this remedy as an essential ingredient of the right. The contrariety of views of the States is particularly impressive in view of the careful reconsideration which they have given the problem in the light of the *Weeks* decision. * * *

Justice Murphy in his dissent called attention to the illusory features of the "other remedies" available if the words are to mean "a positive deterrent to police and prosecutors tempted to violate the Fourth Amendment." He contended that the only real deterrent is the exclusion of evidence. If it is known that evidence obtained in violation of the Fourth Amendment will not be admitted in court, police and prosecutors will restrict their effort to procuring evidence by legally admissible means. But in a number of cases from state courts evidence was obtained by what would be a clear violation of the Fourth Amendment in a federal case before the Court was ready to apply the Fourth Amendment to state procedure.

Probably *Rochin* v. *California* provides the most vivid factual picture of what could occur in a search and seizure without the federal view of the Fourth Amendment's protection.

Rochin v. *California*, 342 U.S. 165, 72 S. Ct. 205 (1952)

MR. JUSTICE FRANKFURTER delivered the opinion of the Court.

Having "some information that [the petitioner here] was selling narcotics," three deputy sheriffs of the County of Los Angeles, on the morning of July 1, 1949, made for the two-story dwelling house in which Rochin lived with his mother, common-law wife, brothers and sisters. Finding the outside door open, they entered and then forced open the door to Rochin's room on the second floor. Inside they found petitioner sitting partly dressed on the side of the bed, upon which his wife was lying. On a "night stand" beside the bed the deputies spied two capsules. When asked "Whose stuff is this?" Rochin seized the capsules and put them in his mouth. A struggle ensued, in the course of which the three officers "jumped upon him" and attempted to extract the capsules. The force they applied proved unavailing against Rochin's resistance. He was handcuffed and taken to a hospital. At the direction of one of the officers a doctor forced an emetic solution through a tube into Rochin's stomach against his will. This "stomach pumping" produced vomiting. In the vomited matter were found two capsules which proved to contain morphine.

Rochin was brought to trial before a California Superior Court, sitting without a jury, on the charge of possessing "a preparation of morphine" in violation of the California Health and Safety Code 1947, §11500. Rochin was convicted and sentenced to sixty days' imprisonment. The chief evidence against him was the two capsules. They were admitted over petitioner's objection, although the means of obtaining them was frankly set forth in the testimony by one of the deputies, substantially as here narrated.

On appeal, the District Court of Appeal affirmed the conviction, despite the finding that the officers "were guilty of unlawfully breaking into and entering defendant's room and were guilty of unlawfully assaulting and battering defendant while in the room", and "were guilty of unlawfully assaulting, battering, torturing and falsely imprisoning the defendant at the alleged hospital." 101 Cal.App.2d 140, 143. . . . The Supreme Court of California denied without opinion Rochin's petition for a hearing. Two justices dissented . . . and in doing so expressed themselves thus: "* * * [We] find no valid ground of distinction between a verbal confession extracted by physical abuse and a confession wrested from defendant's body by physical abuse." 101 Cal.App.2d 143, 149–150. . . .

This Court granted certiorari, 341 U.S. 939, because a serious question is raised as to the limitations which the Due Process Clause of the Fourteenth Amendment imposes on the conduct of criminal proceedings by the States.

In our federal system the administration of criminal justice is predominantly committed to the care of the States. . . . Broadly speaking, crimes in the United States are what the laws of the individual States make them, subject to the limitations of Art. I, §10, cl. 1, in the original Constitution, prohibiting bills of attainder and *ex post facto* laws, and of the Thirteenth and Fourteenth Amendments.

These limitations in the main, concern . . . restrictions upon the manner in which the States may enforce their penal codes. Accordingly . . . we must be deeply mindful of the responsibilities of the States for the enforcement of criminal laws, and exercise with due humility our merely negative function in subjecting convictions from state courts to the very narrow scrutiny which the Due Process Clause of the Fourteenth Amendment authorizes." *Malinski* v. *People of State of New York* 324 U.S. 401, 412, 418. . . .

However, this Court too has its responsibility. Regard for the requirements of the Due Process Clause "inescapably imposes upon this Court an exercise of judgment upon the whole course of the proceedings [resulting in a conviction] in order to ascertain whether they offend those canons of decency and fairness which express the notions of justice of English-speaking peoples even toward those charged with the most heinous offenses." Malinski v. People of State of New York, *supra*, 324 U.S. at pages 416–417. These standards of justice are not authoritatively formulated anywhere as though they were specifics. Due process of law is a summarized constitutional guarantee of respect for those personal immunities which, as Mr. Justice Cardozo twice wrote for the Court, are "so rooted in the traditions and conscience of our people as to be ranked as fundamental", *Snyder* v. *Commonwealth of Massachusetts*, 291 U.S. 97, 105, or are "implicit in the concept of ordered liberty". *Palko* v. *State of Connecticut*, 302 U.S. 319, 325. . . .

In dealing . . . with human rights, the absence of formal exactitude, or want of fixity of meaning, is not an unusual or even regrettable attribute of constitutional provisions. Words being symbols do not speak without a gloss. On the one hand the gloss may be the deposit of history, whereby a term gains technical content. Thus the requirements of the Sixth and Seventh Amendments for trial by jury in the federal courts have a rigid meaning. . . . On the other hand, the gloss of some of the verbal symbols of the Constitution does not give them a fixed technical content. It exacts a continuing process of application.

When the gloss has thus not been fixed but is a function of the process of judgment, the judgment is bound to fall differently at different times and differently at the same time through different judges. . . . Even though the concept of due process of law is not final and fixed, these limits are derived from considerations that are fused in the whole nature of our judicial process. . . .

Restraints on our jurisdiction are self-imposed only in the sense that there is from our decisions no immediate appeal short of impeachment or constitutional amendment. But that does not make due process of law a matter of judicial caprice. The faculties of the Due Process Clause may be indefinite and vague, but the mode of their ascertainment is not self-willed. In each case "due process of law" requires an evaluation based on a disinterested inquiry pursued in the spirit of science, on a balanced order of facts exactly and fairly stated, on the detached consideration of conflicting claims . . . on a judgment not *ad hoc* and episodic but duly mindful of reconciling the needs both of continuity and of change in a progressive society.

Applying these general considerations to the circumstances of the present case we are compelled to conclude that the proceedings by which this conviction was obtained do more than offend some fastidious squeamishness or private sentimentalism about combatting crime too energetically. This is conduct that shocks the conscience. Illegally breaking into the privacy of the petitioner, the struggle to open his mouth and remove what was there, the forcible extraction of his stomach's contents — this course of proceeding by agents of government to obtain evidence is bound to offend even hardened sensibilities. They are methods too close to the rack and the screw to permit of constitutional differentiation.

It has long since ceased to be true that due process of law is heedless of the means by which otherwise relevant and credible evidence is obtained. This was not true even before the series of recent cases enforced the constitutional principle that the States may not base convictions upon confessions, however much verified, obtained by coercion. These decisions are . . . only instances of the general requirement that States in their prosecutions respect certain decencies of civilized conduct. . . . It would be a stultification of the responsibility which the course of constitutional history has cast upon this Court to hold that in order to convict a man the police cannot extract by force what is in his mind but can extract what is in his stomach. . . .

Coerced confessions offend the community's sense of fair play and decency. So here, to sanction the brutal conduct which naturally enough was condemned by the court whose judgment is before us, would be to afford brutality the cloak of law. Nothing would be more calculated to discredit law and thereby to brutalize the temper of a society. * * *

On the facts of this case the conviction of the petitioner has been obtained by methods that offend the Due Process Clause. The judgment below must be reversed.   *Reversed.* . . .

MR. JUSTICE BLACK, concurring. . . .

In the view of a majority of the Court, . . . the Fifth Amendment imposes no restraint of any kind on the states. They nevertheless hold that California's use of this evidence violated the Due Process Clause of the Fourteenth Amendment. Since they hold as I do in this case, I regret my inability to accept their interpretation without protest. But I believe that faithful adherence to the specific guarantees in the Bill of Rights insures a more permanent protection of individual liberty than that which can be afforded by the nebulous standards stated by the majority. * * *

The *Rochin* case arose, as many difficult cases do, as a result of effort by the state to control a species of crime particularly abhorrent to the community. The *Breithaupt* case, (*Breithaupt* v. *Abram*, 352 U.S. 432, 77 S. Ct. 408; 1957) had as its source the concern for highway accidents, especially when one of the drivers involved has been drinking alcoholic beverages. In this case an invasion of the body of Breithaupt was countenanced: while Breithaupt was unconscious, a doctor took a sample of his blood to determine its content of alcohol. As a result of the test, he was tried, convicted, and sentenced for involuntary manslaughter. Justice Clark, for the Court, in distinguishing this case from the *Rochin* case, said:

> Basically the distinction rests on the fact that there is nothing "brutal" or "offensive" in the taking of a sample of blood when done, as in this case, under the protective eye of a physician. . . . Furthermore, due process is . . . measured . . . by that whole community sense of "decency and fairness" that has been woven by common experience into the fabric of acceptable conduct. It is on this bedrock that this Court has established the concept of due process.[7]

Mr. Chief Justice Warren, Mr. Justice Black and Mr. Justice Douglas joined in a dissent, believing that the essential elements of *Rochin* and this case were the same, and therefore the decision should be the same.

> We should, in my opinion, hold that due process means at least that law-enforcement officers in their efforts to obtain evidence from persons suspected of crime must stop short of bruising the body, breaking skin, puncturing tissue or extracting body fluids, whether they contemplate doing it by force or by stealth.[8]

A resolution of the conflicts between state and federal standards, and the possibility of a greater protection for the individual, came with the case of *Mapp* v. *Ohio*, which could have been decided on the authority of *Wolf* v. *Colorado*.

Mapp v. *Ohio*, 367 U.S. 643, 81 S. Ct. 1684 (1961)

MR. JUSTICE CLARK delivered the opinion of the Court.
Appellant stands convicted of knowingly having had in her possession and under her control certain lewd and lascivious books, pictures, and photographs in violation of § 2905.34 of Ohio's Revised

---

[7]*Breithaupt* v. *Abram*, 352 U.S. 432, pp. 435, 436. [8]*Ibid.*, p. 442.

Code. As officially stated in the syllabus to its opinion, the Supreme Court of Ohio found that her conviction was valid though "based primarily upon the introduction in evidence of lewd and lascivious books and pictures unlawfully seized during an unlawful search of defendant's home. ° ° °"

On May 23, 1957, three Cleveland police officers arrived at appellant's residence in that city pursuant to information that "a person [was] hiding out in the home who was wanted for questioning in connection with a recent bombing, and that there was a large amount of policy paraphernalia being hidden in the home." . . .. Upon their arrival at that house, the officers knocked on the door and demanded entrance but appellant, after telephoning her attorney, refused to admit them without a search warrant. They advised their headquarters of the situation and undertook a surveillance of the house.

The officers again sought entrance some three hours later when four or more additional officers arrived on the scene. When Miss Mapp did not come to the door immediately, at least one of the several doors to the house was forcibly opened and the policemen gained admittance. Meanwhile Miss Mapp's attorney arrived, but the officers, having secured their own entry, and continuing in their defiance of the law, would permit him neither to see Miss Mapp nor to enter the house. . . . Miss Mapp . . . demanded to see the search warrant. A paper, claimed to be a warrant, was held up by one of the officers. She grabbed the "warrant" and placed it in her bosom. A struggle ensued in which the officers recovered the piece of paper and as a result of which they handcuffed appellant because she had been "belligerent" in resisting their official rescue of the "warrant" from her person. Running roughshod over appellant, a policeman "grabbed" her, "twisted [her] hand," and she "yelled [and] pleaded with him" because "it was hurting." Appellant, in handcuffs, was then forcibly taken upstairs to her bedroom where the officers searched a dresser, a chest of drawers, a closet and some suitcases. They also looked into a photo album and through personal papers belonging to the appellant. The search spread to the rest of the second floor including the child's bedroom, the living room, the kitchen and a dinette. The basement of the building and a trunk found therein were also searched. The obscene materials for possession of which she was ultimately convicted were discovered in the course of that widespread search.

At the trial no search warrant was produced by the prosecution, nor was the failure to produce one explained or accounted for. At best, "There is, in the record, considerable doubt as to whether there ever was any warrant for the search of defendant's home." 170 Ohio St. at p. 430. The Ohio Supreme Court believed a "reasonable argument" could be made that the conviction should be reversed "because the 'methods' employed to obtain the [evidence]were such as to offend 'a sense of justice'" but the court found determinative the fact that the evidence had not been taken "from defendant's person by the use of brutal or offensive physical force against defendant." 170 Ohio St. at p. 431.

The State says that even if the search were made without authority, or otherwise unreasonably, it is not prevented from using the
unconstitutionally seized evidence at trial, citing *Wolf* v. *People of
State of Colorado*, 1949, 338 U.S. 25, at page 33, . . . in which this
Court did indeed hold that in a prosecution in a State court for a
State crime the Fourteenth Amendment does not forbid the admission of evidence obtained by an unreasonable search and seizure."
On this appeal, . . . it is urged once again that we review that
holding.

Seventy-five years ago, in *Boyd* v. *United States*, 116 U.S. 616,
630 (1886), considering the Fourth and Fifth Amendments as running
"almost into each other" on the facts before it, this Court held that
the doctrines of those Amendments

"apply to all invasions on the part of the government and its em-
ployes of the sanctity of a man's home and the privacies of life. . . .
[A]ny forcible and compulsory extortion of a man's own testimony or
of his private papers to be used as evidence to convict him of crime
or to forfeit his goods, is within the condemnation * * * [of those
Amendments]." * * *

Less than 30 years after *Boyd*, this Court, in *Weeks* v. *United
States*, 232 U.S. 383 (1914), at pages 391 – 392, stated that

"the 4th Amendment * * * put the courts of the United States and
Federal officials, in the exercise of their power and authority, under
limitations and restraints [and] * * * forever secure[d] the people,
their persons, houses, papers, and effects, against all unreasonable
searches and seizures under the guise of law. * * *

Finally, the Court in that case clearly stated that use of the seized
evidence involved "a denial of the constitutional rights of the accused." At page 398. * * *

[T]he plain and unequivocal language of *Weeks* — and its later
paraphrase in *Wolf* — to the effect that the *Weeks* rule is of constitutional origin, remains entirely undisturbed. * * *

. . . While in 1949, prior to the *Wolf* case, almost two-thirds of the
States were opposed to the use of the exclusionary rule, now, despite
the *Wolf* case, more than half of those since passing upon it, by their
own legislative or judicial decision, have wholly or partly adopted or
adhered to the *Weeks* rule * * * The obvious futility of relegating
the Fourth Amendment to the protection of other remedies has,
moreover, been recognized by this Court since *Wolf*. * * *

* * * [O]nly last Term, . . . in *Elkins* v. *United States*, *supra*,
the Court pointed out that "the controlling principles" as to search
and seizure and the problem of admissibility "seemed clear" (364
U.S. at page 212) until the announcement in *Wolf* "that the Due
Process Clause of the Fourteenth Amendment does not itself require state courts to adopt the exclusionary rule" of the *Weeks* case.
At page 213 of 364 U.S. . . . At the same time, the Court pointed
out, "the underlying constitutional doctrine which *Wolf* established * * * that the Federal Constitution * * * prohibits un-

reasonable searches and seizures by state officers" had undermined the "foundation upon which the admissibility of state-seized evidence in a federal trial originally rested * * *" *Ibid.* . . . Today we once again examine Wolf's constitutional documentation of the right to privacy free from unreasonable state intrusion. . . . We hold that all evidence obtained by searches and seizures in violation of the Constitution is, by that same authority, inadmissible in a state court.

Since the Fourth Amendment's right of privacy has been declared enforceable against the States through the Due Process Clause of the Fourteenth, it is enforceable against them by the same sanction of exclusion as is used against the Federal Government. * * * Only last year the Court itself recognized that the purpose of the exclusionary rule "is to deter—to compel respect for the constitutional guaranty in the only effectively available way—by removing the incentive to disregard it." *Elkins* v. *U.S., supra,* 364 U.S. at page 217. * * *

Moreover, our holding that the exclusionary rule is an essential part of both the Fourth and Fourteenth Amendments is not only the logical dictate of prior cases, but it also makes very good sense. There is no war between the Constitution and common sense. * * * If the fruits of an unconstitutional search had been inadmissible in both state and federal courts, this inducement to evasion would have been sooner eliminated. * * *

The ignoble shortcut to conviction left open to the State tends to destroy the entire system of constitutional restraints on which the liberties of the people rest. Having once recognized that the right to privacy embodied in the Fourth Amendment is enforceable against the States, and that the right to be secure against rude invasions of privacy by state officers is, therefore, constitutional in origin, we can no longer permit that right to remain an empty promise. Because it is enforceable in the same manner and to like effect as other basic rights secured by the Due Process Clause, we can no longer permit it to be revocable at the whim of any police officer who, in the name of law enforcement itself, chooses to suspend its enjoyment. Our decision, founded on reason and truth, gives to the individual no more than that which the Constitution guarantees him, to the police officer no less than that to which honest law enforcement is entitled, and, to the courts, that judicial integrity so necessary in the true administration of justice.

The judgment of the Supreme Court of Ohio is reversed and the cause remanded for further proceedings not inconsistent with this opinion.   *Reversed and remanded.*

MR. JUSTICE BLACK and MR. JUSTICE DOUGLAS concurred in separate opinions.

MR. JUSTICE HARLAN, whom MR. JUSTICE FRANKFURTER and MR. JUSTICE WHITTAKER join, dissenting.

In overruling the *Wolf* case the Court, in my opinion, has forgotten the sense of judicial restraint which, with due regard for *stare decisis,* is one element that should enter into deciding whether a past decision of this Court should be overruled. Apart from that I also believe that the *Wolf* rule represents sounder Constitutional doctrine than the new rule which now replaces it.

From the Court's statement of the case one would gather that the central, if not controlling, issue on this appeal is whether illegally state-seized evidence is Constitutionally admissible in a state prosecution, an issue which would of course face us with the need for reexamining *Wolf.* However, such is not the situation. For, although that question was indeed raised here and below among appellant's subordinate points, the new and pivotal issue brought to the Court by this appeal is whether §2905.34 of the Ohio Revised Code making criminal the *mere* knowing possession or control of obscene material, and under which appellant has been convicted, is consistent with the rights of free thought and expression assured against state action by the Fourteenth Amendment. That was the principal issue which was decided by the Ohio Supreme Court, which was tendered by appellant's Jurisdictional Statement, and which was briefed and argued in this Court. * * *

The action of the Court finds no support in the rule that decision of Constitutional issues should be avoided wherever possible. For in overruling *Wolf* the Court, instead of passing upon the validity of Ohio's §2905.34, has simply chosen between two Constitutional questions. * * *

The occasion which the Court has taken here is in the context of a case where the question was briefed not at all and argued only extremely tangentially. * * *

It cannot be too much emphasized that what was recognized in *Wolf* was not that the Fourth Amendment *as such* is enforceable against the States as a facet of due process, a view of the Fourteenth Amendment which, as *Wolf* itself pointed out (338 U.S. at page 26), has long since been discredited, but the principle of privacy "which is at the core of the Fourth Amendment." *Id.,* 338 U.S. at page 27. * * * Since there is not the slightest suggestion that Ohio's policy is "affirmatively to sanction * * * police incursion into privacy" . . . what the Court is now doing is to impose upon the States not only federal substantive standards of "search and seizure" but also the basic federal remedy for violation of those standards. For I think it entirely clear the *Weeks* exclusionary rule is but a remedy which, by penalizing past official misconduct, is aimed at deterring such conduct in the future. * * *

In conclusion, it should be noted that the majority opinion in this case is in fact an opinion only for the *judgment* overruling Wolf, and not for the basic rationale by which four members of the majority have reached that result. . . .

I regret that I find so unwise in principle and so inexpedient in policy a decision motivated by the high purpose of increasing respect for Constitutional rights. But in the last analysis I think this

Court can increase respect for the Constitution only if it rigidly respects the limitations which the Constitution places upon it, and respects as well the principles inherent in its own processes. In the present case I think we exceed both, and that our voice becomes only a voice of power, not of reason.

But in *Linkletter* v. *Walker*, 381 U.S. 618, 85 S. Ct. 1731 (1965), the Court refused to apply *Mapp* v. *Ohio* retroactively. The petitioner had been convicted of burglary on May 28, 1959; the Supreme Court of Louisiana affirmed the judgment in March, 1960. On June 19, 1961, the *Mapp* decision was announced, and the petitioner filed an application for a writ of habeas corpus. Ultimately his appeal reached the U.S. Supreme Court. The question was whether the exclusionary rule of *Mapp* applied to state court convictions which had become final before the *Mapp* decision. The Court held that it did not, saying:

. . . All that we decide today is that though the error complained of might be fundamental it is not of the nature requiring us to overturn all final convictions based upon it. After full consideration of all the factors we are not able to say that the Mapp rule requires retrospective application.

Mr. Justice Black, joined by Mr. Justice Douglas, dissented, pointing out that although the seizure in the *Mapp* case occurred before that in the *Linkletter* case, Mr. Linkletter was actually convicted before Miss Mapp was.

. . . [T]here is no experience of the past that justifies a new Court-made rule to perpetrate a grossly invidious and unfair discrimination against Linkletter simply because he happened to be prosecuted in a State that was evidently well up with its criminal docket. * * *

The plain facts here are that the Court's opinion cuts off many defendants who are now in jail from any hope of relief from unconstitutional convictions. . . . No State should be considered to have a vested interest in keeping prisoners in jail who were convicted because of lawless conduct by the State's officials. . . .

Self-Incrimination

The Fifth Amendment provides a broad range of protections for the individual:

No person shall be held to answer for a capital, or otherwise infamous crime, unless on a presentment or indictment of a Grand Jury, except in cases arising in the land or naval forces, or in the Militia, when in actual service in time of War or public danger; nor shall any person be subject for the same offense to be twice put in jeopardy of life or limb, nor shall be compelled in any criminal case to be a witness against himself, nor be deprived of life, liberty, or property, without due process of law; nor shall private property be taken for public use, without just compensation.

In the clause "nor shall any person . . . be compelled in any criminal case to be a witness against himself . . ." the emphasis may well be placed upon the verb, for there is no objection to the admission of voluntary confessions. The problem is twofold: what the definition of a "voluntary" confession is, and what standards the Supreme Court may apply to the procedures which are under the control of the state.

It was not until 1936 that a decision from a state Supreme Court was reversed on the grounds that the confessions of the defendants were coerced. The petitioners were indicted for murder on April 4, 1934, were arraigned, and pleaded not guilty.

Brown v. *Mississippi,* 297 U.S. 278, 56 S. Ct. 461 (1936)

MR. CHIEF JUSTICE HUGHES delivered the opinion of the Court.

The question in this case is whether convictions, which rest solely upon confessions shown to have been extorted by officers of the State by brutality and violence, are consistent with the due process of law required by the Fourteenth Amendment of the Constitution of the United States. . . .

Petitioners were indicted for . . . murder. . . . Counsel were appointed by the court to defend them. Trial was begun the next morning and was concluded on the following day, when they were found guilty and sentenced to death.

Aside from the confessions, there was no evidence sufficient to warrant the submission of the case to the jury. . . .

On their appeal to the Supreme Court of the State, defendants assigned as error the inadmissibility of the confessions. The judgment was affirmed. * * *

. . . We granted a writ of certiorari. . . .

The opinion of the state court did not set forth the evidence as to the circumstances in which the confessions were procured. That the evidence established that they were procured by coercion was not questioned. . . .

There is no dispute as to the facts upon this point and as they are clearly and adequately stated in the dissenting opinion of Judge Griffith (with whom Judge Anderson concurred) . . . we' quote this part of his opinion in full, as follows (*Id.,* pp. 470, 471):

"The crime with which these defendants, all ignorant negroes, are charged, was discovered about one o'clock p. m. on Friday, March 30, 1934. On that night one Dial, a deputy sheriff, accompanied by others, came to the home of Ellington, one of the defendants, and requested him to accompany them to the house of the deceased, and there a number of white men were gathered, who began to accuse the defendant of the crime. Upon his denial they seized him, and with the participation of the deputy they hanged him by a rope to the limb of a tree, and having let him down, they hung him again, and when he was let down the second time, and he still protested his innocence, he was tied to a tree and whipped, and still declining to accede to the demands that he confess, he was finally released and he returned with some difficulty to his home, suffering intense pain and agony. The record of the testimony shows that the signs of the rope on his neck were plainly visible during the so-called trial. A day or two thereafter the said deputy, accompanied by another, . . . departed with the prisoner towards the jail . . . and while on the way, . . . the deputy stopped and again severely whipped the defendant, declaring that he would continue the whipping until he confessed, and the defendant then agreed to confess to such a statement as the deputy would dictate, and he did so, after which he was delivered to jail.

"The other two defendants, Ed Brown and Henry Shields, were also arrested and taken to the same jail. On Sunday night, April 1, 1934, the same deputy, accompanied by a number of white men, one of whom was also an officer, and by the jailer, came to the jail, and the two last named defendants were made to strip and they were laid over chairs and their backs were cut to pieces with a leather strap with buckles on it, and they were likewise made by the said deputy definitely to understand that the whipping would be continued unless and until they confessed, and not only confessed, but confessed in every matter of detail as demanded by those present; and in this manner the defendants confessed the crime, and as the whippings progressed and were repeated, they changed or adjusted their confession in all particulars of detail so as to conform to the demands of their torturers. . . .

"Further details of the brutal treatment to which these helpless prisoners were subjected need not be pursued. It is sufficient to say that in pertinent respects the transcript reads more like pages torn from some medieval account, than a record made within the confines of a modern civilization which aspires to an enlightened constitutional government.

"All this having been accomplished, on the next day, that is, on Monday, April 2, when the defendants had been given time to recuperate somewhat from the tortures to which they had been subjected, the two sheriffs, one of the county where the crime was committed, and the other of the county of the jail in which the prisoners were confined, came to the jail, accompanied by eight other persons, some of them deputies, there to hear the free and voluntary confession of these miserable and abject defendants. The sheriff of the county of the crime admitted that he had heard of the whipping, but averred that he had no personal knowledge of it. He admitted that one of the defendants, when brought before him to confess, was limping and did not sit down, and that this particular defendant then and there stated that he had been strapped so severely that he could not sit down, and as already stated, the signs of the rope on the neck of another of the defendants were plainly visible to all. Nevertheless the solemn farce of hearing the free and voluntary confessions was gone through with, and these two sheriffs and one other person then present were the three witnesses used in court to establish the so-called confessions, which were received by the court and admitted in evidence over the objections of the defendants duly entered of record as each of the said three witnesses delivered their alleged testimony. There was thus enough before the court when these confessions were first offered to make known to the court that they were not, beyond all reasonable doubt, free and voluntary; and the failure of the court then to exclude the confessions is sufficient to reverse the judgment, under every rule of procedure that has heretofore been prescribed, and hence it was not necessary subsequently to renew the objections by motion or otherwise.

"The spurious confessions having been obtained . . . the court, then in session, . . . ordered the grand jury to reassemble on the succeeding day, April 4, 1934, at nine o'clock, and on the morning of the day last mentioned the grand jury returned an indictment against the defendants for murder. Late that afternoon the defendants were . . . arraigned. . . . The court thereupon appointed counsel, and set the case for trial for the following morning at nine o'clock. . . .

"The defendants were brought to the courthouse of the county on the following morning, April 5th, and the so-called trial was opened, and was concluded on the next day, April 6, 1934, and resulted in a pretended conviction with death sentences. The evidence upon which the conviction was obtained was the so-called confessions. Without this evidence a peremptory instruction to find for the defendants would have been inescapable. The defendants were put on the stand, and by their testimony the facts and the details thereof as to the manner by which the confessions were extorted from them were fully developed, and it is further disclosed by the record that the same deputy, Dial, under whose guiding hand and active participation the tortures to coerce the confessions were administered, was actively in the performance of the supposed duties of a court deputy in the courthouse and in the presence of the prisoners during what is denominated, in complimentary terms, the trial of these defendants. This deputy was put on the stand by the state in rebuttal, and admitted the whippings. . . . The facts are not only undisputed, they are admitted, and admitted to have been done by officers of the state, in conjunction with other participants, and all this was definitely well known to everybody connected with the trial, and during the trial, including the state's prosecuting attorney and the trial judge presiding." . . .

The State is free to regulate the procedure of its courts in accordance with its own conceptions of policy, unless in so doing it "offends some principle of justice so rooted in the traditions and conscience of our people as to be ranked as fundamental." *Snyder* v. *Massachusetts, supra*. . . . But the freedom of the State in establishing its policy is the freedom of constitutional government and limited by the requirement of due process of law. Because a State may dispense with a jury trial, it does not follow that it may substitute trial by ordeal. The rack and torture chamber may not be substituted for the witness stand. . . . It would be difficult to conceive of methods more revolting to the sense of justice than those taken to procure the confessions of these petitioners, and the use of the confessions thus obtained as the basis for conviction and sentence was a clear denial of due process. . . .

In the instant case, the trial court was fully advised by the undisputed evidence of the way in which the confessions had been procured. The trial court knew that there was no other evidence upon which conviction and sentence could be based. Yet it proceeded to permit conviction and to pronounce sentence. The conviction and sentence were void for want of the essential elements of due process, and the proceeding thus vitiated could be challenged in any appropriate manner. . . . It was challenged before the Supreme Court of the State by the express invocation of the Fourteenth Amendment. That court . . . declined to enforce petitioners' constitutional right. The court thus denied a federal right fully established and specially set up and claimed and the judgment must be

Reversed

But there are more subtle ways to obtain a confession than by physical torture. Many factors may contribute to breaking down the resistance of the suspect. Exhaustion may help; so may isolation from others except the interrogators; the putting of the defendant in fear because of the possibility of mob action; the use of false confessions claimed to have been given by others involved in the crime; the refusal to allow the defendant to talk to anyone, attorney or family, until he has confessed; the taking advantage of the suggestibility of an emotionally ill or mentally deficient suspect; the use of a psychiatrist to "prepare" the suspect, so that he is willing to confess; the use of a "lie detector"; the failure or refusal to arraign the suspect, even though required by statute to do so promptly.

These particular situations arose in state cases, but similar situations have arisen in federal cases. The *Mallory* case (*Mallory* v. *U.S.*, 354 U.S. 449, 77 S. Ct. 1356; 1957) is probably the best known of the recent cases of federal origin, but, because there was a clear violation of the rules of federal procedure, no constitutional issue had to be decided. The petitioner, age nineteen, of limited intelligence and suspected of rape, was taken to police headquarters when he was apprehended. There he was questioned by "at least four officers" for about 45 minutes, and was later asked to take a "lie detector" test, to which he agreed. The test did not begin until 8 o'clock in the evening; he admitted he was responsible for the crime. Thereafter, about 10, after repeating his confession to other officers, an attempt was made to reach a Commissioner to have the defendant arraigned. He was not actually arraigned until the next morning. The Court held that his arraignment was not "without unnecessary delay," as required by the federal rules, and the lower court decision was reversed.

The power of persuasion, if the suspect is held long enough by the police, even though no physical abuse is involved, is illustrated by *Culombe* v. *Connecticut*, 367 U.S. 568, 81 S. Ct. 1860 (1961).

A series of holdups and killings in and around New Britain had terrorized the small shop owners in the area, for they had been the victims of the holdups. Two friends, Arthur Culombe and Joseph Taborsky, were requested to come to the state police headquarters on February 23, 1957.

> They were never again out of police custody. In the Headquarters' interrogation room and elsewhere, they were questioned about the . . . holdups and other matters. Within ten days Culombe had five times confessed orally to participation in the Kurp's Gasoline Station affair—once re-enacting the holdup for the police—and had signed three typed statements incriminating himself and Taborsky in the Kurp's killings. Taborsky also confessed.[9]

Culombe was of subnormal intelligence, with a mental age of about nine and a half years. He had been in trouble with the law since his adolescence, and had been in a mental hospital for treatment. He had escaped from a Massachusetts training school for mental defectives, and had been in prison at least twice. However, during the three years immediately preceding his arrest he had been working steadily, and was supporting his wife and two children. A psychiatrist described him as highly suggestible, and said he could be intimidated. He was illiterate: his reading and writing ability was limited to signing his name and recognizing his own signature, a fact known to the police.

No physical brutality was inflicted upon Culombe, no eight- or ten-hour sessions of unremitting questioning by relays of officers. But gradually, over a period of five days, his resistance was broken down, and bit by bit he incriminated himself, and finally confessed in detail.

Culombe v. *Connecticut*, 367 U.S. 568 81 S. Ct. 1860 (1961)

MR. JUSTICE FRANKFURTER announced the judgment of the court* * *

[9]*Culombe* v. *Connecticut*, 367 U.S. 586, p. 570.

The critical elements of the problem may be quickly isolated. . . . Its first pole is the recognition that "Questioning suspects is indispensable in law enforcement." . . . But if it is once admitted that questioning of suspects is permissible, whatever reasonable means are needed to make the questioning effective must also be conceded to the police. . . .

At the other pole is a cluster of convictions each expressive, in a different manifestation, of the basic notion that the terrible engine of the criminal law is not to be used to overreach individuals who stand helpless against it. Among these . . . is the conviction, basic to our legal order, that men are not to be exploited for the information necessary to condemn them before the law, that, in Hawkins' words, a prisoner is not "to be made the deluded instrument of his own conviction." . . . An extra-judicial confession, if . . . offered in evidence against a man, must be the product of his own free choice. . . . And, in a long series of cases, this Court has held that the Fourteenth Amendment does not prohibit a state from such detention and examination of a suspect as, under all the circumstances, is found not to be coercive. * * *

What appears in this case, then, is this. Culombe was taken by the police and held in the carefully controlled environment of police custody for more than four days before he confessed. During that time he was questioned—questioned every day about the Kurp's affair—and with the avowed intention, not merely to check his story to ascertain whether there was cause to charge him, but to obtain a confession if a confession was obtainable.

All means found fit were employed to this end. Culombe was not told that he had a right to remain silent. Although he said that he wanted a lawyer, the police made no attempt to give him the help he needed to get one. Instead of bringing him before a magistrate with reasonable promptness, as Connecticut law requires, to be duly presented for the grave crimes of which he was in fact suspected (and for which he had been arrested under the felony-arrest statute), he was taken before the New Britain Police Court on the palpable ruse of a breach-of-the-peace charge concocted to give the police time to pursue their investigation. This device is admitted. It had a twofold effect. First, it kept Culombe in police hands without any of the protections that a proper magistrate's hearing would have assured him. Certainly, had he been brought before it charged with murder instead of an insignificant misdemeanor, no court would have failed to warn Culombe of his rights and arrange for appointment of counsel. Second, every circumstance of the Police Court's procedure was, in itself, potentially intimidating. Culombe had been told that morning that he would be presented in a court of law and would be able to consult counsel. Instead, he was led into a crowded room, penned in a corner, and, without ever being brought before the bench or given a chance to participate in any way, his case was disposed of. Culombe had been convicted of crimes before and presumably was not ignorant of the way in which justice is regularly done. It would deny the impact of experience to believe that the impression which even his limited mind drew from this appearance before a court which did not even hear him, a court which may well have appeared a mere tool in the hands of the police, was not intimidating.

That same evening, by arrangement of the State Police, Culombe's wife and daughter appeared at Headquarters for the interview that left him sobbing in his cell. The next morning, although the mittimus of the New Britain Police Court had committed Culombe to the Hartford jail until released by due course of law, the police "borrowed" him, and later the questioning resumed. There can be no doubt of its purpose at this time. For Paige then "knew"—if he was ever to know—that Culombe was guilty. Paige opened by telling Culombe to stop lying and to say instead that he did not want to answer. But when Culombe said that he did not want to answer, Detective Murphy took over and repeated the same questions that Paige had asked.

It is clear that this man's will was broken Wednesday afternoon. It is no less clear that his will was broken Wednesday night when, after several hours in a car with four policemen, two interviews with his wife and his apparently ill child, further inquiries made of him in the presence of the Police Commissioner, and a four and a half-hour session which left him (by police testimony) "tired," he agreed to the composition of a statement that was not even cast in his own words. We do not overlook the fact that Culombe told his wife at their apartment that he wanted to cleanse his conscience and make a clean breast of things. This item, in the total context, does not overbalance the significance of all else, particularly since it was his wife who the day before, at the request of Lieutenant Rome, had asked him to confess. Neither the Wednesday-afternoon nor the Wednesday-midnight statement may be proved against Culombe, and he convicted by their use, consistently with the Constitution. . . .

Regardful as one must be of the problems of crime-detection confronting the States, one does not reach the result here as an easy decision. In the case of such unwitnessed crimes as the Kurp's killings, the trails of detection challenge the most imaginative capacities of law enforcement officers. Often there is little else the police can do than interrogate suspects as an indispensable part of criminal investigation. But when interrogation of a prisoner is so long continued, with such a purpose, and under such circumstances, as to make the whole proceeding an effective instrument for extorting an unwilling admission of guilt, due process precludes the use of the confes-confession thus obtained. Under our accusatorial system, such an exploitation of interrogation, whatever its usefulness, is not a permissible substitute for judicial trial.   *Reversed.*

Obviously, a detailed examination of the facts was essential to the Court's decision, for the Court was not dealing with a clear-cut instance of physical brutality. The totality of the facts led to the conclusion, even though the standards applied were those of the due process clause of the Fourteenth Amendment in which the right of the state to set its standards, within limits, was recognized.

As in the cases which led up to the School Desegregation cases of 1954, the Court was dealing with and assessing events accompanied by imponderables which made clear distinctions difficult. The next logical step was to apply the federal standard—a step which had long been urged by Justices Black and Douglas. That step was taken in *Malloy* v. *Hogan,* 378 U.S. 1 (1964). *Griffin* v. *California,* 380 U.S. 609 (1965), extended the principle to the particular circumstances prevailing in California.

Malloy v. *Hogan,* 378 U.S. 1, 84 S. Ct. 1489 (1964)

MR. JUSTICE BRENNAN delivered the opinion of the Court.

In this case we are asked to reconsider prior decisions holding that the privilege against self-incrimination is not safeguarded against state action by the Fourteenth Amendment. . . .

The petitioner was arrested during a gambling raid in 1959 by Hartford, Connecticut police. He pleaded guilty to the crime of pool-selling, a misdemeanor, and was sentenced to one year in jail and fined $500. The sentence was ordered to be suspended after 90 days, at which time he was to be placed on probation for two years. About 16 months after his guilty plea, petitioner was ordered to testify before a referee appointed by the Superior Court of Hartford County to conduct an inquiry into alleged gambling and other criminal activities in the county. The petitioner was asked a number of questions related to events surrounding his arrest and conviction. He refused to answer any question "on the grounds it may tend to incriminate me." The Superior Court adjudged him in contempt, and committed him to prison until he was willing to answer the questions. Petitioner's application for a writ of habeas corpus was denied by the Superior Court of Errors and the Connecticut Supreme Court affirmed. . . . The latter court held that the Fifth Amendment's privilege against self-incrimination was not available to a witness in a state proceeding, that the Fourteenth Amendment extended no privilege to him, and that the petitioner had not properly invoked the privilege available under the Connecticut Constitution. We granted certiorari. . . . We reverse. We hold that the Fourteenth Amendment guaranteed the petitioner the protection of the Fifth Amendment's privilege against self-incrimination, and that under the applicable federal standard, the Connecticut Supreme Court of Errors erred in holding that the privilege was not properly invoked.

The extent to which the Fourteenth Amendment prevents state invasion of rights enumerated in the first eight Amendments has been considered in numerous cases in this Court since the Amendment's adoption in 1868. . . .

The Court has not hesitated to re-examine past decisions according the Fourteenth Amendment a less central role in the preservation of basic liberties than that which was contemplated by its Framers when they added the Amendment to our constitutional scheme. Thus, although the Court as late as 1922 said that "neither the Fourteenth Amendment nor any other provision of the Constitution of the United States imposes upon the States any restrictions about 'freedom of speech' * * *," *Prudential Ins. Co. of America* v. *Cheek,* 259 U.S. 530, 543, three years later *Gitlow* v. *New York,* 268 U.S. 652, initiated a series of decisions which today holds immune from state invasion every First Amendment protection for the cherished rights of mind and spirit—the freedoms of speech, press, religion, assembly, association, and petition for redress of grievances. . . .

We hold today that the Fifth Amendment's exception from compulsory self-incrimination is also protected by the Fourteenth Amendment against abridgment by the States. Decisions of the Court since *Twining* and *Adamson* have departed from the contrary view expressed in those cases. We discuss first the decisions which forbid the use of coerced confessions in state criminal prosecutions. . . .

The Court in *Brown* v. *Mississippi,* 297 U.S. 278, felt impelled, in light of *Twining,* to say that its conclusion did not involve the privilege against self-incrimination. "Compulsion by torture to extort a confession is a different matter." 297 U.S. 285. But this distinction was soon abandoned, and today the admissibility of a confession in a state criminal prosecution is tested by the same standard applied in federal prosecutions since 1897. . . . Under this test, the constitutional inquiry is whether the confession is "free and voluntary." . . . In other words the person must not have been compelled to incriminate himself. . . .

The marked shift to the federal standard in state cases began with *Lisenba* v. *California,* 314 U.S. 219, where the Court spoke of accused's "free choice to admit, to deny, or to refuse to answer." *Id.,* 314 U.S. at 241. . . . The shift reflects recognition that the American system of criminal prosecution is accusatiorial, not inquisitorial, and that the Fifth Amendment privilege is its essential mainstay. *Rogers* v. *Richmond,* 365 U.S. 534, 541. . . . Since the Fourteenth Amendment prohibits the States from inducing a person to confess through "sympathy falsely aroused," *Spano* v. *New York, supra,* 360 U.S. at p. 323, or other like inducement far short of "compulsion by torture," *Haynes* v. *Washington, supra,* it follows *a fortiori* that it also forbids the States to resort to imprisonment, as here, to compel him to answer questions that might incriminate him. The Fourteenth Amendment secures against state invasion the same privilege that the Fifth Amendment guarantees against federal infringement—the right of a person to remain silent unless he chooses to speak in the unfettered exercise of his own will, and to suffer no penalty, as held in *Twining,* for such silence.

This conclusion is fortified by our recent decision in *Mapp* v.

Ohio, 367 U.S. 643, overruling *Wolf* v. *Colorado, supra,* which had held "that in a prosecution in a State court for a State crime the Fourteenth Amendment does not forbid the admission of evidence obtained by an unreasonable search and seizure," 338 U.S., at 33. . . . We relied upon the great case of *Boyd* v. *United States,* 116 U.S. 616, decided in 1886, which, considering the Fourth and Fifth Amendments as running "almost into each other," *id.,* 116 U.S., 630, held that "Breaking into a house and opening boxes and drawers are circumstances of aggravation; but any forcible and compulsory extortion of a man's own testimony, or of his private papers to be used as evidence to convict him of crime, or to forfeit his goods, is within the condemnation of [those Amendments] * * *." 116 U.S., at 630.

In thus returning to the *Boyd* view that the privilege is one of the "principles of a free government," 116 U.S., at 632, *Mapp* necessarily repudiated the *Twining* concept of the privilege as a mere rule of evidence. . . .

. . . . We have held that guarantees of the First Amendment . . . the prohibition of unreasonable searches and seizures of the Fourth Amendment . . . and the right to counsel guaranteed by the Sixth Amendment . . . are all to be enforced against the States under the Fourteenth Amendment according to the same standards that protect those personal rights against federal encroachment. . . . The Court thus has rejected the notion that the Fourteenth Amendment applies to the states only a "watered-down, subjective version of the individual guarantees of the Bill of Rights," *Ohio ex rel. Eaton* v. *Price,* 364 U.S. 263, 275 . . . (dissenting opinion). . . . It would be incongruous to have different standards determine the validity of a claim of privilege based on the same feared prosecution, depending on whether the claim was asserted in a state or federal court. Therefore, the same standards must determine whether an accused's silence in either a federal or state proceeding is justified. * * *

The State of Connecticut argues that the Connecticut courts properly applied the federal standards to the facts of this case. We disagree.

The investigation in the course of which petitioner was questioned began when the Superior Court in Hartford County appointed the Honorable Ernest A. Inglis, formerly Chief Justice of Connecticut, to conduct an inquiry into whether there was reasonable cause to believe that crimes, including gambling, were being committed in Hartford County. Petitioner appeared on January 16 and 25, 1961, and in both instances he was asked substantially the same questions about the circumstances surrounding his arrest and conviction for pool-selling in late 1959. The questions which petitioner refused to answer may be summarized as follows: (1) for whom did he work on September 11, 1959; (2) who selected and paid his counsel in connection with his arrest on that date and subsequent conviction; (3) who selected and paid his bondsman; (4) who paid his fine; (5) what was the name of the tenant in the apartment in which he was arrested; and

(6) did he know John Bergoti. The Connecticut Supreme Court of Errors ruled that the answers to these questions could not tend to incriminate him because the defenses of double jeopardy and the running of the one-year statute of limitations on misdemeanors would defeat any prosecution growing out of his answers to the first five questions. . . .

The conclusions of the Court of Errors, tested by the federal standard, fails to take sufficient account of the setting in which the questions were asked. The interrogation was part of a wide-ranging inquiry into crime, including gambling, in Hartford. It was admitted on behalf of the State at oral argument . . . that the State desired to elicit from the petitioner the identity of the person who ran the pool-selling operation in connection with which he had been arrested in 1959. It was apparent that petitioner might apprehend that if this person were still engaged in unlawful activity, disclosure of his name might furnish a link in a chain of evidence sufficient to connect the petitioner with a more recent crime for which he might still be prosecuted.

Analysis of the sixth question, concerning whether petitioner knew Bergoti, yields a similar conclusion. . . . An affirmative answer to the question might well have either connected petitioner with a more recent crime, or at least have operated as a waiver of his privilege with reference to his relationship with a possible criminal. . . . See *Rogers* v. *United States*, 340 U.S. 367. We conclude, therefore, that as to each of the questions, it was "evident from the implications of the question, in the setting in which it [was] asked, that a responsive answer to the question or an explanation of why it [could not] be answered might be dangerous because injurious disclosure could result," *Hoffman* v. *United States, supra*, 341 U.S. 486–487. . . .

Reversed

While MR. JUSTICE DOUGLAS joins the opinion of the Court, he also adheres to his concurrence in *Gideon* v. *Wainwright*, 372 U.S. 335, 345.

MR. JUSTICE HARLAN, whom MR. JUSTICE CLARK joins, dissenting.

Connecticut has adjudged this petitioner in contempt for refusing to answer questions in a state inquiry. The courts of the State, whose laws embody a privilege against self-incrimination, refused to recognize the petitioner's claim of privilege, finding that the questions asked him were not incriminatory. This Court now holds the contempt adjudication unconstitutional because, it is decided: (1) the Fourteenth Amendment makes the Fifth Amendment privilege against self-incrimination applicable to the States; (2) the federal standard justifying a claim of this privilege likewise applies to the States; and (3) judged by that standard the petitioner's claim of privilege should have been upheld.

Believing that the reasoning behind the Court's decision carries extremely mischievous, if not dangerous consequences for our federal system in the realm of criminal law enforcement, I must dissent. The importance of the issue presented and the serious incursion which the Court makes on time-honored, basic constitutional principles justifies a full exposition of my reasons.

I can only read the Court's opinion as accepting in fact what it rejects in theory: the application to the States, via the Fourteenth Amendment, of the forms of federal criminal procedure embodied within the first eight Amendments to the Constitution. . . .

In particular in this case, I agree that principles of justice to which due process gives expression, as reflected in decisions of this Court, prohibit a State, as the Fifth Amendment prohibits the Federal Government, from imprisoning a person *solely* because he refuses to give evidence which may incriminate him under the laws of the State. I do not understand, however, how this process of re-examination, which must refer always to the guiding standard of due process of law, including, of course, reference to the particular guarantees of the Bill of Rights, can be short-circuited by the simple device of incorporating into due process, without critical examination, the whole body of law which surrounds a specific prohibition directed against the Federal Government. The consequence of such an approach to due process as it pertains to the States is inevitably disregard of all relevant differences which may exist between state and federal criminal law and its enforcement. The ultimate result is compelled uniformity, which is inconsistent with the purpose of our federal system and which is achieved either by encroachment on the States' sovereign powers or by dilution in federal law enforcement of the specific protections found in the Bill of Rights. . . .

The Court suggests that this consistent line of authority has been undermined by the concurrent development of constitutional doctrine in the areas of coerced confessions and search and seizure. That is *post facto* reasoning at best. Certainly there has been no intimation until now that *Twining* has been tacitly overruled. * * *

The coerced confession cases are relevant to the problem of this case not because they overruled *Twining sub silentio,* but rather because they applied the same standard of fundamental fairness which is applicable here. . . .

The elaboration of *Mapp* in *Ker* v. *California,* 374 U.S. 23, did in my view make the Fourth Amendment applicable to the States through the Fourteenth; but there is nothing in it to suggest that the Fifth Amendment went along as baggage.

The previous discussion shows that this Court's decisions do not dictate the "incorporation" of the Fifth Amendment's privilege against self-incrimination into the Fourteenth Amendment. * * *

Seen in proper perspective, therefore, the fact that First Amendment protections have generally been given equal scope in the federal and state domains or that in some areas of criminal procedure the Due Process Clause demands as much of the States as the Bill of Rights demands of the Federal Government, is only tangentially relevant to the question now before us. . . . It is toying with constitutional principles to assert that the Court has "rejected the notion that the Fourteenth Amendment applies to the states only a watered-down, subjective version of the Bill of Rights,'" *ante,* p. 10. What the Court has with the single exception of the *Ker* case, *supra,* . . . consistently rejected is the notion that the Bill of Rights, as such, applies to the States in any aspect at all. * * *

The Court's approach in the present case is in fact nothing more or less than "incorporation" in snatches. If, however, the Due Process Clause *is* something more than a reference to the Bill of Rights and protects only those rights which derive from fundamental principles, as the majority purports to believe, it is just as contrary to precedent and just as illogical to incorporate the provisions of the Bill of Rights one at a time as it is to incorporate them all at once.

The Court's undiscriminating approach to the Due Process Clause carries serious implications for the sound working of our federal system in the field of criminal law.

The Court concludes, almost without discussion, that "the same standards must determine whether an accused's silence in either a federal or state proceeding is justified," *ante,* p. 11. About all that the Court offers in explanation of this conclusion is the observation that it would be "incongruous" if different standards governed the assertion of a privilege to remain silent in state and federal tribunals. Such "incongruity," however, is at the heart of our federal system. * * *

I do not understand how anyone could read the opinion of the Connecticut court and conclude that the state law which was the basis of its decision or the decision itself was lacking in fundamental fairness. The truth of the matter is that under any standard — state or federal — the commitment for contempt was proper. Indeed, as indicated above, there is every reason to believe that the Connecticut court did apply the *Hoffman* standard quoted approvingly in the majority's opinion. . . . The Court's reference to a federal standard is, to put it bluntly, simply an excuse for the Court to substitute its own superficial assessment of the facts and state law for the careful and better informed conclusions of the state court. No one who scans the two opinions with an objective eye will, I think, reach any other conclusion.

I would affirm.

MR. JUSTICE WHITE, with whom MR. JUSTICE STEWART joins, dissenting.

The Fifth Amendment safeguards an important complex of values, but it is difficult for me to perceive how these values are served by the Court's holding that the privilege was properly invoked in this case. While purporting to apply the prevailing federal standard of incrimination — the same standard of incrimination that the Connecticut courts applied — the Court has all but stated that a witness' invocation of the privilege to any question is to be automatically, and without more, accepted. With deference, I prefer the rule permitting the judge rather than the witness to determine when an answer sought is incriminating.

The established rule has been that the witness' claim of the privilege is not final, for the privilege qualifies a citizen's general duty of disclosure only when his answers would subject him to danger from the criminal law. The privilege against self-incrimination or any other evidentiary privilege does not protect silence which is solely an expression of political protest, a desire not to inform, a fear of social obloquy or economic disadvantage or fear of prosecution for future crimes. *Smith* v. *United States,* 337 U.S. 137, 147. . . . If the general duty to testify when subpoenaed is to remain and the privilege is to be retained as a protection against compelled incriminating answers, the trial judge must be permitted to make a meaningful determination of when answers to tend to incriminate. . . .

Answers which would furnish a lead to other evidence needed to prosecute or convict a claimant of a crime—clue evidence—cannot be compelled, but "this protection must be confined to instances where the witness has reasonable cause to apprehend danger from a direct answer." *Hoffman* v. *United States,* 341 U.S. 479, at 486. . . . Of course the witness is not required to disclose so much of the danger as to render his privilege nugatory. But that does not justify a flat rule of no inquiry and automatic acceptance of the claim of privilege. In determining whether the witness has a reasonable apprehension, the test in the federal courts has been that the judge is to decide from the circumstances of the case, his knowledge of matters surrounding the inquiry and the nature of the evidence which is demanded from the witness. *Hoffman* v. *United States,* 341 U.S. 479. This rule seeks and achieves a workable accommodation between what are obviously important competing interests. . . .

. . . In order to allow the judge passing on the claim to understand how the answers sought are incriminating, I would at least require the claimant to state his grounds for asserting the privilege to questions seemingly irrelevant to any incriminating matters. . . .

I would affirm. . . .

Griffin v. *California,* 380 U.S. 609, 85 S. Ct. 1229 (1965)

MR. JUSTICE DOUGLAS delivered the opinion of the Court.

Petitioner was convicted of murder in the first degree after a jury trial in the California court. He did not testify at the trial on the issue of guilt, though he did testify at the separate trial on the issue of penalty. The trial court instructed the jury on the issue of guilt, stating that a defendant has a constitutional right not to testify. But it told the jury:

"As to any evidence or facts against him which the defendant can reasonably be expected to deny or explain because of facts within his knowledge, if he does not testify, or if, though he does testify, he fails to deny or explain such evidence, the jury may take that failure into consideration as tending to indicate the truth of such evidence and as indicating that among the inferences that may be reasonably drawn therefrom those unfavorable to the defendant are the more probable."

It added, however, that no such inference could be drawn as to evidence respecting which he had no knowledge. It stated that failure of a defendant to deny or explain the evidence of which he had knowledge does not create a presumption of guilt nor by itself warrant an inference of guilt nor relieve the prosecution of any of its burden of proof.

Petitioner had been seen with the deceased the evening of her death, the evidence placing him with her in the alley where her body was found. The prosecutor made much of the failure of petitioner to testify:

"The defendant certainly knows whether Essie Mae had this beat up appearance at the time he left her apartment and went down the alley with her. . . .

"He would know that. He would know how she got down the alley. He would know how the blood got on the bottom of the concrete steps. He would know how long he was with her in that box. He would know how her wig got off. He would know whether he beat her or mistreated her. He would know whether he walked away from that place cool as a cucumber when he saw Mr. Villasenor because he was conscious of his own guilt and wanted to get away from that damaged or injured woman.

"These things he has not seen fit to take the stand and deny or explain.

"And in the whole world, if anybody would know, this defendant would know.

"Essie Mae is dead, she can't tell you her side of the story. The defendant won't."

The death penalty was imposed and the California Supreme Court affirmed. 60 Cal.2d 182. The case is here . . . to consider the single question whether comment on the failure to testify violated the Self-Incrimination Clause of the Fifth Amendment which we made applicable to the States by the Fourteenth in *Malloy* v. *Hogan,* 378 U.S. 1, decided after the Supreme Court of California had affirmed the present conviction.

If this were a federal trial, reversible error would have been committed. *Wilson* v. *United States,* 149 U.S. 60, so holds. It is said, however, that the *Wilson* decision rested not on the Fifth Amendment, but on an Act of Congress. 18 U.S.C. § 3481. . . . But that is the beginning, not the end of our inquiry. The question remains whether, statute or not, the comment rule, approved by California, violates the Fifth Amendment.

We think it does. It is in substance a rule of evidence that allows the State the privilege of tendering to the jury for its consideration the failure of the accused to testify. No formal offer of proof is made as in other situations; but the prosecutor's comment and the court's acquiescence are the equivalent of an offer of evidence and its acceptance. . . . For comment on the refusal to testify . . . a remnant of the . . . is a penalty imposed by courts for exercising a constitutional privilege. It cuts down on the privilege by making its assertion costly. It is said, however, that the inference of guilt for failure to testify as to facts peculiarly within the accused's knowledge is in any event natural and irresistible, and that comment on the failure does not magnify that inference into a penalty for asserting a constitutional privilege. . . . What the jury may infer given no help from the court is one thing. What they may infer when the court solemnizes the silence of the accused into evidence against him is quite another. . . .

We said in *Malloy* v. *Hogan, supra,* . . . that "the same standards must determine whether an accused's silence in either a federal or state proceeding is justified." We take that in its literal sense and hold that the Fifth Amendment, in its direct application to the federal government and its bearing on the States by reason of the Fourteenth Amendment, forbids either comment by the prosecution on the accused's silence or instructions by the court that such silence is evidence of guilt. *Reversed.* . . .

MR. JUSTICE HARLAN, concurring.

I agree with the Court that within the federal judicial system the Fifth Amendment bars adverse comment by federal prosecutors and judges on a defendant's failure to take the stand in a criminal trial, a right accorded him by that amendment. And given last Term's decision in *Malloy* v. *Hogan,* . . . that the Fifth Amendment applies to the States in all its refinements, I see no legitimate escape from today's decision and therefore concur in it. I do so, however, with great reluctance, since for me the decision exemplifies the creeping paralysis with which this court's recent adoption of the "incorporation" doctrine is infecting the operation of the federal system. * * *

MR. JUSTICE STEWART, with whom MR. JUSTICE WHITE joins, dissenting. * * *

No claim is made that the prosecutor's argument or the trial judge's instructions to the jury in this case deprived the petitioner of due process of law as such. This Court long ago decided that the Due Process Clause of the Fourteenth Amendment does not of its own force forbid this kind of comment on a defendant's failure to testify. . . . The Court holds, however, that the California constitutional provision violates the Fifth Amendment's injunction that no person "shall be compelled in any criminal case to be a witness against himself," an injunction which the Court less than a year ago for the first time found was applicable to trials in the courts of the several States. . . .

We must determine whether the petitioner has been "compelled to be a witness against himself." Compulsion is the focus of the inquiry. . . . I think that the Court in this case stretches the concept of compulsion beyond all reasonable bounds, and that whatever compulsion may exist derives from the defendant's choice not to testify, not from any comment by court or counsel. * * *

Sixth Amendment Rights to Counsel and Confrontation

Amendment VI of the Bill of Rights makes provision for the right to

a speedy and public trial, by an impartial jury of the State and district wherein the crime shall have been committed, which district shall have been previously ascertained by law, and to be informed of the nature and cause of the accusation, to be confronted with the witnesses against him; to have the compulsory process for obtaining witnesses in his favor, and to have the Assistance of Counsel for his defence.

But this is a limitation on the federal government; each state has its own provisions. Under the Fourteenth Amendment the state must provide the accused with "equal protection of the law" and with "due process of law." The right to counsel, therefore, depends upon whether a denial of counsel would deny the accused either "equal protection of the law" or "due process of law." Of course there is no problem if the accused can afford an attorney; the question has arisen when the accused was indigent and had to rely upon the state's provisions for counsel. When the crime was a capital one, an attorney was appointed. But if the crime did not carry a death sentence as a penalty, the practice varied. *Betts* v. *Brady,* 316 U.S. 455 (1941), involved a non-capital crime.

Betts v. *Brady,* 316 U.S. 455, 62 S. Ct. 1252 (1941)

MR. JUSTICE ROBERTS delivered the opinion of the Court.

The petitioner was indicted for robbery in the Circuit Court of Carroll County, Maryland. Due to lack of funds, he was unable to employ counsel, and so informed the judge at his arraignment. He requested that counsel be appointed for him. The judge advised him that this would not be done, as it was not the practice in Carroll County to appoint counsel for indigent defendants, save in prosecutions for murder and rape.

Without waiving his asserted right to counsel, the petitioner pleaded not guilty and elected to be tried without a jury. . . . The judge found him guilty and imposed a sentence of eight years. . . .

Some months later, a petition for a writ of habeas corpus was presented to . . . the Court of Appeals of Maryland, setting up the same grounds for the prisoner's release as the former petition. The respondent answered, a hearing was afforded, at which an agreed statement of facts was offered by counsel for the parties, the evidence taken at the petitioner's trial was incorporated in the record, and the cause was argued. . . .

The petitioner applied to this court for certiorari directed to Judge

Bond. The writ was issued on account of the importance of the jurisdictional questions involved . . . and conflicting decisions upon the constitutional question presented. * * *

Was the petitioner's conviction and sentence a deprivation of his liberty without due process of law, in violation of the Fourteenth Amendment, because of the court's refusal to appoint counsel at his request?

The Sixth Amendment of the national Constitution applies only to trials in federal courts. The due process clause of the Fourteenth Amendment does not incorporate, as such, the specific guarantees found in the Sixth Amendment, although a denial by a State of rights or privileges specifically embodied in that and others of the first eight amendments may, in certain circumstances, or in connection with other elements, operate, in a given case, to deprive a litigant of due process of law in violation of the Fourteenth. Due process of law is secured against invasion by the federal Government by the Fifth Amendment, and is safeguarded against state action in identical words by the Fourteenth. The phrase formulates a concept less rigid and more fluid than those envisaged in other specific and particular provisions of the Bill of Rights. Its application is less a matter of rule. Asserted denial is to be tested by an appraisal of the totality of facts in a given case. . . .

The petitioner, in this instance, asks us, in effect, to apply a rule in the enforcement of the due process clause. He says the rule to be deduced from our former decisions is that, in every case, whatever the circumstances, one charged with crime, who is unable to obtain counsel, must be furnished counsel by the State. . . .

[I]n the great majority of the States, it has been the considered judgment of the people, their representatives and their courts that appointment of counsel is not a fundamental right, essential to a fair trial. On the contrary, the matter has generally been deemed one of legislative policy. In the light of this evidence, we are unable to say that the concept of due process incorporated in the Fourteenth Amendment obligates the States, whatever may be their own views, to furnish counsel in every such case. Every court has power, if it deems proper, to appoint counsel where that course seems to be required in the interest of fairness.

The practice of the courts of Maryland gives point to the principle that the States should not be straight-jacketed in this respect, by a construction of the Fourteenth Amendment. * * *

To deduce from the due process clause a rule binding upon the States in this matter would be to impose upon them, as Judge Bond points out, a requirement without distinction between criminal charges of different magnitude or in respect of courts of varying jurisdiction. . . . And, indeed, it was said by petitioner's counsel both below and in this court, that as the Fourteenth Amendment extends the protection of due process to property as well as to life and liberty, if we hold with the petitioner, logic would require the furnishing of counsel in civil cases involving property.

As we have said, the Fourteenth Amendment prohibits the conviction and incarceration of one whose trial is offensive to the common and fundamental ideas of fairness and right, and while want of counsel in a particular case may result in a conviction lacking in such fundamental fairness, we cannot say that the Amendment embodies an inexorable command that no trial for any offense, or in any court, can be fairly conducted and justice accorded a defendant who is not represented by counsel.

The judgment is   *Affirmed.*

MR. JUSTICE BLACK, dissenting, with whom MR. JUSTICE DOUGLAS and MR. JUSTICE MURPHY concur.

. . . This case can be determined by a resolution of a narrower question: whether in view of the nature of the offense and the circumstances of his trial and conviction, this petitioner was denied the procedural protection which is his right under the Federal Constitution. I think he was.

The petitioner, a farm hand, out of a job and on relief, was indicted in a Maryland state court on a charge of robbery. . . . The court below found that the petitioner had "at least an ordinary amount of intelligence." It is clear from his examination of witnesses that he was a man of little education. . . .

I believe that the Fourteenth Amendment made the Sixth Applicable to the States. But this view, although often urged in dissents, has never been accepted by a majority of this Court and is not accepted today. * * *

The right to counsel in a criminal proceeding is "fundamental." *Powell* v. *Alabama,* 287 U.S. 45, 70; *Grojean* v. *American Press Co.,* 297 U.S. 233, 243–244. It is guarded from invasion by the Sixth Amendment, adopted to raise an effective barrier against arbitrary or unjust deprivation of liberty by the Federal Government. *Johnson* v. *Zerbst,* 304 U.S. 458, 462. * * *

A practice cannot be reconciled with "common and fundamental ideas of fairness and right," which subjects innocent men to increased dangers of conviction merely because of their poverty. Whether a man is innocent cannot be determined from a trial in which, as here, denial of counsel has made it impossible to conclude, with any satisfactory degree of certainty, that the defendant's case was adequately presented. . . .

Denial to the poor of the request for counsel in proceedings based on charges of serious crime has long been regarded as shocking to the "universal sense of justice" throughout this country. . . .

Twenty-two years later, the *Gideon* case determined that the right to counsel is "fundamental and essential to a fair trial." In *Escobedo* v. *Illinois,* that right was extended to an accused who was denied the right to consult his attorney. But there were strong dissents.

In *Pointer* v. *Texas* the right to confront one's accusers, delineated in the Sixth Amendment, was also included in the Fourteenth Amendment.

Gideon v. *Wainwright*, 372 U.S. 335, 83 S. Ct. 792 (1963)

MR. JUSTICE BLACK delivered the opinion of the Court.

Petitioner was charged in a Florida state court with having broken and entered a poolroom with intent to commit a misdemeanor. This offense is a felony under Florida law. Appearing in court without funds and without a lawyer, petitioner asked the court to appoint counsel for him, whereupon the following colloquy took place: "The *Court:* Mr. Gideon, I am sorry, but I cannot appoint Counsel to represent you in this case. Under the laws of the State of Florida, the only time the Court can appoint Counsel to represent a Defendant is when that person is charged with a capital offense. I am sorry, but I will have to deny your request to appoint Counsel to defend you in this case.

"The *Defendant:* The United States Supreme Court says I am entitled to be represented by Counsel."

Put to trial before a jury, Gideon conducted his defense about as well as could be expected from a layman. . . . The jury returned a verdict of guilty, and petitioner was sentenced to serve five years in the state prison. . . . Since 1942, when *Betts* v. *Brady,* 316 U.S. 455, was decided by a divided Court, the problem of a defendant's federal constitutional right to counsel in a state court has been a continuing source of controversy and litigation in both state and federal courts. To give this problem another review here, we granted certiorari. . . .

The facts upon which Betts claimed that he had been unconstitutionally denied the right to have counsel appointed to assist him are strikingly like the facts upon which Gideon here bases his federal constitutional claim. . . . Like Gideon, Betts sought release by habeas corpus, alleging that he had been denied the right to assistance of counsel in violation of the Fourteenth Amendment. Betts was denied any relief, and on review this Court affirmed. It was held that a refusal to appoint counsel for an indigent defendant charged with a felony did not necessarily violate the Due Process Clause of the Fourteenth Amendment, which for reasons given the Court deemed to be the only applicable federal constitutional provision. . . .

Treating due process as "a concept less rigid and more fluid than those envisaged in other specific and particular provisions of the Bill of Rights," the Court held that refusal to appoint counsel under the particular facts and circumstances in the *Betts* case was not so "offensive to the common and fundamental ideas of fairness" as to amount to a denial of due process. Since the facts and circumstances of the two cases are so nearly indistinguishable, we think the *Betts* v. *Brady* holding if left standing would require us to reject Gideon's claim that the Constitution guarantees him the assistance of counsel. Upon full reconsideration we conclude that *Betts* v. *Brady* should be overruled.

The Sixth Amendment provides, "In all criminal prosecutions, the accused shall enjoy the right * * * to have the Assistance of Counsel for his defence." We have construed this to mean that in federal courts counsel must be provided for defendants unable to employ counsel unless the right is competently and intelligently waived. Betts argued that this right is extended to indigent defendants in state courts by the Fourteenth Amendment. * * *

We think the Court in *Betts* had ample precedent for acknowledging that those guarantees of the Bill of Rights which are fundamental safeguards of liberty immune from federal abridgment are equally protected against state invasion by the Due Process Clause of the Fourteenth Amendment. This same principle was recognized, explained, and applied in *Powell* v. *Alabama,* 287 U.S. 45 (1932), a case upholding the right of counsel where the Court held that . . . the Fourteenth Amendment "embraced" those "'fundamental principles of liberty and justice which lie at the base of all our civil and political institutions,'" even though they had been "specifically dealth with in another part of the Federal Constitution." 287 U.S., at 67. . . . Explicitly recognized to be of this "fundamental nature" and therefore made immune from state invasion by the Fourteenth, or some part of it, are the First Amendment's freedoms of speech, press, religion, assembly, association, and petition for redress of grievances. For the same reason, though not always in precisely the same terminology, the Court has made obligatory on the States the Fifth Amendment's command that private property shall not be taken for public use without just compensation, the Fourth Amendment's prohibition of unreasonable searches and seizures, and the Eighth's ban on cruel and unusual punishment. . . .

We accept *Betts* v. *Brady's* assumption, based as it was on our prior cases, that a provision of the Bill of Rights which is "fundamental and essential to a fair trial" is made obligatory upon the States by the Fourteenth Amendment. We think the Court in *Betts* was wrong, however, in concluding that the Sixth Amendment's guarantee of counsel is not one of these fundamental rights. * * *

. . . In returning to these old precedents, sounder we believe than the new, we but restore constitutional principles established to achieve a fair system of justice. Not only these precedents but also reason and reflection require us to recognize that in our adversary system of criminal justice, any person haled into court, who is too poor to hire a lawyer, cannot be assured a fair trial unless counsel is provided for him. This seems to us to be an obvious truth. . . . From the very beginning, our state and national constitutions and laws have laid great emphasis on procedural and substantive safeguards designed to assure fair trials before impartial tribunals in which every defendant stands equal before the law. This noble ideal cannot be realized if the poor man charged with crime has to face his accusers without a lawyer to assist him. . . .

. . . The Court in *Betts* v. *Brady* departed from the sound wisdom upon which the Court's holding in *Powell* v. *Alabama* rested. Florida, supported by two other States, has asked that *Betts* v. *Brady* be left intact. Twenty-two States, as friends of the Court, argue that *Betts* was "an anachronism when handed down" and that it should now be overruled. We agree.

The judgment is reversed and the cause is remanded to the Supreme Court of Florida for further action not inconsistent with this opinion.   *Reversed.*

MR. JUSTICE DOUGLAS.
I join the opinion of the Court. * * *

MR. JUSTICE CLARK, concurring in the result. . . .
That the Sixth Amendment requires appointment of counsel in "all criminal prosecutions" is clear, both from the language of the Amendment and from this Court's interpretation. . . .

I must conclude here . . . that the Constitution makes no distinction between capital and noncapital cases. The Fourteenth Amendment requires due process of law for the deprival of "liberty" just as for deprival of "life," and there cannot constitutionally be a difference in the quality of the process based merely upon a supposed difference in the sanction involved. . . .

MR. JUSTICE HARLAN, concurring.
I agree that *Betts* v. *Brady* should be overruled, but consider it entitled to a more respectful burial than has been accorded, at least on the part of those of us who were not on the Court when that case was decided. . . .

When this Court . . . decided *Betts* v. *Brady*, it did no more than to admit of the possible existence of special circumstances in noncapital as well as capital trials, while at the same time to insist that such circumstances be shown in order to establish a denial of due process. . . .

In noncapital cases, the "special circumstances" rule has continued to exist in form while its substance has been substantially and steadily eroded. * * *

In what is done today I do not understand the Court to depart from the principles laid down in *Palko* v. *Connecticut,* 302 U.S. 319, or to embrace the concept that the Fourteenth Amendment "incorporates" the Sixth Amendment as such. . . .

I join in the judgment of the Court.

Escobedo v. *State of Illinois* 378 U.S. 478, 84 S. Ct. 1758 (1964)

MR. JUSTICE GOLDBERG delivered the opinion of the Court.
The critical question in this case is whether, under the circumstances, the refusal by the police to honor petitioner's request to consult with his lawyer during the course of an interrogation constitutes a denial of "the Assistance of Counsel" in violation of the Sixth Amendment to the Constitution as "made obligatory upon the States

by the Fourteenth Amendment," *Gideon* v. *Wainwright,* 372 U.S. 335, 342, and thereby renders inadmissible in a state criminal trial any incriminating statement elicited by the police during the interrogation.

On January 30, . . . petitioner and his sister, the widow of the deceased, were arrested and taken to police headquarters. . . . Petitioner testified without contradiction, that the "detectives said they had us pretty well, up pretty tight, and we might as well admit to this crime," and that he replied, "I am sorry but I would like to have advice from my lawyer." A police officer testified that although petitioner was not formally charged "he was in custody" and "couldn't walk out the door."

Shortly after petitioner reached police headquarters, his retained lawyer arrived. The lawyer described the ensuing events in the following terms:

"On that day . . . I asked Sergeant Pidgeon for permission to speak to my client, Danny Escobedo. * * * . . , . He told me I could not see him. Then I went upstairs to the Homicide Bureau. . . . I identified myself as Escobedo's attorney and asked permission to see him. They said I could not. * * *. . . I identified myself to Chief Flynn and asked permission to see my client. He said I could not. . . . He said I couldn't see him because they hadn't completed questioning. * * * [F]or a second or two I spotted him in an office in the Homicide Bureau. The door was open and I could see through the office. * * * I waved to him and he waved back and then the door was closed, by one of the officers at Homicide. . . . I filed an official complaint with Commissioner Phelan of the Chicago Police Department. I had a conversation with every police officer I could find. . . . I had no opportunity to talk to my client that night. I quoted to Captain Flynn the Section of the Criminal Code which allows an attorney the right to see his client."

Petitioner testified that during the course of the interrogation he repeatedly asked to speak to his lawyer and that the police said that his lawyer "didn't want to see" him. The testimony of the police officers confirmed these accounts in substantial detail.

Notwithstanding repeated requests by each, petitioner and his retained lawyer were afforded no opportunity to consult during the course of the entire interrogation. . . .

It is undisputed that during the course of the interrogation Officer Montejano . . . conferred alone with petitioner "for about a quarter of an hour * * *." Petitioner testified that the officer said to him "in Spanish that my sister and I could go home if I pinned it on Benedict DiGerlando," that "he would see to it that we would go home and be held only as witnesses, if anything, if we had made a statement against DiGerlando * * *, that we would be able to go home that night." Petitioner testified that he made the statement in issue because of this assurance. Officer Montejano denied offering any such assurance. . . .

Mr. Cooper, an experienced lawyer who was assigned to the Homicide Division to take "statements from some defendants and some prisoners that they had in custody," "took" petitioner's statement by asking carefully framed questions apparently designed to assure the admissibility into evidence of the resulting answers. Mr. Cooper testified that he did not advise petitioner of his constitutional rights, and it is undisputed that no one during the course of the interrogation so advised him.

Petitioner moved both before and during trial to suppress the incriminating statement, but the motions were denied. Petitioner was convicted of murder and he appealed the conviction. * * *

The interrogation here was conducted before petitioner was formally indicted. But in the context of this case, that fact should make no difference. When petitioner requested, and was denied, an opportunity to consult with his lawyer, the investigation had ceased to be a general investigation of "an unsolved crime." *Spano* v. *New York*, 360 U.S. 315, 327. . . . Petitioner, a layman, was undoubtedly unaware that under Illinois law an admission of "mere" complicity in the murder plot was legally as damaging as an admission of firing of the fatal shots. . . . The "guiding hand of counsel" was essential to advise petitioner of his rights in this delicate situation. *Powell* v. *Alabama*, 287 U.S. 45, 69. . . .

In *Gideon* v. *Wainwright*, 372 U.S. 335, we held that every person accused of a crime, whether state or federal, is entitled to a lawyer at trial. The rule sought by the State here, however, would make the trial no more than an appeal from the interrogation; and the "right to use counsel at the formal trial [would be] a very hollow thing [if], for all practical purposes, the conviction is already assured by pretrial examination." *In re Groban*, 352 U.S. 330, 344. . . .

It is argued that if the right to counsel is afforded prior to indictment, the number of confessions obtained by the police will diminish significantly, because most confessions are obtained during the period between arrest and indictment, and "any lawyer worth his salt will tell the suspect in no uncertain terms to make no statement to police under any circumstances." *Watts* v. *Indiana*, 388 U.S. 49, 59. . . .

The right to counsel would indeed be hollow if it began at a period when few confessions were obtained. . . .

Our Constitution, unlike some others, strikes the balance in favor of the right of the accused to be advised by his lawyer of his privilege against self-incrimination.

We have learned the lesson of history, ancient and modern, that a system of criminal law enforcement which comes to depend on the "confession" will, in the long run, be less reliable and more subject to abuses than a system which depends on extrinsic evidence independently secured through skillful investigation. . . .

We have also learned the companion lesson of history that no system of criminal justice can, or should, survive if it comes to depend for its continued effectiveness on the citizens' abdication through unawareness of their constitutional rights. No system worth preserving should have to *fear* that if an accused is permitted to consult with a lawyer, he will become aware of, and exercise, these rights. . . .

We hold, therefore, that where, as here, the investigation is no longer a general inquiry into an unsolved crime but has begun to focus on a particular suspect, the suspect has been taken into police custody, the police carry out a process of interrogations that lends itself to eliciting incriminating statements, the suspect has requested and been denied an opportunity to consult with his lawyer, and the police have not effectively warned him of his absolute constitutional right to remain silent, the accused has been denied "the Assistance of Counsel" in violation of the Sixth Amendment to the Constitution as "made obligatory upon the States by the Fourteenth Amendment," *Gideon* v. *Wainwright,* 372 U.S., at 342, and that no statement elicited by the police during the interrogation may be used against him at a criminal trial. . . .

Nothing we have said today affects the powers of the police to investigate "an unsolved crime," *Spano* v. *New York,* 360 U.S. 315, 327, (STEWART, J., concurring) by gathering information from witnesses and by other "proper investigative efforts." *Haynes* v. *Washington,* 373 U.S. 503, 519. We hold only that when the process shifts from investigatory to accusatory—when its focus is on the accused and its purpose is to elicit a confession—our adversary system begins to operate, and, under the circumstances here, the accused must be permitted to consult with his lawyer. . . .

The judgment of the Illinois Supreme Court is reversed and the case remanded for proceedings not inconsistent with this opinion.

Reversed and remanded.

MR. JUSTICE HARLAN, dissenting. . . .

. . . Like my Brother WHITE, *post,* . . . I think the rule announced today is most ill-conceived and that it seriously and unjustifiably fetters perfectly legitimate methods of criminal law enforcement.

MR. JUSTICE STEWART, dissenting. . . .

. . . . Under our system of criminal justice the institution of formal, meaningful judicial proceedings, by way of indictment, information, or arraignment, marks the point at which a criminal investigation has ended and adversary litigative proceedings have commenced. It is at this point that the constitutional guarantees attach which pertain to a criminal trial. Among those guarantees are the right to a speedy trial, the right of confrontation, and the right to trial by jury. Another is the guarantee of the assistance of counsel. *Gideon* v. *Wainwright,* 372 U.S. 335. . . .

The confession which the Court today holds inadmissible was a voluntary one. . . .

The Court says that what happened during this investigation

"affected" the trial. I had always supposed that the whole purpose of a police investigation of a murder was to "affect" the trial of the murderer, and that it would be only an incompetent, unsuccessful, or corrupt investigation which would not do so. The Court further says that the Illinois police officers did not advise the petitioner of his "constitutional rights" before he confessed to the murder. This Court has never held that the Constitution requires the police to give any "advice" under circumstances such as these. . . .

MR. JUSTICE WHITE, with whom MR. JUSTICE CLARK and MR. JUSTICE STEWART join, dissenting.

In *Massiah* v. *United States,* 377 U.S. 201, the Court held that as of the date of the indictment the prosecution is disentitled to secure admissions from the accused. The Court now moves that date back to the time when the prosecution begins to "focus" on the accused. . . .

By abandoning the voluntary-involuntary test for admissibility of confessions, the Court seems driven by the notion that it is uncivilized law enforcement to use an accused's own admissions against him at his trial. . . .

It is incongruous to assume that the provision for counsel in the Sixth Amendment was meant to amend or supersede the self-incrimination provision of the Fifth Amendment, which is now applicable to the States, *Malloy* v. *Hogan,* 378 U.S. 1. . . .

Today's decision cannot be squared with other provisions of the Constitution which, in my view, define the system of criminal justice this Court is empowered to administer. . . .

This new American judge's rule, which is to be applied in both federal and state courts, is perhaps thought to be a necessary safeguard against the possibility of extorted confessions. To this extent it reflects a deep seated distrust of law enforcement officers everywhere, unsupported by relevant data or current material based upon our own experience. Obviously law enforcement officers can make mistakes and exceed their authority, as today's decision shows that even judges can do, but I have somewhat more faith than the Court evidently has in the ability and desire of prosecutors and of the power of the appellate courts to discern and correct such violations of the law.

The Court may be concerned with a narrower matter: the unknowing defendant who responds to police questioning because he mistakenly believes that he must and that his admissions will not be used against him. But this worry hardly calls for the broadside the Court has now fired. . . .

I do not suggest for a moment that law enforcement will be destroyed by the rule announced today. The need for peace and order is too insistent for that. But it will be crippled and its task made a great deal more difficult, all in my opinion, for unsound, unstated reasons, which can find no home in any of the provisions of the Constitution.

Pointer v. *State of Texas,* 380 U.S. 400, 85 S. Ct. 1065 (1965)

MR. JUSTICE BLACK delivered the opinion of the court.

The Sixth Amendment provides in part that:

"In all criminal prosecutions, the accused shall enjoy the right ° ° ° to be confronted with the witnesses against him ° ° ° and to have the Assistance of Counsel for his defence."

Two years ago in *Gideon* v. *Wainwright,* 372 U.S. 335, we held that the Fourteenth Amendment makes the Sixth Amendment's guarantee of right to counsel obligatory upon the States. The question we find necessary to decide in this case is whether the Amendment's guarantee of a defendant's right "to be confronted with the witnesses against him," which has been held to include the right to cross-examine those witnesses, is also made applicable to the States by the Fourteenth Amendment.

The petitioner Pointer and one Dillard were arrested in Texas and taken before a state judge for a preliminary hearing (in Texas called the "examining trial") on a charge of having robbed Kenneth W. Phillips of $375 "by assault, or violence, or by putting in fear of life or bodily injury," in violation of Texas Penal Code Art. 1408. At this hearing an Assistant District Attorney conducted the prosecution and examined witnesses, but neither of the defendants, both of whom were laymen, had a lawyer. Phillips as chief witness for the State gave his version of the alleged robbery in detail, identifying petitioner as the man who robbed him at gunpoint. . . . Petitioner was subsequently indicted on a charge of having committed the robbery. Some time before the trial was held, Phillips moved to California. After putting in evidence to show that Phillips had moved and did not intend to return to Texas, the State at the trial offered the transcript of Phillips' testimony given at the preliminary hearing as evidence against petitioner. Petitioner's counsel immediately objected to introduction of the transcript, stating, "Your Honor, we will object to that, as it is a denial of the confrontation of the witnesses against the Defendant." Similar objections were repeatedly made by petitioner's counsel but were overruled by the trial judge, apparently in part because, as the judge viewed it, petitioner had been present at the preliminary hearing and therefore had been "accorded the opportunity of cross examining the witnesses there against him." The Texas Court of Criminal Appeals . . . affirmed petitioner's conviction, rejecting his contention that use of the transcript to convict him denied him rights guaranteed by the Sixth and Fourteenth Amendments. . . . We granted certiorari to consider the important constitutional question the case involves. . . .

. . . In this case the objections and arguments in the trial court as well as the arguments in the Court of Criminal Appeals and before us make it clear that petitioner's objection is based . . . on the fact that use of the transcript of that statement at the trial denied petitioner any opportunity to have the benefit of counsel's cross-examination of the principal witness against him. It is that . . . question which we decide here. . . .

[L]ast Term in *Malloy* v. *Hogan*, 378 U.S. 1, in holding that the Fifth Amendment's guarantee against self-incrimination was made applicable to the States by the Fourteenth, we reiterated the holding of *Gideon* that the Sixth Amendment's right-to-counsel guarantee is "'a fundamental right, essential to a fair trial,'" and "thus was made obligatory on the States by the Fourteenth Amendment." 378 U.S., at 6. . . . We hold today that the Sixth Amendment's right of an accused to confront the witnesses against him is likewise a fundamental right and is made obligatory on the States by the Fourteenth Amendment.

It cannot seriously be doubted at this late date that the right of cross-examination is included in the right of an accused in a criminal case to confront the witnesses against him. And probably no one, certainly no one experienced in the trial of lawsuits, would deny the value of cross-examination in exposing falsehood and bringing out the truth in the trial of a criminal case. . . . The fact that this right appears in the Sixth Amendment of our Bill of Rights reflects the belief of the Framers of those liberties and safeguards that confrontation was a fundamental right essential to a fair trial in a criminal prosecution. . . .

There are few subjects, perhaps, upon which this Court and other courts have been more nearly unanimous than in their expressions of belief that the right of confrontation and cross-examination is an essential and fundamental requirement for the kind of fair trial which is this country's constitutional goal. . . .

. . . We hold that petitioner was entitled to be tried in accordance with the protection of the confrontation guarantee of the Sixth Amendment, and that that guarantee, like the right against compelled self-incrimination, is "to be enforced against the States under the Fourteenth Amendment according to the same standards that protect those personal rights against federal encroachment." *Malloy* v. *Hogan, supra,* 378 U.S., at 10. . . .

Under this Court's prior decisions, the Sixth Amendment's guarantee of confrontation and cross-examination was unquestionably denied petitioner in this case. . . . Since we hold that the right of an accused to be confronted with the witnesses against him must be determined by the same standards whether the right is denied in a federal or state proceeding, it follows that use of the transcript to convict petitioner denied him a constitutional right, and that his conviction must be reversed.

Reversed and remanded.

MR. JUSTICE HARLAN, concurring in the result.

I agree that in the circumstances the admission of the statement in question deprived the petitioner of a right of "confrontation" assured by the Fourteenth Amendment. I cannot subscribe, however, to the constitutional reasoning of the Court.

. . . This is another step in the onward march of the long-since discredited ·"incorporation" doctrine, . . . which for some reason that I have not yet been able to fathom has come into the sunlight in recent years. . . .

For me this state judgment must be reversed because a right of confrontation is "implicit in the concept of ordered liberty," *Palko* v. *State of Connecticut,* 302 U.S. 319, 325, reflected in the Due Process Clause of the Fourteenth Amendment independently of the Sixth.

While either of these constitutional approaches brings one to the same end result in this particular case, there is a basic difference between the two in the kind of future constitutional development they portend. The concept of Fourteenth Amendment due process embodied in *Palko* and a host of other thoughtful past decisions now rapidly falling into discard, recognizes that our Constitution tolerates, indeed encourages, differences between the methods used to effectuate legitimate federal and state concerns, subject to the requirements of fundamental fairness "implicit in the concept of ordered liberty." The philosophy of "incorporation," on the other hand, subordinates all such state differences to the particular requirements of the Federal Bill of Rights . . . and increasingly subjects state legal processes to enveloping federal judicial authority. "Selective" incorporation . . . ignores the possibility that not all phases of any given guaranty described in the Bill of Rights are necessarily fundamental.

It is too often forgotten in these times that the American federal system is itself constitutionally ordained, that it embodies values profoundly making for lasting liberties in this country, and that its legitimate requirements demand continuing solid recognition in all phases of the work of this Court. The "incorporation" doctrines, whether full blown or selective, are both historically and constitutionally unsound and incompatible with the maintenance of our federal system on even course.

MR. JUSTICE STEWART, concurring.

I join in the judgment reversing his conviction, for the reason that the petitioner was denied the opportunity to cross-examine, through counsel, the chief witness for the prosecution. But I do not join in the Court's pronouncement which makes "the Sixth Amendment's right of an accused to confront the witnesses against him ° ° ° obligatory on the States." That questionable *tour de force* seems to me entirely unnecessary to the decision of this case, which I think is directly controlled by the Fourteenth Amendment's guarantee that no State "shall ° ° ° deprive any person of life, liberty, or property, without due process of law.". . .

Here that right was completely denied. . . .

MR. JUSTICE GOLDBERG, concurring.

I agree with the holding of the Court that "the Sixth Amendment's right of an accused to confront the witnesses against him is * * * a fundamental right and is made obligatory on the States by the Fourteenth Amendment." I therefore join in the opinion and judgment of the Court. . . .

. . . I do not see that my Brother HARLAN'S view would further any legitimate interests of federalism. It would require this Court to intervene in the state judicial process with considerable lack of predictability and with a consequent likelihood of considerable friction. . . .

On June 13, 1966, in *Miranda* v. *Arizona,* 86 S. Ct. 1602 (1966), Chief Justice Warren delivered an opinion which extended the protections given a suspect in the *Escobedo* case. The Court outlined the safeguards to which the suspect is entitled in a police interrogation. He must be "adequately and effectively apprised of his rights," and, the Court added, "the exercise of those rights must be fully honored." A person in custody must be informed "in clear and unequivocal terms" of his right to be silent, and that if he speaks what he says can be used against him in court. He also has a right to have counsel with him at the interrogation, to advise him. If the accused wishes an attorney, but cannot afford one, he must be told that an attorney will be appointed to represent him. Moreover, if the suspect does want an attorney, there can be no further interrogation until the lawyer is present. Although it is possible for the suspect to waive his constitutional rights, the Court specified that the waiver must be "meaningful" — surely a term subject to interpretation.

Although the decision may increase the work of the police, it will certainly help protect the multitudes of the poor and ignorant who are unaware of their legal rights, and rarely have counsel.

On June 20, 1966, in *Johnson* v. *New Jersey,* 86 S. Ct. 1772, the Court refused to apply the *Escobedo* v. *Illinois* and *Miranda* v. *Arizona* cases retroactively.

Also on that date, in *Schmerber* v. *California,* 86 S. Ct. 1826, Justice Brennan spoke for a majority of the Court in an opinion which found that under the circumstances of the case the taking of a blood sample for analysis of its alcoholic content, although the taking was protested, was not a violation of either the Fifth or Fourth Amendments as they apply to the states through the Fourteenth Amendment. Chief Justice Warren and Justices Black, Douglas and Fortas all dissented.

★ ★ ★

CHAPTER EIGHT

Voting

THE THIRTEENTH, FOURTEENTH, and Fifteenth Amendments freed the slaves, made them "citizens of the United States and of the State wherein they reside," and gave them, as citizens, the right to vote without abridgment "by the United States or by any State on account of race, color, or previous condition of servitude." These amendments provide only the basic framework for the creation of free men and citizens. The problem has been to implement the promise, despite opposition.

The ways of evading the requirements of the Amendments are many, and have been believed necessary. They are logical if the basic premises of the evaders can be accepted, and not infrequently are devious in operation. Aside from the methods ranging from "suggestions" through economic pressure to terror, physical violence, and murder, the processes normally employed to assure orderly participation in electoral rights have been adapted to deny the vote to Negroes and to citizens of Mexican descent, particularly in the south and southwest.

Citizens may be obliged to satisfy certain prerequisites in order to qualify to vote. Many requirements protect against fraud, if nothing else. Probably the most common is residence for a specified time in the state and city or town where the voter wishes to cast his ballot. The length of time required for eligibility is usually determined by statute, and varies from state to state.

Registration is another common requirement, and it is not illogical to require it sufficiently in advance of an election to allow the preparation of voting lists. A reading test is a requisite, for ballots are printed with words, not symbols. A written application to register, in addition to giving necessary information, can show that the applicant is able to read and write. Unless there are objective standards of performance to guide the registrar, however, the possibilities of discrimination are infinite, but hard to prove in a court of law.

After the adoption of the Thirteenth, Fourteenth, and Fifteenth Amendments, a variety of methods was used to keep the new citizens from voting. A literacy test was not effective, for it barred illiterate whites as well as Negroes. More effective was a "grandfather" clause, which allowed the franchise without a literacy test to those whose direct ancestors had qualified to vote on or before a specified date. In *Guinn* v. *U.S.* (238 U.S. 347, 35 S. Ct. 926; 1915), the date specified in an amendment to the Oklahoma constitution was January 1, 1866, over forty years before Oklahoma became a state. The Court held that this provision was a clear violation of the Fifteenth Amendment.

Although this kind of evasion was found to be unconstitutional, there were other methods, a number of which were centered around the definition of a "political" party. Since private associations may limit their membership and elect such officers or other functionaries as they desire, the effort in certain states was to have what was, in fact, a political party organized as a private association. The private association then chose its membership and officers, nominated candidates for the primary, and elected its nominees, who then became candidates on the ballot at the regular election. The effort, of course, was to avoid "state action" and a state-sponsored slate for the election, because such state-sponsored action would be a clear violation of the Fourteenth and Fifteenth Amendments.

Because in a one-party state the only meaningful choice of candidates is in the primary, non-members of the organization were effectively barred from participation in the choice of public office holders. A series of cases which reached the U.S. Supreme Court from Texas had shown the Democratic Party how to avoid associations which would make Party conduct state action. *Smith* v. *Allwright* (1944) re-examined the status of the Democratic Party in Texas.

Smith v. *Allwright,* 321 U.S. 649, 64 S. Ct. 757 (1944)

MR. JUSTICE REED delivered the opinion of the Court.

This writ of certiorari brings here for review a claim for damages in the sum of $5,000 on the part of petitioner, a Negro citizen of the 48th precinct of Harris County, Texas, for the refusal of respondents, election and associate election judges respectively of that precinct, to give petitioner a ballot or to permit him to cast a ballot in the primary election of July 27, 1940, for the nomination of Democratic candidates for the United States Senate and House of Represntatives, and Governor and other state officers. The refusal is alleged to have been solely because of the race and color of the proposed voter.

The actions of respondents are said to violate § § 31 and 43 of Title 8 of the United States Code in that petitioner was deprived of rights secured by § § 2 and 4 of Article I and the Fourteenth, Fifteenth and Seventeenth Amendments to the United States Constitution. . . .

We granted the petition for certiorari to resolve a claimed inconsistency between the decision in the *Grovey* case and that of *United States* v. *Classic*, 313 U.S. 299. 319 U.S. 738.

The State of Texas by its Constitution and statutes provides that every person, if certain other requirements are met which are not here in issue, qualified by residence in the district or county "shall be deemed a qualified elector." Constitution of Texas, Article VI, § 2. . . . Primary elections for United States Senators, Congressmen and state officers are provided for by Chapters Twelve and Thirteen of the statutes. Under these chapters, the Democratic party was required to hold the primary which was the occasion of the alleged wrong to petitioner. . . . These nominations are to be made by the qualified voters of the party. . . .

The Democratic party of Texas is held by the Supreme Court of that State to be a "voluntary association," *Bell* v. *Hill*, 123 Tex. 531, 534, protected by § 27 of the Bill of Rights, Art. 1, Constitution of Texas, from interference by the State. . . .

That court stated further:

"Since the right to organize and maintain a political party is one guaranteed by the Bill of Rights of this State, it necessarily follows that every privilege essential or reasonably appropriate to the exercise of that right is likewise guaranteed, — including, of course, the privilege of determining the policies of the party and its membership. . . ."

The Democratic party on May 24, 1932, in a state convention adopted the following resolution, which has not since been "amended, abrogated, annulled or avoided":

"Be it resolved that all white citizens of the State of Texas who are qualified to vote under the Constitution and laws of the State shall be eligible to membership in the Democratic party and, as such, entitled to participate in its deliberations."

It was by virtue of this resolution that the respondents refused to permit the petitioner to vote.

Texas is free to conduct her elections and limit her electorate as she may deem wise, save only as her action may be affected by the prohibitions of the United States Constitution or in conflict with powers delegated to and exercised by the National Government. . . . Respondents . . . defended on the ground that the Democratic party of Texas is a voluntary organization with members banded together for the purpose of selecting individuals of the group representing the common political beliefs as candidates in the general election. . . .

Such action, the answer asserted, does not violate the Fourteenth, Fifteenth or Seventeenth Amendment as officers of government cannot be chosen at primaries and the Amendments are applicable only to general elections where governmental officers are actually elected. Primaries, it is said, are political party affairs, handled by party, not governmental, officers. . . .

The right of a Negro to vote in the Texas primary has been considered heretofore by this Court. The first case was *Nixon* v. *Herndon,* 273 U.S. 536. . . . Without consideration of the Fifteenth, this Court held that the action of Texas in denying the ballot to Negroes by statute was in violation of the equal protection clause of the Fourteenth Amendment and reversed the dismissal of the suit.

The legislature of Texas reenacted the article but gave the State Executive Committee of a party the power to prescribe the qualifications of its members for voting or other participation. This article remains in the statutes. . . . Nixon was refused again the privilege of voting in a primary and again brought suit for damages. . . . This Court again reversed the dismissal of the suit for the reason that the Committee action was deemed to be state action and invalid as discriminatory under the Fourteenth Amendment. The test was said to be whether the Committee operated as representative of the State in the discharge of the State's authority. *Nixon* v. *Condon,* 286 U. S. 73. The question of the inherent power of a political party in Texas "without restraint by any law to determine its own membership" was left open. *Id.,* 84–85.

In *Grovey* v. *Townsend,* 295 U. S. 45, this Court had before it another suit for damages for the refusal in a primary of a county clerk, a Texas officer with only public functions to perform, to furnish petitioner, a Negro, an absentee ballot. The refusal was solely on the ground of race. . . . It was decided that the determination by the state convention of the membership of the Democratic party made a significant change from a determination by the Executive Committee. The former was party action, voluntary in character. The latter, as had been held in the *Condon* case, was action by authority of the State. The managers of the primary election were therefore declared not to be state officials in such sense that their action was state action. A state convention of a party was said not to be an organ of the State. . . . Consequently, there was found no ground for holding that the county clerk's refusal of a ballot because of racial ineligibility for party membership denied the petitioner any right under the Fourteenth or Fifteenth Amendment.

Since *Grovey* v. *Townsend* and prior to the present suit, no case from Texas involving primary elections has been before this Court. We did decide, however, *United States* v. *Classic,* 313 U.S. 299. We there held that § 4 of Article I of the Constitution authorized Congress to regulate primary as well as general elections, 313 U.S. at 316, 317, "where the primary is by law made an integral part of the election machinery." 313 U.S. at 318. Consequently, in the *Classic* case, we upheld the applicability to frauds in a Louisiana primary of §§ 19 and 20 of the Criminal Code. . . . This decision depended, too, on the determination that under the Louisiana statutes the primary was a part of the procedure for choice of federal officials. . . . The *Nixon Cases* were decided under the equal protection clause of the Fourteenth Amendment without a determination of the status of the primary as a part of the electoral process. The exclusion of Negroes from the primaries by action of the State was held invalid under that Amendment. The fusing by the *Classic* case of the primary and general elections into a single instrumentality for choice of officers has a definite bearing on the permissibility under the Constitution of excluding Negroes from primaries. . . . *Classic* bears upon *Grovey* v. *Townsend* not because exclusion of Negroes from primaries is any more or less state action by reason of the unitary character of the electoral process but because the recognition of the place of the primary in the electoral scheme makes clear that state delegation to a party of the power to fix the qualifications of primary elections is delegation of a state function that may make the party's action the action of the State. . . . As the Louisiana statutes for holding primaries are similar to those of Texas, our ruling in *Classic* as to the unitary character of the electoral process calls for a reexamination as to whether or not the exclusion of Negroes from a Texas party primary was state action.

The statutes of Texas relating to primaries and the resolution of the Democratic party of Texas extending the privileges of membership to white citizens only are the same in substance and effect today as they were when *Grovey* v. *Townsend* was decided by a unanimous Court. The question as to whether the exclusionary action of the party was the action of the State persists as the determinative factor. . . .

It may now be taken as a postulate that the right to vote in such a primary for the nomination of candidates without discrimination by the State, like the right to vote in a general election, is a right secured by the Constitution. . . . Under our Constitution the great privilege of the ballot may not be denied a man by the State because of his color.

We are thus brought to an examination of the qualifications for Democratic primary electors in Texas, to determine whether state action or private action has excluded Negroes from participation. . . . Texas requires electors in a primary to pay a poll tax. Every person who does so pay and who has the qualifications of age and residence is an acceptable voter for the primary. . . . Texas requires by the law the election of the county officers of a party. These compose the county executive committee. . . . Statutes provide for the election by the voters of precinct delegates to the county convention of a party and the selection of delegates to the district and state conventions by the county convention. . . .

Primary elections are conducted by the party under state statutory authority. . . . These party committees or the state convention certify the party's candidates to the appropriate officers for inclusion on the official ballot for the general election. No name which has not been so certified may appear upon the ballot for the general election as a candidate of a political party. No other name may be printed on the ballot which has not been placed in nomination by qualified voters. . . .

We think that this statutory system for the selection of party nominees for inclusion on the general election ballot makes the party which is required to follow these legislative directions an agency of the State in so far as it determines the participants in a primary election. The party takes its character as a state agency from the duties imposed upon it by state statutes; the duties do not become matters of private law because they are performed by a political party. The plan of the Texas primary follows substantially that of Louisiana. . . . In numerous instances, the Texas statutes fix or limit the fees to be charged. Whether paid directly by the State or through state requirements, it is state action which compels. When primaries become a part of the machinery for choosing officials, state and national, as they have here, the same tests to determine the character of discrimination or abridgment should be applied to the primary as are applied to the general election. If the State requires a certain electoral procedure, prescribes a general election ballot made up of party nominees so chosen and limits the choice of the electorate in general elections for state offices, practically speaking, to those whose names appear on such a ballot, it endorses, adopts and enforces the discrimination against Negroes, practiced by a party entrusted by Texas law with the determination of the qualifications of participants in the primary. This is state action within the meaning of the Fifteenth Amendment. *Guinn* v. *United States,* 238 U.S. 347, 362.

The United States is a constitutional democracy. Its organic law grants to all citizens a right to participate in the choice of elected officials without restriction by any State because of race. This grant to the people of the opportunity for choice is not to be nullified by a State through casting its electoral process in a form which permits a private organization to practice racial discrimination in the election. Constitutional rights would be of little value if they could be thus indirectly denied. *Lane* v. *Wilson,* 307 U.S. 268, 275.

The privilege of membership in a party may be, as this Court said in *Grovey* v. *Townsend,* 295 U.S. 45, 55, no concern of a State. But when, as here, that privilege is also the essential qualification for voting in a primary to select nominees for a general election, the State makes the action of the party the action of the State. In reaching this conclusion we are not unmindful of the desirability of continuity of decision in constitutional questions. However, when convinced of former error, this Court has never felt constrained to follow precedent. In constitutional questions, where correction depends upon amendment and not upon legislative action this Court throughout its history has freely exercised its power to reexamine the basis of its constitutional decisions. This has long been accepted practice, and this practice has continued to this day. This is particularly true when the decision believed erroneous is the application of a constitutional principle rather than an interpretation of the Constitution to extract the principle itself. Here we are applying, contrary to the recent decision in *Grovey* v. *Townsend,* the well-established principle of the Fifteenth Amendment, forbidding the abridgement by a State of a citizen's right to vote. *Grovey* v. *Townsend* is overruled.

Judgment reversed. . . .

MR. JUSTICE ROBERTS:

In *Mahnich* v. *Southern Steamship Co.*, 321 U.S. 96, 105, I have expressed my views with respect to the present policy of the court freely to disregard and to overrule considered decisions and the rules of law announced in them. This tendency, it seems to me, indicates an intolerance for what those who have composed this court in the past have conscientiously and deliberately concluded, and involves an assumption that knowledge and wisdom reside in us which was denied to our predecessors. I shall not repeat what I there said for I consider it fully applicable to the instant decision, which but points the moral anew. * * *

The reason for my concern is that the instant decision, overruling that announced about nine years ago, tends to bring adjudications of this tribunal into the same class as a restricted railroad ticket, good for this day and train only. * * *

Only two years later the Court decided *Colegrove* v. *Green*. Although the number of members of the U. S. House of Representatives is fixed at 435, and single-member districts are required, the Congress has left the delineation of districts to each state. Not all states have changed their districts to conform to population changes, with the result that there are large disparities in the number of people represented by members of the House of Representatives. In 1946 Illinois had not changed its districting since 1901, with a resulting disparity as great as nine to one in the numbers of voters in different districts. Three voters questioned the constitutionality of this disparity, claiming they had been denied the equal protection of the laws. But the majority of the Court found this a political question, not a constitutional issue.

Traditionally, the Court has not decided "political questions," for the function of the Court is to interpret the Constitution and laws of the United States. The difficulty, however, is in part one of the definition: the majority's "political question" was a violation of Article One and the Fourteenth Amendment of the Constitution to Mr. Justice Black and those who joined him in dissent.

Colegrove v. *Green*, 328 U.S. 549, 66 S. Ct. 1198 (1946)

MR. JUSTICE FRANKFURTER announced the judgment of the Court and an opinion in which MR. JUSTICE REED and MR. JUSTICE BURTON concur. * * *

We are of opinion that the petitioners ask of this Court what is beyond its competence to grant. This is one of those demands on judicial power which cannot be met by verbal fencing about "juris-diction." It must be resolved by considerations on the basis of which this Court, from time to time, has refused to intervene in controversies. It has refused to do so because due regard for the effective working of our Government revealed this issue to be of a peculiarly political nature and therefore not meet for judicial determination.

. . . The basis for the suit is not a private wrong, but a wrong suffered by Illinois as a polity. . . . In effect this is an appeal to the federal courts to reconstruct the electoral process of Illinois in order that it may be adequately represented in the councils of the Nation. Because the Illinois legislature has failed to revise its Congressional Representative districts in order to reflect great changes, during more than a generation, in the distribution of its population, we are asked to do this, as it were, for Illinois.

Of course no court can affirmatively remap the Illinois districts so as to bring them more in conformity with the standards of fairness for a representative system. At best we could only declare the existing electoral system invalid. The result would be to leave Illinois undistricted and to bring into operation, if the Illinois legislature chose not to act, the choice of members for the House of Representatives on a state-wide ticket. The last stage may be worse than the first. The upshot of judicial action may defeat the vital political principle which led Congress, more than a hundred years ago, to require districting. . . . Assuming acquiescence on the part of the authorities of Illinois in the selection of its Representatives by a mode that defies the direction of Congress for selection by districts, the House of Representatives may not acquiesce. In the exercise of its powers to judge the qualifications of its own members, the House may reject a delegation of Representatives-at-large. . . . Nothing is clearer than that this controversy concerns matters that bring courts into immediate and active relations with party contests. From the determination of such issues this Court has traditionally held aloof. It is hostile to a democratic system to involve the judiciary in the politics of the people. And it is not less pernicious if such judicial intervention in an essentially political contest be dressed up in the abstract phrases of the law. . . . Authority for dealing with such problems resides elsewhere. * * *

To sustain this action would cut very deep into the very being of Congress. Courts ought not to enter this political thicket. The remedy for unfairness in districting is to secure State legislatures that will apportion properly, or to invoke the ample powers of Congress. The Constitution has many commands that are not enforceable by courts because they clearly fall outside the conditions and purposes that circumscribe judicial action. * * * The Constitution has left the performance of many duties in our governmental scheme to depend on the fidelity of the executive and legislative action and ultimately, on the vigilance of the people in exercising their political rights.

Dismissal of the complaint is affirmed. * * *

MR. JUSTICE BLACK, dissenting. * * *

. . . Petitioners claim that since they live in the heavily populated districts their vote is much less effective than the vote of those living in a district which under the 1901 Act is also allowed to choose one Congressman, though its population is sometimes only one-ninth that of the heavily populated districts. Petitioners contend that this reduction of the effectiveness of their vote is the result of a wilful legislative discrimination against them and thus amounts to a denial of the equal protection of the laws guaranteed by the Fourteenth Amendment. . . . It is my judgment that the District Court had jurisdiction; that the complaint presented a justiciable case and controversy, and that petitioners had standing to sue, since the facts alleged show that they have been injured as individuals. . . . The complaint attacked the 1901 Apportionment Act as unconstitutional and alleged facts indicating that the Act denied petitioners the full right to vote and the equal protection of the laws. These allegations have not been denied. Under these circumstances, and since there is no adequate legal remedy for depriving a citizen of his right to vote, equity can and should grant relief. * * *

It is true that the States are authorized by Section 2 of Article One of the Constitution to legislate on the subject of Congressional elections to the extent that Congress has not done so. Thus the power granted to the State Legislature on this subject is primarily derived from the Federal and not from the State Constitution. But this federally-granted power with respect to elections of Congressmen is not to formulate policy but rather to implement the policy laid down in the Constitution, that, so far as feasible, votes be given equally effective weight. . . . It can no more destroy the effectiveness of their vote in part and no more accomplish this in the name of "apportionment" than under any other name. For legislation which must inevitably bring about glaringly unequal representation in the Congress in favor of special classes and groups should be invalidated, "whether accomplished ingeniously or ingenuously." *Smith* v. *Texas,* 311 U.S. 128, 132. * * *

It is true that voting is a part of elections and that elections are "political." But as this Court said in *Nixon* v. *Herndon, supra,* it is a mere "play on words" to refer to a controversy such as this as "political" in the sense that courts have nothing to do with protection and vindicating the right of a voter to cast an effective ballot. * * *

In this case, no supervision over elections is asked for. What is asked is that this Court . . . declare a state apportionment bill invalid and to enjoin state officials from enforcing it. . . .

What is involved here is the right to vote guaranteed by the Federal Constitution. It has always been the rule that where a federally protected right has been invaded the federal courts will provide the remedy to rectify the wrong done. Federal courts have not hesitated to exercise their equity power in cases involving deprivation of property and liberty. . . . There is no reason why they should do so where the case involves the right to choose representatives that make laws affecting liberty and property. * * *

MR. JUSTICE DOUGLAS and MR. JUSTICE MURPHY join in this dissent.

This decision did not end the effort to have voting districts reapportioned on a more equitable basis. Some nine other cases reached the Supreme Court, but all were decided on the authority of the *Colegrove* case. *Gomillion* v. *Lightfoot*, 364 U.S. 339, 81 S. Ct. 125 (1960), presented a somewhat different problem. The boundaries of the city of Tuskegee, Alabama, had been redrawn, reshaping the city from a square to what Justice Frankfurter described as "an uncouth twenty-eight-sided figure."[1] The change removed 400 of the 404 or 405 Negro voters from the city's voting rolls, but did not remove a single white person. The Supreme Court held that the petitioners should have an opportunity to prove that the state power to redistrict was in fact "used as an instrument for circumventing a federally protected right."[2]

Baker v. *Carr* (1962) marked the real change in the point of view of the majority. Brought under the Civil Rights Acts of 1875, and claiming a deprivation of equal protection of the law "by virtue of the debasement of their votes" in state elections, the plaintiffs' case had been dismissed by the District Court because of lack of jurisdiction of the subject matter, and because no claim had been stated upon which relief could be granted. The Supreme Court disagreed.

Baker v. *Carr*, 369 U.S. 186, 82 S. Ct. 691 (1962)

MR. JUSTICE BRENNAN delivered the opinion of the Court.

This civil action was brought . . . to redress the alleged deprivation of federal constitutional rights. The complaint, alleging that by means of a 1901 statute of Tennessee apportioning the members of the General Assembly among the State's 95 counties, "these plaintiffs and others similarly situated, are denied the equal protection of the laws accorded them by the Fourteenth Amendment to the Constitution of the United States by virtue of the debasement of their votes," was dismissed. . . . The court held that it lacked jurisdiction of the subject matter and also that no claim was stated upon which relief could be granted. . . . We hold that the dismissal was error, and remand the cause to the District Court for trial and further proceedings consistent with this opinion.

The General Assembly of Tennessee consists of the Senate with 33 members and the House of Representatives with 99 members. * * *

Tennessee's standard for allocating legislative representation among her counties is the total number of qualified voters resident in

[1]*Gomillion* v. *Lightfoot*, 364 U.S. 339, p. 340. [2]*Ibid.*, p. 347.

the respective counties, subject only to minor qualifications. Decennial reapportionment in compliance with the constitutional scheme was effected by the General Assembly each decade from 1871 to 1901. . . . In 1891 there was both an enumeration and an apportionment. In 1901 the General Assembly abandoned separate enumeration in favor of reliance upon the Federal Census and passed the Apportionment Act here in controversy. In the more than 60 years since that action, all proposals in both Houses of the General Assembly for reapportionment have failed to pass.

Between 1901 and 1961, Tennessee has experienced substantial growth and redistribution of her population. In 1901 the population was 2,020,616 of whom 487,380 were eligible to vote. The 1960 Federal Census reports the State's population at 3,567,089 of whom 2,092,891 are eligible to vote. The relative standings of the counties in terms of qualified voters have changed significantly. It is primarily the continued application of the 1901 Apportionment Act to this shifted and enlarged voting population which gives rise to the present controversy.

Indeed, the complaint alleges that the 1901 statute, even as of the time of its passage, "made no apportionment of Representatives and Senators in accordance with the constitutional formula * * *, but instead arbitrarily and capriciously apportioned representatives in the Senate and House without reference * * * to any logical or reasonable formula whatever." It is further alleged that "because of the population changes since 1900, and the failure of the legislature to reapportion itself since 1901," the 1901 statute became "unconstitutional and obsolete." Appellants also argue that, because of the composition of the legislature effected by the 1901 apportionment act, redress in the form of a state constitutional amendment to change the entire mechanism for reapportioning, or any other change short of that, is difficult or impossible. The complaint concludes that "these plaintiffs and others similarly situated, are denied the equal protection of the laws accorded them by the Fourteenth Amendment to the Constitution of the United States by virtue of the debasement of their votes. They seek a declaration that the 1901 statute is unconstitutional and an injunction restraining the appellees from acting to conduct any further elections under it. They also pray that unless and until the General Assembly enacts a valid reapportionment, the District Court should either decree a reapportionment by mathematical application of the Tennessee constitutional formulae to the most recent Federal Census figures, or direct the appellees to conduct legislative elections, primary and general, at large. . . . .

. . . The dismissal order recited that the court sustained the appellees' grounds: (1) that the Court lacks jurisdiction of the subject matter, and (2) that the complaint fails to state a claim upon which relief can be granted. * * *" . . .

We treat the first ground of dismissal as "lack of jurisdiction of the subject matter." The second we consider to result in a failure to state a justiciable cause of action. . . .

The court proceeded to explain its action as turning on the case's presenting a "question of the distribution of political strength for legislative purposes." . . .

The court went on to express doubts as to the feasibility of the various possible remedies sought by the plaintiffs. . . . Then it made clear that its dismissal reflected a view not of doubt that violation of constitutional rights was alleged, but of a court's impotence to correct that violation. . . .

In light of the District Court's treatment of the case, we hold today only (a) that the court possessed the jurisdiction of the subject matter; (b) that a justiciable cause of action is stated upon which appellants would be entitled to appropriate relief; and (c) because appellees raise the issue before this Court, that the appellants have standing to challenge the Tennessee apportionment statutes. Beyond noting that we have no cause at this stage to doubt the District Court will be able to fashion relief if violations of constitutional rights are found, it is improper now to consider what remedy would be most appropriate if appellants prevail at the trial. . . .

The District Court was uncertain whether our cases withholding federal judicial relief rested upon a lack of federal jurisdiction or upon the inappropriateness of the subject matter for judicial consideration—what we have designated "nonjusticiability." The distinction between the two grounds is significant. In the instance of nonjusticiability, consideration of the cause is not wholly and immediately foreclosed; rather, the Court's inquiry necessarily proceeds to the point of deciding whether the duty asserted can be judicially identified and its breach judicially determined, and whether protection for the right asserted can be judicially molded. In the instance of lack of jurisdiction the cause either does not "arise under" the Federal Constitution, laws or treaties (or fall within one of the other enumerated categories of Art. III, § 2), or is not a "case or controversy" within the meaning of that section, or the cause is not one described by any jurisdictional statute. Our conclusion . . . that this cause presents no nonjusticiable "political question" settles the only possible doubt that it is a case or controversy. Under the present heading of "Jurisdiction of the Subject Matter" we hold only that the matter set forth in the complaint does arise under the Constitution and is within 28 U.S.C. § 1343. . . .

. . . Since the District Court obviously and correctly did not deem the asserted federal constitutional claim unsubstantial and frivolous, it should not have dismissed the complaint for want of jurisdiction of the subject matter. . . .

Since the complaint plainly sets forth a case arising under the Constitution, the subject matter is within the federal judicial power defined in Art. III. §2, and so within the power of Congress to assign to the jurisdiction of the District Courts. Congress has exercised that power in 28 U.S.C. §1343(3). * * *

The appellees refer to *Colegrove* v. *Green,* 323 U.S. 549, as authority that the District Court lacked jurisdiction of the subject matter. Appellees misconceive the holding of that case. The holding was precisely contrary to their reading of it. * * *

We hold that the District Court has jurisdiction of the subject matter of the federal constitutional claim asserted in the complaint. . . .

A federal court cannot "pronounce any statute, either of a state or of the United States, void, because irreconcilable with the constitution, except as it is called upon to adjudge the legal rights of litigants in actual controversies." *Liverpool* v. *Commissioners* 113 U.S. 33, 39 . . . Have the appellants alleged such a personal stake in the outcome of the controversy as to assure that concrete adverseness which sharpens the presentation of issues upon which the court so largely depends for illumination of difficult constitutional questions? This is the gist of the question of standing. It is, of course, a question of federal law.

The complaint was filed by residents of Davidson, Hamilton, Knox, Montgomery, and Shelby Counties. Each is a person allegedly qualified to vote for members of the General Assembly representing his county. These appellants sued "on their own behalf and on behalf of all qualified voters of their respective counties, and further, on behalf of all voters of the State of Tennessee who are similarly situated". . . .

We hold that the appellants do have standing to maintain this suit. * * *

A citizen's right to vote free of arbitrary impairment by state action has been judicially recognized as a right secured by the Constitution. . . .

Appellants are entitled to a hearing and to the District Court's decision on their claims. . . .

In holding that the subject matter of this suit was not justiciable, the District Court relied on *Colegrove* v. *Green, supra,* and subsequent per curiam cases. . . . We understand the District Court to have read the cited cases as compelling the conclusion that since the appellants sought to have a legislative apportionment held unconstitutional, their suit presented a "political question" and therefore nonjusticiable. We hold that this challenge to an apportionment presents no nonjusticiable "political question." The cited cases do not hold the contrary.

Of course the mere fact that the suit seeks protection of a political right does not mean it presents a political question. . . .

We hold that the claim pleaded here neither rests upon nor implicates the Guaranty Clause and that its justiciability is therefore not foreclosed by our decisions of cases involving that clause. . . . Appellants' claim that they are being denied equal protection is justiciable, and if "discrimination is sufficiently shown, the right to relief under the equal protection clause is not diminished by the fact that the discrimination relates to political rights." *Snowden* v. *Hughes,* 321 U.S. 1,11. To show why we reject the argument based on the Guaranty Clause, we must examine the authorities under it.

But because there appears to be some uncertainty as to why those cases did present political questions, and specifically as to whether this apportionment case is like those cases, we deem it necessary first to consider the contours of the "political question" doctrine. * * *

Deciding whether a matter has in any measure been committed by the Constitution to another branch of government or whether the action of that branch exceeds whatever authority has been committed, is itself a delicate exercise in constitutional interpretation, and is a responsibility of this Court as ultimate interpreter of the Constitution. * * *

We come, finally, to the ultimate inquiry whether our precedents as to what constitutes a nonjusticiable "political question" bring the case before us under the umbrella of that doctrine. . . . We find none. The question here is the consistency of state action with the Federal Constitution. We have no question decided, or to be decided, by a political branch of government coequal with this Court. . . . Judicial standards under the Equal Protection Clause are well developed and familiar, and it has been open to courts since the enactment of the Fourteenth Amendment to determine, if on the particular facts they must, that a discrimination reflects *no* policy, but simply arbitrary and capricious action.

This case does, in one sense, involve the allocation of political power within a State. * * *

We conclude then that the nonjusticiability of claims resting on the Guaranty Clause which arises from their embodiment of questions that were thought "political," can have no bearing upon the justiciability of the equal protection claim presented in this case. Finally, we emphasize that it is the involvement in Guaranty Clause claims of the elements thought to define "political questions," and no other feature, which could render them nonjusticiable. Specifically, we have said that such claims are not held nonjusticiable because they touch matters of state governmental organization. * * *

We conclude that the complaint's allegations of a denial of equal protection present a justiciable constitutional cause of action upon which appellants are entitled to a trial and a decision. The right asserted is within the reach of judicial protection under the Fourteenth Amendment.

The judgment of the District Court is reversed and the cause is remanded for further prceedings consistent with this opinion.

Reversed and remanded. * * *

MR. JUSTICE DOUGLAS, concurring.

While I join the opinion of the Court and, like the Court, do not reach the merits, a word of explanation is necessary. . . . We have here a phase of the recurring problem of the relation of the federal courts to state agencies. More particularly, the question is the extent to which a State may weight one person's vote more heavily than it does another's.

So far as voting rights are concerned, there are large gaps in the

Constitution. Yet the right to vote is inherent in the republican form of government envisaged by Article IV, Section 4 of the Constitution. . . . That the States may specify the qualifications for voter is implicit in Article I, section 2, Clause 1. . . . Yet . . . those who vote for members of Congress do not "owe their right to vote to the state law, in any sense which makes the exercise of the right to depend exclusively upon the law of the state." [*Ex parte Yarbrough*, 110 U.S. 651, 663 – 4] The power of Congress to prescribe the qualifications for voters and thus override state law is not an issue here. It is, however, clear that by reason of the commands of the Constitution there are several qualifications that a State may not require. * * *

There is no doubt that the federal courts have jurisdiction of controversies concerning voting rights. The Civil Rights Act gives them authority to redress the deprivation "under color of any state law" of any "right, privilege or immunity secured by the Constitution of the United States or by any Act of Congress providing for equal rights of citizens * * * 28 U.S.C. §1343(3). And 28 U.S.C. §1343(4) gives the federal courts authority to award damages or issue an injunction to redress the violation of "any Act of Congress providing for the protection of civil rights, including *the right to vote*." The element of state action covers a wide range. * * *

With the exceptions of *Colgrove* v. *Green*, 328 U.S. 549; *MacDougall* v. *Green*, 335 U.S. 281; *South* v. *Peters*, 339 U.S. 276, and the decisions they spawned, the Court has never thought that protection of voting rights was beyond judicial cognizance. . . .

The justiciability of the present claims being established, any relief accorded can be fashioned in the light of well-known principles of equity.

MR. JUSTICE CLARK, concurring.

One emerging from the rash of opinions with their accompanying clashing of views may well find himself suffering a mental blindness. The Court holds that the appellants have alleged a cause of action. However, it refuses to award relief here—although the facts are undisputed—and fails to give the District Court any guidance whatever. * * *

The controlling facts cannot be disputed. It appears from the record that 37% of the voters of Tennessee elect 20 of the 33 Senators while 40% of the voters elect 63 of the 99 members of the House. But this might not on its face be an "invidious discrimination." *Williamson* v. *Lee Optical of Oklahoma*, 348 U.S. 483, 489 (1955). For a "statutory discrimination will not be set aside if any state of facts reasonably may be conceived to justify it.". *McGowan* v. *Md.*, 366 U.S. 420, 426 (1961).

It is true that the apportionment policy incorporated in Tennessee's Constitution, i.e., state-wide numerical equality of representation with certain minor qualifications, is a rational one. . . . However, the root of the trouble is not in Tennessee's Constitution, for admittedly its policy has not been followed. The discrimination lies in the action of Tennessee's Assembly in allocating legislative seats to counties or districts created by it. Try as one may, Tennessee's apportionment just cannot be made to fit the pattern cut by its Constitution. * * *

The truth is that—although this case has been here for two years and had over six hours' argument (three times the ordinary case) and has been most carefully considered over and over again by us in Conference and individually—no one, not even the State nor the dissenters, has come up with any rational basis for Tennessee's apportionment statute.

No one . . . contends that mathematical equality among voters is required by the Equal Protection Clause. But certainly there must be some rational design to a State's districting. . . .

Although I find the Tennnessee apportionment statute offends the Equal Protection Clause, I would not consider intervention by this Court into so delicate a field if there were any other relief available to the people of Tennessee. . . . Tennessee has no initiative and referendum. I have searched diligently for other "practical opportunities" present under the law. I find none other than through the federal courts. * * *

MR. JUSTICE STEWART, concurring. . . .

. . . I think it appropriate, in joining the opinion of the Court, to emphasize in a few words what the opinion does and does not say.

The Court today decides three things and no more: "(a) that the court possessed jurisdiction of the subject matter; (b) that a justiciable cause of action is stated upon which appellants would be entitled to appropriate relief; and (c) * * * that the appellants have standing to challenge the Tennessee apportionment statutes." [Pp. 197, 198.]

The complaint in this case asserts that Tennessee's system of apportionment is utterly arbitrary—without any possible justification in rationality. * * *

The merits of this case are not before us now. The defendants have not yet had an opportunity to be heard in defense of the State's system of apportionment; indeed, they have not yet even filed an answer to the complaint. As in other cases, the proper place for the trial is in the trial court, not here.

MR. JUSTICE FRANKFURTER, whom MR. JUSTICE HARLAN joins, dissenting.

The Court today reverses a uniform course of decision established by a dozen cases, including one by which the very claim now sustained was unanimously rejected only five years ago. * * *

A hypothetical claim resting on abstract assumptions is now for the first time made the basis for affording illusory relief for a particular evil even though it foreshadows deeper and more pervasive difficulties in consequence. . . . For this Court to direct the District Court to enforce a claim to which the Court has over the years consistently found itself required to deny legal enforcement and at the same time to find it necessary to withhold any guidance to the lower court how to enforce this turnabout, new legal claim, manifests an odd — indeed an esoteric — conception of judicial propriety. * * *

In this situation, as in others of like nature, appeal for relief does not belong here. Appeal must be to an informed, civically militant electorate. In a democratic society like ours, relief must come through an aroused popular conscience that sears the conscience of the people's representatives. * * *

In sustaining appellants' claim, based on the Fourteenth Amendment, that the District Court may entertain this suit, this Court's uniform course of decision over the years is overruled or disregarded. Explicitly it begins with *Colegrove* v. *Green, supra,* decided in 1946, but its roots run deep in the Court's historic adjudicatory process. * * *

The *Colegrove* doctrine, in the form in which repeated decisions have settled it, was not an innovation. It represents long judicial thought and experience. . . . To classify the various instances as "political questions" is rather a form of stating this conclusion than revealing of analysis. * * *

The present case involves all of the elements that have made the Guarantee Clause cases non-justiciable. It is, in effect, a Guarantee Clause claim masquerading under a different label. But it cannot make the case more fit for judicial action that appellants invoke the Fourteenth Amendment rather than Art. IV, § 4, where, in fact, the gist of their complaint is the same — unless it can be found that the Fourteenth Amendment speaks with greater particularity to their situation. * * *

. . . What is actually asked of the Court in this case is to choose among competing bases of representation — ultimately, really, among competing theories of political philosophy — in order to establish an appropriate frame of government for the State of Tennessee and thereby for all the States of the Union. * * *

The stark fact is that if among the numerous widely varying principles and practices that control state legislative apportionment today there is any generally prevailing feature, that feature is geographic inequality in relation to the population standard. * * *

Manifestly, the Equal Protection Clause supplies no clearer guide for judicial examination of apportionment methods than would the Guarantee Clause itself. Apportionment, by its character, is a subject of extraordinary complexity, involving — even after the fundamental theoretical issues concerning what is to be represented in a representative legislature have been fought out or compromised — considerations of geography, demography, electoral convenience, economic and social cohesions or divergencies among particular local groups, communication, the practical effects of political institutions like the lobby and the city machine, ancient traditions and ties of settled usage, respect for proven incumbents of long experience and senior status, mathematical mechanics, censuses compiling relevant data, and a host of others. * * *

Dissenting opinion of MR. JUSTICE HARLAN, whom MR. JUSTICE FRANKFURTER joins. . . .

Once one cuts through the thicket of discussion devoted to "jurisdiction," "standing," "justiciability," and "political question," there emerges a straightforward issue which, in my view, is determinative of this case. Does the complaint disclose a violation of a federal constitutional right, in other words, a claim over which a United States District Court would have jurisdiction under 28 U.S.C. § 1343 (3), . . . and 42 U.S.C. § 1983? The majority opinion does not actually discuss this basic question, but, as one concurring Justice observes, seems to decide it *"sub silentio."* p. 261. However, in my opinion, appellants' allegations, accepting all of them as true, do not, parsed down or as a whole, show an infringement by Tennessee of any rights assured by the Fourteenth Amendment. Accordingly, I believe the complaint should have been dismissed for "failure to state a claim upon which relief can be granted." Fed. Rules Civ. Proc. rule 12(b) (6), 28 U.S.C.

It is at once essential to recognize this case for what it is. The issue here relates not to a method of state electoral apportionment by which seats in the federal House of Representatives are allocated, but solely to the right of a State to fix the basis of representation in its *own* legislature. * * *

I can find nothing in the Equal Protection Clause or elsewhere in the Federal Constitution which expressly or impliedly supports the view that state legislatures must be so structured as to reflect with approximate equality the voice of every voter. * * *

In short, there is nothing in the Federal Constitution to prevent a State, acting not irrationally, from choosing any electoral legislative structure it thinks best suited to the interests, temper, and customs of its people. * * *

It is not inequality alone that calls for a holding of unconstitutionality; only if the inequality is based on an impermissible standard may this Court condemn it. * * *

It is my view that the majority opinion has failed to point to any recognizable constitutional claim alleged in this complaint. * * *

In conclusion, it is appropriate to say that one need not agree, as a citizen, with what Tennessee has done or failed to do, in order to deprecate, as a judge, what the majority is doing today. Those observers of the Court who see it primarily as the last refuge for the correction of all inequality or injustice, no matter what its nature or source, will no doubt applaud this decision and its break with the past. Those who consider that continuing national repsect for the Court's authority depends in large measure upon its wise exercise of self-restraint and discipline in constitutional adjudication, will view the decision with deep concern.

I would affirm.

On the basis of this case a variety of apportionment plans were open for decision. The next case was *Gray* v. *Sanders* (1963), in which the

Georgia county unit system was questioned. That case was followed in 1964 by decisions in seven other cases. All were decided on the basis of "equal representation for equal numbers of people." The first was *Wesberry* v. *Sanders* (376 U.S. 1, 84 S. Ct. 524; 1964) in which the Court determined that the Georgia apportionment statute of 1931 grossly discriminated against voters in the district where the appellants lived. That district's Congressmen represented

> from two to three times as many people as do Congressmen from some of the other Georgia districts. . . . We hold that, construed in its historical context, the command of Art. I, § 2, that Representatives by chosen "by the People of the several States" means that as nearly as practicable one man's vote in a congressional election is to be worth as much as another's. . . . We do not believe that the Framers of the Constitution intended to permit the same vote-diluting discrimination to be accomplished through the device of districts containing widely varied numbers of inhabitants.[3]

It was, however, *Reynolds* v. *Sims* which reached most deeply into the States' apportionment rules. Involved were cases from Georgia, Alabama, New York, Maryland, Virginia, Delaware, and Colorado. The decision in the Colorado case makes it clear that not even a majority of the people of a state may violate the "one person, one vote" principle. The voters of Colorado had rejected a constitutional amendment which would have put both houses of the legislature on a population basis, and adopted an amendment which used population and other factors, including geographic features which naturally divided the state into four regions. In all these cases, it was the apportionment of the state legislature, not districts for representation in the Congress, which was in question.

Gray v. *Sanders*, 372 U.S. 368, 83 S. Ct. 801 (1963)

This suit was instituted by appellee, who is qualified to vote in primary and general elections in Fulton County, Georgia, to restrain appellants from using Georgia's county unit system as a basis for counting votes in a Democratic primary for the nomination of a United States Senator and statewide officers, and for declaratory relief. . . . Appellee alleges that the use of the county unit system in counting, tabulating, consolidating, and certifying votes cast in primary elections for statewise offices violates the Equal Protection Clause and the Due Process Clause of the Fourteenth Amendment and the Seventeenth Amendment. . . .

Under Georgia law each county is given a specified number of representatives in the lower House of the General Assembly. . . .

Appellee asserted that . . . one unit vote in Echols County repre-

[3] *Wesberry* v. *Sanders*, 376 U.S. 1, pp. 7, 8.

sented 938 residents, whereas one unit vote in Fulton County represented 92,721 residents. Thus, one resident in Echols County had an
influence in the nomination of candidates equivalent to 99 residents
of Fulton County.

On the same day as the hearing in the District Court, Georgia
amended the statutes challenged in the complaint. This amendment
modified the county unit system by allocating units to counties in
accordance with a "bracket system" instead of doubling the number
of representatives of each county in the lower House of the Georgia
Assembly. . . . Under the amended Act, all candidates for statewide
office (not merely for Senator and Governor as under the earlier Act)
are required to receive a majority of the county unit votes to be
entitled to nomination in the first primary. . . .

Appellee was allowed to amend his complaint so as to challenge
the amended Act. The District Court held that the amended Act had
some of the vices of the prior Act. It stated that under the amended
Act "the vote of each citizen counts for less and less as the population of the county of his residence increases." . . .

The District Court held that as a result of *Baker* v. *Carr*, 369 U.S.
186, it had jurisdiction, that a justiciable case was stated, that appellee had standing, and that the Democratic primary in Georgia is
"state" action within the meaning of the Fourteenth Amendment. It
held that the county unit system as applied violates the Equal Protection Clause, and it issued an injunction, not against conducting
any party primary election under the county unit system, but against
conducting such an election under a county unit system that does not
meet the requirements specified by the court. . . . The District
Court . . . allowed a county unit system to be used in weighting the
votes if the system showed no greater disparity against a county than
exists against any State in the conduct of national elections. . . .

We agree with the District Court that the action of this party in the
conduct of its primary constitutes state action within the meaning of
the Fourteenth Amendment. . . .

We . . . conclude that state regulation of this preliminary phase
of the election process makes it state action. . . .

We also agree that appellee, like any person whose right to vote is
impaired . . . has standing to sue.

Moreover, we think the case is not moot by reason of the fact that
the Democratic Committee voted to hold the 1962 primary on a
popular vote basis. . . .

On the merits we take a different view of the nature of the problem than did the District Court. . . .

The present case is only a voting case. *Cf. Nixon* v. *Herndon*, 273
U.S. 536. . . .

The Fifteenth Amendment prohibits a State from denying or
abridging a Negro's right to vote. The Nineteenth Amendment does
the same for women. If a State in a statewide election weighted the
male vote more heavily than the female vote or the white vote more
heavily than the Negro vote, none could successfully contend that

that discrimination was allowable. See *Terry* v. *Adams*, 345 U.S. 461. How then can one person be given twice or 10 times the voting power of another person in a statewide election merely because he lives in a rural area or because he lives in the smallest rural county? Once the geographical unit for which a representative is to be chosen is designated, all who participate in the election are to have an equal vote — whatever their race, whatever their sex, whatever their occupation, whatever their income, and wherever their home may be in that geographical unit. This is required by the Equal Protection Clause of the Fourteenth Amendment. The concept of "we the people" under the Constitution visualizes no preferred class of voters but equality among those who meet the basic qualifications. The idea that every voter is equal to every other voter in his State, when he casts his ballot in favor of one of several competing candidates, underlies many of our decisions.

The Court has consistently recognized that all qualified voters have a constitutionally protected right "to cast their ballots and have them counted at Congressional elections." *United States* v. *Classic*, 313 U.S. 299, 315. Every voter's vote is entitled to be counted once. It must be correctly counted and reported. . . . It can be protected from the diluting effect of illegal ballots. *Ex Parte Siebold*, 100 U.S. 371. And these rights must be recognized in any preliminary election that in fact determines the true weight a vote will have. . . . The concept of political equality in the voting booth contained in the Fifteenth Amendment extends to all phases of state elections, see *Terry* v. *Adams, supra;* and, as previously noted, there is no indication in the Constitution that homesite or occupation affords a permissible basis for distinguishing between qualified voters within the State.

The only weighting of votes sanctioned by the Constitution concerns matters of representation, such as the allocation of Senators irrespective of population and the use of the electoral college in the choice of a President. Yet when Senators are chosen, the Seventeenth Amendment states the choice must be made "by the people." . . . But once the class of voters is chosen and their qualifications specified, we see no constitutional way by which equality of voting power may be evaded. . . . The conception of political equality from the Delcaration of Independence, to Lincoln's Gettysburg Address, to the Fifteenth, Seventeenth, and Nineteenth Amendments can mean only one thing — one person, one vote.

While we agree with the District Court on most phases of the case and think it was right in enjoining the use of the county unit system in tabulating the votes, we vacate its judgment and remand the case so that a decree in conformity with our opinion may be entered.

It is so ordered. . . .

MR. JUSTICE STEWART, whom MR. JUSTICE CLARK joins, concurring. . . .

MR. JUSTICE HARLAN, dissenting.

When *Baker* v. *Carr*, 369 U.S. 186, was argued at the last Term we were assured that if this Court would only remove the roadblocks of *Colegrove* v. *Green*, 328 U.S. 549, this Court in all likelihood would never have to get deeper into such matters. State legislatures, it was predicted, would be prodded into taking satisfactory action by the mere prospect of legal proceedings.

These predictions have not proved true. As of November 1, 1962, the apportionment of seats in at least 30 state legislatures had been challenged in state and federal courts, and, besides this one, 10 electoral cases of one kind or another are already on this Court's docket. The present case is the first of these to reach plenary consideration. . . .

. . . The Court . . . strikes down Georgia's County Unit System *as such,* a holding which the District Court declined to make. . . .

The Court's holding surely flies in the face of history. For, as impressively shown by the opinion of Frankfurter, J., in *Baker* v. *Carr,* 369 U.S., at 301–324, "one person, one vote" has never been the universally accepted political philosophy in England, the American Colonies, or in the United States. . . .

Indeed this Court itself some 15 years ago rejected, in a comparable situation, the notion of political equality now pronounced. . . .

Certainly no support for this equal protection doctrine can be drawn from the Fifteenth, Seventeenth, or Nineteenth Amendments. . . .

A violation of the Equal Protection Clause thus cannot be found in the *mere* circumstance that the Georgia County Unit System results in disproportionate vote weighting. It "is important for this court to avoid extracting from the very general language of the Fourteenth Amendment a system of delusive exactness. . . ." *Louisville & Nashville R. Co.* v. *Barber Asphalt Co.,* 197 U.S. 430, 434 (Holmes, J.). . . .

At the core of Georgia's diffusion of voting strength which favors the small as against the large counties is the urban-rural problem, so familiar in the American political scene. In my dissent in *Baker* v. *Carr,* 369 U.S., at 336, I expressed the view that a State might rationally conclude that its general welfare was best served by apportioning more seats in the legislature to agricultural communities than to urban centers, lest the legitimate interests of the former be submerged in the stronger electoral voice of the latter. In my opinion, recognition of the same factor cannot be deemed irrational in the present situation even though all of the considerations supporting its use in a legislative apportionment case are not present here.

. . . I do not understand how, on the basis of these mere numbers, unilluminated as they are by any of the complex and subtle political factors involved, a court of law can say, except by judicial fiat, that these disparities are in themselves constitutionally invidious.

. . . It is . . . apparent that a slight modification of the Georgia plan could bring it within the tolerance permitted in the federal scheme.

It was of course imponderables like these that lay at the root of the Court's steadfast pre-*Baker* v. *Carr* refusal "to enter [the] political thicket." *Colegrove* v. *Green, supra,* 328 U.S. at 556.

What then should be the test of "rationality" in this judicially unfamiliar field? My Brother CLARK has perhaps given us a clue in the "legislative inactivity—absence of any other remedy—crazy quilt" approach contained in his concurring opinion in *Baker* v. *Carr, supra,* at 369 U.S. 253–262. But I think a formulation of the basic ground rules in this untrod area of judicial competence should await a fully developed record. This case is here at an interlocutory stage. . . . No full-dress exploration of any of the many intricate questions involved in establishing criteria for judging "rationality" took place. . . .

Surely, if the Court's "one person, one vote" ideology is constitutionally untenable, as I think it clearly is, the basic ground rules implementing *Baker* v. *Carr* should await the trial of this or some other case in which we have before us a fully developed record. Only then can we know what we are doing. . . . A matter which so profoundly touches the barriers between the federal judicial and state legislative authority demands nothing less.

I would vacate the judgment of the District Court and remand the case for trial.

Reynolds v. *Sims,* 377 U.S. 533, 84 S. Ct. 1362 (1964)

MR. CHIEF JUSTICE WARREN delivered the opinion of the Court. . . .

I.

On August 26, 1961, the original plaintiffs (appellees in No. 23), residents, taxpayers and voters of Jefferson County, Alabama, filed a complaint in the United States District Court . . . challenging the apportionment of the Alabama Legislature. Defendants below . . . were various state and political party officials charged with the performance of certain duties in connection with state elections. The complaint alleged a deprivation of rights under the Alabama Constitution and under the Equal Protection Clause of the Fourteenth Amendment, and asserted that the District Court had jurisdiction under provisions of the Civil Rights Act, 42 U. S. C. §§ 1983, 1988, as well as under 28 U.S. C. § 1343 (3).

The complaint stated that the Alabama Legislature was composed of a Senate of 35 members and a House of Representatives of 106 members. It set out relevant portions of the 1901 Alabama Constitution, which prescribe the number of members of the two bodies of the State Legislature and the method of apportioning the seats among the State's 67 counties. * * *

Plaintiffs below alleged that the last apportionment of the Alabama Legislature was based on the 1900 federal census, despite the requirement of the State Constitution that the legislature be reapportioned decennially. They asserted that, since the population growth in the State from 1900 to 1960 had been uneven, Jefferson and other counties were now victims of serious discrimination with respect to the allocation of legislative representation. As a result of the failure of the legislature to reapportion itself, plaintiffs asserted, they were denied "equal suffrage in free and equal elections . . . and the equal protection of the laws" in violation of the Alabama Constitution and the Fourteenth Amendment to the Federal Constitution. The complaint asserted that plaintiffs had no other adequate remedy, and that they had exhausted all forms of relief other than that available through the federal courts. They alleged that the Alabama Legislature had established a pattern of prolonged inaction from 1911 to the present which "clearly demonstrates that no reapportionment . . . shall be effected"; that representation at any future constitutional convention would be established by the legislature, making it unlikely that the membership of any such convention would be fairly representative; and that, while the Alabama Supreme Court had found that the legislature had not complied with the State Constitution in failing to reapportion according to population decennially, that court had nevertheless indicated that it would not interfere with matters of legislative reapportionment. . . .

On March 29, 1962, just three days after this Court had decided *Baker* v. *Carr*, 369 U.S. 186, plaintiffs moved for a preliminary injunction requiring defendants to conduct at large the May 1962 Democratic primary election and the November 1962 general election for members of the Alabama Legislature. . . . On April 14, 1962, the District Court reset the case for hearing on July 16. . . . Relying on our decision in *Baker* v. *Carr*, the Court found jurisdiction, justiciability and standing. It stated that it was taking judicial notice of the facts that there had been population changes in Alabama's counties since 1901, that the present representation in the State Legislature was not on a population basis, and that the legislature had never reapportioned its membership as required by the Alabama Constitution. Continuing, the Court stated that if the legislature complied with the Alabama constitutional provision requiring legislative representation to be based on population there could be no objection on federal constitutional grounds to such an apportionment. The Court further indicated that, if the legislature failed to act, or if its actions did not meet constitutional standards, it would be under a "clear duty" to take some action on the matter prior to the November 1962 general election. . . . Subsequently, plaintiffs were permitted to amend their complaint by adding a further prayer for relief, which asked the District Court to reapportion the Alabama Legislature provisionally so that the rural strangle hold would be relaxed enough to permit it to reapportion itself.

On July 12, 1962, an extraordinary session of the Alabama Legislature adopted two reapportionment plans to take effect for the 1966 elections. One was a proposed constitutional amendment, referred to as the "67-Senator Amendment." . . .

The other reapportionment plan was embodied in a statutory

measure adopted by the legislature and signed into law by the Alabama Governor, and was referred to as the "Crawford-Webb Act." It was enacted as standby legislation to take effect in 1966 if the proposed constitutional amendment should fail of passage by a majority of the State's voters, or should the federal courts refuse to accept the proposed amendment (though not rejected by the voters) as effective action in compliance with requirements of the Fourteenth Amendment. . . .

The evidence adduced at trial before the three-judge panel consisted primarily of figures showing the population of each Alabama county and senatorial district according to the 1960 census, and the number of representatives allocated to each county under each of the three plans at issue in the litigation—the existing apportionment (under the 1901 constitutional provisions and the current statutory measures substantially reenacting the same plan), the proposed 67-Senator constitutional amendment, and the Crawford-Webb Act. Under all three plans, each senatorial district would be represented by only one senator.

On July 21, 1962, the District Court held that the inequality of the existing representation in the Alabama Legislature violated the Equal Protection Clause of the Fourteenth Amendment, a finding which the Court noted had been "generally conceded" by the parties to the litigation, since population growth and shifts had converted the 1901 scheme, as perpetuated some 60 years later, into an invidiously discriminatory plan completely lacking in rationality. . . . Under the existing provisions, applying 1960 census figures, only 25.1% of the State's total population resided in districts represented by a majority of the members of the Senate, and only 25.7% lived in counties which could elect a majority of the members of the House of Representatives. Population-variance ratios of up to about 41-to-1 existed in the Senate, and up to about 16-to-1 in the House. . . .

The Court then considered both the proposed constitutional amendment and the Crawford-Webb Act to ascertain whether the legislature had taken effective action to remedy the unconstitutional aspects of the existing apportionment. In initially summarizing the result which it had reached, the Court stated:

"This Court has reached the conclusion that neither the '67-Senator Amendment,' nor the 'Crawford-Webb Act' meets the necessary constitutional requirements. We find that each of the legislative acts, when considered as a whole, is so obviously discriminatory, arbitrary and irrational that it becomes unnecessary to pursue a detailed development of each of the relevant factors of the [federal constitutional] test."

The Court stated that the apportionment of one senator to each county, under the proposed constitutional amendment, would "make the discrimination in the Senate even more invidious than at present." Under the 67-Senator Amendment, as pointed out by the court below, "[t]he present control of the Senate by members representing 25.1% of the people of Alabama would be reduced to control by members representing 19.4% of the people of the State," the 34 smallest counties, with a total population of less than that of Jefferson County, would have a majority of the senatorial seats, and senators elected by only about 14% of the State's population could prevent the submission to the electorate of any future proposals to amend the State Constitution (since a vote of two-fifths of the members of one house can defeat a proposal to amend the Alabama Constitution). Noting that the "only conceivable rationalization" of the senatorial apportionment scheme is that it was based on equal representation of political subdivisions within the State and is thus analogous to the Federal Senate, the District Court rejected the analogy on the ground that Alabama counties are merely involuntary political units of the State created by statute to aid in the administration of state government. . . .

The Court also noted that the senatorial apportionment proposal "may not have complied with the State Constitution," since not only is it explicitly provided that the population basis of legislative representation "shall not be changed by constitutional amendments," but the Alabama Supreme Court had previously indicated that that requirement could probably be altered only by constitutional convention. The Court concluded, however, that the apportionment of seats in the Alabama House, under the proposed constitutional amendment, was "based upon reason, with a rational regard for known and accepted standards of apportionment." . . . About 43% of the State's total population would live in counties which could elect a majority in that body. And, under the provisions of the 67-Senator Amendment, while the maximum population-variance ratio was increased to about 59-to-1 in the Senate, it was significantly reduced to about 4.7-to-1 in the House of Representatives. . . . Even so, serious disparities from a population-based standard remained. . . .

Turning next to the provision of the Crawford-Webb Act, the District Court found that its apportionment of the 106 seats in the Alabama House of Representatives, by allocating one seat to each county and distributing the remaining 39 to the more populous counties in diminishing ratio to their populations, was "totally unacceptable." Under this plan, about 37% of the State's total population would reside in counties electing a majority of the members of the Alabama House, with a maximum population-variance ratio of about 5-to-1. . . .

The Court pointed out that, under the Crawford-Webb Act, the vote of a person in the senatorial district consisting of Bibb and Perry Counties would be worth 20 times that of a citizen in Jefferson County, and that the vote of a citizen in the six smallest districts would be worth 15 or more times that of a Jefferson County voter. . . .

Under the detailed requirements of the various constitutional provisions relating to the apportionment of seats in the Alabama Senate and House of Representatives, the Court found, the membership of neither house can be apportioned solely on a population basis. . . .

The District Court then directed its concern to the providing of an effective remedy. It indicated that it was adopting and ordering into effect for the November 1962 election a provisional and temporary reapportionment plan composed of the provisions relating to the House of Representatives contained in the 67-Senator Amendment and the provisions of the Crawford-Webb Act relating to the Senate. The Court noted, however, that "[t]he proposed reapportionment of the Senate in the 'Crawford-Webb Act,' unacceptable as a piece of permanent legislation, may not even break the strangle hold." Stating that it was retaining jurisdiction and deferring any hearing on plaintiffs' motion for a permanent injunction "until the Legislature, as provisionally reapportioned . . . , has an opportunity to provide for a true reapportionment of both Houses of the Alabama Legislature." . . .

[T]he present Alabama Legislature is apportioned in accordance with the temporary plan prescribed by the District Court's decree. All members of both houses of the Alabama Legislature serve four-year terms, so that the next regularly scheduled election of legislators will not be held until 1966. The 1963 regular session of the Alabama Legislature produced no legislation relating to legislative apportionment, and the legislature, which meets biennially, will not hold another regular session until 1965.

No effective political remedy to obtain relief against the alleged malapportionment of the Alabama Legislature appears to have been available. No initiative procedure exists under Alabama law. Amendment of the State Constitution can be achieved only after a proposal is adopted by three-fifths of the members of both houses of the legislature and is approved by a majority of the people, or as a result of a constitutional convention convened after approval by the people of a convention call initiated by a majority of both houses of the Alabama Legislature. . . .

II.

Undeniably the Constitution of the United States protects the right of all qualified citizens to vote, in state as well as in federal elections. A consistent line of decisions by this Court in cases involving attempts to deny or restrict the right of suffrage has made this indelibly clear. It has been repeatedly recognized that all qualified voters have a constitutionally protected right to vote, *Ex parte Yarbrough*, 110 U.S. 651, and to have their votes counted, *United States v. Mosley*, 238 U.S. 383. In *Mosley* the Court stated that it is "as equally unquestionable that the right to have one's vote counted is as open to protection . . . as the right to put a ballot in a box." 238 U.S., at 386. The right to vote can neither be denied outright, *Guinn*

v. *United States,* 238 U.S. 347, *Lane* v. *Wilson,* 307 U. S. 268, nor destroyed by alteration of ballots, see *United States* v. *Classic,* 313 U. S. 299, 315, nor diluted by ballot-box stuffing, *Ex parte Siebold,* 100 U. S. 371, *United States* v. *Saylor,* 322 U. S. 385. As the Court stated in *Classic,* "Obviously included within the right to choose, secured by the Constitution, is the right of qualified voters within a state to cast their ballots and have them counted. . . ." 313 U.S., at 315. Racially based gerrymandering, *Gomillion* v. *Lightfoot,* 364 U.S. 339, and the conducting of white primaries, *Nixon* v. *Herndon,* 273 U.S. 536, *Nixon* v. *Condon,* 286 U.S. 73, *Smith* v. *Allwright,* 321 U.S. 649, *Terry* v. *Adams,* 345 U.S. 461, both of which result in denying to some citizens their right to vote, have been held to be constitutionally impermissible. And history has seen a continuing expansion of the scope of the right of suffrage in this country. The right to vote freely for the candidate of one's choice is of the essence of a democratic society, and any restrictions on that right strike at the heart of representative government. And the right of suffrage can be denied by a debasement or dilution of the weight of a citizen's vote just as effectively as by wholly prohibiting the free exercise of the franchise.

In *Baker* v. *Carr,* 369 U.S. 186, we held that a claim asserted under the Equal Protection Clause challenging the constitutionality of a State's apportionment of seats in its legislature, on the ground that the right to vote of certain citizens was effectively impaired since debased and diluted in effect, presented a justiciable controversy subject to adjudication by federal courts. The spate of similar cases filed and decided by lower courts since our decision in *Baker* amply shows that the problem of state legislative malapportionment is one that is perceived to exist in a large number of the States. . . . We indicated in *Baker* . . . that the Equal Protection Clause provides discoverable and manageable standards for use by lower courts in determining the constitutionality of a state legislative apportionment scheme. . . . Subsequent to *Baker,* we remanded several cases to the courts below for reconsideration in light of that decision. * * * Of course, in these cases we are faced with the problem not presented in *Gray*—that of determining the basic standards and stating the applicable guidelines for implementing our decision in *Baker* v. *Carr.*

In *Wesberry* v. *Sanders,* 376 U.S.1, . . . we concluded that the constitutional prescription for election of members of the House of Representatives "by the People," construed in its historical context, "means that as nearly as is practicable one man's vote in a congressional election is to be worth as much as another's." . . . We found further, in *Wesberry,* that "our Constitution's plain objective" was that "of making equal representation for equal numbers of people the fundamental goal. . . ." . . .

Gray and *Wesberry* are of course not dispositive of or directly controlling on our decision in these cases involving state legislative apportionment controversies. Admittedly, those decisions, in which we held that, in statewide and in congressional elections, one person's vote must be counted equally with those of all other voters in a State, were based on different constitutional considerations and were addressed to rather distinct problems. But neither are they wholly inapposite. *Gray* . . . established the basic principle of equality among voters within a State, and held that voters cannot be classified, constitutionally, on the basis of where they live, at least with respect to voting in statewide elections. And our decision in *Wesberry* was of course grounded on that language of the Constitution which prescribes that members of the Federal House of Representatives are to be chosen "by the People," while attacks on state legislative apportionment schemes, such as that involved in the instant cases, are principally based on the Equal Protection Clause of the Fourteenth Amendment. Nevertheless, *Wesberry* clearly established that the fundamental principle of representative government in this country is one of equal representation for equal numbers of people, without regard to race, sex, economic status, or place of residence within a State. Our problem, then, is to ascertain, in the instant cases, whether there are any constitutionally cognizable principles which would justify departures from the basic standard of equality among voters in the apportionment of seats in state legislatures.

III.

A predominant consideration in determining whether a State's legislative apportionment scheme constitutes an invidious discrimination violative of rights asserted under the Equal Protection Clause is that the rights allegedly impaired are individual and personal in nature. . . . While the result of a court decision in a state legislative apportionment controversy may be to require the restructuring of the geographical distribution of seats in a state legislature, the judicial focus must be concentrated upon ascertaining whether there has been any discrimination against certain of the State's citizens which constitutes an impermissible impairment of their constitutionally protected right to vote. . . . Especially since the right to exercise the franchise in a free and unimpaired manner is preservative of other basic civil and political rights, any alleged infringement of the right of citizens to vote must be carefully and meticulously scrutinized. . . .

Legislators represent people, not trees or acres. Legislators are elected by voters, not farms or cities or economic interests. As long as ours is a representative form of government, and our legislatures are those instruments of government elected directly by and directly representative of the people, the right to elect legislators in a free and unimpaired fashion is a bedrock of our political system. . . .

Overweighting and overvaluation of the votes of those living here has the certain effect of dilution and undervaluation of the votes of those living there. The resulting discrimination against those individual voters living in disfavored areas is easily demonstrable mathematically. . . . Two, five or 10 of them must vote before the effect of their voting is equivalent to that of their favored neighbor. Weighting the votes of citizens differently, by any method or means, merely because of where they happen to reside, hardly seems justifiable. One must be ever aware that the Constitution forbids "sophisticated as well as simple-minded modes of discrimination." *Lane* v. *Wilson,* 307 U.S. 268, 275, *Gomillion* v. *Lightfoot,* 364 U.S. 339, 342. . . .

With the birth of our National Government, and the adoption and ratification of the Federal Constitution, state legislatures retained a most important place in our Nation's governmental structure. But representative government is in essence self-government through the medium of elected representatives of the people, and each and every citizen has an inalienable right to full and effective participation in the political processes of his State's legislative bodies. Most citizens can achieve this participation only as qualified voters through the election of legislators to represent them. Full and effective participation by all citizens in state government requires, therefore, that each citizen have an equally effective voice in the election of members of his state legislature. Modern and viable state government needs, and the Constitution demands, no less. . . .

Since legislatures are responsible for enacting laws by which all citizens are to be governed, they should be bodies which are collectively responsive to the popular will. And the concept of equal protection has been traditionally viewed as requiring the uniform treatment of persons standing in the same relation to the governmental action questioned or challenged. With respect to the allocation of legislative representation, all voters, as citizens of a State, stand in the same relation regardless of where they live. Any suggested criteria for the differentiation of citizens are insufficient to justify any discrimination, as to the weight of their votes, unless relevant to the permissible purposes of legislative apportionment. Since the achieving of fair and effective representation for all citizens is concededly the basic aim of legislative apportionment, we conclude that the Equal Protection Clause guarantees the opportunity for equal participation by all voters in the election of state legislators. Diluting the weight of votes because of place of residence impairs basic constitutional rights under the Fourteenth Amendment just as much as invidious discriminations based upon factors such as race, *Brown* v. *Board of Education,* 347 U.S. 483, or economic status, *Griffin* v. *Illinois,* 351 U.S. 12, *Douglas* v. *California,* 372 U.S. 353. Our constitutional system amply provides for the protection of minorities by means other than giving them majority control of state legislatures. And the democratic ideals of equality and majority rule, which have served this Nation so well in the past, are hardly of any less significance for the present and the future.

We are told that the matter of apportioning representation in a state legislature is a complex and many-faceted one. We are advised that States can rationally consider factors other than population in apportioning legislative representation. We are admonished not to restrict the power of the States to impose differing views as to political philosophy on their citizens. We are cautioned about the dangers of entering into political thickets and mathematical quagmires. Our answer is this: a denial of constitutionally protected rights demands judicial protection; our oath and our office require no less of us. . . . To the extent that a citizen's right to vote is debased, he is that much less a citizen. The fact that an individual lives here or there is not a legitimate reason for overweighting or diluting the efficacy of his vote. The complexions of societies and civilizations change, often with amazing rapidity. . . . But the basic principle of representative government remains, and must remain, unchanged — the weight of a citizen's vote cannot be made to depend on where he lives. . . .

IV.

We hold that, as a basic constitutional standard, the Equal Protection Clause requires that the seats in both houses of a bicameral state legislature must be apportioned on a population basis. Simply stated, an individual's right to vote for state legislators is unconstitutionally impaired when its weight is in a substantial fashion diluted when compared with votes of citizens living in other parts of the State. Since, under neither the existing apportionment provisions nor either of the proposed plans was either of the houses of the Alabama Legislature apportioned on a population basis, the District Court correctly held that all three of these schemes were constitutionally invalid. Furthermore, the existing apportionment, and also to a lesser extent the apportionment under the Crawford-Webb Act, presented little more than crazy quilts, completely lacking in rationality, and could be found invalid on that basis alone. . . . While mathematical nicety is not a constitutional requisite, one could hardly conclude that the Alabama House, under the proposed constitutional amendment, had been apportioned sufficiently on a population basis to be sustainable under the requirements of the Equal Protection Clause. And none of the other apportionments . . . under the three plans considered by the District Court, came nearly as close to approaching the required constitutional standard as did that of the House of Representatives under the 67-Senator Amendment.

Legislative apportionment in Alabama is signally illustrative and symptomatic of the seriousness of this problem in a number of the States. At the time this litigation was commenced, there had been no reapportionment of seats in the Alabama Legislature for over 60 years. * * *

V.

Since neither of the houses of the Alabama Legislature, under any of the three plans considered by the District Court, was apportioned on a population basis, we would be justified in proceeding no further. . . .

Much has been written since our decision in *Baker* v. *Carr* about the applicability of the so-called federal analogy to state legislative apportionment arrangements. After considering the matter, the court below concluded that no conceivable analogy could be drawn between the federal scheme and the apportionment of seats in the Alabama Legislature under the proposed constitutional amendment. We agree with the District Court, and find the federal analogy inapposite and irrelevant to state legislative districting schemes. Attempted reliance on the federal analogy appears often to be little more than an after-the-fact rationalization offered in defense of maladjusted state apportionment arrangements. The original constitutions of 36 of our States provided that representation in both houses of the state legislatures would be based completely, or predominantly, on population. And the Founding Fathers clearly had no intention of establishing a pattern or model for the apportionment of seats in state legislatures when the system of representation in the Federal Congress was adopted. . . .

The system of representation in the two Houses of the Federal Congress is one ingrained in our Constitution, as part of the law of the land. It is one conceived out of compromise and concession indispensable to the establishment of our federal republic. Arising from unique historical circumstances, it is based on the consideration that in establishing our type of federalism a group of formerly independent States bound themselves together under one national government. Admittedly, the original 13 States surrendered some of their sovereignty in agreeing to join together "to form a more perfect Union." But at the heart of our constitutional system remains the concept of separate and distinct governmental entities which have delegated some, but not all, of their formerly held powers to the single national government. The fact that almost three-fourths of our present States were never in fact independently sovereign does not detract from our view that the so-called federal analogy is inapplicable as a sustaining precedent for state legislative apportionments. . . .

Political subdivisions of States—counties, cities, or whatever—never were and never have been considered as sovereign entities. Rather, they have been traditionally regarded as subordinate governmental instrumentalities created by the State to assist in the carrying out of state governmental functions. . . . The relationship of the States to the Federal Government could hardly be less analogous.

Thus, we conclude that the plan contained in the 67-Senator Amendment for apportioning seats in the Alabama Legislature cannot be sustained by recourse to the so-called federal analogy. . . . We conclude simply that such a plan is impermissible for the States under the Equal Protection Clause, since perforce resulting, in virtually every case, in submergence of the equal-population principle in at least one house of a state legislature.

Since we find the so-called federal analogy inapposite to a consideration of the constitutional validity of state legislative apportionment schemes, we necessarily hold that the Equal Protection Clause requires both houses of a state legislature to be apportioned on a population basis. . . . In summary, we can perceive no constitutional difference, with respect to the geographical distribution of state legislative representation, between the two houses of a bicameral state legislature.

We do not believe that the concept of bicameralism is rendered anachronistic and meaningless when the predominant basis of representation in the two state legislative bodies is required to be the same—population. A prime reason for bicameralism, modernly considered, is to insure mature and deliberate consideration of, and to prevent precipitate action on, proposed legislative measures. Simply because the controlling criterion for apportioning representation is required to be the same in both houses does not mean that there will be no differences in the composition and complexion of the two bodies. Different constituencies can be represented in the two houses. One body could be composed of single-member districts while the other could have at least some multimember districts. The length of terms of the legislators in the separate bodies could differ. The numerical size of the two bodies could be made to differ, even significantly, and the geographical size of districts from which legislators are elected could also be made to differ. And apportionment in one house could be arranged so as to balance off minor inequities in the representation of certain areas in the other house. In summary, these and other factors could be, and are presently in many States, utilized to engender differing complexions and collective attitudes in the two bodies of a state legislature, although both are apportioned substantially on a population basis.

VI.

By holding that as a federal constitutional requisite both houses of a state legislature must be apportioned on a population basis, we mean that the Equal Protection Clause requires that a State make an honest and good faith effort to construct districts, in both houses of its legislature, as nearly of equal population as is practicable. . . . Mathematical exactness or precision is hardly a workable constitutional requirement.

In *Wesberry* v. *Sanders, supra,* the Court stated that congressional representation must be based on population as nearly as is practicable. In implementing the basic constitutional principle of representative government as enunciated by the Court in *Wesberry*—equality of population among districts—some distinctions may well be made between congressional and state legislative representation. . . . Somewhat more flexibility may therefore be constitutionally permissible with respect to state legislative apportionment than in congressional districting. Lower courts can and assuredly will work out more concrete and specific standards for evaluating state legislative apportionment schemes in the context of actual litigation. For the present, we deem it expedient not to attempt to spell out any precise constitutional tests. What is marginally permissible in one

State may be unsatisfactory in another, depending on the particular circumstances of the case. . . . Single-member districts may be the rule in one State, while another State might desire to achieve some flexibility by creating multimember or floterial districts. Whatever the means of accomplishment, the overriding objective must be substantial equality of population among the various districts, so that the vote of any citizen is approximately equal in weight to that of any other citizen in the State. . . . So long as the divergences from a strict population standard are based on legitimate considerations incident to the effectuation of a rational state policy, some deviations from the equal-population principle are constitutionally permissible with respect to the apportionment of seats in either or both of the two houses of bicameral state legislature. But neither history alone, nor economic or other sorts of groups interests, are permissible factors in attempting to justify disparities from population-based representation. Citizens, not history or economic interests, cast votes. Considerations of area alone provide an insufficient justification for deviations from the equal-population principle. . . .

A consideration that appears to be of more substance in justifying some deviations from population-based representation in state legislatures is that of insuring some voice to political subdivisions, as political subdivisions. . . . However, permitting deviations from population-based representation does not mean that each local governmental unit or political subdivision can be given separate representation, regardless of population. . . . And careful judicial scrutiny must of course be given, in evaluating state apportionment schemes, to the character as well as the degree of deviations from a strict population basis. But if, even as a result of a clearly rational state policy of according some legislative representation to political subdivisions, population is submerged as the controlling consideration in the apportionment of seats in the particular legislative body, then the right of all of the State's citizens to cast an effective and adequately weighted vote would be unconstitutionally impaired.

VII.

One of the arguments frequently offered as a basis for upholding a State's legislative apportionment arrangement, despite substantial disparities from a population basis in either or both houses, is grounded on congressional approval, incident to admitting States into the Union, of state apportionment plans containing deviations from the equal-population principle. . . . [C]ongressional approval, however well-considered, could hardly validate an unconstitutional state legislative apportionment. Congress simply lacks the constitutional power to insulate States from attack with respect to alleged deprivations of individual constitutional rights.

VIII.

That the Equal Protection Clause requires that both houses of a state legislature be apportioned on a population basis does not mean that States cannot adopt some reasonable plan for periodic revision of their apportionment schemes. . . . While we do not intend to indicate that decennial reapportionment is a constitutional requisite, compliance with such an approach would clearly meet the minimal requirements for maintaining a reasonably current scheme of legislative representation. . . . But if reapportionment were accomplished with less frequency, it would assuredly be constitutionally suspect. . . .

IX.

Although general provisions of the Alabama Constitution provide that the apportionment of seats in both houses of the Alabama Legislature should be on a population basis, other more detailed provisions clearly make compliance with both sets of requirements impossible. With respect to the operation of the Equal Protection Clause, it makes no difference whether a State's apportionment scheme is embodied in its constitution or in statutory provisions. . . .

X.

We do not consider here the difficult question of the proper remedial devices which federal courts should utilize in state legislative apportionment cases. . . . It is enough to say now that, once a State's legislative apportionment scheme has been found to be unconstitutional, it would be the unusual case in which a court would be justified in not taking appropriate action to insure that no further elections are conducted under the invalid plan. . . .

We feel that the District Court in this case acted in a most proper and commendable manner. . . .

We find, therefore, that the action taken by the District Court in this case, in ordering into effect a reapportionment of both houses of the Alabama Legislature for purposes of the 1962 primary and general elections, by using the best parts of the two proposed plans which it had found, as a whole, to be invalid, was an appropriate and well-considered exercise of judicial power. . . . In retaining jurisdiction while deferring a hearing on the issuance of a final injunction in order to give the provisionally reapportioned legislature an opportunity to act effectively, the court below proceeded in a proper fashion. . . . [W]e affirm the judgment below and remand the cases for further proceedings consistent with the views stated in this opinion.   *It is so ordered.*

MR. JUSTICE CLARK, concurring in the affirmance.

The Court goes much beyond the necessities of this case in laying down a new "equal population" principle for state legislative apportionment. This principle seems to be an offshoot of *Gray* v. *Sanders*, 372 U.S. 368, 381 (1963), *i.e.*, "one person, one vote," modified by the "nearly as is practicable" admonition of *Wesberry* v. *Sanders*, 376 U.S. 1, 8 (1964). Whether "nearly as is practicable" means "one person, one vote" qualified by "approximately equal" or "some deviations" or by the impossibility of "mathematical nicety" is not clear from the majority's use of these vague and meaningless phrases. But whatever the standard, the Court applies it to each house of the State Legislature.

It seems to me that all that the Court need say in this case is that each plan considered by the trial court is "a crazy quilt," clearly revealing invidious discrimination in each house of the Legislature and therefore violative of the Equal Protection Clause. ⁎ ⁎ ⁎

MR. JUSTICE HARLAN, dissenting.⁎

In these cases the Court holds that seats in the legislatures of six States are apportioned in ways that violate the Federal Constitution. Under the Court's ruling it is bound to follow that the legislatures in all but a few of the other 44 States will meet the same fate. These decisions, with *Wesberry* v. *Sanders,* 376 U. S. 1, involving congressional districting by the States, and *Gray* v. *Sanders,* 372 U. S. 368, relating to elections for statewide office, have the effect of placing basic aspects of state political systems under the pervasive over-lordship of the federal judiciary. Once again, I must register my protest. . . .

CONCLUSION.

With these cases the Court approaches the end of the third round set in motion by the complaint filed in *Baker* v. *Carr.* What is done today deepens my conviction that judicial entry into this realm is profoundly ill-advised and constitutionally impermissible. As I have said before, *Wesberry* v. *Sanders, supra,* at 48, I believe that the vitality of our political system, on which in the last analysis all else depends, is weakened by reliance on the judiciary for political reform; in time a complacent body politic may result.

These decisions also cut deeply into the fabric of our federalism. . . . [T]he aftermath of these cases, however desirable it may be thought in itself, will have been achieved at the cost of a radical alteration in the relationship between the States and the Federal Government, more particularly the Federal Judiciary. Only one who has an overbearing impatience with the federal system and its political processes will believe that that cost was not too high or was inevitable.

Finally, these decisions give support to a current mistaken view of the Constitution and the constitutional function of this Court. This view, in a nutshell, is that every major social ill in this country can find its cure in some constitutional "principle," and that this Court should "take the lead" in promoting reform when other branches of government fail to act. The Constitution is not a panacea for every blot upon

⁎This opinion applies also to No. 20, *WMCA, Inc., et al.* v. *Lomenzo, Secretary of State of New York, et al., post,* p. 633; No. 29, *Maryland Committee for Fair Representation et al.* v. *Tawes, Governor, et al., post,* p. 656; No. 69, *Davis, Secretary, State Board of Elections, et al.* v. *Mann et al., post,* p. 678; No. 307, *Roman, Clerk, et al.* v. *Sincock et al., post,* p. 695; and No. 508, *Lucas et al.* v. *Forty-Fourth General Assembly of Colorado et al., post,* p. 713. [Footnote included in opinion. — Ed.]

the public welfare, nor should this Court, ordained as a judicial body, be thought of as a general haven for reform movements. The Constitution is an instrument of government, fundamental to which is the premise that in a diffusion of governmental authority lies the greatest promise that this Nation will realize liberty for all its citizens. This Court, limited in function in accordance with that premise, does not serve its high purpose when it exceeds its authority, even to satisfy justified impatience with the slow workings of the political process. For when, in the name of constitutional interpretation, the Court *adds* something to the Constitution that was deliberately excluded from it, the Court in reality substitutes its view of what should be so for the amending process.

I dissent in each of these cases, believing that in none of them have the plaintiffs stated a cause of action. To the extent that *Baker* v. *Carr,* expressly or by implication, went beyond a discussion of jurisdictional doctrines independent of the substantive issues involved here, it should be limited to what it in fact was: an experiment in venturesome constitutionalism. . . .

"Vote diluting" discrimination is not the only method used to deny the right to an effective vote. Both Mississippi and Louisiana had adopted requirements for registration which left much discretion in the hands of the registrars of voters. In Mississippi applicants were obliged to "demonstrate . . . a reasonable understanding of the duties and obligations of citizenship under a constitutional form of government; and to demonstrate to the county registrar that applicant is a person of good moral character. . . ." The Louisiana statute required that the applicant be able to "give a reasonable interpretation" of any clause of the Louisiana or the United States constitution. In the Mississippi case (*U.S.* v. *Mississippi,* 380 U.S. 128, 85 S. Ct. 808; 1965), the Court held that the United States Attorney General had power to bring suit against a state and its officials to protect the voting rights of Negroes guaranteed by statute and by the Fourteenth and Fifteenth Amendments. In the Louisiana case, the court found that the "interpretation test vested in the voting registrars a virtually uncontrolled discretion as to who should vote and who should not."[4] There were no standards to guide them, and there was evidence that the test was used to "deprive otherwise qualified Negroes of their right to vote."[5] Although a new "citizenship" test had been adopted after the action had been filed, the Court affirmed the District Court's decision to postpone the use of the new test until there had been a complete reregistration of all voters, so that the new test would apply to all, not merely to previously unreg-

[4]*U.S.* v. *Mississippi,* 380 U.S. 128, p. 150
[5]*Loc. cit.*

istered Negroes. The court also found it "appropriate" to have monthly reports on registration of voters in the 20 parishes in question.

Not all limitations on the registration of new voters have been on the basis of race. In states having a large number of servicemen among their inhabitants it has been common to put special restrictions on their acquisition of voting rights. The mere fact that an individual is living in a particular state does not make him "domiciled" in the state, or even a legal resident for voting purposes. Domicile is dependent on two factors: the intent of the individual to make a particular state his permanent home, and his actual and voluntary physical presence in the state.

Texas had this provision in its constitution:

> Any member of the Armed Forces of the United States or component branches thereof, or in the military service of the United States, may vote only in the county in which he or she resided at the time of entering such service so long as he or she is a member of the Armed Forces.

This restriction effectively prevented all persons in the Armed Forces who were stationed in Texas from changing their legal residence, whether that residence was a county in Texas different from the one in which they had lived before serving, or a different state.

In *Carrington* v. *Rash,* 380 U.S. 89, 85 S. Ct. 775 (1965), the petitioner, who was a sergeant in the Army, had been living in Texas since 1962, and intended to make his home there. He owned a small business and also a home in which he lived with his wife and two children. He commuted regularly to his Army post in New Mexico. He paid property taxes in Texas, and had his car registered there. Texas conceded that had he not been a member of the Armed Forces he would have been a bona fide resident of the state, and entitled to vote. At issue, technically, was the classification used. Texas argued that the state "has a legitimate interest in immunizing its elections from the concentrated balloting of military personnel, whose collective voice may overwhelm a small local civilian community." Secondly, the State said

> it has a valid interest in protecting the franchise from infiltration by transients, and it can reasonably assume that those servicemen who fall within the constitutional exclusion will be within the State for only a short period of time.[6]

The Supreme Court pointed out that Texas had been able to make special provisions for other groups, such as civilian employees of the

[6]*Carrington* v. *Rash,* 380 U.S. 89, p. 93

federal government, and the residence of service men for purposes of divorce. Although recognizing that special problems existed, "By forbidding a soldier ever to controvert the presumption of non-residence, the Texas Constitution imposes an invidious discrimination in violation of the Fourteenth Amendment."[7]

A common method of restricting the right to vote has been to require the payment of a poll tax as a prerequisite to registering to vote. In order to prevent the use of this tax as a method of disenfranchising Negroes in an election of federal officers, the Twenty-fourth Amendment was ratified in 1964.

Harman v. *Forssenius*, 380 U.S. 528, 85 S. Ct. 1177 (1965)

MR. CHIEF JUSTICE WARREN delivered the opinion of the Court.

We are called upon in this case to construe, for the first time, the Twenty-fourth Amendment to the Constitution of the United States:

"The right of citizens of the United States to vote in any primary or other election for President or Vice President, for electors for President or Vice President, or for Senator or Representative in Congress, shall not be denied or abridged by the United States or any State by reason of failure to pay any poll tax or other tax."

The precise issue is whether § 24–17.2 of the Virginia Code—which provides that in order to qualify to vote in federal elections, one must either pay a poll tax or file a witnessed or notarized certificate of residence—contravenes this command. . . .

In 1963, in anticipation of the promulgation of the Twenty-fourth Amendment, the Governor of Virginia convened a special session of the Virginia General Assembly. On November 21 of that year, the General Assembly enacted two Acts designed

"(1) to enable persons to register and vote in federal elections without the payment of poll tax or other tax as required by the 24th Amendment to the Constitution of the United States, (2) to continue in effect in all other elections the present registration and voting requirements of the Constitution of Virginia, and (3) to provide methods by which all persons registered to vote in federal or other elections may prove that they meet the residence requirements of § 18 of the Constitution of Virginia."

No changes were made with regard to qualification for voting in state elections. With regard to federal elections, however, the payment of a poll tax as an absolute prerequisite to registration and voting was eliminated, and a provision was added requiring the federal voter to file a certificate of residence in each election year or, at his option, to pay the customary poll taxes. The statute provides that the certificate of residence must be filed no earlier than October 1 of the year immediately preceding that in which the voter desires to vote and not later than six months prior to the election. The voter must state in

[7]*Ibid.*, p. 96.

the certificate (which must be notarized or witnessed) his present address, that he is currently a resident of Virginia, that he has been a resident since the date of his registration, and that he does not presently intend to remove from the city or county of which he is a resident prior to the next general election. . . . Thus, as a result of the 1963 Acts, a citizen after registration may vote in both federal and state elections upon the payment of all assessable poll taxes. . . . If he has not paid such taxes he cannot vote in state elections, and may vote in federal elections only upon filing a certificate of residence in each election year. . . .

The present appeal originated as two separate class actions, brought by appellees in the United States District Court for the Eastern District of Virginia, attacking the foregoing provisions of the 1963 Virginia legislation as violative of Art. I, § 2, of the Constitution of the United States, and the Fourteenth, Seventeenth, and Twenty-fourth Amendments thereto. * * *

We hold that § 24–17.2 is repugnant to the Twenty-fourth Amendment and affirm the decision of the District Court on that basis. We therefore find it unnecessary to determine whether that section violates Art. I, § 2, and the Seventeenth Amendment. . . .

. . . We hold that the District Court did not abuse its discretion in refusing to postpone the exercise of its jurisdiction.

In applying the doctrine of abstention, a federal district court is vested with discretion to decline to exercise or to postpone the exercise of its jurisdiction in deference to state court resolution of underlying issues of state law. . . . If the state statute in question, although never interpreted by a state tribunal, is not fairly subject to an interpretation which will render unnecessary or substantially modify the federal constitutional question, it is the duty of the federal court to exercise its properly invoked jurisdiction. *Baggett* v. *Bullitt*, 377 U.S. 360, 375–379. . . .

The state statutes involved here are clear and unambiguous in all material respects. . . .

In addition to the clarity of Virginia statutes in issue, support for the District Court's refusal to stay the proceedings is found in the nature of the constitutional deprivation alleged and the probable consequences of abstaining. . . . As this Court has stressed on numerous occasions. "[T]he right to vote freely for the candidate of one's choice is of the essence of a democratic society, and any restrictions on that right strike at the heart of representative government." *Reynolds* v. *Sims*, 377 U.S. 533, 555. Given the importance and immediacy of the problem, and the delay inherent in referring questions of state law to state tribunals, it is evident that the District Court did not abuse its discretion in refusing to abstain. *Griffin* v. *County School Board of Prince Edward County*, 377 U.S. 218, 229; *Baggett* v. *Bullitt*, 377 U.S. 360, 375–379. . . .

Reaching the merits, it is important to emphasize that the question presented is . . . whether the State of Virginia may constitutionally confront the federal voter with a requirement that he *either* pay the cutomary poll taxes as required for state elections *or* file a certificate of residence. We conclude that this requirement constitutes an abridgment of the right to vote in federal elections in contravention of the Twenty-fourth Amendment. * * *

It has long been established that a State may not impose a penalty upon those who exercise a right guaranteed by the Constitution. . . . Significantly, the Twenty-fourth Amendment does not merely insure that the franchise shall not be "denied" by reason of failure to pay the poll tax; it expressly guarantees that the right to vote shall not be "denied or abridged" for that reason. Thus, like the Fifteenth Amendment, the Twenty-fourth "nullifies sophisticated as well as simple-minded modes" of impairing the right guaranteed. *Lane* v. *Wilson*, 307 U.S. 268, 275. . . .

Thus, in order to demonstrate the invalidity of § 24–17.2 of the Virginia Code, it need only be shown that it imposes a material requirement solely upon those who refuse to surrender their constitutional right to vote in federal elections without paying a poll tax. Section 24–17.2 unquestionably erects a real obstacle to voting in federal elections for those who assert their constitutional exemption from the poll tax. As previously indicated, the requirement for those who wish to participate in federal elections without paying the poll tax . . . is plainly a cumbersome procedure. In effect, it amounts to annual re-registration which Virginia officials have sharply contrasted with the "simple" poll tax system. . . . In addition, the certificate must be filed six months before the election, thus perpetuating one of the disenfranchising characteristics of the poll tax which the Twenty-fourth Amendment was designed to eliminate. We are thus constrained to hold that the requirement imposed upon the voter who refuses to pay the poll tax constitutes an abridgment of his right to vote by reason of failure to pay the poll tax. . . .

. . . For federal elections, the poll tax is abolished absolutely as a prerequisite to voting, and no equivalent or milder substitute may be imposed. Any material requirement imposed upon the federal voter solely because of his refusal to waive the constitutional immunity subverts the effectiveness of the Twenty-fourth Amendment and must fall under its ban. . . .

The Virginia poll tax was born of a desire to disenfranchise the Negro. . . . The poll tax was later characterized by the Virginia Supreme Court of Appeals as a device limiting "the right of suffrage to those who took sufficient interest in the affairs of the State to qualify themselves to vote." *Campbell* v. *Goode*, 172 Va. 463, 466. . . . For federal elections the poll tax, regardless of the services it performs, was abolished by the Twenty-fourth Amendment. That Amendment was also designed to absolve all requirements impairing the right to vote in federal elections by reason of failure to pay the poll tax. Section 24–17.2 of the Virginia Code falls within this proscription.

The judgment of the District Court is affirmed.

On June 13, 1966, in *Katzenbach* v. *Morgan,* 86 S. Ct. 1717 (1966), the Supreme Court upheld the constitutionality of Section 4(E) of the Voting Rights Act of 1965, which provides that persons who have successfully completed the sixth grade in public school, or in a private school accredited by the Commonwealth of Puerto Rico in which instruction was not in English, shall not be denied the right to vote in any election because of an inability to read or write English. The challenge to the act was brought on the grounds that the legislation in part prevents the enforcement of the laws of New York, which require the ability to read and write English. Mr. Justice Brennan said:

Katzenbach v. *Morgan,* 86 S. Ct. 1717 (1966)

We hold that, in the application challenged in this case, Section 4(E) is a proper exercise of the powers granted to Congress by Section 5 of the Fourteenth Amendment and that by force of the Supremacy Clause, Article VI, the New York English literacy requirement cannot be enforced to the extent that it is inconsistent with section 4(E).

Under the distribution of powers effected by the Constitution, the states establish qualifications for voting for state officers. . . . But, of course, the states have no power to grant or withhold the franchise on conditions that are forbidden by the Fourteenth Amendment, or any other provision of the Constitution. . . .

There can be no doubt that Section 4(E) may be regarded as an enactment to enforce the equal protection clause. . . .

The persons referred to include those who have migrated from the Commonwealth of Puerto Rico to New York and who have been denied the right to vote because of their inability to read and write English. . . .

Section 4(E) may be readily seen as "plainly adapted" to furthering these aims of the equal protection clause. . . . Congress has thus prohibited the state from denying that community the right that "is preservative of all rights." This enhanced political power will be helpful in gaining nondiscriminatory treatment in public services for the entire Puerto Rican community.

It was well within Congressional authority to say that this need of the Puerto Rican minority for the vote warranted Federal intrusion upon any state interests served by the English literacy requirement. It was for Congress, as the branch that made this judgment, to assess and weigh the various conflicting considerations. . . .

It is not for us to review the Congressional resolution of these factors. It is enough that we are able to perceive a basis upon which the Congress might resolve the conflict as it did. There plainly was such a basis to support Section 4(E) in the application in question in this case. Any contrary conclusion would require us to be blind to the realities familiar to the legislators. . . .

The Court also found that the means used were not prohibited by the Constitution, and that the legislation was appropriate to the enforcement of the Equal Protection Clause. Mr. Justice Harlan, joined by Mr. Justice Potter, disagreed.

> . . . The question here is not whether the statute is appropriate remedial legislation to cure an established violation of a constitutional command, but whether there has in fact been an infringement of that constitutional command. . . .
>
> To hold . . . that Section 4(E) overrides the New York literacy requirement seems to be tantamount to allowing the Fourteenth Amendment to swallow the state's constitutionally ordained primary authority in this field. For if Congress . . . can set that otherwise permissible requirement partially at naught I see no reason why it could not also substitute its judgment for that of the states in other fields of their exclusive primary competence as well. . . .
>
> I would affirm the judgments in each of these cases.

CHAPTER NINE

★ ★ ★

Aliens and Citizens

WITH THE PASSAGE of time and the development of the country, attitudes toward aliens have changed. When aliens were needed to settle and develop the land there were few restrictions put upon them, either at entry or after their arrival. With our diminishing need for people to develop the country, laws limiting the entrance of aliens have become increasingly important, and have varied greatly in the restrictions imposed. There have been statutes which excluded Chinese and Japanese persons, and prevented those residing here from becoming citizens. In 1921, an act restricting immigration to "quotas" from named nations became the basic law, which was not changed until 1965.

Although Congress is given the power "To establish an uniform Rule of Naturalization . . ." in Article I, Section 8 of the Constitution, there is no definition of eligibility either for admission or for qualification for citizenship. Congress alone has the power to set the requirements for the acquisition of citizenship, may determine eligibility for admission, and may restrict those who are admitted.

Once lawfully admitted, even though the alien may never be eligible for citizenship, he is entitled to due process and equal protection of the law under the Fourteenth Amendment, and to the protection of the First and Fifth Amendments (*Kwong Hai Chew* v. *Colding*, 344 U.S. 590, 73 S. Ct. 472; 1953). He is entitled to be heard in opposition to an order of deportation, as a matter of procedural due process, although that hearing may be administrative, rather than judicial. He is also entitled to notice of the charges against him. But his position may be precarious, because the rules which governed when he entered may change, even years later, with the result that acts which were innocent when done may be the basis for deportation when the rules are changed.

Harisiades v. *Shaughnessy,* 342 U.S. 580, 72 S. Ct. 512 (1952)

These aliens ask us to forbid their expulsion by a departure from the long-accepted application to such cases of the Fifth Amendment provision that no person shall be deprived of life, liberty or property without due process of law. Their basic contention is that admission for permanent residence confers a "vested right" on the alien, equal to that of the citizen, to remain within the country, and that the alien is entitled to constitutional protection in that matter to the same extent as the citizen. . . .

Under our law, the alien in several respects stands on an equal footing with citizens, but in others has never been conceded legal parity with the citizen. Most importantly, to protract this ambiguous status within the country is not his right but is a matter of permission and tolerance. The Government's power to terminate its hospitality has been asserted and sustained by this Court since the question first arose. . . .

. . . [I]t does not require war to bring the power of deportation into existence or to authorize its exercise. Congressional apprehension of foreign or internal dangers short of war may lead to its use. So long as the alien elects to continue the ambiguity of his allegiance his domicile here is held by a precarious tenure.

. . . [E]xpulsion . . . is a weapon of defense and reprisal confirmed by international law as a power inherent in every sovereign state. . . .

This brings us to the alternative defense under the Due Process Clause — that, granting the power, it is so unreasonably and harshly exercised by this enactment that it should be held unconstitutional.

In historical context the Act before us stands out as an extreme application of the expulsion power. * * *

. . . Certainly, . . . nothing in the structure of our Government or the text of our Constitution would warrant judicial review by standards which would require us to equate our political judgment with that of Congress. * * *

We are urged, because the policy inflicts severe and undoubted hardship on affected individuals, to find a restraint in the Due Process Clause. * * *

We think that, in the present state of the world, it would be rash and irresponsible to reinterpret our fundamental law to deny or qualify the Government's power of deportation. . . .

. . . Reform in this field must be entrusted to the branches of the Government in control of our international relations and treaty-making powers.

We hold that the Act is not invalid under the Due Process Clause. . . .

The First Amendment is invoked as a barrier against this enactment. The claim is that in joining an organization advocating overthrow of government by force and violence the alien has merely exercised freedom of speech, press and assembly which that Amendment guarantees to him. . . .

Our Constitution sought to leave no excuse for violent attack on the status quo by providing a legal alternative—attack by ballot. To arm all men for orderly change, the Constitution put in their hands a right to influence the electorate by press, speech and assembly. This means freedom to advocate or promote Communism by means of the ballot box, but it does not include the practice or incitement of violence.

True, it often is difficult to determine whether ambiguous speech is advocacy of political methods or subtly shades into a methodical but prudent incitement to violence. . . . We apprehend that the Constitution enjoins upon us the duty, however, difficult, of distinguishing between the two. We think the First Amendment does not prevent the deportation of these aliens. * * *

We find none of the constitutional objections to the Act well founded. The judgments accordingly are affirmed.

Affirmed. . . .

MR. JUSTICE DOUGLAS, with whom MR. JUSTICE BLACK concurs, dissenting.

There are two possible bases for sustaining this Act:

(1) A person who was once a Communist is tainted for all time and forever dangerous to our society; or

(2) Punishment through banishment from the country may be placed upon an alien not for what he did, but for what his political views once were.

Each of these is foreign to our philosophy. We repudiate our traditions of tolerance and our articles of faith based upon the Bill of Rights when we bow to them by sustaining an Act of Congress which has them as a foundation. * * *

The power of Congress to exclude, admit, or deport aliens flows from sovereignty itself and from the power "To establish an uniform Rule of Naturalization." U.S. Const., Art. I, §8, cl. 4. The power of deportation is therefore an *implied* one. The right to life and liberty is an *express* one. Why this *implied* power should be given priority over the *express* guarantee of the Fifth Amendment has never been satisfactorily answered. * * *

The right to be immune from arbitrary decrees of banishment certainly may be more important to "liberty" than the civil rights which all aliens enjoy when they reside here. Unless they are free from arbitrary banishment, the "liberty" they enjoy while they live here is indeed illusory. Banishment is punishment in the practical sense. It may deprive a man and his family of all that makes life worth while. * * *

This drastic step may at times be necessary in order to protect the national interest. . . . But unless such condition is shown, I would stay the hand of the Government and let those to whom we have extended our hospitality and who have become members of our communities remain here and enjoy the life and liberty which the Constitution guarantees.

Congress has not proceeded by that standard. It has ordered these aliens deported not for what they are but for what they once were. Perhaps a hearing would show that they continue to be people dangerous and hostile to us. But the principle of forgiveness and the doctrine of redemption are too deep in our philosophy to admit that there is no return for those who have once erred.

The Constitution makes only one basic distinction between "natural born citizens" and those who acquire citizenship by naturalization: only the former are "eligible to the Office of President. . . ." A Representative must have been a citizen for seven years, and a Senator for nine, but these are the only other distinctions in the Constitution. Section 1 of the Fourteenth Amendment says, "All persons born or naturalized in the United States and subject to the jurisdiction thereof are citizens of the United States and of the State wherein they reside." No power to deprive an individual of his citizenship is mentioned.

If, however, Congress has power to determine the qualifications for naturalization, may it not also deprive one so naturalized of his citizenship? May a person "born . . . in the United States" be deprived of his citizenship? The first case to determine the meaning of that Fourteenth Amendment phrase, "born or naturalized in the United States and subject to the jurisdiction thereof," was *U.S.* v. *Wong Kim Ark.* Wong Kim Ark was born in California, of Chinese parents who were not in the diplomatic service. He grew up in the United States, and visited China without incident, but on his return from a second visit to China he was denied readmission to the United States.

United States v. *Wong Kim Ark,* 169 U.S. 649, 18 S. Ct. 456 (1898)

* * * The Constitution of the United States, as originally adopted, uses the words "citizen of the United States," and "natural born citizen of the United States."

The Constitution nowhere defines the meaning of these words, either by way of inclusion or of exclusion, except in so far as this is done by the affirmative declaration that "all persons born or naturalized in the United States, and subject to the jurisdiction thereof, are citizens of the United States." In this, as in other respects, it must be interpreted in the light of the common law, the principles and history of which were familiarly known to the framers of the Constitution. * * *

The first section of the Fourteenth Amendment of the Constitution begins with the words, "All persons born or naturalized in the United States, and subject to the jurisdiction thereof, are citizens of the United States and of the State wherein they reside." As appears from the face of the amendment, as well as from the history of the times, this was not intended to impose any new restrictions upon citizenship, or to prevent any persons from becoming citizens by the fact of birth within the United States, who would thereby have become citizens according to the law existing before its adoption. It is declaratory in form, and enabling and extending in effect. * * *

The foregoing considerations . . . irresistibly lead us to these conclusions: the Fourteenth Amendment affirms the ancient and fundamental rule of citizenship by birth within the territory, in the allegiance and under the protection of the country, including all children here born of resident aliens, with the exceptions or qualifications (as old as the rule itself) of children of foreign sovereigns or their ministers, or born on foreign public ships, or of enemies within and during hostile occupation of part of our territory, and with the single additional exception of children of members of the Indian tribes owing direct allegiance to their several tribes. The Amendment, in clear words and in manifest intent, includes the children born, within the territory of the United States, of all other persons, of whatever race or color, domiciled within the United States. * * *

The Fourteenth Amendment of the Constitution, in the declaration that "all persons born or naturalized in the United States, and subject to the jurisdiction thereof, are citizens of the United States and of the States wherein they reside," contemplates two sources of citizenship, and two only; birth and naturalization. Citizenship by naturalization can only be acquired by naturalization under the authority and in the forms of law. But citizenship by birth is established by the mere fact of birth under the circumstances defined in the Constitution. Every person born in the United States, and subject to the jurisdiction thereof, becomes at once a citizen of the United States, and needs no naturalization. A person born out of the jurisdiction of the United States can only become a citizen by being naturalized, either by treaty, as in the case of the annexation of foreign territory, or by authority of Congress, exercised either by declaring certain classes of persons to be citizens, as in the enactments conferring citizenship upon foreign-born children of citizens, or by enabling foreigners individually to become citizens by proceedings in the judicial tribunals, as in the ordinary provisions of the naturalization acts.

The power of naturalization, vested in Congress by the Constitution, is a power to confer citizenship, not a power to take it away. "A naturalized citizen," said Chief Justice Marshall "becomes a member of the society, possessing all the rights of a native citizen, and standing, in the view of the Constitution, on the footing of a native. The Constitution does not authorize Congress to enlarge or abridge those rights. The simple power of the National Legislature is to prescribe a uniform rule of naturalization, and the exercise of this power exhausts it, so far as respects the individual. The Constitution then takes him up, and, among other rights, extends to him the capacity of suing in the courts of the United States precisely under the same circumstances under which a native might sue." *Osborn* v. *United States Bank*, 9 Wheat. 738, 827. Congress having no power to abridge the rights conferred by the Constitution upon those who have become naturalized citizens by virtue of acts of Congress, a fortiori no act or omission of Congress, as to providing for the naturalization of parents or children of a particular race, can affect citizenship acquired as a birthright, by virtue of the Constitution itself, without any aid of legislation. The Fourteenth Amendment, while it leaves the power where it was before, in Congress, to regulate naturalization, has conferred no authority upon Congress to restrict the effect of birth, declared by the Constitution to constitute a sufficient and complete right to citizenship. * * *

The evident intention, and the necessary effect, of the submission of this case to the decision of the court upon the facts agreed by the parties, were to present for examination the single question, stated at the beginning of this opinion, namely, whether a child born in the United States, of parents of Chinese descent, who, at the time of his birth, are subjects of the Emperor of China, but have a permanent domicile and residence in the United States, and are there carrying on business, and are not employed in any diplomatic or official capacity under the Emperor of China, becomes at the time of his birth a citizen of the United States. For the reasons above stated, this court is of opinion that the question must be answered in the affirmative.

A citizen may voluntarily relinquish his citizenship, either by a formal renunciation or by action which is clearly inconsistent with the citizen's duty to the United States. Voluntarily taking an oath of allegiance to a foreign sovereign, for instance, constitutes a renunciation of citizenship. Recognition of such a renunciation by the United States also reduces possible foreign policy entanglements. But problems arise when Congress enumerates the acts which, if undertaken, constitute a surrender of citizenship. Congress has made a distinction between natural-born citizens, and those who have acquired their citizenship by naturalization under the Nationality Act of 1940: only the latter could lose citizenship by residing in a foreign country for five years.

There is, of course, a distinction between acts which clearly indicate a surrender of citizenship (such as a formal renunciation) and those which may be subject to other explanations. Residing in a foreign country for five years may, for example, be required by work or other reasons which prevent a return to the United States. In more recent statutes, the latter action is "considered prima facie evidence of a lack of intention on the part of such person to reside permanently in the United States at the time of filing his petition for naturalization. . . ."[1] Technically, it is possible to introduce evidence to prove that no such purpose existed.

Revocation of naturalized citizenship on grounds of fraud is some-

[1]Immigration and Nationality Act, June, 1952, as amended, 1954, 8 U.S.C. § 1451 (d).

what different. One theory is that the sovereign has been induced to consent to the naturalization because of false or fraudulent information, and there is, in fact, no consent.

In *Perez* v. *Brownell*, 356 U.S. 44, the Court affirmed the loss of citizenship by one who was born in the United States. Born in 1909, Perez had lived in Mexico without interruption from the time he was about 11 until he was about 34. When he was about 18, he was told that he had been born in the United States. He had entered this country in 1943, and again in 1952, both times claiming to be a native-born citizen of Mexico. In 1946 he had voted in a Mexican political election. The Court found that by virtue of voting in that election, and by remaining out of the United States to avoid military service, both of which facts Perez admitted, he had expatriated himself.

The Court found the authority of Congress to make such acts reason for expatriation in the power to enact legislation for the "effective regulation of foreign affairs."

Perez v. *Brownell*, 356 U.S. 46, 78 S. Ct. 568 (1958)

* * * The question must finally be faced whether, given the power to attach some sort of consequence to voting in a foreign political election, Congress, acting under the Necessary and Proper Clause, Art. I, § 8, cl. 18, could attach loss of nationality to it. Is the means, withdrawal of citizenship, reasonably calculated to effect the end that is within the power of Congress to achieve, the avoidance of embarrassment in the conduct of our foreign relations attributable to voting by American citizens in foreign political elections? . . . The critical connection between this conduct and loss of citizenship is the fact that it is the possession of American citizenship by a person committing the act that makes the act potentially embarrassing to the American Government and pregnant with the possibility of embroiling this country in disputes with other nations. The termination of citizenship terminates the problem. Moreover, the fact is not without significance that Congress has interpreted this conduct, not irrationally, as importing not only something less than complete and unswerving allegiance to the United States but also elements of an allegiance to another country in some measure, at least, inconsistent with American citizenship.

Of course, Congress can attach loss of citizenship only as a consequence of conduct engaged in voluntarily. To deny the power of Congress to enact the legislation challenged here would be to disregard the constitutional allocation of governmental functions that it is this Court's solemn duty to guard. . . .   *Judgment affirmed.*

MR. CHIEF JUSTICE WARREN, with whom MR. JUSTICE BLACK and MR. JUSTICE DOUGLAS join, dissenting.

The Congress of the United States had decreed that a citizen of the United States shall lose his citizenship by performing certain designated acts. The petitioner in this case, a native-born American, is declared to have lost his citizenship by voting in a foreign election. Whether this forfeiture of citizenship exceeds the bounds of the Constitution is the issue before us. The problem is fundamental and must be resolved upon fundamental considerations. . . .

. . . This Government was born of its citizens, it maintains itself in a continuing relationship with them, and, in my judgment, it is without power to sever the relationship that gives rise tó its existence. I cannot believe that a government conceived in the spirit of ours was established with power to take from the people their most basic right.

Citizenship *is* man's basic right for it is nothing less than the right to have rights. . . .

It has long been recognized that citizenship may not only be voluntarily renounced through exercise of the right of expatriation but also by other actions in derogation of undivided allegiance to this country. While the essential qualities of the citizen-state relationship under our Constitution preclude the exercise of governmental power to divest United States citizenship, the establishment of that relationship did not impair the principle that conduct of a citizen showing a voluntary transfer of allegiance is an abandonment of citizenship. . . . In recognizing the consequence of such action, the Government is not taking away United States citizenship to implement its general regulatory powers. . . . Rather, the Government is simply giving formal recognition to the inevitable consequence of the citizen's own voluntary surrender of his citizenship. * * *

. . . [T]he purpose of governing the formulation of most of the loss-of-nationality provisions of the codification was the specification of acts that would of themselves show a voluntary abandonment of citizenship. Congress did not assume it was empowered to use denationalization as a weapon to aid in the exercise of its general powers. Nor should we. * * *

My conclusions are as follows. The Government is without power to take citizenship away from native-born or lawfully naturalized American. The Fourteenth Amendment recognizes that this priceless right is immune from the exercise of governmental powers. If the Government determines that certain conduct by United States citizens should be prohibited because of anticipated injurious consequences to the conduct of foreign affairs or to some other legitimate governmental interest, it may within the limits of the Constitution proscribe such activity and assess appropriate punishment. But every exercise of governmental power must find its source in the Constitution. The power to denationalize is not within the letter or the spirit of the powers with which our Government was endowed. The citizen may elect to renounce his citizenship, and under some circumstances he may be found to have abandoned his status by voluntarily performing acts that compromise his undivided allegiance to his country. The mere act of voting in a foreign election, however, without regard to the circumstances attending the participation, is not sufficient to show a voluntary abandonment of citizenship. The record in this case does not disclose any of the circumstances under which this petitioner voted. We know only the bare fact that he cast a ballot. The basic right of American citizenship has been too dearly won to be so lightly lost. * * *

In *Trop* v. *Dulles*, decided the same day (356 U.S. 86, 78 S. Ct. 590; 1958), the Court held that Congress had exceeded its power in declaring that a conviction by court-martial for wartime desertion is reason for forfeiture of citizenship. The petitioner, a native-born American, had become a stateless person as a result of his conviction for such desertion. The punishment was held to be within the proscription of the Eighth Amendment, as "cruel and unusual" punishment, and the decision was reversed.

There is . . . the total destruction of the individual's status in organized society. It is a form of punishment more primitive than torture, for it destroys for the individual the political existence that was centuries in the development. The punishment strips the citizen of his status in the national and international political community. . . .[2]

The power to divest an American of his citizenship was also in issue in *Kennedy* v. *Mendoza-Martinez* and *Rusk* v. *Cort,* both decided in 1963. The decision was, however, based on different constitutional grounds.

Kennedy v. *Mendoza-Martinez; Rusk* v. *Cort,* 372 U.S. 144, 83 S. Ct. 554 (1963)

MR. JUSTICE GOLDBERG delivered the opinion of the Court.

We are called upon in these two cases to decide the grave and fundamental problem, common to both, of the constitutionality of Acts of Congress which divest an American of his citizenship, for "departing from or remaining outside of the jurisdiction of the United States in time of war or * * * national emergency for the purpose of evading or avoiding training and service" in the Nation's armed forces.[1]

A. *Mendoza-Martinez*—No. 2

The facts of both cases are not in dispute. Mendoza-Martinez, the appellee in No. 2, was born in this country and therefore acquired American citizenship by birth. By reason of his parentage, he also, under Mexican law, gained Mexican citizenship, thereby possessing dual nationality. In 1942 he departed from this country and went to

[2]*Trop* v. *Dulles,* 356 U.S. 86, p. 101.
[1]In question in No. 2, Kennedy v. Mendoza-Martinez, is § 401(j) of the Nationality Act of 1940, added in 1944, 58 Stat. 746. . . . [From the opinion—Ed.]

Mexico solely, as he admits, for the purpose of evading military service in our armed forces. He concedes that he remained there for that sole purpose until November 1946, when he voluntarily returned to this country. In 1947 . . . he pleaded guilty to and was convicted of evasion of his service obligations. . . . He served the imposed sentence. . . . [A]fter a lapse of five years, he was served with a warrant of arrest in deportation proceedings. This was premised on the assertion that, by remaining outside the United States to avoid military service after September 27, 1944, when § 401(j), took effect, he had lost his American citizenship. . . . [T]he Board of Immigration Appeals of the Department of Justice . . . dismissed his appeal.

Thereafter, Mendoza-Martinez brought a declaratory judgment action . . . seeking a declaration of his status as a citizen, of the unconstitutionality of § 401(j), and of the voidness of all orders of deportation directed against him. A single-judge District Court . . . entered judgment against Mendoza-Martinez in 1955. . . . This Court, in 1958, . . . vacated the judgment, and remanded the cause to the District Court for reconsideration in light of its decision a week earlier in *Trop* v. *Dulles,* 356 U.S. 86. . . .

The District Court on remand . . . reaffirmed its previous holding that § 401(j) is unconstitutional, holding that § 401 is "essentially penal in character and deprives the plaintiff of procedural due process. . . ." * * *

B. *Cort* — No. 3.

Cort, . . . is also a native-born American. . . . Unlike Mendoza-Martinez, he has no dual nationality. His wife and two young children are likewise American citizens by birth. Following receipt of his M.D. degree from the Yale University School of Medicine in 1951, he went to England for the purpose of undertaking a position as a Research Fellow at Cambridge University. He had earlier registered in timely and proper fashion for the draft and shortly before his departure supplemented his regular Selective Service registration by registering under the newly enacted Doctor's Draft Act. In late 1951 he received a series of letters from the American Embassy in London instructing him to deliver his passport to it to be made "valid only for return to the United States." He did not respond to these demands because, he now says . . . "I believed that they were unlawful and I did not wish to subject myself to this and similar forms of political persecution then prevalent in the United States. * * *" Cort had been a member of the Communist Party while he was a medical student at Yale from 1946 to 1951, except for the academic year 1948–1949 when he was in England. In late 1952, while still in England at Cambridge, he accepted a teaching position for the following academic year at Harvard University Medical School. When, however, the school discovered . . . that he had not yet fulfilled his military obligations, it advised him that it did not regard his teaching position as essential enough to support his deferment from military service in order to enter upon it. Thereafter, his local draft board in Brookline, Massachusetts, notified him . . . that he should report within 30 days. . . . He did not appear . . . and the board on August 13 ordered him to report for induction on September 14, 1953. He did not report, and consequently he was indicted in December 1954 for violation of § 12(a) of the Selective Service Act of 1948 by reason of his failure to report for induction. This indictment is still outstanding. His complaint in this action states that he did not report for induction because he believed "that the induction order was not issued in good faith to secure his military services, that his past political associations and present physical disabilities made him ineligible for such service, and that he was being ordered to report back to the United States to be served with a Congressional committee subpoena or indicted under the Smith Act ° ° °" In mid-1954 he and his family moved to Prague, Czechoslovakia, where he took a position as Senior Scientific Worker at the Cardiovascular Institute. He has lived there since.

In April 1959, his previous United States passport having long since expired, Cort applied at the American Embassy in Prague for a new one. His complaint in this action states that he wanted the passport "in order to return to the United States with his wife and children so that he might fulfill his obligations under the Selective Service laws and his wife might secure medical treatment for multiple sclerosis." Mrs. Cort received a passport and came to this country temporarily in late 1959. . . . Cort's application, however, was denied on the ground that he had, by his failure to report for induction on September 14, 1953, as ordered, remained outside the country to avoid military service and thereby automatically forfeited his American citizenship by virtue of § 349(a) (10) of the Immigration and Nationality Act of 1952, which had superseded § 401(j). The State Department's Passport Board of Review affirmed the finding of expatriation, and the Department's legal adviser affirmed the decision. Cort, through counsel, thereupon brought this suit . . . for a declaratory judgment that he is a citizen of the United States, for an injunction against enforcement of § 349(a) (10) because of its unconstitutionality, and for an order directing revocation of the certificate of loss of nationality and issuance of a United States passport to him. . . . The court held that he had remained outside the United States to evade military service, but that § 349(a) (10) is unconstitutional because "We perceive no substantial difference between the constitutional issue in the *Trop* case and the one facing us." It therefore concluded that Cort is a citizen of this country and enjoined the Secretary of State from withholding a passport from Cort on the ground that he is not a citizen and from otherwise interfering with his rights of citizenship. ° ° °

Since the validity of an Act of Congress is involved, we begin our analysis mindful that the function we are now discharging is "the gravest and most delicate duty that this Court is called upon to perform." *Blodgett* v. *Holden,* 275 U.S. 142, 148 (separate opinion of Holmes, J.) This responsibility we here fulfill with all respect for the powers of Congress but with recognition of the transcendent status of our Constitution.

We deal with the contending constitutional arguments in the context of certain basic and sometimes conflicting principles. Citizenship is a most precious right. It is expressly guaranteed by the Fourteenth Amendment to the Constitution, which speaks in the most positive terms. The Constitution is silent about the permissibility of involuntary forfeiture of citizenship rights. While it confirms citizenship rights, plainly there are imperative obligations of citizenship, performance of which Congress in the exercise of its powers may constitutionally exact. One of the most important of these is to serve the country in time of war and national emergency. . . . Similarly, Congress has broad power under the Necessary and Proper Clause to enact legislation for the regulation of foreign affairs. Latitude in this area is necessary to ensure effectuation of this indispensable function of government.

These principles . . . are urged upon us by the parties here. The Government argues that §§ 401 (j) and 349(a) (10) are valid as an exercise of Congress' power over foreign affairs, of its war power, and of the inherent sovereignty of the Government. Appellees urge the provisions' invalidity as not within any of the powers asserted, and as imposing a cruel and unusual punishment.

We recognize at the outset that we are confronted here with an issue of the utmost import. Deprivation of citizenship . . . has grave practical consequences. An expatriate who, like Cort, had no other nationality becomes a stateless person—a person who not only has no rights as an American citizen, but no membership in any national entity whatsoever. . . .

The basic principles here involved, the gravity of the issue, and the arguments bearing upon Congress' power to forfeit citizenship were considered by the Court in relation to different provisions of the Nationality Act of 1940 in two cases decided on the same day less than five years ago: *Perez* v. *Brownell,* 356 U.S. 44, and *Trop* v. *Dulles,* 356 U.S. 86. . . .

In *Perez,* § 401(e), which imposes loss of nationality for "[v]oting in a political election in a foreign state or participating in an election or plebiscite to determine the sovereignty over foreign territory," was upheld by a closely divided Court as a constitutional exercise of Congress' power to regulate foreign affairs. . . .

In *Trop,* § 401(g), forfeiting the citizenship of any American who is guilty of "[d]eserting the military or naval forces of the United States in time of war, provided he is convicted thereof by court martial and as the result of such conviction is dismissed or dishonorably discharged * * *" was declared unconstitutional. There was no opinion of the Court. . . .

The present cases present for decision the constitutionality of a section not passed upon in either *Perez* or *Trop.* . . . [section] 401 (j), added in 1944, and its successor and present counterpart, § 349 (a) (10) of the Immigration and Nationality Act of 1952. We have come to the conclusion that there is a basic question in the present cases, the answer to which obviates a choice here between the powers of Congress and the constitutional guarantee of citizenship. That issue is whether the statutes here, which automatically—without prior court or administrative proceedings—forfeit citizenship, are essentially penal in character, and consequently have deprived the appellees of their citizenship without due process of law and without according them the rights guaranteed by the Fifth and Sixth Amendments, including notice, confrontation, compulsory process for obtaining witnesses, trial by jury, and assistance of counsel. . . .

It is fundamental that the great powers of Congress to conduct war and to regulate the Nation's foreign relations are subject to the constitutional requirements of due process. The imperative necessity for safeguarding these rights to procedural due process under the gravest of emergencies has existed throughout our constitutional history, for it is then, under the pressing exigencies of crisis, that there is the greatest temptation to dispense with fundamental constitutional guarantees which, it is feared, will inhibit governmental action. . . . *Ex parte Milligan*, 4 Wall. 2. . . . The rights guaranteed by the Fifth and Sixth Amendments are "preserved to every one accused of crime who is not attached to the army, or navy, or militia in actual service." *Id.* at 123. . . .

We hold § 401(j) and 349(a) (10) invalid because in them Congress has plainly employed the sanction of deprivation of nationality as a punishment—for the offense of leaving or remaining outside the country to evade military service—without affording the procedural safeguards guaranteed by the Fifth and Sixth Amendments. . . .

As the Government concedes, § 401(j) and 349(a) (10) automatically strip an American of his citizenship, with concomitant deprivation "of all that makes life worth living," *Ng Fung Ho* v. *White*, 259 U.S. 276, 284–285, whenever a citizen departs from or remains outside the jurisdiction of this country for the purpose of evading his military obligations. Conviction for draft evasion . . . is not prerequisite to the operation of this sanction. Independently of prosecution, forfeiture of citizenship attaches when the statutory set of facts develops. . . . [F]orfeiture of citizenship is a penalty for the act of leaving or staying outside the country to avoid the draft. This being so, the Fifth and Sixth Amendments mandate that this punishment cannot be imposed without a prior criminal trial and all its incidents, including indictment, notice, confrontation, jury trial, assistance of counsel, and compulsory process for obtaining witnesses. If the sanction these sections impose is punishment, and it plainly is, the procedural safeguards required as incidents of a criminal prosecution are lacking. We need go no further. * * *

We conclude, for the reasons stated, that §§ 401(j) and 349(a) (10) are punitive and as such cannot constitutionally stand, lacking as they do the procedural safeguards which the Constitution commands. . . . What we hold is only that, in keeping with this cherished tradition, punishment cannot be imposed "without due process of law." Any lesser holding would ignore the constitutional mandate upon which our essential liberties depend. Therefore the judgments of the District Courts in these cases are affirmed. . . .

MR. JUSTICE DOUGLAS and MR. JUSTICE BLACK, while joining the opinion of the Court, adhere to the views expressed in the dissent of MR. JUSTICE DOUGLAS, in which MR. JUSTICE BLACK joined, in *Perez* v. *Brownell,* 356 U.S. 44, 79, . . . that Congress has no power to deprive a person of the citizenship granted the native born by § 1, cl. 1, of the Fourteenth Amendment.

MR. JUSTICE BRENNAN [concurred]. * * *

MR. JUSTICE STEWART, with whom MR. JUSTICE WHITE joins, dissenting.

The Court's opinion is lengthy, but its thesis is simple: (1) The withdrawal of citizenship which these statutes provide is "punishment." (2) Punishment cannot constitutionally be imposed except after a criminal trial and conviction. (3) The statutes are therefore unconstitutional. As with all syllogisms, the conclusion is inescapable if the premises are correct. But I cannot agree with the Court's major premise—that the divestiture of citizenship which these statutes prescribe is punishment in the constitutional sense of that term. . . .

. . . The Court as I understand it does not hold that involuntary deprivation of citizenship is inherently and always a penal sanction—requiring the safeguards of a criminal trial. . . .

. . . [I]t has been established for almost 50 years that Congress under some circumstances may, without providing for a criminal trial, make expatriation the consequence of the voluntary conduct of a United States citizen, irrespective of the citizen's subjective intention to renounce his nationality, and irrespective too of his awareness that denationalization will be the result of his conduct. . . .

The position taken by the Court today is simply that . . . the statutes at issue in the present case employ deprivation of citizenship as a penal sanction. . . .

In these cases, however, we have before us statutes which were enacted in 1944 and 1952, respectively. . . . Unlike the 1865 law, the legislation at issue in the cases before us is *not* "in terms penal." And there is nothing in the history of *this* legislation which persuades me that these statutes, though not in terms penal, nonetheless embody a purpose of the Congress which enacted them to impose criminal punishment without the safeguards of a criminal trial. * * *

The question of whether or not a statute is punitive ultimately depends upon whether the disability it imposes is for the purpose of vengeance or deterrence, or whether the disability is but an incident to some broader regulatory objective. . . . In commenting on the nature of this kind of inquiry, the Court said in *Flemming* v. *Nestor,* "We observe initially that only the clearest proof could suffice to establish the unconstitutionality of a statute on such a ground. Judicial inquiries into Congressional motives are at best a hazardous matter, and when that inquiry seeks to go behind objective manifestations it becomes a dubious affair indeed. Moreover, the presumption of constitutionality with which this enactment, like any other, comes to us forbids us lightly to choose that reading of the statute's setting which will invalidate it over that which will save it." 363 U.S., at 617.

In the light of the standard enunciated in *Nestor,* I can find no clear proof that the prime purpose of this legislation was punitive. * * *

. . . [T]he statute seems to me precisely the same kind of regulatory measure, rational and efficacious, which this Court upheld against similar objections in *Perez* v. *Brownell, supra.* . . .

For the reasons stated I cannot find in the terms of these statutes or in their legislative history anything close to the "clearest proof" that the basic congressional purpose was to impose punishment. * * *

In the view I take of this case, it is unnecessary to pursue further an inquiry as to whether the power to regulate foreign affairs could justify denationalization for the conduct in question. For I think it apparent that Congress in enacting the statute was drawing upon another power broad and far-reaching.

A basic purpose of the Constitution was "to provide for the common defence." . . .

It seems to me evident that Congress was drawing upon this power when it enacted the legislation before us. * * *

For the reasons stated, I believe the substantive provisions of § 401(j) of the 1940 Act and of § 349(a) (10) of the 1952 Act are constitutionally valid. In addition to its substantive provisions, however, § 349(a) (10) declares:

"For the purposes of this paragraph failure to comply with any provision of any compulsory service laws of the United States shall raise the presumption that the departure from or absence from the United States was for the purpose of evading or avoiding training and service in the military, air, or naval forces of the United States."

I think the evidentiary presumption which the statute creates is clearly invalid, and that it fatally infected the administrative determination that Joseph Henry Cort had lost his citizenship.

The District Court did not mention this statutory presumption.

But it is clear that the final reviewing agency in the State Department relied heavily upon this presumption in determining that Cort had lost his citizenship. * * *

. . . [T]he statute . . . creates a presumption of an expatriating act from failure to comply with "*any* provision of *any* compulsory service laws" by a citizen abroad, regardless of the nature of the violations and regardless of the innocence of his purpose in originally leaving the United States. * * *

In No. 3, *Rusk* v. *Cort,* I would vacate the judgment of the District Court and remand the case with instructions to declare null and void the certificate of loss of nationality issued to Cort by the Secretary of State, so that upon Cort's renewed application for a passport, an administrative hearing could be had, free of the evidentiary presumption of § 349(a) (10). . . .

In No. 2, *Kennedy* v. *Mendoza-Martinez,* I would reverse the judgment of the District Court.

In *Schneider* v. *Rusk* a majority of the Court refused to make a distinction between the rights of a natural-born citizen and one who has been naturalized. The distinction was one which had long been on the statute books.

Schneider v. *Rusk,* 377 U.S. 163, 84 S. Ct. 1187 (1964)

MR. JUSTICE DOUGLAS delivered the opinion of the Court.

The Immigration and Nationality Act of 1952, 66 Stat. 163, 269, 8 U.S. C. §§ 1101, 1484, provides by § 352:

"(a) A person who has become a national by naturalization shall lose his nationality by—

"(1) *having a continuous residence for three years* in the territory of a foreign state of which he was formerly a national or in which the place of his birth is situated, except as provided in section 353 of this title, whether such residence commenced before or after the effective date of this Act * * *." [Italics added.]

Appellant, a German national by birth, came to this country with her parents when a small child, acquired derivative American citizenship at the age of 16 through her mother, and after graduating from Smith College, went abroad for postgraduate work. In 1956 while in France she became engaged to a German national, returned here briefly, and departed for Germany, where she married and where she has resided ever since. Since her marriage she has returned to this country on two occasions for visits. Her husband is a lawyer in Cologne where appellant has been living. Two of her four sons, born in Germany, are dual nationals, having acquired American citizenship under § 301(a) (7) of the 1952 Act. The American citizenship of the other two turns on this case. In 1959 the United States denied her a passport, the State Department certifying that she had lost her American citizenship under § 352(a) (1), quoted above. Appellant sued for a declaratory judgment that she still is an American citizen. The District Court held against her, . . . and the case is here on appeal. 375 U.S. 893.

The Solicitor General makes his case along the following lines.

Over a period of many years this Government has been seriously concerned by special problems engendered when naturalized citizens return for a long period to the country of their former nationalities. It is upon this premise that the argument derives that Congress, through its power over foreign relations, has the power to deprive such citizen of his or her citizenship.

Other nations, it is said, frequently attempt to treat such persons as their own citizens, thus embroiling the United States in conflicts when it attempts to afford them protection. It is argued that expatriation is an alternative to withdrawal of diplomatic protection. . . . The argument continues that it is not invidious discrimination for Congress to treat such naturalized citizens differently from the manner in which it treats native-born citizens and that Congress has the right to legislate with respect to the general class without regard to each factual violation. It is finally argued that Congress here, unlike the situation in *Kennedy* v. *Mendoza-Martinez,* 372 U.S. 144, was aiming only to regulate and not to punish. . . .

We start from the premise that the rights of citizenship of the native born and of the naturalized person are of the same dignity and are coextensive. The only difference drawn by the Constitution is that only the "natural born" citizen is eligible to be President. Art. II, § 1.

While the rights of citizenship of the native born derive from § 1 of the Fourteenth Amendment and the rights of the naturalized citizen derive from satisfying, free of fraud, the requirements set by Congress, the latter, apart from the exception noted, "becomes a member of the society, possessing all the rights of a native citizen, and standing, in view of the constitution, on the footing of a native. The constitution does not authorize Congress to enlarge or abridge those rights. The simple power of the national Legislature is to prescribe a uniform rule of naturalization, and the exercise of this power exhausts it, so far as respects the individual." *Osborn* v. *Bank of United States,* 9 Wheat. 738, 827. . . .

Views of the Justices have varied when it comes to the problem of expatriation.

There is one view that the power of Congress to take away citizenship for activities done by the citizens is nonexistent absent expatriation by the voluntary renunciation of nationality and allegiance. See *Perez* v. *Brownell,* 356 U.S. 44, 79. That view has not yet commanded a majority of the entire Court. Hence we are faced with the issue presented and decided in *Perez* v. *Brownell, supra,* i.e., whether the present Act violates due process. That in turn comes to the question put in the following words in *Perez:*

"Is the means, withdrawal of citizenship, reasonably calculated to effect the end that is within the power of Congress to achieve, the avoidance of embarrassment in the conduct of our foreign relations * * * ?" 356 U.S., at 60.

In that case, where an American citizen voted in a foreign election, the answer was in the affirmative. In the present case the question is whether the same answer should be given merely because the naturalized citizen lived in her former homeland for three years. We think not. . . .

As stated by JUDGE FAHY, dissenting below, such legislation, touching as it does on the "most precious right" of citizenship (*Kennedy* v. *Mendoza-Martinez,* 372 U.S., at 159), would have to be justified under the foreign relations power "by some more urgent public necessity than substituting administrative convenience for the individual right of which the citizen is deprived." 218 F. Supp. 302, 320. * * *

This statute proceeds on the impermissible assumption that naturalized citizens as a class are less reliable and bear less allegiance to this country than do the native born. This is an assumption that is impossible for us to make. Moreover, while the Fifth Amendment contains no equal protection clause, it does forbid discrimination that is "so unjustifiable as to be violative of due process." *Bolling* v. *Sharpe,* 347 U.S. 497, 499. A native-born citizen is free to reside abroad indefinitely without suffering loss of citizenship. The discrimination aimed at naturalized citizens drastically limits their rights to live and work abroad in a way that other citizens may. It creates indeed a second-class citizenship. Living abroad, whether the citizen be naturalized or native born, is no badge of lack of allegiance and in no way evidences a voluntary renunciation of nationality and allegiance. It may indeed be compelled by family, business, or other legitimate reasons.

Reversed.

MR. JUSTICE CLARK, whom MR. JUSTICE HARLAN and MR. JUSTICE WHITE join, dissenting.

The appellant, a derivative citizen since 1950, has voluntarily absented herself from the United States for over a decade, living in her native Germany for the last eight years. In 1956 she married a German citizen there; she has since borne four (German national) sons there, and now says she has no intention to return to the United States. . . .

. . . I cannot say that Congress made her a second-class citizen by enacting § 352(a) (1), placing a "badge of lack of allegiance" upon her because she chose to live permanently abroad in her native land. If there is such a citizenship or badge, appellant, not the Congress, created it through her own actions. All that Congress did was face up to problems of the highest national importance by authorizing expatriation, the only adequate remedy. Appellant, with her eyes open to the result, chose by her action to renounce her derivative citizenship. Our cases have so interpreted such action for half a century. *Mackenzie* v. *Hare,* 239 U.S. 299, (1915). As applied to her I cannot say, as does the Court, that the command of Congress in § 352(a) (1) is discriminatory and, therefore, violative of due process. *Mackenzie* decided just the contrary. . . .

I.

There is nothing new about the practice of expatriating naturalized citizens who voluntarily return to their native lands to reside. It has a long established and widely accepted history. * * *

II.

This historical background points up the international difficulties which led to the adoption of the policy announced in § 352(a)(1). Residence of United States nationals abroad has always been the source of much international friction and the ruling today will expand these difficulties tremendously. In 1962 alone 919 persons were expatriated on the basis of residence in countries of former nationality. The action of the Court in voiding these expatriations will cause no end of difficulties because thousands of persons living throughout the world will come under the Court's broad sweep. It is estimated that several thousand of these American expatriates reside in iron curtain countries alone. . . . The protection of American citizens abroad has always been a most sensitive matter and continues to be so today. This is especially true in Belgium, Greece, France, Iran, Israel, Switzerland and Turkey, because of their refusal to recognize the expatriation of their nationals to acquire American citizenship. The dissension that springs up in some of these areas adds immeasurably to the difficulty.

Nor is the United States alone in making residence abroad cause for expatriation. Although the number of years of foreign residence varies from two to 10 years, 20 countries, including the United Kingdom and seven commonwealth countries, expatriate naturalized citizens residing abroad. . . . Even the United Nations sanctions different treatment for naturalized and native-born citizens. . . .

III.

The decisions of this Court have consistently approved the power of Congress to enact statutes similar to the one here stricken down. Beginning with *Mackenzie* v. *Hare, supra,* . . . the Court has invariably upheld expatriation when there is a concurrence on the part of the citizen. In *Mackenzie* exactly the same argument was made that appellant urges here. Indeed, the Court uses the same opinion in this case to strike down § 352(a) (1) as was urged in MacKenzie, namely, *Osborn* v. *Bank of the United States,* 9 Wheat. 738 (1824) * * *

. . . Appellant's prolonged residence in her former homeland, the allegiance her husband and children owe to it, and her intention not to return to the United States all show some measure of allegiance to Germany. At the very least, these factors show much less than "unswerving allegiance to the United States" and are "inconsistent with American citizenship." . . .

. . . In adopting the classification "naturalized citizen" has the Congress acted with reason? Many times this Court has upheld classifications of more significance. . . . Distinctions between native-born and naturalized citizens in connection with foreign residence are drawn in the Constitution itself. . . . During the entire nineteenth century only naturalized citizens were, as a general rule, expatriated on the grounds of foreign residence, and for nearly 100 years our naturalization treaties have contained provisions authorizing the expatriation of naturalized citizens residing in their native lands. . . . It is a little late for the Court to decide in the face of this mountain of evidence that the section has suddenly become so invidious that it must be stricken as arbitrary under the Due Process Clause. * * *

I dissent.

Case Index

341

Index of Justices

Topical Index

Abstention, doctrine of, 317
Acts of Congress
  Alien and Sedition, 96
  Civil Rights Act of 1866, 222, 297
  Civil Rights Act of 1875, 222, 287
  Civil Rights Act of 1964, 220, 221, 222, 223, 292
  Federal Communications Act, 236; evidence procured by violation of, 237
  Foreign Agents Registration Act of 1938, 140
  Immigration and Nationality Act of June, 1952, 326, 330, 331, 332, 333, 334, 335, 336
  Internal Security Act (McCarran Act), 97, 98, 203
  Postal Service and Federal Employees Salary Act of 1962, 140
  Universal Military Training and Service Act, 76
  Smith Act, 82, 83, 85, 88, 90, 91, 97
  Subversive Activities Control Act, 204 *et seq.*; §6 unconstitutional on face, 207; whole act unconstitutional, 208; as Bill of Attainder, 208; as violation of procedural protections, 208
Advocacy of action to overthrow government, abstract doctrine of, 90, 91
Alien
  limitations upon, 320, 322
  powers of Congress over, 323
  rights of, 321, 322
Apportionment
  constitutionality of, 312
  floterial districts, 311
  no rational basis for, 292
  population as basis for, 304, 311
  Sixty-seven Senator Amendment, 308
  temporary, 304
Arraignment, right to, without unnecessary delay, 252
Association, right of
  absorbed by Fourteenth, 201
  activities of groups protected, 199
  limitations on, property rights, 189; fitness of teachers, 194, 195
  reasonableness of inquiries re, 196
  right of state to compel disclosures, 194
  (*see also* First Amendment; Fourteenth Amendment)

Balancing test, 201
Belief, freedom of, 160
  (*see also* First Amendment; Fourteenth Amendment)
Bill of Attainder, 208
Bill of Rights
  applicable to states (*see* Fourteenth Amendment)
  fundamental nature of some of, 268
  "penumbras" of, 144 *et seq.*